# China's Leaders

# China's Leaders

## The New Generation

Cheng Li

ROWMAN & LITTLEFIELD PUBLISHERS, INC.
*Lanham · Boulder · New York · Oxford*

ROWMAN & LITTLEFIELD PUBLISHERS, INC.

Published in the United States of America
by Rowman & Littlefield Publishers, Inc.
4720 Boston Way, Lanham, Maryland 20706
www.rowmanlittlefield.com

12 Hid's Copse Road, Cumnor Hill, Oxford OX2 9JJ, England

British Library Cataloguing in Publication Information Available

**Library of Congress Cataloging-in-Publication Data**
Li, Cheng, 1956–
    China's leaders: the new generation / Cheng Li.
       p. cm.
    Includes bibliographical references and index.
    ISBN 0-8476-9496-8 (alk. paper)—ISBN 0-8476-9497-6 (pbk.: alk.paper)
    1. Communist leadership—China. 2. Political leadership—China. 3. China—Politics and govern-
ment—1976– I. Title.
HX518.L4 L48 2000
320.951—dc21          00-062539

Printed in the United States of America

♾ ™The paper used in this publication meets the minimum requirements of American National
Standard for Information Sciences—Permanence of Paper for Printed Library Materials, ANSI/NISO
Z39.48-1992.

*To Yinsheng Li*

# Contents

# Figures

# Tables

# Abbreviations

| | |
|---|---|
| ACSF | All-China Students Federation |
| CAC | Central Advisory Commission |
| CASS | Chinese Academy of Social Sciences |
| CC | Central Committee |
| CCDI | Central Commission for Discipline Inspection |
| CCP | Chinese Communist Party |
| CCTV | China's Central Television |
| CCYL | Chinese Communist Youth League |
| CITIC | China International Trust and Investment Corporation |
| CMC | Central Military Commission |
| CPPCC | Chinese People's Political Consultative Conference |
| CPS | Central Party School |
| CR | Cultural Revolution |
| ENA | Ecole Nationale d'Administration |
| KMT | Kuomintang |
| MFN | Most Favored Nation |
| MITI | Ministry of International Trade and Industry |
| NATO | North Atlantic Treaty Organization |
| NDU | National Defense University |
| NPC | National People's Congress |
| OECD | Organization of Economic Cooperation and Development |
| PLA | People's Liberation Army |
| PNTR | Permanent Normal Trade Relations |
| PRC | People's Republic of China |
| SOE | State-Owned Enterprises |

| | |
|---|---|
| SPC | System of Political Counselors |
| TMD | Theater Missile Defense |
| TVE | Township and Village Enterprises |
| WTO | World Trade Organization |
| WWII | World War II |

# Acknowledgments

The initial idea for this book was the result of a conversation with Peter Geithner in December 1997. Peter is a senior adviser at the Asia Center of Harvard University and has spent much time in China during the past two decades. Both of us were disturbed by two contradictory themes in Western studies of China at that time. While Chinese political leaders were often portrayed as ineffective, incompetent, narrow-minded and shortsighted, China actually achieved remarkable economic growth and social stability. This occurred despite all the odds against this country, such as poor natural resources and the heavy burden of surplus laborers. Because of the nature of Peter's work, he had broad contacts with many provincial and ministerial-level leaders in China. He told me that he was particularly impressed by the new generation of leaders in their forties and early fifties. Many of these leaders were sent down to the countryside during the Cultural Revolution, some studied abroad in the 1980s and then returned to China, and all had a strong commitment to the continuing political and economic transformation of the country.

What followed this conversation was two years of extensive research, including five trips to China, which ultimately led to this book. I am deeply grateful to my friend Peter Geithner for his inspiration and insights, without which I would not have pursued a focused study of this new generation of Chinese leaders. The purpose of this book is *not* to argue that post-Deng leaders should receive the bulk of credit for China's development at the turn of the century. (I believe that societal forces have played a principal role in China's progress.) My intention is to analyze the characteristics of new Chinese leaders—their merits and weaknesses, their life experiences and political attitudes—in a more objective way, instead of demonizing them, as often reflected in the media and in some writings of the scholarly community in the West.

Intellectual inquiry is like a process of wave formation—each succeeding wave owes its momentum to the strength of those that went before. Much of the analysis in this book is also built on the works of many scholars, in both China and abroad, who have studied and written on leadership, elite transformation, political socialization and networking, technocracy and democracy, generational change, China's Cultural Revolution generation, and other related subjects. My debt to them is acknowledged only inadequately by references to their works in the notes and bibliography. My gratitude to them, however, is profound.

Some of my friends and colleagues have also had a direct hand in contributing to the content of this intellectual inquiry; I would like to acknowledge their help. My deepest thanks go to Sally Carman, my friend and colleague at Hamilton College, for proofreading the manuscript, polishing my English, and producing the figures as they are presented in the book. I am grateful for the care and long hours she lavished at a critical point in the preparation of this book, which was also a very difficult period of her life when Dick Carman, her husband and my dear friend, passed away in September 1999. Words can hardly convey my appreciation to Sally and my fond memories of Dick.

I am also indebted to John Farranto, my research assistant and the most brilliant undergraduate any college professor could possibly hope to have, for his thorough library research and meticulous scrutiny of the manuscript. At Hamilton, I wish also to thank Michael Debraggio, Antonis Ellinas, Sharon Rippey, Dawn Woodward, and Benjamin Zoll for their helpful comments on part of the manuscript. Reference librarians at the College, Lynn Mayo, Julia Dickinson, and Kristin Strohmeyer, provided much needed support at various stages of my work, from the initial search for relevant literature to the final verification of complete citations.

Hamilton College offered substantial financial aid, through the Office of the President, the Office of the Dean of Faculty, the Department of Government, and the Levitt Public Affairs Center. These funds supported a range of activities, from travels across the Pacific and fieldwork to student assistantship and data analysis. The Chiang Ching-Kuo Foundation for International Scholarly Exchange very generously granted me a postdoctoral fellowship in 1999–2000, the period during which the book was written. I am enormously grateful to each of these institutions and to the individuals who administer them.

Three of my graduate school teachers (and sometime coauthors) actually made this work a collaboration. Professor Robert Scalapino, who introduced me to the field of Chinese politics at University of California, Berkeley, has been a source of encouragement ever since. He helped me to realize, when I started to write my master's thesis under his direction in 1987, the great importance of studying the elite transformation in post-Mao China. Professor David Bachman has offered continued critiques on my study of Chinese technocrats—from my dissertation, in which I tried to redefine Chinese politics in the light of the theory of technocracy, to the proposal I wrote for this book. Many of the improvements in the manuscript's contents must be attributed to his insightful comments. My greatest intellectual debt in the research and writing of this book is to Professor Lynn White. As a scholar, he set a high standard for thoroughness of research, depth of thinking, and elegance of style. As a teacher, he has dedicated an extraordinary amount of time and energy to his students, both current and former. He has been an enthusiastic supporter of this book project from its inception. I am very grateful to all of these teachers and my lifelong friends.

I am indebted to the late A. Doak Barnett, who has had a great impact in shaping my analysis of Chinese political leaders. For many decades, Professor Barnett constantly stressed the importance of studies of Chinese leaders, especially the need to analyze them in a less ideological manner. In the fall of 1993, Doak and I had a three-hour conversation in Shanghai during which he explained to me that Jiang Zemin might not be as dumb as most people thought, and China's political succession might not be as abrupt and violent as many China experts predicted. That was the first time that I heard anyone speak positively about Jiang's ability to succeed Deng Xiaoping. What has happened during the past seven years proved the truth of Doak's prediction. Doak's brilliance as a dean of American Studies of China, and his voice of reason during a perplexing time in U.S.–China relations, will be greatly missed.

I want to extend particular gratitude to Joseph Fewsmith, who took the time to read the entire manuscript with exceptional care. This book would have been immeasurably weaker without his criticism and suggestions. I am indebted to him for pointing out factual errors, infelicities of language, and not-well-grounded assessments that I would not have noticed otherwise. His own writings on Chinese leadership and political debates in reform China have always provided great inspiration for my work on similar subjects.

Some of the findings in this book were presented at a number of conferences and workshops in Washington, D.C., New York, and San Diego during the past two years. I am very grateful for the invaluable advice offered by distinguished China experts: Scott Douglus Bellard, Zhiyue Bo, Thomas Fingar, Dru Gladney, David D. Gries, Carol Lee Hamrin, Kurt Hockstein, Lyman Miller, Barry Naughton, Stephen Schlaikjer, David Shambaugh, Dorothy Solinger, Robert G. Sutter, Ezra F. Vogel, Martin Whyte, and Dali L. Yang, among many others.

Susan L. McEachern at Rowman & Littlefield was the best editor a China scholar could imagine—exceptionally knowledgeable about the field of Chinese studies, ineffably encouraging and patient while listening to an author's needs and concerns, and meticulously caring about the quality of writing. This is the second book that I have written for Rowman & Littlefield, and it has been a great joy and a remarkable learning experience to work with Susan. In addition, Janice Braunstein, production editor, and Chrisona Schmidt, copy editor, did a superb job in providing constructive editorial help on the manuscript and efficiently bringing this book into being.

I greatly appreciate all these individuals and institutions for their interest in my work, for the financial support they provided, and for the contribution they made to improving the quality of this intellectual inquiry. As for any errors of fact, argument, data analysis, interpretation or conceptualization, I naturally bear full responsibility.

Parts of chapter 3 were first published in my article, "Jiang Zemin's Successors: The Rise of the Fourth Generation of Leaders in the PRC," *China Quarterly* 161 (March 2000): 1–40; and the article coauthored with Lynn White, "The Fifteenth Central Committee of the Chinese Communist Party: Full Fledged Technocratic Leadership with Partial Control by Jiang Zemin," *Asian Survey* 38, no. 3 (March 1998): 231–264. Parts of chapter 4 were also printed in my article, "University Networks and the Rise of Qinghua Graduates in China's Leadership," *Australian Journal of Chinese Affairs* 32 (July 1994): 1–32.

Finally, my warmest thanks go to my parents from whom I have inherited, among many traits, a sense of optimism about the future, even during the horrible years of the "red terror"; to my siblings who are members of the Cultural Revolution generation and whose life experiences have taught me a great deal about dramatic changes in China, and, most of all, to Yinsheng Li for all these years of constant companionship in trying to understand our native land from both sides of the Pacific.

# 1

〜

# Coming of Age: A New
# Generation of Leaders

If you want to plan for a year, plant a seed. If for ten years, plant a tree.
If for a hundred years, train the leaders.

                —A Chinese Proverb

L eadership and succession have long been at the crux of Chinese political studies. In a society such as China, where the process of succession is not fully institutionalized, an evaluation of political events and a prediction of the future rely
extensively on analyses of leaders and their generational characteristics. The history of the People's Republic of China (PRC) indicates that changes in the composition of the political elite often reflect—and sometimes herald—broad social,
economic, and political changes in the country at large. This study focuses on the
new generation of PRC political elite, the so-called fourth generation of leaders—
those officials who are now in their late forties and fifties.

## SIGNIFICANCE OF THE NEW GENERATION LEADERSHIP

Three particular reasons highlight the importance—for both the scholarly community and policy makers—of paying close attention to this new generation of
Chinese leaders. First, shortly after Jiang Zemin and his so-called third generation
of leaders replaced Deng Xiaoping, China began to face a new round of political
succession. This is no surprise because Jiang, at the time of this writing, is already
seventy-four years old, and two other top leaders, Premier Zhu Rongji and Li

Peng, head of the people's congress, are also in their early seventies. The average ages of members of the Standing Committee, Politburo, and secretariat of the Fifteenth Central Committee of the Chinese Communist Party (CCP) in 2000 are sixty-eight, sixty-six, and sixty-six, respectively.[1]

Jiang and his generation of leaders are certainly aware of the importance of selecting their own successors. The Hong Kong media recently reported that Jiang will hand over, one at a time, three important posts that he currently holds (president, secretary-general of the Party, and chairman of the Central Military Commission) to the new generation of leaders.[2] In a Politburo meeting held in the spring of 2000, Jiang said that a majority of Politburo members, including five standing members who are in their late sixties and early seventies, will be too old to remain in the next Politburo, which will be formed during the Sixteenth Party Congress in 2002.[3] Jiang expressed his intention to resign his post as secretary-general of the CCP during the next Party congress.[4] Jiang stressed the fact that a number of world powers, such as the United States, Great Britain, and Russia, are now run by leaders in their fifties. Jiang used this as a rationale for promoting the Chinese fifty-somethings to the top leadership.[5]

On a few occasions, Jiang said that the "issue of succession is better handled now than later."[6] The elevation of fifty-five-year-old Hu Jintao to vice president of the state during the Ninth National People's Congress in 1998 was the first major sign of the rise of the new generation of leaders. In the PRC, the position of vice president of the state used to be a ceremonial one held by a non-Communist Party figurehead or a semiretired Communist veteran. Madame Song Qinling (widow of Sun Yat-sen), for example, held the post for decades. Rong Yiren, Hu's immediate predecessor, was a former leading industrialist in the pre-Communist era. But the selection of Hu, the youngest standing member of the Politburo, as President Jiang's deputy suggests that Hu will play an even more active role in national affairs in the beginning of the new century. In 1999, Hu was appointed vice chair of the Central Military Commission (CMC), another step toward succeeding Jiang Zemin. This also places Hu at the "core of fourth generation of leaders in the PRC," a term often used by both the Chinese and some China watchers abroad.[7] During the Politburo meeting held in April 2000, Jiang asked others to support his proposal that Hu be appointed as secretary-general of the Party during the Sixteenth CCP Congress.[8]

Along with Hu, two other Politburo members in their fifties, Wu Bangguo and Wen Jiabao, are now in charge of China's industrial, agricultural, and financial affairs on the State Council, where they serve as vice premiers. Zeng Qinghong, an alternate member of the Politburo who is in his late fifties and is a long-time confidant of Jiang, was recently appointed head of the Party's Organization Department and is in charge of personnel affairs in the CCP. It was reported that Hu Jintao, Wen Jiabao, Zeng Qinghong, Luo Gan (secretary of the Work Committee for Central Government Organizations), Wang Gang (director of the General Office of CCP Central Committee), Wang Zhaoguo (director of the CCP United Front

Department), Wang Zhongyu (secretary-general of the State Council), He Chun-lin (secretary-general of the National People's Congress), and He Yong (minister of supervision) have formed a leadership group responsible for the appointment and promotion of both Party and government officials.[9]

The rise of the fourth generation of leaders is most evident at the ministry and provincial levels. In 1999, all ministries and provinces in the country experienced a reshuffling of their top leadership. After the reshuffling, fifteen of the twenty-nine ministers in the State Council were born in the 1940s, as were eighteen Party bosses (58 percent), as well as twenty-three governors/mayors (77 percent) in thirty-one provinces and directly administered cities.[10] Li Changchun, fifty-five, the youngest member of the Politburo and a native of Liaoning, serves as Party boss of Guangdong Province (now China's richest province). Li Changchun has lately been seen as a dark horse for a top leadership post on the forthcoming Sixteenth Central Party Committee.[11] Another rising star in China's provincial leadership, Li Keqiang, forty-four, was recently appointed governor of Henan Province (now China's most populous province). Zhao Leji, newly appointed governor of Qinghai Province, is only forty-three years old.

In 1998, the central authorities instituted a rule stating that all provincial Party standing committees must have at least three members in their fifties or younger, and there must also be at least two people in their fifties or younger who are governors or vice governors in each province.[12] In fact, the number of governors and vice governors who are under fifty increased from twenty-seven to sixty-one after the reshuffling, and their average age is now 52.3.[13] Both Hu Jintao and Zeng Qinghong recently called for the promotion of a large number of younger leaders to national and provincial leadership posts.[14] They argued that the age distribution of Chinese officials at various levels of leadership is not conducive to political succession. To make the generational transition more "rational" and "smooth" for the next Party congress, the CCP Organization Department now requires top posts in provincial and ministry governments be held by more leaders in their fifties and deputy posts be held by more leaders in their forties.[15] While at present the top Chinese leadership is still largely ruled by the third generation of cadres, political elites in their fifties and late forties (young by Chinese standards) are aggressively beginning to take the helm in both central and regional administrations.

It is, of course, too early to suggest that the political future of these prominent individuals in the new generation leadership is assured. In PRC history many appointed heirs (e.g., Liu Shaoqi, Lin Biao, and Wang Hongwen under Mao; Hu Yaobang and Zhao Ziyang under Deng) fell suddenly from favor. However, it is likely that, if not Hu Jintao, one of the current front-runners in the fourth generation of leaders will succeed Jiang in the not-too-distant future.

Second, the replacement of an older generation of leaders by a younger one in any society can be viewed as a "regenerative force" for a stagnant country or as a stimulus for greater change.[16] This is particularly relevant to China today. The country is undergoing rapid, sometimes painful, socioeconomic transformation.

The Chinese authorities face many perplexing problems such as urban unemployment, surplus rural laborers, income disparity, official corruption, and environmental degradation. The scale of each of these problems is enormous, and none of them has an easy solution. The Chinese economy, after over a decade of double-digit growth, has slowed since the late 1990s. This is related partly to the East Asian financial crisis but mainly to the decline in domestic consumer spending. The Chinese people are not willing to spend money despite the fact that private savings are remarkably high. The total bank savings of Chinese citizens increased from 21 billion yuan in 1978 to 4,628 billion yuan in 1998, a 220-fold growth in two decades.[17] Although the annual interest rate is now 2.5 percent, the lowest in twenty years, people still want to save money, and they feel insecure and uncertain about the future.

Under these circumstances, the rise of younger and more capable leaders at the national level will psychologically influence the behavior of consumers. Consumer confidence will contribute to the economic growth of the country. Nothing seems more essential and more advantageous to China now than a young, dynamic Chinese leader, a figure like Mikhail Gorbachev in the mid-1980s or Bill Clinton in the early 1990s. The future of the Chinese Communist Party will largely depend on whether, as Hu Jintao recently said, the new Chinese leadership can win over the support of the public, especially the country's younger generations.[18]

Meanwhile, in the wake of the U.S. bombing of the Chinese embassy in Belgrade and the subsequent mass protest against the United States and the North Atlantic Treaty Organization (NATO), China is undergoing a momentous rethinking of its foreign policy. Anti-American sentiment in China did not rise solely from that tragic bombing incident but was brought about by a series of episodes. These include the demonization of China in the American media after the Tiananmen incident, the U.S. role as a world police force, the difficulties of the World Trade Organization (WTO) negotiations, and allegations of illegal campaign contributions and technological espionage. It is critically important to understand the way in which Chinese policy makers, especially the new generation of leaders, respond both economically and militarily to the ongoing crisis in Sino-U.S. relations and to perplexing regional and global challenges.

As David Shambaugh observed, "That China will grow stronger is not in doubt. Nor is the prospect of enhanced Chinese military capability. What is uncertain is the question of how China will perceive its regional environment and define its national interests."[19] The answer to this question relies heavily on a study of the views and behavior of Chinese policy makers, especially the rising generation of leadership. The highly personalized quality of the Chinese political process, including the making of foreign policy, highlights the great importance of a better understanding of the new Chinese leaders.[20]

The third reason for paying close attention to the rise of the fourth generation of leaders is the fact that this generation consists mainly of members of the so-called Cultural Revolution generation. This is particularly evident among leaders at both the province-ministry level and the county-bureau level, who grew up during the Cultural Revolution (CR). This experience had a great impact on their formative years, and this generation of leaders is accustomed to coping with hardship; it is politically sophisticated but ideologically disillusioned.

Western studies of China, of course, do not lack research on the Cultural Revolution. But surprisingly, there has been little effort, in either the scholarly community or public policy circles in the West, to assess the implications of the CR generation's coming of age.[21] Thomas Gold's 1991 study of young adults in the first three decades of the PRC showed generational differences in values and behavioral tendencies among the cohorts of each decade, including the CR generation.[22] No one seems to doubt that the CR left enduring and distinctive imprints on the political views and behavior of this generation. Yet relatively little is known about the political implications as members of the CR generation now become the backbone of Chinese political leadership.

Despite the great importance of the subject, no one has yet undertaken a focused analysis of this generation of leaders. Indeed, no broad (either quantitative or qualitative) comparison of political elites by age-groups has been published during the past two decades.[23] As Carol Lee Hamrin observes, although sinologists recognize generational differences or "gaps" as "both very evident and important in understanding China," no systematic generational approach has been applied to empirical studies in the recent literature.[24] Bruce Gilley's recent book, *Tiger on the Brink: Jiang Zemin and China's New Elite*, focuses on the life and politics of Jiang Zemin rather than analyzing the characteristics of Jiang's generation, or of Jiang's successors.[25] In fact, the elite transformation during the reform era has not received as much scholarly attention as it deserves. Only a few books published in the West, for example, Hong Yung Lee's 1991 book, *From Revolutionary Cadres to Party Technocrats: The Changing Cadre System in Socialist China*, have focused on elite transformation during the reform era.[26] Thus the many important changes in the Chinese leadership that have taken place during recent years are being ignored in Western studies of Chinese politics.

This neglect is in sharp contrast to the enormous number of Chinese writings about the CR generation published since the mid-1990s.[27] Topics such as the legacy of the CR, generational identity and consciousness, the uniqueness of the CR generation, and differences within the new generation of leaders are heatedly discussed. More importantly, members of the Cultural Revolution generation actually govern China today, since they already occupy most ministerial and provincial leadership posts.

What are the main characteristics of the fourth generation of leaders? In what ways do they resemble or differ from their predecessors—the third generation of leaders? What are their social backgrounds and career paths? What are the principal criteria for advancement to high office in this generation? How did their life experiences, especially those of their formative years, shape their political values and worldviews? To what extent does the fourth generation of leaders share similar convictions about the Communist political system, and thereby maintain loy-alty and commitment to it? In addition to inter-generational differences, are there any important intra-generational differences among leaders of the fourth genera-tion? How much will their coming of age change Chinese politics?

The fourth generation of leaders emerges at a time when China faces many per-plexing economic and sociopolitical choices; dealing with problems such as un-employment, disparity, and corruption will be more difficult than during the Deng era. What initiatives and constraints does the fourth generation of leaders face in responding to all these challenges? What new vision, if any, does this new gener-ation of leaders bring with it to power? Research on Chinese politics in general, and its leadership in particular, will be invaluable if it begins to address any of these questions.

## POLITICAL GENERATIONS: THEORY AND PRACTICE

The term "political generations" is frequently used but not carefully defined. Like many other biological and sociological categories—ethnicity, class, ideology, in-come—"generation can be imprecise at the boundaries."[28] In the literature, gen-erational boundaries are often defined by a combination of birth year and the characteristics of peer groups. The latter includes shared major life experiences and collective sociopolitical attitudes. A political generation is often defined as a group of cohorts born during a period of about twenty-two years.[29] The literature on generational studies in contemporary China, however, tends to depict general breaks at shorter intervals of fifteen years.[30] These same-age cohorts have experi-enced the same major historical events during their formative years (described as approximately 17–25).[31]

A generation named and defined by a major historical event is certainly not unique to China. Many Western scholars use major historical events such as the Depression, the Holocaust, the Second World War, and the Vietnam War as "a way to show how cohorts adapt and societies reconstitute themselves after such dis-ruptions."[32] Karl Mannheim, a prominent social scientist who has contributed some seminal theoretical works in the study of generations, draws a primary dis-tinction between a generation as a single age-group based entirely on year of birth and a generation based on collective social and political experiences. Mannheim uses the term "location" to refer to the former and the term "actuality" to refer to the latter. Mannheim's emphasis on the actuality of a generation highlights the im-portance of collective social and political experiences.[33] These experiences often lead to a shared consciousness and a unique worldview. According to Mannheim, a purely age-based definition of a generation "does not fully account for the for-mation of a specific identity and self-consciousness of a particular generation."[34]

In Mannheim's view, a political generation becomes "sociologically significant only when it also involves participation in the same historical and social circum-stances."[35] This relates to another important concept of Mannheim's theory of generation, "generational units," which posits that subgroups within a generation may experience the world differently as a result of differences in race, class, gender, education, and even region of residence. The concept of generational units notes intra-generational differences as well as inter-generational contrasts, and makes it easier to consider differences and conflicts within, as well as between, generations. It therefore develops a more valid picture of a variety of subgroups rather than what Pat McNeill calls "an over-simplified and monolithic portrayal" of a generation, all with the same shared experience and supposedly the same values.[36]

Mannheim's conceptual assumptions have profound implications for the study of Chinese political generations. The concept of political generations in China has often been based on the distinctive political experience of elites, for example, the "Long March generation." The term "political generations," which many sinologists have used in their studies, may be more accurately identified as "political elite generations." Political and socioeconomic events do not affect all generational units or social groups in the same way. Technocrats in the fourth generation of leadership, for example, may have more in common with technocrats in the previous generation than with nonelites in the same age-group.

It is also important, as Mannheim suggests, to pay attention to the tensions and differentiations within a political elite generation and, therefore, to search for contrasts and sources of conflict among various elite groups, even within the same age range. An elite generation may not be homogeneous in some crucial aspect of its members' backgrounds, views, and values, even though they have experienced similar major historical events at a similar point in their personal development. This assumption, which is reinforced in this study, differs profoundly from some more rigid definitions of elite generation. Seweryn Bialer, a student of the post-Stalin Soviet Union, for example, defines "elite generation as an age group whose membership is homogeneous with respect to a particular life experience at a similar point in its development."[37]

Keeping all these concepts and modifications in mind, one can identify five political elite generations in contemporary Chinese history: (1) the Long March veterans, (2) the Anti-Japanese War officers, (3) the Socialist Transformation cadres, (4) the CR grown-ups, and (5) the Economic Reform elites (see table 1.1).[38] Some Western sinologists have used similar terms to identify selected political elite generations in Communist China.[39] Cohort membership in a political elite generation has often been considered an important social attribute in an analysis of PRC politics. The differences between political elite generations, as some political scientists have observed, constitute an "important milestone in the evolution of the society's elite system in particular, and of the political system in general."[40] The hardship of the Long March and the Yan'an periods are seen to have molded the members of that cohort in particular ways. Meanwhile, the strong bond that derived from this shared experience has created a "sense of collective identity and solidarity among them."[41] The Chinese Communist Party itself, as Michael Yahuda noted, "has classified its members in terms of the historical periods during which they joined the Party, and their participation in key events during the Party's history such as the Long March, the War of Resistance to Japan, and so forth."[42]

This categorization is also identical to the generational classification of China's leadership used by current Chinese authorities. Leaders in their late forties and early fifties often identify themselves as members of the fourth generation.[43] This categorization is, of course, highly political in terms of all the major actors involved. First, it was Deng Xiaoping who initiated this categorization during his meeting with other top leaders on June 16, 1989, soon after the Tiananmen crackdown. While admitting his two previous failures in arranging for succession (in the cases of Hu Yaobang and Zhao Ziyang), Deng pushed for the establishment of a new collective leadership under Jiang Zemin. He called this collective leadership the third generation and Jiang its "core" (hexin). Deng said, "There should be a core in any collective. A leadership without a core is unreliable. . . . [We] must make a conscious effort to uphold the leadership core in Comrade Jiang Zemin, whom we agree to select."[44] Deng's pronouncement showed his determination to make the succession smooth despite all the crises he faced.

Jiang Zemin was more than ready to identify himself as the "core of the third generation of leaders" and used this identity to consolidate his political legitimacy as an heir to Deng. During the mid-1990s, when Deng's health deteriorated, Jiang frequently referred to this categorization in order to secure his position as the "core" of the third-generation leadership.[45] As both a Communist student activist in France in the early 1920s and a member of the Long March, Deng should not be seen in the same generation as Hu Yaobang and Zhao Ziyang. But by identifying Deng as the core of the second generation and himself as the core of the third, Jiang skipped the real core members of the second generation such as Zhao Ziyang and Wan Li.[46] More importantly, by appointing Hu Jintao as core member of the next generation, Jiang has attempted to diminish the pressure of contenders for power in his own generation such as Li Peng, Zhu Rongji and Li Ruihuan. And finally, Hu Jintao, Zeng Qinghong, and their same-age cohorts, who used to be identified as the "third echelon" (disan tidui), are now more inclined to be seen as the core of the fourth generation that is in line to succeed Jiang.

There are, of course, many ambiguities in terms of boundaries between generations. It is rather arbitrary to define "where one generation begins and another ends," as Ruth Cherrington noted.[47] Political leadership does not always consist exclusively of political elites in the same generation, although members of that generation may dominate the most important power positions. In empirical studies of Chinese political elites, generational classification based on age should also allow for some exceptions. For instance, Hu Yaobang is usually seen as a member of the second generation of Chinese leaders, although he took part in the Long March (Hu was one of the youngest people in the march).

Most political leaders in the PRC, however, fit in the generational classification listed on table 1.1. For example, the formative years of a majority of the third

**Table 1.1  Political Elite Generations in Communist China**

| Generation of Leaders | Major Historical Event | Period of Event | Paramount Leader ("Core Figure") | Representative Figures | Primary Age Group by 1999 |
|---|---|---|---|---|---|
| 1st Generation | The Long March | 1934–1935 | Mao Zedong | Zhou Enlai, Liu Shaoqi, Lin Biao, Deng Xiaoping | Late 80s or older |
| 2d Generation | The Anti-Japanese War | 1937–1945 | Deng Xiaoping | Hu Yaobang, Zhao Ziyang, Hua Guofeng, Qiao Shi | Late 70s and 80s |
| 3d Generation | The Socialist Transformation | 1949–1958 | Jiang Zemin | Li Peng, Zhu Rongji, Li Lanqing, Li Ruihuan | 60s and early 70s |
| 4th Generation | The Cultural Revolution | 1966–1976 | Hu Jintao? | Wen Jiabao, Zeng Qinghong, Wu Bangguo, Li Changchun | Late 40s and 50s |
| 5th Generation | The Economic Reform | 1978– | Unknown | Unknown | Early 40s |

generation of leaders occurred after the Japanese occupation. Among the twenty-four members of the Politburo in 1998, only one joined the Party before 1945.[48] Most of them began their political careers during the socialist transformation in the 1950s, and many went to the Soviet Union and other Eastern European countries for higher education (including four standing members of the Politburo— Jiang Zemin, Li Peng, Wei Jianxing, and Li Lanqing—and a few other members of the Politburo—Li Tieying, Luo Gan, and Qian Qichen).

Among the fourth generation of leaders, some senior members such as Hu Jintao and Wen Jiabao graduated from college prior to the beginning of the CR. They were often identified as "red and expert" cadre. In contrast, some junior members of the fourth generation such as Li Keqiang and Xi Jinping (governor of Fujian) were sent to the countryside after attending middle school.[49] They were called sent-down youth. These two subgroups of the fourth generation may differ from each other in some important ways but both were profoundly affected by the political turmoil of the Cultural Revolution.

## THE CULTURAL REVOLUTION GENERATION AND THE FOURTH GENERATION OF LEADERS

How is the fourth generation of leaders defined? On what basis are the age cohorts of this generation determined? As noted before, the fourth generation is composed of those who grew up or experienced their formative years during the CR. In addition, they usually acquired their first political experiences during the course of the CR. This study defines the CR generation as the one born between 1941 and 1956, making them ten to twenty-five years of age when the CR began in 1966 and forty-four to fifty-nine in 2000 (see figure 1.1).

Determining a cut-off age for this generation is somewhat arbitrary. Yet this definition is largely based on both the "fifteen-year span of a generation" and "formative years between seventeen and twenty-five." The oldest among this group were twenty-five when the CR began in 1966, and some may have finished college and started working by the mid-1960s. The youngest members were ten years old—a bit too young to be an active participant, but certainly old enough to have memories of the CR. Most of them were either in high school or in college when the CR began, and therefore a majority of them served as Mao's "Red Guards." They were the most active participants of the CR. During this extraordinary period, these CR youths developed a generational consciousness out of what Mannheim called the process of "fresh contact," developing a unique set of values and bonding with others their own age.[50]

The so-called three old classes (*laosanjie*)—the high school classes of 1966, 1967, and 1968—constituted a large portion of the CR generation. Some were among the 30 million young men and women who were sent to the countryside in the late 1960s and early 1970s. Many of them were members of the so-called

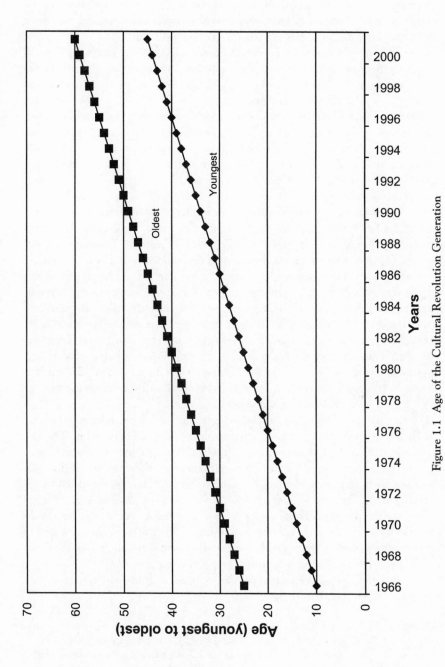

Figure 1.1 Age of the Cultural Revolution Generation

lost generation.[51] Some later returned to school to complete their education, especially after 1977 when reformers reinstituted entrance examinations for higher education. They managed to get their careers back on track.

The CR certainly affected this generation of leaders in ways that were remarkably different from other generations. Despite some important differences between subgroups of this generation, virtually all of them believed in Mao and Maoism (at least during the early stages of the CR). Later, however, they were disillusioned and felt manipulated or even betrayed. Their idealism was shattered, their energy wasted, their education lost, and their careers interrupted. Some scholars argue that, as a result of the CR, this generation also "acquired a variety of political skills and . . . the habit of independent thinking."[52] As a Western journalist described them, the CR generation "learned hard lessons about their society and its political system."[53]

One important conceptual distinction should be made here: the fourth generation of leaders is the CR generation, but not vice versa. This is the distinction between a political elite generation and a political generation. Those members of the CR generation who had a college education and/or became political leaders were only the tip of the iceberg. An overwhelming majority of the CR generation lost the opportunity to be educated during the CR and now face unemployment and other problems, such as the increasing cost of educating their children and caring for their parents. A Chinese scholar recently wrote that political, economic, and cultural elites do not have the right to represent "this generation" (*zheyidai*). They are only the lucky ones in the generation. If based only on age, this generation accounts for one-fifth of China's population—roughly 250 million people. According to the author, an overwhelming majority of this generation are "laid-off" (*xiagang*) rural and urban workers.[54]

During the late 1990s, many of the leading critics of China's reform, for example, He Qinglian and Yang Fan, are also members of the CR generation. The former works in Shenzhen, the frontier of capitalist development in southern China, and the latter in northern China. Their outrage about the current political system has earned them the sobriquet "*nan* He *bei* Yang" (He in the South and Yang in the North). They are sharply critical of the pitfalls of reform, especially regarding the rampancy of official corruption and growing disparities in Chinese society. Both He and Yang are very aware of their CR identities. In the afterword to her best-selling book, *China's Pitfall*, He Qinglian writes that she formed her "basic outlook on life and society" during those disturbing years.[55]

Yang Fan sees the CR generation as the most unfortunate generation in contemporary China. He writes:

> This generation not only bore the burden of the cost of the CR, but also has to bear the cost of the reform. They lost much during the CR, but did not receive any compensation in the reform era. . . . This generation has been extremely unlucky: during their childhood, they experienced "three bad years;" during the normal years of

schooling, they were sent to the countryside to do manual labor; when they became adults, they lived in a time of sexual restraint; when they wanted to have children, they could have only one child. When they became experienced workers, they were unemployed, they needed to care for their elderly and paid a great deal for their children's education.[56]

In another recently published article, Yang criticizes the argument made by some Chinese policy makers and economists that the difficulties experienced by this generation are the necessary costs of the structural transition in the country.[57] Yang states that "the reform should not sacrifice one generation." Yang believes that the increasing "generational disparity" should be considered the fifth way in which the country is unevenly divided. The other four dichotomies are occupational differences, the east-west geographical division, urban-rural distinctions, and the disparity between rich and poor.[58]

Both He Qinglian and Yang Fan observe profound differences among the CR generation. This observation is backed up by the fact that some leading overseas political dissidents, for example, Wei Jingsheng, Wang Juntao, Wang Xize and Dai Qing, are also members of the CR generation. They are counterelites rather than members of the political elite generation. In fact, as Erling Hoh observes, the Chinese overseas dissident leaders are currently drawn from three diverse eras of protest: the 1957 "Let a Hundred Flowers Bloom" liberalization, the 1979 democracy wall demonstration and the 1989 Tiananmen student rally.[59] Indeed, they represent three generations, and each was profoundly influenced by the political era during which they grew up. Writer Liu Binyan and astrophysicist Fang Lizhi belong to the older generation whose dissent against totalitarianism started during the brief period of liberation in 1957. The members of the 1979 democracy wall generation, such as Wei Jingsheng and Wang Xize, battled with "mental scars from the CR," and the 1989 Tiananmen generation has a different set of political challenges and psychological problems to overcome.

To a certain extent, the infighting seen in dissident communities reflects generational differences.[60] For example, when student leaders of the 1989 movement such as Chai Ling and Wuer Kaixi accused older generations of dissidents of bossing young students, older generations of dissidents denounced students for being ultraradical and egoistic. Liu Binyan criticized his junior colleagues for being more interested in factionalism than in fighting for democracy. Liu was afraid that "when China does become democratic, there will be a thousand political parties."[61] But this does not mean the infighting occurs only across generations. One of the ugliest instances of infighting in the overseas dissident movement recently took place among Wei Jingsheng, Xu Wenli, and Wang Xize, all of whom belong to the CR generation.[62] Some Chinese dissidents attribute the infighting to the political upbringing of their rivals—Wei, Wang, and Xu all grew up during the anarchic CR, when factional politics was widespread.[63]

Similarly, within the fourth generation of leaders, there are important contrasting subgroups shaped by variables such as what they studied in college, when they graduated from college, when they joined the Party (i.e., prior to, during, or after the CR), and what their class or family backgrounds were. Probably similar to the leadership in post-Communist Russia, China's fourth generation of leaders may lack a common ideology and a willingness to commit to the existing political system. They also lack a fundamental consensus on major socioeconomic policies.[64] This study will elaborate on both the commonalties and differences among the fourth generation of leaders, as well as their demographic and sociological characteristics in contrast to their predecessors' generation.

Although we are primarily concerned with the fourth generation of leaders, not the CR generation per se, we will find it valuable to have the broader perspective of an intra-generational comparison. Whether the emerging fourth generation of leaders will have a better understanding of their peers' needs and concerns, and therefore make the regime more accountable to its people than their predecessors, remains to be seen.

## SOURCES OF DATA AND METHODOLOGY

The data of this study are largely drawn from three different sources: (1) a quantitative analysis of biographical information about members of the fourth generation of leaders and both inter- and intra-generational comparisons; (2) case studies of formal and informal networks of prominent figures in the new generation; and (3) a qualitative examination of the values and policies of new leaders. Each source represents a particular methodological approach. By putting all of them together, however, we can develop a comprehensive understanding of the main characteristics of the fourth generation of leaders.

### Quantitative Analysis of Biographical Data

The quantitative analysis is based on two pools of comprehensive biographical data. The first pool includes data on 298 Chinese political elites, obtained exclusively from the 1994 revised edition of *Zhongguo renming da cidian xiandai dangzhengjun lingdaorenwujuan* (Who's who in China: The volume on current Party, government, and military leaders), which lists a total of 2,121 current leaders at all levels above medium-sized city government.[65] The 298 leaders studied are members of the youngest group included in the volume. They were all born between 1941 and 1956 and are therefore considered part of the CR generation. Many of them occupy some of the most important positions in the Party, government, and army. For example, forty are ministers and deputy ministers of the central government, and 101 are provincial governors and vice governors. For the sake of comparison, a total of 2,121 current leaders have been coded using Microsoft Excel.

The second pool is based exclusively on biographical data of all members of the Fifteenth Central Committee of the Chinese Communist Party and the Central Commission for Discipline Inspection (CCDI), which were released to the public in 1999.[66] This pool contains a total of 459 top Party leaders, including 193 full members and 151 alternates of the Fifteenth Central Committee of the CCP and 115 members of the Central Commission for Discipline Inspection. Almost half of them, 224, were born between 1941 and 1956; the other half were mainly members of the third generation leadership. This allows us to compare various aspects of these two generations.

This study codes three types of data for analysis: (1) demographic distribution, including age, sex, nationality, birthplace, and, for provincial and municipal leaders, the province or city in which they were born and the province and city in which they now serve as leaders; (2) their educational backgrounds, including schools, degree levels, major fields, graduation years, and interval that elapsed between joining the Party and graduating from college; and (3) their career and recruitment paths, including work experiences in different organizations (e.g., Party, government administration, military, youth league), work experiences in different fields (industry, agriculture, propaganda), and work experiences at different levels (grassroots, bureau/county/district, municipal/provincial, central).

In addition, this study uses other sources from Hong Kong, Taiwan, Japan, and elsewhere, seeking verification from multiple Chinese publications and the increasing availability of Internet information from the PRC.[67] These two pools of data, along with additional sources, constitute the first large-scale quantitative study of political elites during the reform era.

## Case Studies of Political Networks

Data about the background characteristics of leaders, of course, cannot give complete information about how they were selected, especially in regard to important formal networks and informal connections among the new generation of leaders. Two case studies provide additional input. The first case study explores school ties, an increasingly important formal network. This study focuses on Qinghua University, the "cradle of the fourth generation of leaders." The second case study examines the role of informal connections such as children of high-ranking officials and *mishu* (personal secretaries).

One of the most important trends regarding the elite transformation during the reform era is the crucial role of school ties in the recruitment of both civilian and military elites.[68] School ties have become the main source of generational identity, replacing other ties, such as field army, birthplace, wartime experience and bureaucratic affiliation.[69] It is now widely known that a significant portion of top leadership posts in both the Party and the state, in both central and provincial government, are occupied by graduates of Qinghua University, China's leading engineering school.[70] For example, among the twenty-two full members of the

Politburo in 1999, five (23 percent) are Qinghua graduates, including two of its standing committee members: Premier Zhu Rongji and Vice President Hu Jintao. In addition, 15 percent of ministers in the cabinet, 11 percent of central committee members of the CCP, dozens of governors, hundreds of mayors and county heads, and thousands of bureau heads and factory directors are Qinghua graduates. As this study will show, no other institution in China can match Qinghua in the number of graduates holding high-ranking political leadership positions during the reform era. The overrepresentation of Qinghua graduates is evident in the fourth generation of leaders.

Qinghua graduates' success in acquiring national leadership positions is partially due to the technical expertise they acquired and mainly due to the political networking that they developed there. This study explores the "Qinghua clique," which was formed in the 1950s by the late president of Qinghua, Jiang Nanxiang. Several prominent figures of the Qinghua clique, especially Hu Jintao, are carefully examined. There are three primary sources for this study: (1) interviews with Qinghua officials and graduates conducted in 1990, 1994, and 1997; (2) a review of Qinghua official documents; and (3) an analysis of biographical data, particularly political associations, of Qinghua graduates who hold national and provincial leadership positions. The Qinghua clique, which has formed on the basis of school ties, may suggest not only the new means of elite formation but also new sources of elite conflict in Chinese politics in the future.

In addition to school ties, blood ties (e.g., being the child of a high-ranking official) are important for the career advancement of the fourth generation of leaders. The second case study therefore investigates informal networks and personal connections among the fourth generation leadership with a focus on some prominent figures known to have high-ranking cadre family backgrounds (called princelings, or *taizi* in Chinese). They advanced quickly with the help of their parents or their parents' comrades in arms. These princelings, whose training in power politics began at an early age, usually grew up in an environment that taught them about political survival in an authoritarian political system.

Studies of the third generation of leaders in the post-Mao era have showed the prevalence of nepotism.[71] There are, however, some important differences between the third and fourth generations of leaders who have high-ranking cadre family backgrounds. The princelings in the third generation usually studied in the Soviet Union and East European countries, while the fourth generation most likely attended elite schools in China, such as Qinghua. Many of the princelings in the third generation of leaders suffered hardships in their childhood. Jiang Zemin, Li Peng, and Zou Jiahua, for example, all came from the families of Communist martyrs. They participated in the Communist revolution during the early years of their political careers. But most princelings of the fourth generation had a privileged life (though in some cases it was interrupted briefly during the first few years of the CR).

Because of this privileged life, *taizi*-turned-leaders in the fourth generation are less secure than their counterparts of the third generation, who generally could stand on their own. This was reflected in both the election of the Fifteenth Central Committee of the Chinese Communist Party in 1997 and the election of members of the State Council and other governmental positions in the Ninth National People's Congress held in March 1998. Many candidates with princeling backgrounds were not elected because the deputies strongly opposed nepotism.[72] In addition, the members of Jiang Zemin's "Shanghai gang" were often embarrassed because they received only a small proportion of the votes. For example, Chen Zhili, minister of education, received the fewest votes among twenty-nine ministers. About 35 percent of the deputies opposed the appointment of Han Zhubin, Jiang's long-time associate in Shanghai, as procurator-general of the state.[73] All these episodes suggest that political nepotism in its various forms has received growing opposition and criticism, not only from Chinese society but also from deputies of both the Party congress and the National People's Congress (NPC) who blocked the election of some princelings and the nominees favored by Jiang.

This, of course, does not mean that political nepotism is no longer crucial in Chinese elite recruitment today. The number of members of the "Shanghai gang" in the central leadership may not be high, but numbers alone are not indicative of the true seat of power. Many of the most important leadership posts are occupied by Jiang's confidants. The most recent example is the appointment of Zeng Qinghong as head of the Department of Organization of the Central Committee of the CCP. He is now the person who chooses leaders on both the central and provincial levels. A detailed analysis of the personality, social backgrounds, and political behavior of two most influential *mishu* in today's China—Wen Jiabao and Zeng Qinghong—follows.

What is most evident in Chinese politics at present is the broad trend away from an all-powerful single leader such as Mao and Deng to greater collective leadership, as is now characteristic of the Jiang era. This study will examine whether or not post-Jiang leaders, because of their restraints and limitations, will rely more on power sharing, negotiation, consultation, and consensus building than their predecessors.

## Qualitative Examination of Outlooks and Policies

Methodologically, getting at elite values and outlooks is difficult even in democratic political systems.[74] For scholars, the questions of how an individual's social background affects his or her outlook, and how the outlook further influences his or her behavior, are theoretically tempting but analytically perplexing. It is even more difficult to conduct research on views and values of political leaders in China because most leaders only reiterate the Party line. For most of PRC history, differences and conflicts in views and policy preferences among leaders have been unknown to the public until the political winner announced the defeat of his enemy. But since the late 1990s, Chinese political leaders have become more accessible and more open about their views and policies. In 1998, for example, almost all newly appointed cabinet ministers appeared, one at a time, on a national news program on China's Central Television.[75] The Internet version of *Renmin ribao* (People's daily) now routinely provides *links* to the writings and speeches of China's ministerial and provincial leaders.

The increasing transparency of views of individual leaders is related to the fact that progress and problems, promises and pitfalls, in the ongoing reform are frequently debated in today's China. Since the mid-1990s, many public intellectuals—who come from various professional backgrounds and diverse political spectra—have openly debated almost all important aspects of the reform. Grave problems that have emerged during the reform era lead its critics to question the direction that China has taken. Some bold critics of government policies have gone far beyond those who criticized the CR when Mao died or those who called for democracy in the spring of 1989. Meanwhile, China's top leaders have clearly been worried about possible loss of control because of high unemployment, income disparity, and the lack of a social safety net. But compared with their predecessors, the current technocratic leaders seem to be more willing to admit problems and mistakes, as well as more tolerant of criticism from public intellectuals in the country.

Some outspoken critics are actually "advisers" and members of "think tanks" for top leaders. This is not entirely new. Earlier intellectual discourses (e.g., those in the 1987 liberal movement and in the 1989 Tiananmen movement prior to the crackdown) also included members of the political establishment and advisers to top leaders. For example, Fang Lizhi, Wen Yuankai, Yan Jiaqi, Su Shaozhi, and Chen Yizhi all had their "patrons" within the top leadership. What distinguishes the present group of critics from their predecessors is that now far more "advisers" join the debates. In addition, one of the major differences between Deng and Jiang is that the latter relies even more on think tanks in the decision-making process.

Liu Ji, a long-time confidant of Jiang Zemin, for example, is also the "chief adviser" to China Today Press, which recently published an influential book series entitled *China's Problems*. This series addresses politically sensitive issues such as unemployment, crime, population pressures, rural-urban migration, and income disparity. It was Liu Ji who endorsed the publication of He Qinglian's controversial book, *China's Pitfall*. Another adviser to President Jiang, Wang Huning, is also a contributor to another controversial book, *Political China: Facing the Era of Choosing a New Structure*. This volume contains thirty-nine recently published essays by thirty-two scholars, journalists, and government officials, including former officials who were dismissed for their liberal views.[76] Although Wang has hardly been seen as a liberal by China watchers, in his essay he suggests some specific measures for consolidating China's legal system in order to deal with corruption and other power abuses. He also calls for greater separation of government and industry.

Some think tank members and public intellectuals make bold and specific suggestions. For example, Hu Angang, a leading economist who is a member of the

Chinese Academy of Social Sciences (CASS) and was once a consultant to Zhu Rongji, even proposed a "one-province, one-vote" system for the Politburo. In his view, this would not only give every province a voice in Party policy but also would lead to a more genuine effort to ease local dissatisfaction with central government and the increasing disparity between coastal and interior provinces.[77] He calls for political reform in China, but he believes that the priority of political reform should be technocratic decision making in social welfare policy, which involves more open discussion and consultation among independent think tanks instead of adoption of the Western multiparty system.[78] Public intellectuals within the establishment disagree among themselves in terms of their emphasis on China's problems, but they all share the conviction that the system must change in a fundamental way. He Xin, a long-time adviser to "conservative" leaders such as Li Peng, also believes that structural economic change in China will be essential as China moves into the twenty-first century.[79]

In the arena of China's foreign policy, new leaders and their advisers also seem less restrained than their predecessors. Two middle-ranking military officers recently published a book entitled *Beyond the Rule of War* in which they offered a new strategy in the era of high-tech warfare.[80] They argued that economically weak and militarily backward countries should not follow the conventional rules of war in order to fight against technologically advanced Western powers. The new strategy for weak countries such as Yugoslavia and Iraq should be one "beyond the rule of war." This means that they should conduct warfare "by hook or by crook" (*buze shouduan*), resorting to Internet viruses, stock market disruptions, and all kinds of terrorism in major cities of Western countries. This controversial book has led to an open debate among some members of military think tanks.[81] Most public intellectuals and scholars with an interest in the debate are critical of the idea that China should adopt an aggressive foreign policy.[82]

This study examines recent writings and speeches of some prominent members of the fourth generation of leaders as well as members of their think tanks, especially their views and policies about urban unemployment, income disparity, prospects for a rule of law, political democracy, social stability, rapid technological changes, China's foreign policy, and economic and cultural globalization. Some possible future scenarios for China's foreign policy are also forecast.

The following is a summary of the remaining six chapters. Chapter 2 gives an overview of the elite transformation from revolutionary veterans to technocrats during the reform era. Chapter 3 consists mainly of the biographical characteristics of the fourth generation of leaders, especially as they differ from those of the third generation of leaders. Chapter 4, based on a case study of Qinghua University, sheds light on the role of school networks in elite recruitment. Chapter 5 presents case studies of two other informal networks of princelings and personal secretaries who are part of the fourth generation of leaders. Institutional opposition to nepotism is also discussed. Chapter 6 explores collective characteristics of the new generation of elites, especially their attitudes and outlooks nurtured during both the Cultural Revolution and the reform era. Chapter 7 highlights the intra-generational diversity of new leaders, including their career paths, occupational backgrounds, and policy preferences. The chapter concludes with a discussion of the implications of the coming of age of the fourth generation of leaders.

## NOTES

1. For a detailed discussion of the age distribution of leadership bodies of the Fifteenth Party Congress and its comparison with previous Party congresses, see Li Cheng and Lynn White, "The Fifteenth Central Committee of the Chinese Communist Party: Full-Fledged Technocratic Leadership with Partial Control by Jiang Zemin," *Asian Survey* 38, no. 3 (March 1998): 231–264.

2. *Jingbao* (Mirror) March 2000, 1; and *Shijie ribao* (World journal), 3 March 1998, A1.

3. *Jingbao*, March 2000, 1.

4. *South China Morning Post*, 4 May 2000, 1.

5. Ibid.

6. *Shijie ribao*, 5 December 1998, A9.

7. Xiao Yu, "New Generation Aims for the Top: 'Fourth Generation' Leaders Are Taking the Helm in both Central and Regional Administrations." *South China Morning Post*, 6 August 1998, 1; and "Hu Jintao: Communist Party 'Golden Boy,'" Agence France Presse, 15 March 1998; *South China Morning Post*, 25 August 1998, 1; and *Shijie ribao*, 25 August 1998, A9.

8. *South China Morning Post*, 4 May 2000, 1.

9. *Shijie ribao*, 11 October 1999, A2.

10. *Renmin ribao* (People's daily), Internet database, July 1999. In 1998, twelve Party secretaries and twenty-one heads of governments in China's thirty-one provinces and directed administered cities were born in the 1940s. *China News Analysis*, 1 April 1998, 4–5; 1–15 July 1998, 18–20.

11. For a detailed discussion of Li Changchun, especially his effort to deal with the so-called Guangdong gang, see Gao Xin, *Xiangfu Guangdong bang* (Taming the Guangdong gang) (Hong Kong: Mingjing chubanshe, 2000).

12. Xiao Yu, "Fourth Generation of Leadership Takes Shape; Hu Groomed to Be Next Helmsman," *South China Morning Post*, 7 July 1998, 1.

13. *Renmin ribao*, 3 August 1998, 1.

14. *Renmin ribao*, 28 April 2000, 1; and www.Chinesenewsnet.com, 21 February 2000.

15. *Shijie ribao*, 14 February 2000, A8.

16. Ruth Cherrington, "Generational Issues in China: A Case Study of the 1980s Generation of Young Intellectuals," *British Journal of Sociology* 48, no. 2 (June 1997): 303.

17. *Renmin ribao*, 24 September 1998, 1.

18. *China Daily*, 20 June 1998, 1.

19. David Shambaugh, "Growing Strong: China's Challenge to Asia Security," *Survival* 36, no. 2 (Summer 1994): 57.

20. Richard H. Solomon observes, "In U.S. dealings with the PRC, two factors have tended to magnify the impact of individual personalities: the highly personalized quality of the Chinese political process, and the remarkable continuity of senior personnel in the PRC leadership that has given a few individuals enormous influence over the PRC's for-

eign relations." *Chinese Political Negotiating Behavior, 1967–1984* (Santa Monica, Calif.: Rand Corporation, 1995), 139.

21. A few exceptions include a thoughtful journalistic series on the CR generation; Steven Mufson, "The Next Generation," *Washington Post*, 14–18 June 1998, A1; and Carol Lee Hamrin, "Perspectives on Generational Change in China," unpublished scope paper for the workshop organized by The Paul H. Nitze School of Advanced International Studies, Johns Hopkins University, June 1993.

22. Thomas Gold, "Youth and State," *China Quarterly* 127 (1991): 594–612. Also see T. David Mason, "Modernization and Its Discontents Revisited: The Political Economy of Urban Unrest in the People's Republic of China," *Journal of Politics* 56, no. 2 (1994): 400–424.

23. Earlier studies based on generational analysis include Michael Yahuda, "Political Generations in China," *China Quarterly* 80 (December 1979): 792–805; and W. William Whitson, "The Concept of Military Generation," *Asian Survey* 11, no. 11 (November 1968).

24. Hamrin, "Perspectives on Generational Change in China."

25. Bruce Gilley, *Tiger on the Brink: Jiang Zemin and China's New Elite* (Berkeley: University of California Press, 1998).

26. Hong Yung Lee, *From Revolutionary Cadres to Party Technocrats: The Changing Cadre System in Socialist China* (Berkeley: University of California Press, 1991).

27. For example, Zhang Kai and Ji Yuan, *Youshuo laosanjie* (The three old classes revisited) (Beijing: Zhongguo Qingnian Chubanshe, 1997); Xiao Chong, *Zhong gong disidai mengren* (The fourth generation of leaders of the Chinese Communist Party) (Hong Kong: Xiafeier guoji chubangongsi, 1998); and Long Xiong, "Sanshinian wandong, sanshinian wanxi" ("Thirty years live east, thirty years live west") *Haishang wentan* (Literary forum of Shanghai) 2 (February 1997): 5–11.

28. William Strauss and Neil Howe, *Generations: The History of America's Future, 1582–2069* (New York: William Morrow, 1992), 59.

29. Strauss and Howe, *Generations*, 60–61.

30. Hamrin, "Perspectives on Generational Change in China," 1.

31. Many scholars define the formative years of personal growth as 17–25. See Michael Yahuda, "Political Generations in China," *China Quarterly* 80 (December 1979): 795; Marvin Rintala, "Generations: Political Generations," in *The International Encyclopedia of the Social Sciences* (New York: Macmillan/Free Press, 1968); and Rodolfo Garza and David Vaughan, "The Political Socialization of Chicano Elites: A Generational Approach," *Social Science Quarterly* 65 (June 1984): 290–307.

32. Thomas Gold, "Youth and State," *China Quarterly* 127 (1991): 594. Also see Ruth Cherrington, *Deng's Generation: Young Intellectuals in 1980s China* (London: Macmillan/St. Martin's, 1997), 14–15.

33. See Karl Mannheim, "Consciousness of Class and Consciousness of Generation," in Karl Mannheim, *Essays on Sociology of Knowledge* (London: RKP, 1952); and Pat McNeill, "The Changing Generation Gap," *New Statesman and Society* 1, no. 16 (September 1988): 30.

34. Quoted from Cherrington, "Generational Issues in China," 304.

35. Mannheim, *Essays on Sociology of Knowledge*, 298.

36. Pat McNeill, "The Changing Generation Gap," *New Statesman and Society* 1, no. 16 (September 1988): 30.

37. See Seweryn Bialer, *Stalin's Successors: Leadership, Stability, and Change in the Soviet Union* (Oxford: Cambridge University Press, 1980), 100.

38. At present, the reform generation, or the fifth generation of leaders, has not emerged as a significant elite group on either the central or provincial levels. It is expected, however, that the fifth generation will be represented on the next central committee of the CCP. Jiang Zemin recently stated that the CCP Organization Department would promote a large number of elites who were born during the 1960s and graduated from college during the 1980s. *Shijie ribao*, 28 August 2000, A7.

39. Yahuda, "Political Generations in China." Carol Lee Hamrin categorizes four political generations: (1) revolutionary elders (seventies and eighties), whose coming of age was most influenced by anti-imperialism and civil war in the 1920s and 1930s; (2) patriotic leaders (fifties and sixties), most influenced by the anti-Japanese and anti-American wars and the adoption of the Soviet model; (3) rebel adults (thirties and forties), shaped by the CR and rural exile and seeking new ideals and values; and (4) open youth (teens and twenties) raised with weak transitional values during the reform era. See Hamrin, "Perspectives on Generational Change in China," 2.

40. Bialer, *Stalin's Successor*, 100.

41. C. Montogomery Broaded, "The Lost and Found Generation: Cohort Succession in Chinese Higher Education," *Australian Journal of Chinese Affairs* 23 (January 1990): 77.

42. Yahuda, "Political Generations in China," 795.

43. Age and generation consciousness, as some scholars have observed, is a primary identification. See Vern L. Bengtson et al., "Generations, Cohorts, and Relations between Age Groups," in *Handbook of Aging and the Social Sciences*, ed. Robert H. Binstock and Ethel Shanas (New York: Van Nostrand Reinhold, 1985), 305.

44. Deng Xiaoping, "Deng's 16 June Speech: Establish the Third-Generation Collective Leadership Now," *World Affairs* 152, no. 3 (Winter 1989–1990): 159.

45. For Jiang's effort, see Paul Cavey, "Building a Power Base: Jiang Zemin and the Post-Deng Succession," *Issues and Studies* 33, no. 11 (November 1997): 1–34.

46. For studies of some members of this age-group of leaders, see David M. Lampton, *Paths to Power: Elite Mobility in Contemporary China* (Ann Arbor: Center for Chinese Studies, University of Michigan, 1986); and John Israel and Donald Klein, *Rebels and Bureaucrats: China's December 9ers* (Berkeley: University of California Press, 1976).

47. Cherrington, "Generational Issues in China," 304.

48. For the average age distribution of the Fifteenth Central Committee of the CCP and its Politburo, see Li and White, "The Fifteenth Central Committee of the Chinese Communist Party," 252, 254.

49. Some observers consider Li, Xi, and others with similar backgrounds as members of the fifth generation of leaders. See www.Chinesenewsnet.com (November 27, 2000). But Li, Xi, and many others in the same age-group often had their formative experiences during the Cultural Revolution rather than during the reform era. Moreover, they constitute a significant segment of the fourth generation leadership.

50. Mannheim, *Essays on Sociology of Knowledge*, 305. Quoted from Charlotte C. Dunham and Vern L. Bengtson, "Generational Continuity and Change," in *Encyclopedia of Adolescence*, ed. Richard M. Lerner, Anne C. Petersen, and Jeanne Brooks-Gunn (New York: Garland, 1991), 392.

51. A discussion of the "lost generation" is found in Marthe Engelborghs-Bertels, "The New Man or a Lost Generation? Education in the Four Modernizations Program of the PRC," *Issues and Studies* 21, no. 9 (September 1985): 87–118; Yahuda, "Political Generations in China," 802–804; and C. Montgomery Broaded, "The Lost and Found Generation," 77–95.

52. Yahuda, "Political Generations in China," 802.

53. Mufson, "The Next Generation," A1.

54. Chen Hanzhong, "Zheyidai: Xiagang gongren" (This generation: Laid-off workers) *Zhongguo Zhichun* (China spring), November 1998.

55. He Qinglian, *Zhongguo de xianjing* (China's pitfall) (Hong Kong: Mingjing chubanshe, 1998).

56. Yang Fan calls the CR generation the "third generation of the republic," which includes those were who born between 1942 and 1958. They were students at elementary schools, junior and senior high schools, and universities. See "Wei 'disandai ren' zheng gongdao" (Justice for the 'third generation'), *Zhongguo yu shijie* (China and the world), December 1997.

57. Yang Fan, "Zhongguo fasheng jingji weiji de keneng yu fanweiji duice" (The possibility of the occurrence of crisis in China and protective measures), *Zhongguo yu shijie* (China and the world), March 1999.

58. Yang Fan, "Wei 'disandai ren' zheng gongdao."

59. Erling Hoh, "Freedom's Factions: Wei Jingsheng Fails to Rally Exiled Dissidents," *Far Eastern Economic Review*, 4 March 1999, 26–27.

60. For a more detailed discussion of the infighting of the Chinese dissident movement, see Ian Buruma, "Tiananmen, Inc.," *New Yorker*, May 1999, 45–52.

61. Quoted from Hoh, "Freedom's Factions," 27.

62. More recently, Wei Jingsheng and Dai Qing had a heated debate in the U.S. media on the issue of whether the United States should grant China PNTR (permanent normal trade relations) status. See Dai Qing, "Keep the Doors to China Wide Open," *Los Angeles Times*, 20 April 2000, 12.

63. *Straits Times*, 14 May 1999, 25.

64. For a discussion of the contrasting subgroups of post-Communist leadership in Russia, see David Lane, "Transition under Eltsin (Yeltsin): The Nomenklatura and Political Elite Circulation," *Political Studies* 45, no. 5 (December 1997): 874.

65. Liao Gailong and Fan Yuan, comps., *Zhongguo renming da cidian xiandai dangzhengjun lingdaorenwujuan* (Who's who in China: The volume on current party, government, and military leaders) (Beijing: Foreign Languages Press, 1994); for the complete list of categories of leaders included in the volume, see pp. xi–xv. An overwhelming majority of the fourth generation of leaders were not included in the 1989 edition.

66. Shen Xueming et al., comps., *Zhonggong di shiwujie zhongyang weiyuanhui zhongyang jilü jiancha weiyuanhui weiyuan minglu* (Who's who of the members of the Fifteenth Central Committee of the Chinese Communist Party and the Fifteenth Central Commission for Discipline Inspection) (Beijing: Zhonggong wenxian chubanshe, 1999).

67. The following sources have been thoroughly verified in regard to career experiences and informal networking of Chinese leaders: *Renmin ribao* (Internet version), *China Directory* (Tokyo: Rapiopress); *China News Analysis* (Taipei); *Guangjiaojing* (Wide Angle), (Hong Kong); and *Zhonggong yanjiu* (Studies of Chinese Communism), (Taipei).

68. For a discussion of school ties of military elites, especially the role of the National Defense University, see Shu Zhan et al., "Guofang daxue, jiangjun de yaolan" (The National Defense University: The cradle of generals), *Zhonghua yingcai* (China's talents) 171 (August 1997): 40–42. Since its founding in 1985, the NDU has graduated 5,000 military officers. They have occupied some of the most important leadership positions in the PLA; also see Li and White, "The Army in the Succession to Deng Xiaoping: Familiar Fealties and Technocratic Trends," *Asian Survey* 33, no. 8 (August 1993): 782–784.

69. Hamrin, "Perspectives on Generational Change in China."

70. For an earlier discussion on the Qinghua network, see Cheng Li, "University Networks and the Rise of Qinghua Graduates in China's Leadership," *Australian Journal of Chinese Affairs* 32 (July 1994): 1–32.

71. For example, Jae-Ho Chung, "The Politics of Prerogatives in Socialism: The Case of Taizidang in China," *Studies in Comparative Communism* 24, no. 1 (March 1991): 58–76.

72. For a discussion of the opposition to nepotism in the selection of the 15th CC members, see Li and White, "The Fifteenth Central Committee of the Chinese Communist Party," 258–262.

73. Willy Wo-Lap Lam, "All the President's Men," *South China Morning Post*, 18 March 1998, 1; Vivien Pik-Kwan Chan, "Strong Opposition as Jiang Man Gets Top Law Job," *South China Morning Post*, 18 March 1998, 1; and *Shijie ribao*, 20 March 1998, A9.

74. Interviews and questionnaires, the two forms that are often used for this inquiry, sometimes are problematic in deriving proper data. See Alex Pravda, "Ideology and the Policy Process," in *Ideology and Soviet Politics*, ed. Stephen White and Alex Pravda (London: Macmillan, 1988), 228.

75. The interview reports have also been collected and published in book form. See Li Dongsheng, ed., *Buzhang fangtan lu* (Interview with ministers) (Beijing: Zhongguo jiancha chubanshe, 1998).

76. Erik Eckholm, "Chinese Book on Political Reform Stirs Hopes for More Debate," *New York Times*, 25 August 1998, 1.

77. Wu An-chia, "Leadership Changes at the Fourth Plenum," *Issues and Studies* 30, no. 10 (October 1994): 134.

78. *Shijie ribao*, 19 June 1999, A9.

79. Tang Dianwei, "Duoqian dongwu He Xin" (He Xin: An all-rounder), *Shijie zhoukan* (World journal weekly) 792 (May 23–May 29, 1999): 26.

80. Qiao Liang and Wang Xianghui, *Chaoxian zhan* (Beyond the rule of war) (Beijing: Jiefangjun wenyi chubanshe, 1999).

81. *Shijie ribao*, 2 July 1999, A9.

82. For example, Ling Zhijun and Ma Licheng, *Huhan: Dangjin Zhongguo de wuzhong shengyin* (Voices: Five voices in present China) (Guangzhou: Guangzhou chubanshe, 1999); and Zhang Yuan, *Chongsu zhengfu: '98 zhengfu jigou gaige jiaodian da toushi* (Remolding the government: An analysis of governmental reform in 1998) (Beijing: Zhonghua gongshang lianhe chubanshe, 1998).

# 2

# The Rise of Technocrats: Elite Transformation in the Reform Era

The heresy of one age becomes the orthodoxy of the next.
—Helen Keller

Each wave of the Yangtze River pushes at the wave ahead.
—A Chinese proverb

In the spring of 1999, Norman Pearlstine, editor in chief of *Time* magazine, visited Beijing. During his trip, he met many current Chinese leaders and had dinner with President Jiang Zemin. Pearlstine was amazed by the fact that the Chinese leadership is overwhelmingly dominated by well-educated and pragmatic technocrats similar to Jiang. He wrote that this trip made him realize "how much China and its leadership had changed and how much America had not."[1] In Pearlstine's view, people in the United States still quite often see this rapidly changing country through Henry Luce's eyes as "Red China."[2]

Pearlstine's observation is accurate—today's China is largely run by technocrats, engineers turned politicians. Three "big bosses" in the third generation leadership, Jiang Zemin, Li Peng, and Zhu Rongji, and three front-runners in the fourth generation, Hu Jintao, Wen Jiabao, and Zeng Qinghong, are all trained engineers. A reporter from *Financial Times* in Great Britain described this trend even more forcefully: to describe the post-Deng government "as technocratic is not remotely controversial."[3] In 2000, of the seven members of the Politiburo's Standing Committee, China's supreme decision-making body, six are engineers and one is an architect.[4] This pattern repeats itself throughout the State Council and the ministerial and provincial government.

The present Chinese technocratic leadership is the product of two concurrent transitions in elite composition during the reform era, one is generational and the other occupational.[5] The current leadership not only reflects the transition from the Long March generation and the Anti-Japanese War generation to the third and fourth generations of leaders; it also represents the transition from revolutionary ideologues and functionalists to technocratic managers—a new type of political elite in CCP history.[6]

Technocratic politics in China, however, has not received the serious scholarly investigation that it deserves. The questions concerning the rule of technocrats have not been adequately addressed, or even raised. It has been almost two decades since technocrats emerged in 1982 as a distinct elite group in Chinese politics at the Twelfth Party Congress. However, only a few books and a handful of scholarly articles published in the West have focused on Chinese technocrats. Western studies of contemporary China have failed to include any serious scholarly inquiries on the implications of the rise of technocrats on Chinese political and socioeconomic life.

This chapter begins with a discussion of the reasons for the underestimation of China's technocratic development and then provides an overview of elite transformation during the reform era. The primary theme is the historical ramification of the rise of young technocratic elites to replace revolutionary veterans. Both the third and fourth generations of leaders are composed largely of technocratic elites. A discussion of China's current leadership that does not explore their technocratic identity is akin to an analysis of the American political system that does not pay attention to the role of lawyers and the legal backgrounds of politicians.

## CHINA'S TECHNOCRATIC DEVELOPMENT

There are three major reasons for the underestimation of power of technocracy in the PRC. First, some students of Chinese politics avoid the word "technocrats" because, in their view, this term is unsatisfactory or ambiguous. Second, those who study Chinese politics have failed to make an accurate assessment of the particular leadership role of Jiang Zemin, who heads China's technocratic elite. And third, Western sinologists have been preoccupied with Communist jargon and have been influenced by the Chinese dissidents' misinterpretation of the nature of post-Mao China.

### Chinese Technocrats Defined

The word "technocrat" does not have a universally accepted definition. Indeed, controversy usually erupts as soon as the term is mentioned, for there are many diverse ideas about how it can or should be used. The term "technocracy" was introduced to China as early as the 1930s. In an article titled "Scott and Technocracy," which was published in *Xinzhonghua zazhi* (New China magazine) in 1933, the author translated it as *jishu zhuyi* (technocratism).[7] It took approximately half a century, however, before the Chinese version of "technocrat," *jishu wenguan* or *jishu guanliao*, came into use in Chinese. Its various forms in Chinese, such as *jishu guanliao* or *jishu ganbu*, however, differ greatly in meaning and connotation.[8]

In the West, some authors have portrayed technocrats as elites whose influence is based entirely on their technical expertise. Technocratic elites, according to these authors, have had nonbureaucratic careers, are nonpolitical or nonideological, and are relatively lacking in close personal ties.[9] Rejecting these inaccurate assumptions, others who study China have adopted terms such as "political technocrats," "bureaucratic technocrats," "marketized technocrats," "Marxist technocrats," or even "marketized Marxist technocrats."[10] Both groups' premises about technocrats, however, deserve to be researched. There is no need to exclude or mystify the political and ideological features of technocrats, and there is also no need to use overly narrow policy or value-laden terms when defining them.

Some scholars deny the existence of technocratic leadership in China because, in their view, technocrats should be genuine technical experts, whereas the current top leaders in China, such as Jiang Zemin, Li Peng, Zhu Rongji, and Hu Jintao, are engineers in name only. Although there is some validity to this argument, it overlooks the possibility that similar occupational training of leaders may affect their political coherence. In China, many top leaders have been trained and have actually served as engineers. A country run by military elites differs fundamentally from a state governed by lawyers. A regime headed by Marxist ideologues is unlike a nation led by capitalist entrepreneurs. The disproportionate representation of leaders with engineering backgrounds in China may be similar to the situation that the United States faces with lawyers, or France with "énarchs" (graduates of ENA, the Ecole Nationale d'Administration).

This study defines a technocrat as a person who is concurrently specialized by training in a technical science, holds a professional occupation, and has a leadership position.[11] "Technical" disciplines are ones that mainly explore "scientific" causations rather than human purposes, often, but not always, using physical or mathematical models. Graduates of the humanities are not technocrats, even if they are professionals with high posts.

How should we regard economists in the Chinese leadership? In his comparative study of Western countries, Robert Putnam argues for distinguishing between elites trained in the natural sciences and those trained in the social sciences.[12] Other studies also indicate that, in contrast to China where a large number of top administrators are engineers by training, countries such as Japan and South Korea have a large number of bureaucrats who are economists by training.[13] For example, when scholars speak of the technocrats at MITI (Japan's Ministry of International Trade and Industry), they are not referring to engineers.[14] A division between broad and narrow definitions of technocrats seems appropriate here. In a broad sense, technocrats are defined as those who have expertise, practical experience, and leadership positions. In a narrow sense, only those who are trained in engineering and natural sciences should be identified as technocrats.

In studies of democratic countries, technocrats are often identified as technically trained elites who are *selected* for power, in contrast to politicians who are *elected*. But in an authoritarian country such as China, no high political leaders are actually elected. In nondemocratic regimes, therefore, a technocrat is always, in one way or another, a political technocrat. Some writings about Chinese technocrats tend to distinguish them from Party cadres in terms of their administrative functions. But at present the technocrats in China are almost all Party officials, and some are also in charge of the Party organization and ideological work even if they were educated in the applied sciences. All technocrats are simultaneously bureaucrats (not vice versa).[15] As will be shown later in this book, Chinese technical elites came to power only partially because of their technical credentials and partly because of their nontechnocratic political or family connections. The emphasis on three objective elements—technical education, professional occupation, and leadership position—avoids value judgments and thus is less subjective.

The fact that many Chinese leaders share the specialized occupation of engineering, especially since the general population of China does not have many engineers, aids communication and mutual recognition among the elite. In the distant Confucian past, and then again in the more recent Marxist-Maoist era, rulers in this vast country were more cohesive because they convinced themselves that they had a common identity and ideology. Currently, technocratic criteria for the promotion of new leaders may serve the same role of fostering a sense of unity among the current elites, who badly need this sense in their fast-changing and decentralizing postrevolutionary situation. This does not mean that technocrats are always on the same side. Zhu Rongji and Li Peng, for example, are known to have conflicting opinions on various policies. Just as cadres of the British Raj in India believed that they should think well of each other because they knew subjects such as Latin, so PRC cadres today recognize each other's right to rule effectively because they have studied subjects such as electrical engineering.[16] In each case, they say their own rare skills are particularly relevant to the business of government. The reason for the large-scale recruitment of engineers to top leadership in reform China is political: to provide a facile standard basis on which leaders can justify each other's legitimacy to rule.

### Jiang Zemin: A Technocratic Leader

A second reason for the inadequacy of most studies of technocratic leadership in China lies in the way in which China experts have assessed the role of Jiang Zemin—China's top technocrat and the "core of the third generation of leadership in the CCP." Prior to Deng's death, many sinologists were extremely suspicious about Jiang's power. Ever since 1989, when Jiang was chosen by Deng to replace Zhao Ziyang, outside observers often considered Jiang to be a "transitional figure" or a "Hua Guofeng–like figure"—a basically incompetent leader whose power depended exclusively on the words of his paramount patron. Ten years have passed and this "transitional figure" has been able to hang on to power much longer than some top leaders in other large countries, such as Mikhail Gorbachev, George Bush, and John Major, who were active during the same time period.

Jiang was often seen as a mere technocrat with no charisma, no common touch, and no solid basis of power in the military or Party hierarchy. Yet Jiang by no means lacks the political determination to get rid of his rivals. Over the past few years, this "uncharismatic, politically fragile"[17] technocrat has surprised observers by defeating his main political rivals, including "generals of the Yang family," "the boss of Beijing"—Chen Xitong and "the next strong man"—the head of the National People's Congress, Qiao Shi. Most importantly, he succeeded Deng Xiaoping smoothly.

What, then, went wrong with outside observers' analysis of Jiang's capacity? Foreign observers failed to understand that Jiang actually represents a powerful political force—technocrats. Most of Jiang's friends in high circles are technocrats. Wu Bangguo and Huang Ju, two Politburo members promoted by Jiang from Shanghai, are both Qinghua University–trained engineers. A recently published book entitled *Jiang Zemin's Counselors* lists four people as Jiang's closest political friends: Wang Daohan, former mayor of Shanghai and the man who has been in charge of China's negotiation with Taiwan; Zeng Qinghong, Jiang's longtime assistant and newly elected Politburo alternate who now runs the powerful Organization Department of the CCP; Chen Zhili, a new full member of the Central Committee and the woman who has recently been chosen to take over the Ministry of Education; and Liu Ji, former vice president of the Chinese Academy of Social Sciences and coauthor of a well-known article, "On Scientific Policy-Making," which advocates technocratic thinking for China's reform.[18] All four are from Shanghai and each has a technical education.

Many foreign observers were suspicious about the ability of technocrats to be their own bosses. Jiang's success in defeating three arch rivals does not necessarily mean any permanent victory of technocrats over nontechnocrats. It is probably just coincidental that the Yang brothers, Chen, and Qiao all happened to be nontechnocrats. Future battles may occur among technocrats themselves. But it should be obvious that technocrats are completely political, both in groups and as individuals. Although technocrats differ from revolutionary veterans in that they are more interested in the means of bureaucratic control than political campaign methods, they are by no means ineffective in seizing and holding political power. As Hans Morgenthau argued, "man [or woman] is a political animal by nature and a scientist [and engineer] by chance or choice."[19]

Ever since the 1989 Tiananmen student movement and subsequent government crackdown, Western sinologists have been reluctant to make any generalizations or predictions about China's future. This is understandable because China

has been undergoing such drastic and complicated socioeconomic changes during
the past decade that students of China have found it very difficult to find the right
way to characterize the reform era. In Lucian Pye's words, "for every valid generalization about Deng's China the exact opposite seems also to apply."[20] For example, during the mid-1990s, Western studies of China were dominated by a contradictory theme: the strongest remaining Communist regime in the world was
rushing toward capitalism![21]

Meanwhile, the fascinating changes that have occurred in China during the reform era, especially the rapid and large-scale elite transformation, have not
spawned many theoretical efforts to redefine the nature of Chinese politics but instead have created, among many sinologists, a strong sense of uncertainty about
the future of China. In recent writings on China, the word "uncertainty" has become one of the most frequently used terms in referring to Chinese politics.[22]
Many prominent political scientists who study contemporary China have offered
a great number of possible scenarios to predict China's developmental path.[23]
With so many scenarios, the reader cannot draw any meaningful conclusions
about the nature of the Chinese political system.

In addition, some essential terms used by China experts are not without ambiguity. As David Bachman noted, China experts often speak of China in transition, but they are usually unclear as "to what the endpoint of the transitional
process may be."[24] This phenomenon in the study of Chinese politics reflects the
theoretical and analytical poverty of the field. China's historical transition to
technocratic rule and the implication for China's future have not received much
scholarly attention. Although it is impossible to predict the fate of an individual
leader or a political faction, one can comment with greater conviction about major political and socioeconomic forces at work, no matter what an individual
leader's fate may be in the future.

## Chinese Dissidents: Misinterpreting Politics in the Reform Era

A third reason for the limited understanding of Chinese technocrats in the West
is that some sinologists have long been preoccupied with the legacy of Mao's anti-
intellectualism and the dichotomy of "red and expert." That the ruling party in
the PRC continues to call itself the Communist Party prevents many Western students of China from identifying these new Chinese leaders differently. They tend
to overlook the fundamental change in the sociopolitical status of knowledge
elites in the reform era.

One important factor that led to overlooking this change is the misinterpretation made by Chinese dissident intellectuals. Since the Tiananmen incident in
1989, many dissident intellectuals and student leaders have been exiled in the
West and have significantly influenced Western studies of Chinese politics. Most
of the Chinese dissidents who have written about social and political issues during the reform era came from technocratic backgrounds themselves. These tech-

nocrats-turned-dissidents preferred to identify their opponents (e.g., Li Peng and Jiang Zemin) as Communist hard-liners rather than as their peers, at least in terms of educational background, if not social values.

Not surprisingly, a great number of books on the Tiananmen crisis written by Western sinologists and Chinese dissidents presented the Tiananmen conflict as a conflict between "gerontocratic, Communist bumpkins" and "younger, well-educated democrats."[25] This view is too simplistic, if not entirely misleading. One may reasonably argue that technical elites were actively involved on all sides of the 1989 conflict. They included, for example, *incumbent technocrats* (Premier Li Peng, and the Party boss in Shanghai and soon-to-be Secretary-General Jiang Zemin), *former technocrats* (dissident astrophysicist Fang Lizhi, mathematician Yan Jiaqi, and many members of Zhao Ziyang's think tank), and *potential technocrats* (many student leaders). Soon after technical elites emerged as a distinctive political force in post-Mao China, they split into various factions. The political dissidents such as Fang and Yan were part of the elite establishment before they were expelled from the Chinese Communist Party in the late 1980s. As a result of misinterpretation, the power struggle between technocrats in government on the one hand, and educated elites in the opposition on the other, was largely neglected. Consequently, the massive elite transformation and its profound political and socioeconomic impact on the country during the reform era was largely overlooked.

## FORMATION OF A CHINESE POLITICAL ELITE: HISTORICAL BACKGROUND

Although this study is primarily concerned with the new generation of leaders and the elite transformation in the 1980s, some brief observations about traditional elites in Chinese society and important changes in the twentieth century, especially the social backgrounds of prereform PRC elites, will be helpful.

### Meritocracy: Confucian Tradition

Traditional China was a meritocratic society. Social stratification in that society was generally based on two reciprocal Confucian social concepts. First, human beings differ from one another in intelligence, knowledge, and ability. Second, because of these differences, the rule of the "wise" and "able" is morally justified.[26] The principle that membership in the ruling class should be based on an individual's educational achievements has prevailed in China since the seventh century, when the competitive examination system was firmly established.[27] In a society under this tradition, education served as the main avenue of upward social mobility. To become a scholar-official (*shidafu*) was the highest goal for almost everyone.

But not everyone who succeeded in educational competition in traditional China was a member of the ruling class. The term *buyi* ("wearers of cotton-cloth garments") was used to identify scholars who were not officials. Also, not all members of the ruling class were educated. Passing official exams was just one of the mechanisms for social and political mobility. Ho Ping-ti observes that "money could be directly translated into higher status through the purchase of studentship, offices, and official titles."[28] For example, a very influential figure at the end of the Qing dynasty, Li Lianying, was born in a humble family and was apprenticed as a cobbler at an early age. He had "no schooling, no money to buy rank, and no military experience," but he rose to power through a "special self-sacrifice"—starting as a eunuch.[29]

During the three centuries before the Qing dynasty collapsed in 1911, intellectual merit was increasingly replaced by parental wealth and status as a basis for elite recruitment.[30] In Chinese history, furthermore, rebellions repeatedly brought some illiterates to power. Education, nevertheless, was the surest "ladder to success" in traditional China.

Men who rose to official positions through examinations were always generalists, not specialists or technocrats in a modern sense. What enabled career advancement was usually their memory of the classics, their talent in writing poetry, or their skill in calligraphy. As Fei Xiaotong described the basis of traditional elites, "in a society in which historic traditions have the only real validity, influence lies not with the innovators but with those who can guide the country along established paths."[31] The official examination system operated well when it fulfilled its basic purposes of channeling social thought and recruiting potential leaders, and it lasted until 1905.

### The Formation of the KMT Elite

Through what channels, then, did new political elites emerge at the beginning of the twentieth century? During the republican period from 1912 to 1949, China experienced ceaseless civil conflicts between warlords, the Japanese invasion, and then the conflicts between the CCP and the KMT (*Kuomintang,* the Chinese Nationalist Party). During the entire period, as Tsai Wen-hui noted, "the foundation of the rulers' political power had to be built upon the personal loyalty of relatives, trusted friends, and members of their own political and military subordinates."[32] A majority of political leaders came from the military, especially in the first part of this period. The distinction between the first part (1912–1928) and the second part (1929–1949) of the period was a transition from domination mainly by military elites to domination by both military elites and KMT party officials.[33]

In their comparative study of the CCP and KMT, Robert North and Ithiel Pool observed that both parties emerged from political and economic chaos, and both were greatly influenced by the Soviet Union; thus, there were initially many similarities between CCP and KMT cadres.[34] The elites of both parties had careers in party organization and military service. According to North and Pool, most of the CCP and KMT high-level cadres received college-level education. But North and Pool's description of educational backgrounds is in one sense misleading. The high percentages of advanced education and foreign study among both the KMT and CCP elites should be interpreted carefully, since much of this education was military training. It is necessary to take a closer look at the formation of the CCP elite before we turn to its transformation in the 1980s.

### The Formation of the CCP Elite prior to the Reform

The Chinese Communist Party rose to power as a military organization; its leaders were mostly soldiers, peasants, and members of the urban lower-middle class.[35] Although many of its key leaders went abroad before they came to power, some, like Zhou Enlai and Deng Xiaoping, were mainly engaged in political activities rather than in formal education. Liu Shaoqi, Ye Jianying, and Yang Shangkun attended college in the Soviet Union but received only military training and lessons in Marxist doctrine. Mao Zedong was never able to fully participate in the few university courses he audited; this, according to many students of Chinese politics, is one of the reasons for his hostility toward intellectuals.[36]

None of the thirteen people who attended the first meeting of the Chinese Communist Party in 1921 had studied the natural sciences.[37] There was a complete absence of specialists such as the engineers in the CCP Central Committee.[38] Furthermore, during the late 1920s and early 1930s, a large number of poor peasants, many illiterate, flocked into the Red Army and the Party.[39] Some of these people, two decades later, became a major part of the ruling elite of the PRC. These people occupied a large majority of leadership posts above the county level after the Communist victory in 1949.

From 1949 to 1978, recruitment to cadre positions and political advancement was usually based on (1) seniority in joining the Party and the revolution, such as taking part in the Long March and the Anti-Japanese War, (2) ideological commitment to Marxism and Mao Zedong thought, (3) political loyalty and activism in the class struggle, and (4) class background from a "proletarian family." None of these criteria changed significantly until the early 1980s.

Therefore, for the first three decades of the PRC regime, the educational level of Party cadres and members was extremely low. In 1955, for example, only 5 percent of the top leaders had a junior high school education or above.[40] During the Cultural Revolution, Mao first used the Red Guards to humiliate intellectuals, then urged workers to destroy the established Party and the state machinery, and finally created a "leadership of the revolutionary triple alliance," consisting of military officers, mass organization leaders, and revolutionary cadres. Under this policy, a large number of peasants, workers, and soldiers entered high-level leadership, including the CCP Central Committee and the Politburo. For example, Chen Yonggui, a peasant from the model Dazhai brigade, became a Politburo member in the 1970s; Wu Guixian, a textile worker, was appointed vice premier.

The formation of Chinese Communist elites thus helps explain the recurring conflict between "reds" and "experts" in Mao's China, especially during the Cul-

tural Revolution. During the 1960s, one of the most important Chinese accusations against "revisionism," in the Soviet Union and domestically, was its technocratic orientation.[41] Intellectuals—those who were college educated in the
Chinese context—were branded the "ninth stinking category," a social stratum
that should always be under revolutionary scrutiny.

The term "technocracy" was translated as the "dictatorship of engineers"
(*gongchengshi zhuanzheng*) in Chinese during the Mao era.[42] As David Bachman
noted, prior to Mao's death in 1976, Party membership was composed overwhelmingly of peasants, who "were seen as its key constituency."[43] Intellectuals,
as such, had no claim on leadership. According to the 1982 PRC census, only 4
percent of the members of the CCP were educated beyond high school level. Most
(52.3 percent) had only a primary school education or were illiterate. In 1980,
among the 450,000 leaders at county level and above, 230,000 (51 percent) had
only a junior high school level education or less.[44]

## THE LARGEST PEACEFUL ELITE
## TURNOVER IN CHINESE HISTORY

The elite transformation from revolutionary veterans to technocrats during the
post-Mao era is not only the largest peaceful elite turnover in Chinese history, but
it is probably the most massive, rapid change of elites within any regime in human
history. The Maoist cadre recruitment policy was reversed soon after Deng Xiaoping moved to the top of the power structure. As early as 1978, when he had just been
"rehabilitated" as vice premier, Deng made a speech at a national conference on science and technology, claiming that "the modernization of science and technology
is the key to the Four Modernizations."[45] Although Deng was hostile to some dissident intellectuals, he constantly urged that intellectuals, as a social stratum, should
not be treated as an "alien force" (*yiji*), as happened during the Mao era, but should
be respected as the "core (*gugan*) of the modernization program." Deng also told a
group of technical experts and scientists that he was willing to serve as "head of the
ministry of logistics for their work."[46] Chen Yun, another veteran leader, also called
for selecting revolutionary successors with advanced educational background.

The most fundamental change in the CCP elite recruitment policy occurred in
the early 1980s when Deng Xiaoping and Hu Yaobang made two important
speeches. Deng Xiaoping's speech was delivered to an enlarged session of the
Politburo of the CCP on August 31, 1980, and Hu's was addressed to a large conference in commemoration of the centenary of Karl Marx's death in 1983.[47] Hu,
then Party general secretary, stated forcefully that the Party should oppose the
tendency to divorce its own leadership from expertise and should no longer oppose experts. Instead, he said, the Party should establish the concept that all leaders must be trained specialists. Hu's speech was a landmark, symbolizing the beginning of a massive elite transformation. Since then, technicians and specialists
have become increasingly prominent in the circle of power.

Although Deng Xiaoping, Chen Yun, Hu Yaobang, and Zhao Ziyang lacked a technical background, they acted as "patrons of technocrats."[48] Zhao Ziyang's favorable view of technocratic leadership, for example, can be traced to the Mao era. In 1962, when he was a provincial leader in Guangdong, Zhao attempted "the coordination of three powers" (Party, administration, and technical).[49] In Zhao's view, a commune's chief agronomist should have the same power as the Party secretary and administrator. When he became premier, Zhao established numerous research centers and think tanks under the State Council. He had close contacts with many famous reform-oriented scholars, such as Li Yining of Beijing University, Wen Yuankai of China's University of Science and Technology, and Qin Benli, editor of *World Economic Herald,* one of the most influential newspapers in China in the 1980s that advocated the rule of technocracy.[50]

## The Meteoric Rise of Chinese Technocrats

Technocrats began to emerge as a distinctive elite in the Twelfth Party Congress in 1982, when a number of technocrats such as Li Peng, Hu Qili, Jiang Zemin, Hu Jintao, Wu Bangguo, and Wang Zhaoguo were recruited to the Central Committee of the CCP. The 1982 congress can be seen as a watershed for CCP leadership.[51] The effort to recruit young technocrats accelerated when 131 high-ranking Party veterans (most in their seventies and eighties) resigned, including fifty-four full members and ten alternates of the Central Committee, during a special Party conference held in 1985.[52] These sixty-four Central Committee retirees were replaced by an equal number of new members, whose average age was barely over fifty; 76 percent of them were college educated.[53] At the subsequent fifth plenum of the Twelfth Central Committee held in the same year, Li Peng and Hu Qili became members of the Politburo.

There was a massive turnover of Chinese leaders at all levels in the 1980s, with a significant number of the promoted elites being technocrats. Table 2.1 shows that an overwhelming majority of political leaders rose to their positions after 1982. Among the eighteen Politburo members in the Thirteenth Central Committee, only two (11 percent), Hu Yaobang and Zhao Ziyang, had assumed their posts before 1980. In the Thirteenth Central Committee of the CCP, 92 percent of the members were promoted after 1982. Among the ministers, top military officers, and mayors, only 2.5 percent of each were appointed before 1981. Only 5 percent of provincial leaders held their posts before 1981.

From 1980 to 1986, more than 1,370,000 senior cadres, all recruited before 1949, retired. At the same time, more than 469,000 college-educated younger cadres came into leadership positions above the county level.[54] This monumental change seems to be the result of the *nomenklatura* requirement that PRC leaders should have college degrees or other tertiary education. The key constituency of the Party, especially the upper- and middle-level leadership, changed from peasants and workers to college-educated elites, especially technical specialists.[55] By the end of

Table 2.1 Year of Assuming Leadership Position among PRC Elites in the 1980s (percentage)

| Leadership Level | Pre-1980 | 1980 | 1981 | 1982 | 1983 | 1984 | 1985 | 1986 | 1987 | 1988 | Total |
|---|---|---|---|---|---|---|---|---|---|---|---|
| Politburo members (N = 18)[a] | 11 | | | 22 | | | 28 | | 39 | | 100 |
| Central Comm. members (N = 285)[b] | 8 | | | 24 | | | | | 68 | | 100 |
| Minister (N = 40)[c] | | 2.5 | | | 5 | 7.5 | 15 | 7.5 | 15 | 42.5 | 100 |
| Provincial leaders (N = 60)[d] | | | 5 | 2 | 13 | 2 | 20 | 10 | 8 | 40 | 100 |
| Military leaders (N = 224)[e] | 2 | | 0.5 | 4 | 5 | 0.5 | 42 | 11 | 18 | 17 | 100 |
| Mayors (N = 221)[f] | 1 | 0.5 | 1 | 1.5 | 27 | 33 | 28 | 8 | | | 100 |

*Note:* Some figures are rounded.

[a]Based on data from 1987. See Li and White, "The Thirteenth Central Committee of the Chinese Communist Party," 383.

[b]See Li and White, "The Thirteenth Central Committee," 382.

[c]Excludes vice ministers of the State Council. Based on data from 1988. See Liao and Fan, *Zhongguo renming da cidian*. Additional data were accumulated and tabulated by the author.

[d]Refers to governors and provincial Party secretaries. Autonomous regions and three municipalities directly under the central government—Beijing, Tianjin, Shanghai, and Chongqing—are also treated as provinces. Based on data from 1988. See Liao and Fan, *Zhongguo renming da cidian*. The data were accumulated and tabulated by the author.

[e]Refers to commanders, vice commanders, commissars, vice commissars, heads and vice heads of staff, and heads and vice heads of political departments at the greater military district level or above. Based on data from 1988. See Liao and Fan, *Zhongguo renming da cidian*. Data were accumulated by the author for this book.

[f]Based on data from 1987. See Li and Bachman, "Localism, Elitism, and Immobilism," 76.

1998, among the total 61 million CCP members, over 11 million were college graduates (17.8 percent), about 4.5 times greater than was true in the 1982 census.[56]

In the mid-1980s, Qian Xuesen, chairman of China's National Committee of Science and Technology, and a good friend of Deng Xiaoping, wrote a proposal to the authorities that by the year 2000 all cadres must be college graduates, all leaders at the county and bureau level must hold M.A. degrees, and all full or deputy ministers must hold Ph.D. degrees.[57] Western academics may find it hard to conceive how anyone could visualize a country run by Ph.D.s, but Qian advocated this. The objectives of his proposal might not have been achieved, but China is rapidly moving in that direction. For example, among a total of eight top municipal leaders (mayor and deputy mayors) in Beijing in 1999, seven held M.A. degrees, including one Ph.D. Five held high professional titles such as senior engineers or professors. Their average age was fifty-two.[58] In Guangdong Province, a large number of newly appointed mayors and municipal Party secretaries held Ph.D. or M.A. degrees.[59]

Table 2.2 supplies an overview of the change in college educational attainment among Chinese leaders at various important levels between 1978 and 1998. It shows a striking increase in college-educated Chinese leaders at all levels: from 23 percent to 92 percent among members of the Politburo; from 38 percent to 95 percent among ministers and deputy ministers; from 4 percent to 78 percent among military leaders; and from 2 percent to 91 percent among municipal and county heads (also see fig. 2.1).

This rapid increase was partly due to the fact that many officials had recently attended training programs in Party cadre schools. Between 1992 and 1996, 500,000 officials above the county level received such training. About 1,000 cadres above the provincial-ministerial level studied at the Central Party School during the same period.[60] Nevertheless, most of the college-educated elites promoted in the 1980s received a regular education and majored in engineering and natural sciences. For example, about three-fourths of the ministers and deputy ministers are engineers or natural scientists by training (see figure 2.2). About 17 percent majored in the social sciences, including economics, and only 7.5 percent received their higher education in the humanities. The same pattern can be found among Chinese mayors (see figure 2.3).

The meteoric rise of technocrats among top leaders is also evident in table 2.3. In the Twelfth CC in 1982, technocrats accounted for just 2 percent, but by 1987 they were 25 percent, and over half by 1997. Four full Central Committee members with technocratic background in 1982 were Yao Yilin, Li Peng, Hu Qili, and Jiang Zemin. The representation of technocrats has also risen dramatically in other high-level leadership categories such as ministers, provincial Party secretaries, and governors. In 1982, no one technocrat served as a provincial secretary or a governor, and just one technocrat, Li Peng, was a minister. Fifteen years later, technocrats accounted for more than 70 percent in each of these three top administrative categories. Although the general secretaries, Hu Yaobang and Zhao

**Table 2.2   Change in College Education of Chinese Elites during the Reform Era (Percentage)**

| Leadership Level/Year | 1978 | 1982 | 1988 | 1992 | 1998 |
| --- | --- | --- | --- | --- | --- |
| Politburo[a] | 23 | 32 | 67 | 86 | 92 |
| Party Central Committee[b] | 26 | 55 | 73 | 84 | 92 |
| Ministry[c] | n/a | 38 | 82 | 88 | 95 |
| Military[d] | n/a | 4 | 58 | 78 | n/a |
| Province[e] | n/a | 20 | 59 | 96 | 95 |
| Municipality/county[f] | 2 | 31 | 78 | 91 | n/a |

Note: Some figures are rounded.

[a]Li and White, "The Thirteenth Central Committee of the Chinese Communist Party," 379; and Li and White, "The Fifteenth Central Committee of the Chinese Communist Party," 249.

[b]Li and White, "The Thirteenth Central Committee of the Chinese Communist Party," 379; Xiaowei Zang, "The Fourteenth Central Committee of the CCP," 796; and Li and White, "The Fifteenth Central Committee of the Chinese Communist Party," 248.

[c]Refers to ministers and deputy ministers of the State Council. Ch'en Yung-sheng, "Reform of Mainland China's Cadre System," *Issues and Studies* 21, no. 12 (December 1985): 102. The 1988 data are based on Liao and Fan, *Zhongguo renming da cidian* (1989). The total number of this group of elites is 191 (data compiled by the author). The 1992 data are based on Liao and Fan, *Zhongguo renming da cidian* (1994). The 1998 data refer to ministers and members of the State Council only. *Jiefang Daily* (Shanghai), 19 March 1998, 1.

[d]Refers to commanders, vice commanders, commissars, vice commissars, heads and vice heads of staff, heads and vice heads of political departments at the greater military district level or above. *Renmin ribao* (overseas edition), 6 July 1987, 1. The 1988 data are based on Liao and Fan, *Zhongguo renming da cidian* (1989). The total number of this group of elites is 224; data were accumulated and tabulated by the author.

[e]Refers to governors, deputy governors, secretaries, and vice secretaries of provincial Party committees. Ch'en Yung-sheng, 1985, p. 102. The 1988 data are based on Liao and Fan, 1989. The total number of this group of elites is 264; data were accumulated and tabulated by the author. The 1992 and 1998 data refer to governors and deputy governors only. *Renmin ribao* (overseas edition), 29 June 1993, 1; and *Renmin ribao*, 3 August 1998, 1.

[f]Refers to mayors, deputy mayors, secretaries, and vice secretaries of municipal Party committees, county heads, deputy county heads, secretaries, and vice secretaries of county Party committees. The 1988 data refer to mayors only and the total number of mayors under study is 247. In the PRC, municipal government can be administratively equivalent to provincial, prefectural, or county government, depending on the size of the city. Wang Junxian and Cui Wunian, "Changes in the Structure of China's Cadres: An Investigation and Analysis of 6,200 Leading Bodies at County and Prefectural Levels," *Zouxiang weilai*, (Toward the future) 2, no. 2 (1988): 27–28; *Guang Jiao Jing* (Wide angle) 16 March 1986, 21; Ch'en Yung-sheng, 1985, 102; and Li and Bachman, "Localism, Elitism, and Immobilism," 73. The 1992 data refer to mayors only, and the total number of mayors under study is 315. *Zhongguo chengshi nianjian* (The almanac of China's cities) 10 (1994); data were accumulated and tabulated by the author.

Ziyang, were purged in the late 1980s, many of Hu's and Zhao's technocrat-protégés remained in power. Over the past decade, this type of leadership has consolidated, even though a few technocrats have fallen in power struggles.

These data are even more striking in light of three facts. First, college graduates made up only 0.8 percent of the Chinese labor force in the 1980s. Second, al-

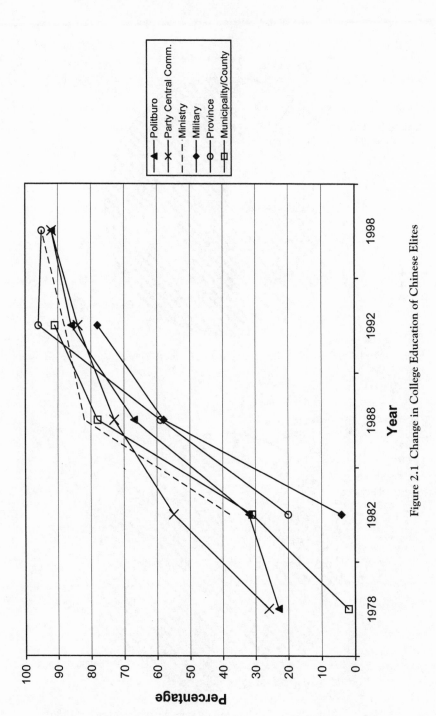

Figure 2.1 Change in College Education of Chinese Elites

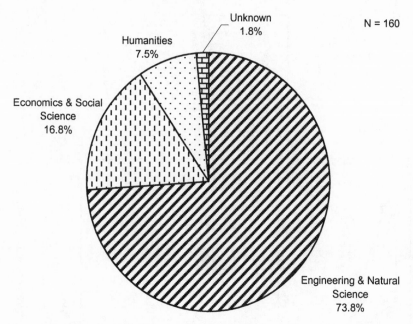

Figure 2.2 Major Field of College Study among Chinese Ministers and Vice Ministers (1988)

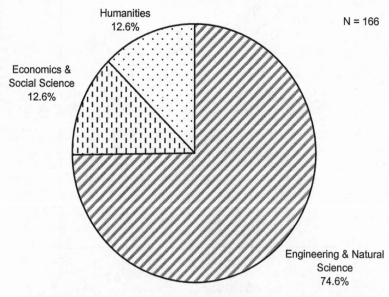

Figure 2.3 Major Field of College Study among Chinese Mayors (1986)

**Table 2.3   Technocrats' Representation in High-Level Leadership, 1982–1997**

| Year | Ministers | | Provincial Secretaries | | Provincial Governors | | Central Committee Full Members | |
|---|---|---|---|---|---|---|---|---|
| | No. | % | No. | % | No. | % | No. | % |
| 1982 | 1 | 2 | 0 | 0 | 0 | 0 | 4 | 2 |
| 1987 | 17 | 45 | 7 | 25 | 8 | 33 | 34 | 26 |
| 1997 | 28 | 70 | 23 | 74 | 24 | 77 | 98 | 51 |

*Sources:* Hong Yung Lee, *From Revolutionary Cadres to Party Technocrats*, 268; Kenneth Lieberthal, *Governing China: From Revolution through Reform* (New York: Norton, 1995), 236; and He Pin, *Zhongguo Xinzhuhou* (The New Lords of China) (Mississauga, Ont.: Canada Mirror Books, 1996).

though China was traditionally a meritocratic society, scientific knowledge and technical competence, which have for centuries been socially esteemed in the West, were always viewed as secondary achievements according to Confucian ideological values.[61] Third, as stated earlier, China's meritocratic tradition underwent an extreme reversal during the Mao era, especially during the Cultural Revolution when professionals were repeatedly targeted.

## The Shadow of Gerontocracy

Elite transformation in post-Mao China was accompanied by an ideological shift and policy changes in Chinese society.[62] The rapid rise of technocratic elites in the leadership was not accomplished without obstacles. Up until the early 1990s, technocrats at various levels, especially in the central government, were often under the shadow of their political patrons or other veteran leaders. For most of the Deng era, revolutionary veterans continued to play a crucial role in Chinese politics. Deng Xiaoping, along with Chen Yun, Wang Zhen, and Yang Shangkun, frequently intervened in major state decisions, although they were officially "retired" from the Politburo and government.

Other relatively young political leaders, including technocrats, as some Western observers have noted, were in many ways caretakers for the policy and legacy of Deng Xiaoping.[63] The fall of Hu Yaobang, the purge of Zhao Ziyang, the demotion of Hu Qili and Yan Mingfu, and the Tiananmen incident are all examples of the power and influence of Chinese octogenarians. To a certain extent, this generation of Communist revolutionaries, reared in the early part of the twentieth century, ruled the PRC from 1949 to the early 1990s.[64]

The tension between the older generation of veterans who spearheaded the revolution and the postrevolutionary generation of technocrats is certainly not unique in China. It also occurred in many third world countries, especially in Communist regimes, as they transitioned into the postrevolutionary era.[65] Murray Tanner and Michael Feder observed that all Marxist-Leninist governments faced two difficult questions: (1) how to develop institutions that allow younger elites to gracefully (or at least nonviolently) replace the aging first generation of revolutionaries and (2) how to recruit elites with the technical skills necessary to make the transition from revolution and social transformation to economic development.[66]

What makes China's transformation distinctive from many others is not only the longevity of Deng Xiaoping but also the historical circumstances of the post–Cultural Revolution era. When Deng returned to power in 1978, he made it very clear that CR activists whom he identified as "beneficiaries of the CR" would be banned from leadership posts at any level. In addition, Deng gradually forced out of power some prominent leaders in the Anti-Japanese War generation whose political careers advanced during the Cultural Revolution, such as Hua Guofeng, Wang Dongxing, and Wu De.

Deng's power base was largely built on those who had been "rehabilitated" after the Cultural Revolution. Most of them belonged to the Long March generation and the Anti-Japanese War generation. Not surprisingly, the average age of the Central Committee of the Chinese Communist Party in 1978 was about sixty-six, the highest in CCP history. In 1980, the average age of provincial leaders was sixty-two, and many of them were well over seventy.[67] Therefore, Deng's effort to promote a new generation of better-educated leaders was only partially achieved.[68] To a certain extent, from the 1980s to the early 1990s China was governed by one strong man who was aided by a group of technocrats.

Deng faced a dilemma in dealing with his fellow revolutionary veterans. On one hand, he understood that these revolutionary veterans were not suitable to the need for rapid change in the social and economic life of the country and would need to move aside to make room for younger and better-educated elites. This was inevitable. But on the other hand, Deng found that he still needed veteran leaders, especially those in the military, when a major crisis such as the 1989 Tiananmen protest occurred. Because of this dilemma, Deng adopted several institutional changes.

During the Twelfth Chinese Communist Party Congress in 1982, Deng formed the Central Advisory Commission (CAC), a Central Committee–level body into which veteran leaders could retire, retaining a voice in Party politics but having no responsibility for the Party's day-to-day affairs.[69] Deng and Chen Yun were chairmen of the first and second CAC, respectively. During the 1980s, the commission played a crucial role in making major decisions. But the CAC gradually withdrew from the decision-making process and was dismantled during the Fourteenth Party Congress in 1992.

During the early 1980s, Deng and the Chinese authorities also institutionalized a system of cadre retirement.[70] Since veteran leaders were reluctant to give up power entirely, some transitional incentives (e.g., financial compensation, maintenance of housing privileges, and affirmative action for their children's employment and promotion) were adopted.[71] Many veteran leaders used this "last opportunity" for abuse of power to make a fortune for their families. According to He Qinglian, the author of the well-known book *China's Pitfalls*, retired officials are among the main beneficiaries of what she calls "agents in the power-money exchange" who stole state assets in the process of "capitalization of power" during the reform.[72]

According to the study of China's provincial leaders conducted by Bo Zhiyue, 1983 was a watershed year. Before 1983, few veteran provincial leaders retired. Only 2 percent of provincial leaders retired in 1980 and 5 percent in 1981. In 1983, however, more than 60 percent of provincial leaders retired. This largely resulted from Deng's proposal at the 1982 Party congress suggesting the retirement of a large number of veteran leaders. Since that proposal was adopted, the retirement of provincial leaders at a certain age has become more or less institutionalized and three waves occurred in 1985 (20 percent), 1988 (15 percent), and 1993 (20 percent).[73] At the central government level, the retirement process occurred even more quickly as Deng Xiaoping, Chen Yun, Li Xiannien, and Bo Yibo vacated their seats on the Politburo and the State Council, although these veteran leaders often had a final say in some major decisions.

Meanwhile, many veteran leaders often requested, either implicitly or explicitly, leadership posts for their children and confidants as a precondition for their retirement. As Hong Yung Lee noted,

> It is easy to understand why children of high-ranking cadres might have benefited most from the system [of retirement]. First of all, it is their parents who have selected the "third echelon" cadres and who have access to information at the top level. Sometimes, high-ranking cadres use their retirement as leverage to gain the appointment of their children to appropriate positions, although the *ting-ti* system [family-line succession in employment] is not officially applicable to cadre positions. Alternatively, they can use their extensive personal networks by offering reciprocal favors to other decision-makers.[74]

In the words of Murray Tanner and Michael Feder, "China's central leadership is pervaded by a Byzantine network of family ties."[75] As a result, the children, relatives, and friends of China's senior leadership have become one of the most significant recruitment pools for China's third and fourth generations of leaders. Chapter 5 provides a detailed discussion of the problem of nepotism in the elite transformation during the reform era. In order to fully understand the process of leadership succession in the reform era, it is important to discuss the notion of the "third echelon."

### "The Third Echelon"

Chen Yun originated the notion of a third echelon. Upon reading reports of the deaths of veteran cadres in the early 1980s, Chen wrote a memo to Deng Xiaoping and Hu Yaobang emphasizing the urgency for developing a succession plan. He argued that the CCP leadership should not only decide on immediate successors but should also train middle-aged and young cadres—"those members of the 'younger generation' who will be targeted for future promotion to specific leadership positions." He suggested that a list of the "third echelon" leaders should be made for each level of leadership, from the central government down to factory administration. They should be considered cadres in "reserve."[76]

According to Chen Yun, veteran revolutionaries such as Deng Xiaoping, Li Xiannian, Bo Yibo, and, of course, Chen Yun himself were members of the "first echelon" or "first front" (*diyixian*) leaders.[77] They were passing the baton to members of the "second echelon" such as Hu Yaobang, Zhao Ziyang, Yao Yilin, and Song Ping, who generally had joined the Communist movement during the war against Japan and were in their sixties. The third echelon referred to Li Peng, Hu Qili, Jiang Zemin, Tian Jiyun, and Ding Guangen, who were in their fifties and had begun their careers during the socialist transformation in the 1950s. The third echelon also referred to those in their forties (e.g., Wang Zhaoguo, Hu Jintao) or even younger, especially in the lower levels of leadership.

Chen Yun's proposal was strongly endorsed by both Deng Xiaoping and Hu Yaobang. Hu declared, "In order to ensure the stability of the state and the continuity in the direction and policies of the Party and the state for an extended period of time, it has become necessary to begin to build up the third echelon."[78] Some top third echelon leaders were Hu's former subordinates in the Chinese Communist Youth League (CCYL).

Deng also played a direct role in selecting members of the third echelon in the central government. In 1986, Deng told an American professor that he would like to promote some thirty- to forty-year-old scientists and engineers to top leadership positions.[79] Deng had already promoted Wang Zhaoguo, Jia Chunwang, and Ding Guangen, three young engineers, to very important positions: director of the General Office of the Central Committee, minister of national security, and minister of transport.[80] They were all Deng's "discoveries."

For example, Deng met Wang Zhaoguo in 1981 when Deng visited the No. 2 Motor Vehicle Plant, where Wang served as deputy director. Deng promoted him immediately to chairman of the national committee of the Chinese Communist Youth League. Deng "discovered" Ding Guangen as they often played bridge together.[81] Another example was the promotion of Hu Jintao to the Politburo. Prior to the Fourteenth Party Congress in 1992, Deng said, "I think Comrade Hu Jintao is not bad." In that congress, Hu was promoted from a member of the Central Committee to standing member of the Politburo.[82]

Deng and Hu Yaobang also decided that the "four general requirements" for the selection of the "third echelon leaders" should be:

young (*nianqinghua*)—usually in their fifties or, preferably, forties
well-educated (*zhishihua*)—usually defined in terms of holding a college degree
  or its equivalent

specialized in training (*zhuanyehua*)—usually with technical training in science and technology

politically reliable (*geminghua*)—usually having a period of service in the Party and no record as a radical activist during the Cultural Revolution[83]

Hu asserted that China could implement "the Four Modernizations" only if the new Chinese leaders possessed the "four general requirements."[84] Personnel offices at various levels of government and Party organization also issued specific guidelines with regard to the age, educational level, functional competency, and political reliability of candidates.[85] The plan to recruit third echelon cadres was implemented on the following three levels:[86]

approximately 1,000 young and middle-aged cadres were immediately appointed to the provincial and ministerial level and were thus in line to replace the first two echelons of China's top leadership

approximately 30,000 were selected to gradually replace senior leaders at the prefectural and municipal levels

an additional 100,000 cadres were selected to gradually replace senior leaders at the county level

As Richard Baum observed, "When selection was completed at all levels, the 131,000 members of the third echelon would form an elite corps" for the new generation of Chinese leadership.[87] The third echelon now, indeed, constitutes the backbone of the fourth generation of leaders. Most of these "third echelon" officials are technocrats. According to a study of 1,500 third echelon cadres, 90 percent of them have a college education, 70 percent are professionals, and most are engineers.[88]

Ten years later, at the turn of the century, the term the "third echelon" is no longer in use, but members of the "third echelon" are also no longer on "reserve." They already occupy some of the most important positions in both the central and provincial levels of leadership in the country.

## NOTES

1. Norman Pearlstine, "My Dinner with Jiang," *Time*, 22 February 1999, 55–56.
2. Pearlstine, "My Dinner with Jiang," 55.
3. James Kynge, "Reform Reaches Top Level," *Financial Times*, 16 November 1998, 6.
4. Li Ruihuan started his professional career as a carpenter. Later he graduated from the Beijing Part-Time Civil Engineering Institute. Although Li, unlike many of his colleagues on the Standing Committee of the Politburo, did not attend an elite school, he did work as an architect in Beijing for many years.
5. For a discussion of the multidimensional transitions in post-Mao leadership, see Lyman Miller, "Overlapping Transitions in China's Leadership," *SAIS Review* 16, no. 2 (Summer-Fall 1996): 22.

6. Li Cheng and Lynn White, "The Thirteenth Central Committee of the Chinese Communist Party: From Mobilizers to Managers," *Asian Survey* 28, no. 4 (April 1988): 371–399.

7. Zhang Sumin, "Makesidier sigaode yu tuikenuokelaxi" (Scott [Marx Jr.] and technocracy), *Xinzhonghua zazhi* (New China Magazine) (Shanghai), 1, no. 4 (February 1933): 28. The article focuses on the ways in which American engineers try to solve social problems by applying the methods of the physical sciences, but it does not discuss in depth any political implications of technocracy.

8. No equivalent term in Chinese was used before *jishu guanliao*, but *guanliao* usually has a negative connotation. The more modern term *jishu ganbu* (technical cadre) mainly refers to engineers and technicians, since all those who have reached the tertiary level of education in the PRC are considered *ganbu* (cadres). A majority of *ganbu* do not hold leadership positions. Thus a more appropriate term increasingly used in China is *jishu wenguan*, since it has neutral connotations.

9. See Hong Yung Lee, *From Revolutionary Cadres to Party Technocrats: The Changing Cadre System in Socialist China* (Berkeley: University of California Press, 1991), 407.

10. Zang Xiaowei, "The Fourteenth Central Committee of the CCP: Technocracy or Political Technocracy?" *Asian Survey* 33, no. 8 (August 1993): 787–803; Zang Xiaowei, "Elite Formation and the Bureaucratic-Technocracy in Post-Mao China," *Studies in Comparative Communism* 24, no. 1 (March 1991): 114–123; and Richard Baum, *Burying Mao: Chinese Politics in the Age of Deng Xiaoping* (Princeton: Princeton University Press, 1994), 381.

11. This discussion is based on Li and White, "Fifteenth Central Committee of the Chinese Communist Party," 231–236. For an earlier discussion of the definition of Chinese technocrats, see Li Cheng and Lynn White, "Elite Transformation and Modern Change in Mainland China and Taiwan: Empirical Data and the Theory of Technocracy," *China Quarterly* 121 (March 1990): 16–26.

12. Robert D. Putnam, "Elite Transformation in Advanced Industrial Societies," *Comparative Political Study* 10, no. 3 (October 1977): 404.

13. For a detailed study of this subject, see Roy Holheinz and Kent Calder, *The Eastasia Edge* (New York: Basic, 1982), 57; Chalmers Johnson, *MITI and the Japanese Miracle: The Growth of Industrial Policy, 1925–1975* (Stanford: Stanford University Press, 1982); and Bae-ho Hahn and Kyu-taik Kim, "Korean Political Leaders (1952–1962): Their Social Origins and Skills" *Asian Survey* (July 1963): 312–313.

14. The author is grateful to Joseph Fewsmith for this observation.

15. The main Chinese translation for "technocrat," *jishu guanliao* ("bureaucrats with technical backgrounds"), demonstrates this.

16. For a discussion of similar occupational identity of a British elite group during the 1950s, see Rupert Wilkinson, *Gentlemanly Power: British Leadership and the Public School Tradition: A Comparative Study in the Making of Rulers* (Oxford: Oxford University Press, 1964).

17. X. Drew Liu, "The Current Power Struggle in the Chinese Communist Party," *China Strategic Review* 2, no. 4 (July–August 1997): 80.

18. Gao Xin, *Jiang Zemin de muliao* (Jiang Zemin's counselors), 4th ed. (Hong Kong: Mingjing chubanshe, 1997), 204–205.

19. Hans J. Morgenthau, *Scientific Man versus Power Politics* (Chicago: University of Chicago Press, 1946), 168.

20. Lucian W. Pye, "Chinese Politics in the Late Deng Era," *China Quarterly* 142 (June 1995): 573–574.

21. See, for example, Nicholas D. Kristof and Sheryl Wudunn, *China Wakes: The Struggle for the Soul of a Rising Power* (New York: Vintage, 1994).

22. For instance, Kenneth C. Walker, "Chinese Uncertainties," *Asian Affairs* 82, no. 2 (June 1995): 183–187; and June Teuffl Dreyer, "The Military's Uncertain Politics," *Current History* 95, no. 603 (September 1996): 254–259.

23. Michel Oksenberg, "China's Political Future," *JETRO China Newsletter* 120 (January–February 1996): 4–5; and Richard Baum, "China after Deng: Ten Scenarios in Search of Reality," *China Quarterly* 145 (March 1996): 154.

24. David Bachman, "Succession, Consolidation, and Transition in China's Future," *Journal of Northeast Asian Studies* 15, no. 1 (Spring 1996): 100.

25. See, for example, Fang Lizhi and James H. Williams, *Bringing Down the Great Wall: Writings on Science, Culture, and Democracy in China* (New York: Norton, 1992); Harrison Evans Salisbury, *Tiananmen Diary: Thirteen Days in June* (Boston: Little, Brown, 1989); and Merle Goldman, *Sowing the Seeds of Democracy in China: Political Reform in the Deng Xiaoping Era* (Cambridge: Harvard University Press, 1994).

26. This discussion is based on Ho Ping-ti, "Aspects of Social Mobility in China, 1368–1911," *Comparative Studies in Society and History* 1, no. 4 (June 1959): 330–359.

27. Ho, "Aspects of Social Mobility in China," 332. Also see Wang Ya'nan, *Zhongguo guanliao zhengzhi yanjiu* (A study of Chinese bureaucratic politics) (Shanghai: Time and Culture Press, 1948); Zhou Gucheng, *Zhongguo shehui zhi jiegou* (The structure of Chinese society) (Shanghai: New Life Press, 1935); and Chang Ching-chien, *Zhongguo wenguan zhidu shi* (The history of Chinese civil service system) (Taipei: Chinese Culture Press, 1955).

28. Ho Ping-ti, *The Ladder of Success in Imperial China: Aspects of Social Mobility, 1368–1911* (New York: Columbia University Press, 1962), 256.

29. Robert North and Ithiel Pool, *Kuomintang and Chinese Communist Elites* (Stanford: Stanford University Press, 1952), 324.

30. Robert Putnam, *The Comparative Study of Political Elites* (Englewood Cliffs, N.J.: Prentice-Hall, 1976), 172.

31. Fei Xiaotong (Fei Hsiao-t'ung), *China's Gentry* (Chicago: University of Chicago Press, 1953), 68.

32. Tsai Wen-hui, "Patterns of Political Elite Mobility in Modern China" (Ph.D. diss., University of California, 1974), 71.

33. Hu Qiuyuan, "Woguo minzhu yundong cuozhe zhi yuanyin yu qusheng zhidao" (The Causes of the failure of the Chinese democracy movement and the road to success), *Zhonghua zazhi* (China magazine) 270 (January 1986): 12.

34. North and Pool, *Kuomintang and Chinese Communist Elites*.

35. Robert A. Scalapino, introduction to *Elites in the People's Republic of China*, ed. Robert A. Scalapino (Seattle: University of Washington Press, 1972); and Kau Ying-mao, "Patterns of Recruitment and Mobility of Urban Cadres," in *The City in Communist China*, ed. John W. Lewis (Stanford: Stanford University Press, 1971), 97–121.

36. Edgar Snow, "The Early Life of Mao Tse-tung," in *Revolutionary Leaders of Modern China*, ed. Chun-tu Hsueh (New York: Oxford University Press, 1971), 395–421. Mao's autobiography, as he told it to Edgar Snow.

37. Among the fifty-three full members of the CCP in 1921, not one was identified as a technician or a scientist. See Fang Chengxiang, "Wusi yundong yu zhishi fengziqun" (The May Fourth movement and the intellectual community), *Shaanxi shida xuebao* (Journal of Shaanxi Normal University) 2 (1989): 3–7.

38. North and Pool, *Kuomintang and Chinese Communist Elites*.

39. Tsai, "Patterns of Political Elite Mobility in Modern China, 1912–1949"; and Paul Wong, *Chinese Higher Leadership in the Socialist Transition* (New York: Free Press, 1976).

40. See *Xinhua banyue kan* (Xinhua bimonthly), 2 January 1957, 89. Quoted from Franz Schurmann, *Ideology and Organization in Communist China*, 2d enl. ed. (Berkeley: University of California Press, 1968), 283.

41. Denis Fred Simon argues that the Cultural Revolution was launched as a result of Mao's concern about the increasing tendency toward technocracy. See "China's S and T Intellectuals in the Post-Mao Era," *Journal of Northeast Asian Studies*, Summer 1980, 62.

42. Jiang Yiwei, "Jishu yu zhengzhi" (Technology and politics), *Xuexi* (Study) 16 (1957): 12.

43. David Bachman, "The Chinese Communist Party: Forty Years in Power," *Fletcher Forum of World Affairs* 14, no. 1 (Winter 1990): 10–17.

44. Hong Yung Lee, "Mainland China's Future Leaders: Third Echelon of Cadres," *Issues and Studies* 24, no. 6 (June 1988): 37.

45. Deng Xiaoping's speech appears in *Hongqi* (Red flag) 4 (1978): 9–18.

46. Quoted from Tang Tsou, "Back from the Brink of Revolutionary "Feudal Totalitarianism," in *State and Society in Contemporary China*, ed. Victor Nee and David Mozingo (Ithaca: Cornell University Press, 1983), 67.

47. Deng's speech was released to the public years later. See Deng Xiaoping, "On the Reform of the System of Party and State Leadership," *Beijing Review*, 3 October 1983, 14–22; and 10 October 1983, 18–22. For Hu's speech, see Hu Yaobang, "Makesizhuyi weidazhenli de guanghui zhaoyao women qianjin," (Great truth of Marxism guides us to move forward), *Hongqi* (Red flag), March 1983, 2–13.

48. For a detailed discussion of the role of patrons of technocrats in both PRC and Taiwan, see Li Cheng and Lynn White, "Elite Transformation and Modern Change in Mainland China and Taiwan: Empirical Data and the Theory of Technocracy," *China Quarterly* 121 (March 1990): 9–16.

49. *Hongweibing ziliao* (Red Guard publications) 6 (1975): 1681. Published by the Center for Chinese Research Materials, Association of Research Libraries, Washington, D.C.

50. For a detailed discussion of the role of the *World Economic Herald* in China's technocratic movement, see Li Cheng and Lynn White, "China's Technocratic Movement and the World Economic Herald," *Modern China* 17, no. 3 (July 1991): 342–388.

51. Hong Yung Lee, "China's Twelfth Central Committee: Rehabilitated Cadres and Technocrats," *Asian Survey* 23, no. 6 (June 1983): 673–691.

52. Richard Baum, "China in 1985: The Greening of the Revolution," *Asian Survey* 26, no. 1 (January 1986): 34.

53. Ibid.

54. *Remin ribao* (overseas edition), 11 October 1987, 1; and 29 June 1986, 1.

55. Bachman, "The Chinese Communist Party: Forty Years in Power," 10–17.

56. *Shijie ribao*, 28 June 1999, A9.

57. Li and White, "China's Technocratic Movement and the World Economic Herald," 361–362.

58. Five joined the Party in the early 1970s, two after the CR. One is not a CCP member. *Renmin ribao*, Internet database. Also *Shijie ribao*, 22 January 1999, A12.

59. www.Chinesenewsnet.com, 4 January 2000.

60. Li and White, "Fifteenth Central Committee of the Chinese Communist Party," 248.

61. Ho, *Ladder of Success,* 259.

62. For a detailed discussion of paralleled development of ideological change and elite transformation, see Li Cheng, "The Rise of Technocracy: Elite Transformation and Ideological Change in Post–Mao China" (Ph.D. diss., Princeton University, 1992).

63. David Bachman, "Succession, Consolidation, and Transition in China's Future," *Journal of Northeast Asian Studies* 15, no. 1 (Spring 1996): 93.

64. Michel C. Oksenberg, Michael D. Swaine, and Daniel C. Lynch, *The Chinese Future* (Santa Monica, Calif.: Pacific Council on International Policy/Rand Center for Asia-Pacific Policy, 1998), 6.

65. James S. Coleman, "The Education of Modern Elites in Developing Countries," in *Education and Political Development,* ed. James S. Coleman (Princeton: Princeton University Press, 1965).

66. Murray Scott Tanner and Michael J. Feder, "Family Politics, Elite Recruitment, and Succession in Post-Mao China," *Australian Journal of Chinese Affairs* 30 (July 1993): 93.

67. Bo Zhiyue, "Economic Performance and Political Mobility: Chinese Provincial Leaders," *Journal of Contemporary China* 5, no. 12 (1996): 140.

68. Kenneth Lieberthal argued that during the 1980s, the Politburo became " a committee of protégés who answered to the real power behind the scenes, the elderly patrons whose deals among themselves determined who would serve in the party's top offices." See *Governing China: From Revolution through Reform.* (New York: Norton, 1995), 224.

69. Miller, "Overlapping Transitions in China's Leadership," 22.

70. For a detailed discussion of the retirement of revolutionary veterans, see Melanie Manion, *Retirement of Revolutionaries in China: Public Policies, Social Norms, Private Interests* (Princeton: Princeton University Press, 1993).

71. Bo, "Economic Performance and Political Mobility," 140.

72. He Qinglian, "Zhongguo dangdai de ziben yuanshi jilei" (Private capital accumulation in contemporary China), *Zhongguo yu shijie* (China and the world), December 1997; and also *Zhongguo de xianjing* (China's pitfall) (Hong Kong: Mingjing chubanshe, 1998).

73. Bo, "Economic Performance and Political Mobility," 141.

74. Lee, "Mainland China's Future Leaders," 52–53.

75. Tanner and Feder, "Family Politics, Elite Recruitment, and Succession in Post-Mao China," 90.

76. *Chen Yun Wenji* (Selected works of Chen Yun) (Beijing: Renmin chubanshi, 1985), 267. Quoted in Hong Yung Lee, "Mainland China's Future Leaders: Third Echelon of Cadres," 39–40; also see Ting Wang, "An Analysis of the P.R.C.'s Future Elite: The Third Echelon," *Journal of Northeast Asian Studies* 4 (Summer 1985): 19–37.

77. For the notion of "first front" leaders, see Frederick C. Teiwes, "The Paradoxical Post-Mao Transition: From Obeying the Leader to "Normal Politics," *China Journal* 34 (July 1995): 62.

78. Quoted from Lee, "Mainland China's Future Leaders, 40–41.

79. *Remin ribao,* 4 November 1986, 1.

80. Currently Wang Zhaoguo is director of the United Front Work Department of the Central Committee of the CCP; Jia Chunwang is minister of public security and Ding Guanggen is the director of the Propaganda Department of the Central Committee of the CCP.

81. Ding was initially recommended to Deng by Wan Li. The author thanks Joseph Fewsmith for this information.

82. *Zhongguo zhichun* (China spring) 12 (1998).

83. Tanner and Feder, "Family Politics, Elite Recruitment, and Succession in Post-Mao China," 99.

84. Quoted from Ting, "An Analysis of the P.R.C.'s Future Elite: The Third Echelon," 22. Hu's words originally appeared in *Renmin ribao*, 10 August 1982.

85. Lee, "Mainland China's Future Leaders," 42.

86. This discussion is based on Baum, "China in 1985," 33.

87. Ibid.

88. Lee, "Mainland China's Future Leaders," 47.

# 3

# The Fourth Generation of Leaders: A Biographical Analysis

Political science without biography is a form of taxidermy.
—Harold Lasswell

This chapter presents two pools of biographical data about the fourth generation of leaders. The first pool is based exclusively on the 1994 revised edition of *Zhongguo renming da cidian* (Who's who in China).[1] This source includes 2,121 current leaders in the Party, government, military, and other areas at all levels above medium-sized city administration. This study concentrates on the 298 leaders born between 1941 and 1956, namely, members of the fourth generation of leaders, although cross-generational comparisons are made if necessary.

The second pool is based on a 1999 reference book of biographical data on all members of the Fifteenth Central Committee (CC) of the Chinese Communist Party and the Central Commission for Discipline Inspection.[2] Among the 459 members in these two CCP leadership bodies, 224 were born between 1941 and 1956. These are the primary focus in this study. The remaining 235 leaders in the second pool include only one member of the second generation (Hua Guofeng, the former chair of the CCP, who was born in 1921), 232 members of the third generation, and two members of the fifth generation who were both born in 1957. The roughly even distribution between the third and fourth generations of leaders in this pool also allows for further cross-generational comparisons.

Both sources are official data released by the Chinese authorities. They also contain the most recent and most comprehensive data available in the quantitative study of Chinese political elites. In addition, by placing the data in the same analytical framework, this study shows patterns and trends of the fourth generation of leaders in the 1990s. For the sake of convenience, this study identifies the first source as the "1994 pool" and the second source on the members of the Fifteenth CC and CCDI as the "1999 pool."[3] A total of 522 elites in the fourth generation from both sources provides sufficient information for quantitative analysis.[4] In addition, a data set of all 2,580 members of the elite from both sources have been coded.[5] This is arguably the most comprehensive quantitative investigation of Chinese political elite in English language studies of contemporary China.

This chapter relies on three types of data for analysis: (1) current leadership positions, (2) demographic distribution, and (3) educational backgrounds. The chapter presents findings in these three broad areas and compares characteristics of the fourth generation of leaders with those of their predecessors.

## CURRENT LEADERSHIP POSITIONS AND TENURES

### Current Posts

Table 3.1 shows the distribution of current posts of two pools of leaders under study. If an official holds more than one leadership post, only the most important and active one is listed. For example, Li Jiating, governor of Yunnan, is also deputy Party secretary of the province, but the table lists only his position as governor (almost all provincial governors in today's China concurrently serve as deputy Party secretaries). For Wen Jiabao, who is concurrently vice premier and member of the Politburo, the table lists only his post of vice premier, since this represents his most active leadership role.

In both pools, most of the fourth generation of leaders are already in very important Party and government positions at both the central and provincial levels. The 1994 pool includes twenty heads and deputy heads of the central departments of the Chinese Communist Party, forty ministers and vice ministers in the State Council, and thirty-eight provincial Party secretaries and deputy secretaries. The three heads of CCP Central Departments in the 1994 pool are Wang Zhaoguo (head of the United Front Department), Liao Hui (head of Overseas Affairs Department), and Wen Jiabao (director of the General Office of the Central Committee). They occupy forty-seven (24.4 percent) of the full membership seats and forty-eight (31.8 percent) of the alternate seats in the Fifteenth Central Committee of the CCP.[6]

The 1999 pool includes 55 (28.5 percent) full members and 112 (74.2 percent) alternates of the Fifteenth Central Committee and 57 (49.6 percent) members of the Fifteenth Central Commission for Discipline Inspection. This means that members of the fourth generation of leaders already occupy 167 out of 344 seats (48.5 percent) in the Central Committee of the CCP. Hu Jintao, Wu Bangguo, Wen Jiabao, and Li Changchun are four leaders who have been in the Politburo

Table 3.1    Distribution of Leadership Posts among the Fourth Generation of Leaders

| Leadership Categories | 1994 Pool No. | 1994 Pool % | 1999 Pool No. | 1999 Pool % |
|---|---|---|---|---|
| Central | | | | |
| Vice president | | | 1 | 0.5 |
| Vice premier | | | 2 | 0.9 |
| Head of CCP Central Dept. | 3 | 1.0 | 2 | 0.9 |
| Deputy head of CCP Central Dept. | 17 | 5.7 | 9 | 4.0 |
| Government minister | 3 | 1.0 | 12 | 5.4 |
| Government vice minister | 37 | 12.4 | 8 | 3.6 |
| Bureau heads of State Council | | | 8 | 3.6 |
| Standing members of NPC | 7 | 2.4 | 1 | 0.5 |
| Standing members of CPPCC | 16 | 5.4 | 2 | 0.9 |
| Secretariat of CCYL | 7 | 2.4 | 1 | 0.5 |
| Editor in chief of major newspaper | 6 | 2.0 | | |
| President/vice president of major bank | 4 | 1.3 | 4 | 1.8 |
| Head of mass org. (e.g., women, union) | 6 | 2.0 | 4 | 1.8 |
| Secretary of discipline commission | | | 10 | 4.5 |
| Head of research institution | | | 6 | 2.7 |
| Provincial and municipal | | | | |
| Provincial Party secretary | 4 | 1.3 | 15 | 6.7 |
| Provincial deputy Party secretary | 34 | 11.4 | 27 | 12.1 |
| Provincial governor | 6 | 2.0 | 22 | 9.8 |
| Vice governor | 95 | 31.9 | 6 | 2.7 |
| Provincial chief procurator | 8 | 2.7 | | |
| President of provincial court | 7 | 2.4 | | |
| Party secretary of major city | 12 | 4.0 | 13 | 5.8 |
| Mayor of major city | 17 | 5.7 | 1 | 0.5 |
| Heads of provincial Party org. | | | 5 | 2.2 |
| Secretary of provincial discipline com. | | | 18 | 8.0 |
| Prefecture Party secretary | | | 10 | 4.5 |
| Head of large enterprise | | | 6 | 2.7 |
| Head of grassroots Party org. | | | 2 | 0.9 |
| Military officer | 9 | 3.0 | 29 | 12.9 |
| Total | 298 | 100.0 | 224 | 100.4 |

*Source:* Liao and Fan, *Zhongguo renming da cidian* (1994); and Shen, *Zhonggong di shiwujie zhongyang weiyuanhui zhongyang jilü jiancha weiyuanhui weiyuan minglu.*

Note: The data were accumulated and tabulated by the author.

and have also served as vice president of the state, vice premiers of the State Council, and Party secretary of Guangdong, respectively.

Comparing these two pools demonstrates that the fourth generation of leaders holds more top posts in ministries, provincial Party committees, and provincial governments in the 1999 pool than in the 1994 pool. The number of ministers increased from three to twelve (despite the fact that the number of ministries under the State Council reduced from 40 to 29 in 1998); the number of provincial Party secretaries increased from four to fifteen and provincial governors from six to twenty-two. This indicates that during the late 1990s the fourth generation of leaders moved from deputy positions to the top positions in ministerial and provincial levels of leadership. The fact that more work on discipline commissions on both central and provincial levels in the 1999 pool is due to the fact that a significant portion of this pool is from the Central Commission for Discipline Inspection of the CCP.

Another important difference between the two pools is the higher representation of military elites in the 1999 pool. The number of fourth generation of leaders in the military in the 1994 pool is remarkably low (3 percent). The Tiananmen incident certainly prolonged the career of many military veteran leaders. This also seems to be consistent with Jiang's political tactic of preventing the formation of any potentially powerful military factions during the early 1990s.[7] As a practical matter, Jiang increased the turnover of senior military officers during the early 1990s and also did not promote young military figures to the top leadership. An alternative explanation is that Jiang might not have been able to enforce the early retirement of senior officers prior to the death of Deng Xiaoping in 1997, especially considering the fact that Jiang's own power was not secured prior to the Fifteenth Party Congress. To a certain extent, the rejuvenation within army ranks has proceeded far more slowly than with civilian posts throughout the reform era. Top military posts on both the central and greater military region levels were long held by those who were in their late sixties and early seventies, although individual officers in this same age-group might have been replaced by their peers quickly.[8]

Some studies of China's high-ranking military elites have described the all-time low percentage of military officers in the Fifteenth Politburo, even though the absolute number was unchanged during the past decade. The percentage of military representatives in the Politburo declined sharply from 40 percent in the Ninth Politburo to 31 percent in the Eleventh, to 11 percent in the Thirteenth, and to 8 percent by 1997.[9] There are no generals serving on the Politburo's standing committee. No successor to "military strongmen" such as Lin Biao, Xu Shiyou, Ye Jianying, Yang Baibing, or Zhang Zhen is among the politicians whom the Party now ranks highest. The two top military officers on the CMC of the Fourteenth Central Committee (eighty-one-year old Liu Huaqing and eighty-three-year old Zhang Zhen) were replaced in the Fifteenth Politburo by two relatively "younger" generals (sixty-eight-year old Chi Haotian and sixty-nine-year old Zhang Wannian).

But more recently, as table 3.1 shows, a group of twenty-nine young, junior-ranking military officers have found their way in the Fifteenth CC and CCDI. The percentage of military elites in the fourth generation of leaders increased from 3 percent in the 1994 pool to 12.9 percent in the 1999 pool. Many new faces with military uniforms have been recruited to these two important leadership bodies. For example, Xu Qiliang, who was born in 1950, was promoted to chief of staff of the PLA air force in the mid-1990s and has served as an alternate in the CC. Li Guoan and Yue Xicui, both with the rank of colonel, were elected to the Fifteenth CC. Several commanders of the group army also entered the Fifteenth CC. Such a pattern suggests that Jiang and top leaders in the PRC now intend to promote more junior officers to the higher military posts rather than allow senior officers in the third generation to gain more power.

Some posts listed on table 3.1, for example, the standing members of NPC and the Chinese People's Political Consultative Conference (CPPCC) in the 1994 pool, are, of course, largely ceremonial figureheads. These positions are usually held by non-Communist figures such as representatives from the sports, arts, philanthropy, and "democratic parties." The number of representatives from other mass organizations, such as the All-China Federation of Trade Unions and China's Federation of Women, is marginal.

The 1999 pool of the Fifteenth CC and CCDI also includes some representatives of mass organizations, local Party officials, and heads of large enterprises such as chief executives of the Baoshan Steel Company, the Anshan Steel Company, the Chunlan Electronic Company, and the Changhong Electronic Company. Although their presence in general may be symbolic, some, especially the chief executives of large enterprises, will likely advance their political careers in the years ahead, especially considering the fact that they are young and have already served on the Central Committee of the CCP.

## Tenure and Upward Mobility

A review of the tenure held by members of the Central Committee of the CCP in the 1999 pool shows that the fourth generation of leaders first emerged during the Twelfth CC in 1982 but did not became a significant part of the CCP Central Committee until the Fourteenth Party Congress in 1992. Among 167 members and alternates of the Fifteenth CC belonging to the fourth generation, ninety-nine (59.3 percent) were newly elected to the Fifteenth Party Congress, forty-six (27.5 percent) were first elected to the Fourteenth Congress in 1992, seven (4.2 percent) in the Thirteenth Congress in 1987, fourteen (8.4 percent) to the Twelfth Congress in the 1982, and one (0.6 percent) to the Eleventh Congress in 1977.[10] This means that about 87 percent of the fourth generation of leaders entered the CC after 1992.

In fact, according to an exclusive study of the Fifteenth Central Committee conducted in 1998, practically all (97.5 percent) of the full CC members joined the committee after 1982.[11] About 57 percent of the full members are first timers. Among the 344 full and alternate members, only five (1.5 percent) were first elected to the committee before 1977. They are Hua Guofeng, former chairman of the CCP; Ni Zhifu, a model worker in the Mao era and vice chairman of the NPC; Lin Liyun, a native of Taiwan and vice chairman of the Overseas Chinese

Affairs Committee; Ismail Amat, a Uygur and minister of the State Nationalities Affairs Commission; and Hao Jianxiu, a model worker in the Mao era and vice minister of the State Planning Commission. The fact that these five have retained their seats in the CC may be a result of some kind of affirmative action.

Most Fifteenth CC members, especially those in the fourth generation, were politically inconspicuous before 1982, when many of them were working as engineers. In a decade and a half, they have risen to China's top leadership. Table 3.2 shows the distribution of the years in which leaders in both pools were appointed to current posts other than membership in the CC and CCDI. The leader who has the longest tenure in the 1994 pool is Zhang Yuqin, vice governor of Guizhou, who has held this post since 1980.[12] Danzim, a Tibetan, has the longest tenure in the 1999 pool. He has served as deputy Party secretary in Tibet since 1985. But as table 3.2 shows, an overwhelming majority of elites in both pools were appointed to their current posts within five years after the data were compiled—87.9 percent in the first pool and 78.9 percent in the second pool.

It is quite common for a member of the fourth generation to stay in a post for two or three years and then move to a higher post. Rapid upward mobility is exemplified by the case of Lu Zhangong, Party secretary of the All-China Federation of Trade Unions. Lu was born in Zhejiang in 1952 and was sent to Heilongjiang to work as a farmer during the Cultural Revolution. In 1978, he enrolled at the Harbin Institute of Architectural Engineering. After graduation in 1982, he worked in a construction company in his native province where he moved from clerk to division head and then to Party secretary. He was appointed Party secretary of the Construction Bureau of Zhejiang in 1985, deputy Party secretary of Jiaxing city in 1988, Party secretary of the city in 1989, deputy head of the Organization Department of Zhejiang Province in 1991, head of the department in 1993, deputy Party secretary of Zhejiang in 1995, deputy Party secretary of Hebei in 1996, before being appointed to his current position in 1998.

The high percentage of elite turnover in 1998 in the second pool might be partially due to the structural changes within the high-level bureaucracy during that year. The complement of ministries was cut from forty to twenty-nine.[13] Nevertheless, table 3.2 reflects the continuing rapid turnover of Chinese political elites during the reform era and the great mobility at high leadership levels.

## DEMOGRAPHIC CHARACTERISTICS

### Age, Gender, and Ethnicity

Table 3.3 shows the distribution by year of birth, gender, and ethnic group. A majority of leaders (92.6 percent in the 1994 pool and 88.7 percent in the second pool) were born between 1941 and 1949. They were between seventeen and twenty-five years old in 1966, when the Cultural Revolution took place. This means that a majority of members of the two pools lived through the CR as young

**Table 3.2   Year Appointed to Current Position among the Fourth Generation of Leaders**

| Year | 1994 Pool | | 1999 Pool | |
|---|---|---|---|---|
| | *No.* | % | *No.* | % |
| 1980 | 1 | 0.3 | | |
| 1981 | | | | |
| 1982 | | | | |
| 1983 | 1 | 0.3 | | |
| 1984 | 2 | 0.7 | | |
| 1985 | 6 | 2.0 | 1 | 0.5 |
| 1986 | 2 | 0.7 | | |
| 1987 | 4 | 1.3 | | |
| 1988 | 9 | 3.0 | 4 | 1.8 |
| 1989 | 5 | 1.7 | | |
| 1990 | 14 | 4.7 | 1 | 0.5 |
| 1991 | 21 | 7.0 | 4 | 1.8 |
| 1992 | 52 | 17.4 | 9 | 4.0 |
| 1993 | 170 | 57.1 | 28 | 12.5 |
| 1994 | 5 | 1.7 | 29 | 12.9 |
| 1995 | | | 26 | 11.6 |
| 1996 | | | 25 | 11.2 |
| 1997 | | | 32 | 14.2 |
| 1998 | | | 65 | 29.0 |
| Unknown | 6 | 2.0 | | |
| Total | 298 | 99.9 | 224 | 100.0 |

*Source:* Liao and Fan, *Zhongguo renming da cidian* (1994); and Shen, *Zhonggong di shiwujie zhongyang weiyuanhui zhongyang jilü jiancha weiyuanhui weiyuan minglu.*

*Note:* The data were accumulated and tabulated by the author.

men and women. The youngest in the first pool, Duan Qiang, vice mayor of Beijing, and the youngest in the second pool, Li Ke, Party secretary of Nanning, were
both ten years old at the beginning of the CR, old enough to remember events
during the first years of the CR.

A striking point, although not really surprising, is the dominance of males
within the fourth generation of leaders. Although the percentage of females in
the fourth generation of leaders (9.4 percent in the 1994 pool and 12.1 percent
in the 1999 pool) is a bit higher than in the entire Fifteenth Central Committee
of the CCP (7.3 percent), female leaders in these two pools have more often than
not been appointed to deputy leadership positions, such as vice governors and vice
ministers. Some serve in ceremonial posts such as deputy chairs of China's Federation of Women (in the case of the first pool) or work in local Party organizations

Table 3.3   Distribution of the Fourth Generation of Leaders by Year of Birth, Gender, and Nationality

|  | 1994 Pool (N = 298) | | 1999 Pool (N = 24) | |
|---|---|---|---|---|
|  | No. | % | No. | % |
| **Year of Birth** | | | | |
| 1941 | 50 | 16.8 | 35 | 15.6 |
| 1942 | 65 | 21.8 | 42 | 18.8 |
| 1943 | 32 | 10.7 | 24 | 10.7 |
| 1944 | 44 | 14.8 | 34 | 15.2 |
| 1945 | 30 | 10.1 | 19 | 8.4 |
| 1946 | 34 | 11.4 | 24 | 10.7 |
| 1947 | 8 | 2.7 | 10 | 4.4 |
| 1948 | 6 | 2.0 | 9 | 4.0 |
| 1949 | 7 | 2.3 | 2 | 0.9 |
| 1950 | 6 | 2.0 | 4 | 1.8 |
| 1951 | 4 | 1.3 | 2 | 0.9 |
| 1952 | 4 | 1.3 | 9 | 4.0 |
| 1953 | 3 | 1.0 | 5 | 2.2 |
| 1954 | 0 | 0 | 1 | 0.5 |
| 1955 | 4 | 1.3 | 3 | 1.3 |
| 1956 | 1 | 0.3 | 1 | 0.5 |
| **Gender** | | | | |
| Male | 270 | 90.6 | 197 | 87.9 |
| Female | 28 | 9.4 | 27 | 12.1 |
| **Nationality** | | | | |
| Han | 260 | 87.2 | 194 | 86.6 |
| Tibetan | 13 | 4.4 | 5 | 2.2 |
| Hui | 8 | 2.7 | 4 | 1.8 |
| Miao | 3 | 1.0 | 2 | 0.9 |
| Uygur | 2 | 0.7 | 1 | 0.5 |
| Tujia | 2 | 0.7 | 2 | 0.9 |
| Korean | 2 | 0.7 | 2 | 0.9 |
| Manchu | 2 | 0.7 | 2 | 0.9 |
| Yi | 1 | 0.3 | 2 | 0.9 |
| Bai | 1 | 0.3 | 2 | 0.9 |
| Zhuang | 1 | 0.3 | 2 | 0.9 |
| Kazak | 1 | 0.3 | 1 | 0.5 |
| Gaoshan | 1 | 0.3 | | |
| Mongolian | 1 | 0.3 | 4 | 1.4 |
| Buyi | | | 1 | 0.5 |

Source: Liao and Fan, Zhongguo renming da cidian (1994); and Shen, Zhonggong di shiwujie zhongyang weiyuanhui zhongyang jilü jiancha weiyuanhui weiyuan minglu.

Note: The data were accumulated and tabulated by the author.

such as deputy Party secretaries on the prefecture levels of leadership (in the case of the second pool). Among fifteen provincial Party secretaries and twenty-two governors who are all members of the fourth generation leadership, not one is a woman. Only one woman in both pools, Chen Zhili, minister of China's Ministry of Education (and a very close friend of Jiang Zemin), is a full member of the CC.[14] She is also the only woman from the fourth generation leadership who heads a ministry under the State Council. Chen is expected to be one of the leading candidates for the Politburo in the next Party congress. Interestingly, in the whole history of the CCP, only six women (including Qiang Qing, Mao's wife; Ye Qun, Lin Biao's wife; and Deng Yingchao, Zhou Enlai's wife) have ever entered the Politburo. In the Chinese leadership, discrimination against women seems to continue into the twenty-first century.

Like all but 7 percent of China's population, most of the fourth generation of leaders are of the Han nationality. During the first three decades of the PRC, representatives from national minorities occupied 4–6 percent of the CC seats.[15] Since the Thirteenth Party Congress in 1987, minorities have increased to over 10 percent of the congress. But most have been alternate members, and no minorities have served in the Politburo or the Secretariat since 1985 when Ulanhu, a Mongolian, resigned.

There are, however, thirteen Tibetans in the 1994 pool, which is more than might be expected. Tibetans also hold more seats in the 1999 pool than other minorities. Some have held important provincial positions: Danzim, deputy Party secretary of Tibet; Legqog, mayor of Lhasa (promoted to governor of Tibet in 1998); Sang Gye Gya, deputy Party secretary of Qinghai; Ou Zegao, vice governor of Sichuan. All four are also alternate members of the Fifteenth Central Committee of the CCP. Another Tibetan, Bu Qiong, serves as secretary of the Commission for Discipline Inspection of the CCP in Tibet. This may reflect a central government policy to select pro-Han Tibetans as a significant part of the local leadership in the areas where Tibetans live, though Hans usually hold the top posts in these areas. In contrast, the representation of Uygur, Kazak, and other ethnic groups in Xinjiang is very low.

### Birthplace: Uneven Distribution

Several recent studies of post-Mao leadership show an overrepresentation of elites who were born in eastern China, especially in Jiangsu and Shandong Provinces. Meanwhile, those from the southern and southwestern provinces such as Guangdong (which produced a significant number of political and military elites during the Nationalist era) and Sichuan (which, until recently, was the most populous province of the country) are underrepresented. This is also in sharp contrast to the Mao era, when the majority of CCP leaders came from central China, especially from Hunan and Hubei Provinces.[16] The Communist movement in the

1920s and 1930s attracted many peasants in central China. For example, approximately one-third of the Eighth Politburo of the CCP formed in 1956 were born in Hunan and about one-third of the Ninth Politburo in 1969 were born in Hubei.[17] The leaders from provinces in central China occupied half the seats in the Politburo in these two Party congresses.

Now, in contrast, Shandong Province accounts for well over one-quarter of China's senior military officers.[18] According to a recent report, of the forty-two highest ranking military officers whose birthplaces are identified, thirteen were born in Shandong and six were born in Jiangsu. Twenty-two military leaders (52.4 percent) are from eastern China.[19] On the 1998 State Council, sixteen out of twenty-nine ministers (55.2 percent) are natives of eastern China, including eight who were born in Jiangsu.[20] The coastal areas are becoming the major recruiting grounds for China's provincial and mayoral elite.

A study of Chinese mayors in the late 1980s shows that Jiangsu, Liaoning, and Shanghai supplied more than 20 percent of China's mayors.[21] Since 1999, Jiangsu natives (Liu Qi, Li Shenglin, and Bao Xuding) have served as mayors of Beijing, Tianjin, and Chongqing, three of China's four municipalities that are directly under control of the central government, respectively. Meanwhile, Shandong natives occupy the seats of Party secretary in five provinces: Henan, Hebei, Shaanxi, Neimenggu, and Xinjiang.

This trend of unbalanced representation by birthplace is also evident in this study of the fourth generation of leaders (see table 3.4). Again, the largest proportion of the fourth generation of leaders in both pools, about 40 percent, are from eastern China, especially from Jiangsu and Shandong Provinces. In contrast, southern China has been badly underrepresented, having only 5.4 percent, 2.7 percent, and 3 percent of the seats in all three categories of leaders, though they make up 10 percent of China's population and about 14 percent of the GDP.[22] In the 1999 pool on the fourth generation of leaders, only 1.8 percent of the leaders were born in Guangdong and 2.7 percent in Sichuan. This is in contrast to the early years of the reform when the country was largely controlled by "strong men" from Guangdong (e.g., Ye Jianying) and Sichuan (e.g., Yang Shangkun, Zhao Ziyang, and indeed Deng Xiaoping himself), who appointed many of their fellow natives to important positions.[23]

A comparison between the third and fourth generations of leaders shows a similar pattern of distribution, except that fewer fourth generation leaders were born in northern China. It is unclear why such a large proportion of the third and fourth generations of leaders were born in either Shandong or Jiangsu Provinces. For the third generation, the higher percentage may be related to the fact that during the final years of the Anti-Japanese War, many young peasants in Shandong joined the Communist army. Two top military officers who are members of the Fifteenth Politburo, Chi Haotian (minister of defense) and Zhang Wannian (vice chair of the Central Military Commission), were both born in Shandong in the late 1920s, and in 1944, as teenagers, they joined the Eighth Route Army un-

Table 3.4 Distribution of Birthplace, by Province, of the Fourth and the Third Generations of Leaders

| Year | 4th Generation | | | | 3d Generation | | | |
|---|---|---|---|---|---|---|---|---|
| | 1994 Pool | | 1999 Pool | | 1999 Pool | | | |
| | No. | % | No. | % | No. | % | Population | GDP |
| North | | | | | | | | |
| Beijing | 3 | 1.0 | 1 | 0.5 | 6 | 2.6 | 1.0 | 2.4 |
| Tianjin | 3 | 1.0 | 7 | 3.1 | 6 | 2.6 | 0.7 | 1.6 |
| Hebei | 22 | 7.4 | 11 | 4.9 | 21 | 9.1 | 5.3 | 5.0 |
| Shanxi | 9 | 3.0 | 7 | 3.1 | 10 | 4.3 | 2.6 | 1.9 |
| Neimenggu | 2 | 0.7 | 3 | 1.3 | 2 | 0.8 | 1.9 | 1.5 |
| Subtotal | 39 | 13.1 | 29 | 12.9 | 45 | 19.4 | 11.5 | 12.4 |
| Northeast | | | | | | | | |
| Liaoning | 16 | 5.4 | 18 | 8.0 | 12 | 5.2 | 3.4 | 4.9 |
| Jilin | 11 | 3.7 | 12 | 5.4 | 12 | 5.2 | 2.2 | 2.0 |
| Heilongjiang | 6 | 2.0 | 5 | 2.2 | 6 | 2.6 | 3.1 | 2.8 |
| Subtotal | 33 | 11.1 | 35 | 15.6 | 30 | 13.0 | 8.7 | 9.7 |
| East | | | | | | | | |
| Shanghai | 5 | 1.7 | 2 | 0.9 | 7 | 3.0 | 1.2 | 4.3 |
| Jiangsu | 39 | 13.1 | 28 | 12.5 | 33 | 14.2 | 5.9 | 9.0 |
| Shandong | 31 | 10.4 | 25 | 11.1 | 36 | 15.5 | 7.2 | 8.7 |
| Zhejiang | 18 | 6.0 | 10 | 4.5 | 13 | 5.6 | 3.6 | 6.2 |
| Anhui | 12 | 4.0 | 14 | 6.2 | 11 | 4.7 | 5.0 | 3.5 |
| Fujian | 11 | 3.7 | 8 | 3.6 | 3 | 1.3 | 2.7 | 3.8 |
| Taiwan | 2 | 0.7 | 0 | 0 | 1 | 0.4 | — | — |
| Subtotal | 118 | 39.6 | 87 | 38.8 | 104 | 44.7 | 25.6 | 35.5 |
| Central | | | | | | | | |
| Henan | 9 | 3.0 | 10 | 4.5 | 7 | 3.0 | 7.5 | 5.2 |
| Hubei | 9 | 3.0 | 6 | 2.7 | 5 | 2.2 | 4.8 | 4.2 |
| Hunan | 13 | 4.4 | 15 | 6.7 | 12 | 5.2 | 5.3 | 3.8 |
| Jiangxi | 3 | 1.0 | 4 | 1.8 | 6 | 2.6 | 3.4 | 2.1 |
| Subtotal | 34 | 11.4 | 35 | 15.6 | 30 | 13.0 | 21.0 | 15.3 |
| South | | | | | | | | |
| Guangdong | 12 | 4.0 | 4 | 1.8 | 6 | 2.6 | 5.7 | 9.4 |
| Guangxi | 3 | 1.0 | 2 | 0.9 | 0 | 0 | 3.8 | 2.8 |
| Hainan | 1 | 0.4 | 0 | 0 | 1 | 0.4 | 0.6 | 0.6 |
| Subtotal | 16 | 5.4 | 6 | 2.7 | 7 | 3.0 | 10.1 | 13.8 |
| Southwest | | | | | | | | |
| Sichuan* | 15 | 5.0 | 6 | 2.7 | 8 | 3.4 | 9.4 | 6.2 |
| Guizhou | 1 | 0.4 | 3 | 1.3 | 2 | 0.8 | 2.9 | 1.1 |
| Yunnan | 6 | 2.0 | 5 | 2.2 | 0 | 0 | 3.3 | 2.1 |
| Xizang (Tibet) | 7 | 2.3 | 3 | 1.3 | 1 | 0.4 | 0.2 | 0.1 |
| Subtotal | 29 | 9.7 | 17 | 7.5 | 11 | 4.6 | 15.8 | 9.5 |

*continued*

**Table 3.4    Continued**

| | 4th Generation | | | | 3d Generation | | | |
| | 1994 Pool | | 1999 Pool | | 1999 Pool | | | |
| Year | No. | % | No. | % | No. | % | Population | GDP |
|---|---|---|---|---|---|---|---|---|
| Northwest | | | | | | | | |
|   Shaanxi | 13 | 4.4 | 11 | 4.9 | 1 | 0.4 | 2.9 | 1.7 |
|   Gansu | 3 | 1.0 | 0 | 0 | 2 | 0.8 | 2.0 | 0.9 |
|   Qinghai | 5 | 1.7 | 1 | 0.5 | 0 | 0 | 0.4 | 0.2 |
|   Ningxia | 5 | 1.7 | 1 | 0.5 | 0 | 0 | 0.4 | 0.2 |
|   Xinjiang | 3 | 1.0 | 2 | 0.9 | 2 | 0.8 | 1.4 | 1.5 |
|     Subtotal | 29 | 9.7 | 15 | 6.7 | 5 | 2.0 | 7.1 | 4.5 |
| Total | 298 | 100.0 | 224 | 99.8 | 232 | 99.7 | 99.8 | 99.7 |

Source: Liao and Fan, Zhongguo renming da cidian (1994); and Shen, Zhonggong di shiwujie zhongyang weiyuanhui zhongyang jilü jiancha weiyuanhui weiyuan minglu. China News Analysis July 1–15, 1997; Li and White, "The Fifteenth Central Committee of the Chinese Communist Party," 246. Population and GDP data are calculated from Zhongguo tongji nianjian, 1996 (China statistical yearbook, 1996), State Statistical Bureau, comp. (Beijing: Zhongguo tongji chubanshe, 1996), 42–43, 73.

Notes: Percentages do not add up to 100 due to rounding. The data were accumulated and tabulated by the author.

*Including Chongqing.

der CCP control. Some senior members of the third generation from Shandong, for example, Tian Jiyun, vice chair of the NPC, and Wang Ruilin, deputy director of the PLA Political Department, had similar experiences.

The high percentage of Jiangsu natives in the civilian leadership may be partially due to the fact that Jiang Zemin, a Jiangsu native, likes to promote his fellow Jiangsuese. His strong endorsement of the promotion of Li Lanqing, a native of Zhenjiang city, Jiangsu Province, to standing member of Politburo and executive vice premier, seems to confirm the practice of favoritism based on a shared birthplace.

But these reasons cannot fully explain the disproportionate overrepresentation of leaders from the east coast. This phenomenon deserves further investigation, including studies of regional educational systems, subcultures, and the correlation between economic wealth and the formation of political elites. The most important finding from this study in terms of geographical distribution of leaders is that the trend of higher representation of East China at the expense of South and Southwest China continues in the fourth generation of leaders.

## Regional Leaders Serving in Their Native Areas

Another important trend in the formation of provincial and municipal leadership in China during the reform era is the selection of local officials for leadership positions in their native areas. This trend challenges the "law of avoidance" by which mandarins were prohibited from serving in their native provinces and counties, a policy characteristic of traditional China for centuries that continued during the Mao era.

In his study of the city of Wuhan during the early decades of the PRC, Ying-mao Kau observed that 91 percent of municipal elites in the city were nonnative "outsiders."[24] Most of the major local leaders (at both the provincial and municipal levels) were not born in the area in which they served. But this "law of avoidance" has changed during the reform era, as demonstrated by some recent studies of local elites, such as the data on Chinese mayors.[25] Among 247 mayors in 1986, 144 (58.2 percent) were natives in the cities that they served and 31 (12.5 percent) were from neighboring areas.

Among the fourth generation of leaders in this study, 187 in the 1994 pool and 124 in the 1999 pool are primarily provincial and municipal leaders.[26] Table 3.5 shows the correlation between their birth provinces and the provinces in which they now serve as leaders, as compared to both the third generation of leaders and the study of Chinese mayors conducted about a decade ago. The trend to select local elites from the same region seems to continue in the new generation of leaders, as shown by the fact that 47 percent of leaders in the 1994 pool and 46 percent in the 1999 pool worked in their native provinces, a higher number than was true of the third generation (37 percent).

These percentages of the fourth generation of leaders working near their birthplaces, however, are lower than for Chinese mayors. This is largely because local government leaders in both the 1994 and 1999 pools were mainly provincial leaders, and thus at a different leadership level. It can be reasonably assumed that lower levels of administration tend to have more leaders born in the same region.

In addition, some nonnative provincial leaders also have some sort of local connection; for example, they graduated from, or had many years of work experience in, the region in which they now serve as leaders. For example, Wang Yunkun, Party secretary of Jilin Province, is a native of Jiangsu, but he worked in Jilin for over thirty years after graduating from college in 1966.

These findings are closely connected with the ongoing reform of the Chinese *nomenklatura* system—the list of positions and the candidates qualified to fill them. The *nomenklatura* system has been the hallmark of the personnel policy during Communist regimes.[27] Since the 1980s, the system has changed in China: in general, the appointment decisions were made by immediate supervisors instead of the more traditional policy of approval by a "two-level" superior organization.[28] In practice, this means that provincial Party secretaries and governors are responsible for appointing the "second tier" provincial level officials and mayoral and prefecture heads of medium- and small-sized cities.

Formerly the appointment of the "second tier" provincial level officials was controlled by the Organization Department of the Central Committee of the CCP. According to Cao Zhi, vice minister of the Organization Department of the

Table 3.5    Distribution of Birthplace of Provincial and Municipal Leaders of the Fourth Generation and a Comparison with the Third Generation and the Study of Chinese Mayors

|  | 4th Generation | | | | 3d Generation | | Mayors (1986) | |
|  | 1994 Pool | | 1999 Pool | | 1999 Pool | | | |
|  | No. | % | No. | % | No. | % | No. | % |
|---|---|---|---|---|---|---|---|---|
| Native province | 88 | 47.1 | 57 | 46.0 | 22 | 37.3 | 144 | 58.2 |
| Neighboring province | 25 | 13.4 | 15 | 12.1 | 15 | 25.4 | 31 | 12.5 |
| Distant province | 74 | 39.6 | 52 | 41.9 | 22 | 37.3 | 59 | 23.8 |
| Unknown | 13 | 5.2 | | | | | | |
| Total | 187 | 100.1 | 124 | 100.0 | 59 | 100.0 | 247 | 99.7 |

Source: Liao and Fan, Zhongguo renming da cidian (1994); Shen, Zhonggong di shiwujie zhongyang weiyuanhui zhongyang jilü jiancha weiyuanhui weiyuan minglu; and Cheng Li and David Bachman, "Localism, Elitism, and Immobilism: Elite Formation and Social Change in Post-Mao China," World Politics 42, no. 1 (October 1989): 64–94.

Note: The data were accumulated and tabulated by the author. Percentages do not add up to 100 due to rounding.

CCP, the central authorities have given provincial leaders autonomy in appointing leaders at the level of mayoral and prefecture heads since the mid-1980s. As a result, the total number of cadres appointed by the CCP Organization Department decreased from 13,000 to 2,700.[29]

The lists of names for the province-level *nomenklatura* are now composed disproportionately of people from the province in question. In view of the degree to which Chinese officials defend their "turf," it is hard to imagine that provincial leaders would choose to search in other jurisdictions to find candidates for their posts.[30] The trend toward recruitment of more native-born elites is strengthened by local cadre elections and by the "election with more candidates than seats" (*cha'e xuanju*), which has been adopted in the Party congress in various levels (from grass roots to the Central Committee) since the Fourteenth Party Congress in 1992. During the 1990s, local officials have wanted a say in the appointments of top leaders in their provinces. As a result, governors and Party secretaries have increasingly acted as representatives of their provincial interests, rather than satraps of the central authorities. Hu Fuguo, a native of Shanxi who serves as Party secretary of Shanxi, told local officials in his "inauguration speech" that he will "fight for the local interests of the Shanxi people."[31]

In local elections, it is highly likely that the people will choose a native candidate to be their local leader if the other candidates' qualifications are roughly equal. These elected local elites may, in turn, make further "localist demands." In the 1990s, local people's congresses sometimes refused even to approve candidates endorsed by the central authorities, producing what the Chinese official journal, *Liaowang,* called, "unexpected results."[32] Wan Xueyuan, a native of Hubei and former head of the CCYL in Shanghai, was appointed by central authorities to be the governor of Zhejiang in 1993 but was then rejected in a legally required election by the Zhejiang People's Congress. Now he serves as director of the Bureau of Foreign Experts, a much lower position than provincial governor.

During the 1990s, the central authorities faced strong local resistance to appointing nonnative leaders to their provinces. Cantonese local officials, for example, were particularly resentful when the central authorities appointed Li Changchun, a native of Liaoning and a new Politburo member, to be Party secretary of Guangdong, replacing Xie Fei, a native Cantonese who was still a member of the Politburo.[33] In most cases, however, the central authorities are able to ensure that nominees from the center are selected for provincial leadership positions. But the interdependence of central and provincial leaders has been consolidated in recent years. As John Burns observes, "appointments are probably often the outcome of negotiation and bargaining among faction leaders mindful of their needs to build and maintain personal relations networks and of the need for factional balance."[34] It took almost a year, in the case of Guangdong mentioned above, for local officials to accept the non-Cantonese Party boss.[35]

Two decades of economic reform and a resurgence of economic localism have also contributed to the erosion of the central authorities' *nomenklatura* system. During the reform era, economic localism reached an unprecedented scale in the PRC history. People within China call this phenomenon "economic warlordism."[36] As a Chinese journal reported, "China today is split into more than 20 independent kingdoms and more than 2,000 fiefdoms."[37] For example, local officials have exerted considerable power over local bank executives—powers that involve the ability to make personnel appointments in local bank branches and thus control the career advancement of bank executives. As Edward S. Steinfeld recently observed, "It is not uncommon for local governments to exert pressure on banks to lend to favored firms or major local employers."[38] In some regions, local officials even side with local banks in refusing to redeem the mature bank deposits of the firms in other regions.

### The Center's Restraint over Localism in Elite Promotion

Since the mid-1980s, the tension between the demand for regional representation and the restraint on the rise of localism has become a crucial issue in Chinese politics in general, and elite recruitment in particular. The central authorities are certainly alert to the trend of selecting local officials from their native place. The Organization Department of the CCP has recently made efforts to limit the number of provincial top leaders who work in their native areas. In June 1999, it issued "The Regulation of Cadre Exchange," which specifies that (1) county and municipal top leaders should not be selected from the same region; (2) those who head a county and city for over ten years should be transferred to another place; and (3) provincial leaders should be transferred more frequently to another province or the central government.[39] In 2000, only four provincial Party secretaries served in the province in which they were born (six in 1999, seven in 1998, and nine in 1997). There are only two provinces (Liaoning and Jiangxi) in which both the Party secretaries and governors are natives.[40] In addition, a head of the public security bureau (*gonganju*) of a provincial government is now required to be transferred to another province after working in the province for a few years.[41]

While a majority of deputy provincial Party secretaries and vice governors often work in the provinces in which they were born, full provincial Party secretaries and full governors are likely to be transferred from other provinces. This means that many current provincial leaders who often formerly served in their native provinces, moving from the level of grassroots leadership to the posts of deputy Party secretary or vice governor, are subsequently transferred to another province to become Party boss or governor.

This pattern can be found among many members in the fourth generation leadership under study. For example, Du Qinglin, a native of Jilin, and Wang Xiaofeng, a native of Hunan, now serve as Party secretary and governor of Hainan, respectively. But prior to their current posts, Du served as deputy Party secretary in Jilin and Wang was deputy Party secretary of Hunan. They had worked in their native provinces for decades. Another example is Qian Yunlu, newly appointed governor of Guizhou. He was born in Hubei in 1944 and after graduating from Hubei University in 1967 worked in his native province as Party secretary of a people's commune, deputy Party secretary in Hanchun county, head of the CCYL in Hubei, Party secretary of Wuhan city, and deputy Party secretary of Hubei before being appointed to his current post in Guizhou.

Meanwhile, the central authorities have also appointed provincial top leaders to the central government in order to restrain local power. For example, Ye Xuanping, son of the late Marshal Ye Jianying, built a solid power base in Guangdong when he served as the Party boss there in the 1980s. The increasing economic and cultural autonomy of Guangdong made the central authorities nervous. To prevent the making of the "Cantonese separationist movement," the central authorities "promoted" Ye to senior vice chair of the Chinese People's Political Consultative Conference. Among the fourteen new Politburo members in the Fourteenth Party Congress in 1992, seven, including Xie Fei, Party secretary of Guangdong, were directly promoted from provinces. Of course, not all of them were promoted for the same reason, but these examples indicate a reduction in the independence of local power.[42]

The central authorities do not treat all the regional administrations in the same manner. Top leaders seem to worry about the threat of localism more in certain regions than in others. Since Jiang Zemin was promoted by Deng from Party secretary of Shanghai to general secretary of the CCP in 1989, no high-ranking officers have been transferred from other regions to the Shanghai administration (either the municipal Party committee or municipal government). Wu Bangguo, former Party secretary, Huang Ju, current Party secretary, and Xu Kuangdi, current mayor, were all born in neighboring provinces and worked in Shanghai soon after they graduated from college. In the 1999 pool, there are five members of the fourth generation of leaders who currently work in Shanghai. They are Chen Liangyu (a Zhejiang native), executive vice mayor; Meng Jianzhu (a Jiangsu native), deputy Party secretary; Zhang Huixin (a Jiangsu native), deputy Party secretary; Wu Yigong (a Zhejiang native), director of the Cultural Bureau; and Xie Qihua (a Zhejiang native), general manager of the Baoshan Steel Company. All of them were born in neighboring provinces and worked in Shanghai for a long time, most since their college graduation about two decades earlier.

In addition to allowing long-time Shanghai leaders to run the city, Jiang has also promoted his friends from Shanghai to important national leadership positions and thus has formed what Western observers call Jiang's "Shanghai gang" in the center. Jiang has apparently cultivated a web of personal ties based on Shanghai connections. Zeng Qinghong, Jiang's chief of staff in Shanghai when Jiang was Party secretary of the city, moved with Jiang to Beijing in 1989. Zeng was promoted from deputy head of the General Office of the CCP to its head, and now to alternate of the Politburo and head of the Organization Department of the CCP. Chen Zhili, Jiang's deputy in the Shanghai Party Committee, now heads the Ministry of Education. You Xigui, Jiang's bodyguard and former commander of the Shanghai Military Garrison Command, also moved to Beijing with Jiang and now serves as director of the Bodyguard Bureau and deputy head of the General Office of the CCP.

Jiang has also promoted his "Shanghai gang" to head the central government's main propaganda organs. Gong Xinhan and Zhou Ruijin were transferred from Shanghai to be deputy head of the Propaganda Department of the CCP and deputy editor in chief of the *People's Daily,* respectively. Xu Guangchun, former head of the Shanghai Branch of Xinhua News Agency, was promoted to editor in chief of *Guangming Daily* and spokesperson for the Fifteenth CCP Congress and is now deputy head of the Propaganda Department of the CCP.[43]

Meanwhile, Zhu Rongji, former mayor of Shanghai, has also promoted his associates in Shanghai to central government positions. For example, when Zhu Rongji took over as governor of the People's Bank of China in 1993, he immediately appointed two close colleagues from Shanghai to the bank as vice governors. They were Dai Xianglong, former governor of the Shanghai-based Bank of Communications and Zhu Xiaohua, former vice governor of the Shanghai branch of the Bank of China.[44]

Favoritism over Shanghai-based leaders shows that the tension between the central government and localism in elite recruitment has centered on political control and countercontrol in central-local relations. The power struggle in central government is the determining factor in the career mobility of top regional leaders. This is certainly not new in the PRC history. What is new is the growing public awareness of this tension and ever stronger resistance toward the central authorities' region-based nepotism and favoritism. Chapter 5 provides more evidence and analysis of this issue.

**Restraining Military Localism**

The central authorities have been even more worried about the potential threat of "military localism" and the formation of military factionalism. The concern about military factionalism is, of course, not new. Mao Zedong and Deng Xiaoping reportedly met when Deng reemerged for the first time in 1973. Mao was beset by the growing power of local military elites and the potential conflicts between them. Deng told Mao he could solve the problem quickly by reassigning the top officers of all military regions at the same time.[45] Deng's tactics worked well, both then and later.

Over the past two decades, no regional military upheaval has occurred, even though the country has gone through periods as potentially (if not actually) turbulent as the 1976 death of Mao, the 1989 Tiananmen incident, the removal of the so-called generals of the Yang family in the early 1990s, and the 1997 death of Deng. The central authorities have achieved such stability through sporadic, large-scale reshuffling of top officers in China's seven greater military regions. Jiang Zemin has also adopted this tactic to prevent the army's propensity to intervene in Chinese politics.

Since the 1940s, the veteran leaders and PLA officers have formed effective bonds that used to be centered in the so-called field armies. As William Whitson observes, a leader's actual power may well depend primarily on the collective status of his field army associates, whether in or out of uniform.[46] The best example is the rise and fall of Lin Biao's Fourth Field Army faction during the Cultural Revolution. An overwhelming majority of top officers from 1966 to 1971 were from that field army, but after Lin fell, many of these officers were purged.[47]

When Deng Xiaoping resumed power in 1978, he promoted some of his Second Field Army associates to key military posts. In 1988, for example, of the seventeen full generals who had the highest rank available after the Cultural Revolution, ten (three-fifths) were from the Second Field Army, especially from Deng's own unit, the 129th Division. These included then defense minister, Qin Jiwei, and director of the PLA General Political Department, Yang Baibing. Of the six noncivilian members on the Central Military Commission, half were originally from the Second Field Army; the Third and Fourth Field Armies each had just one seat. Other veteran leaders resented Deng's favoritism toward the Second Field Army.[48]

In the early 1990s, the rapid military elite transformation and frequent regional reshuffling brought military factions based on the field army systems to an end. Field army association has apparently become irrelevant in appointments of military and civilian leaders.[49] The central authorities, however, face a new challenge, a new kind of military localism: the Chinese military has become involved in business, which has often been regionally based during the reform era. By 1998, the various departments of the PLA (e.g., General Logistics Department, Chief of Staff Headquarters, and the General Political Department) and all greater military regions in the country established over 20,000 business firms. These firms have hired about a million employees, mainly civilians in local areas.[50] What began in the mid-1980s as a means of compensating for inadequate military budgets has burgeoned into an all-purpose "PLA Inc.," providing about one-third of the military's operating expenses but also forging many joint ventures with foreign investors.[51]

During the mid-1990s, the PLA became one of the largest entrepreneurial ventures in the country (and one of the most corrupt institutions as well). In July 1998, Jiang Zemin ordered the country's military to give up commercial activities altogether. Foreign observers believe this was probably "Jiang's boldest move" as well as "one of the biggest gambles of his political career."[52] Jiang's order seems to have worked very well, for almost all the military firms are in the process of converting into enterprises under civilian control. No systematic resistance from the military has been reported thus far.

The frequent reshuffling of top army officers of military regions also echoes Jiang's effort to restrain military localism. This is particularly evident among the military members of the fourth generation leadership. The 1999 pool included nine high-ranking regional officers who belong to the fourth generation. Table 3.6 shows the quick regional reshuffling of these officers during the 1990s. Seven out of nine transferred from other military regions to their current positions.[53] No one has held his current post more than four years. For example, in 1995 Jiang Futang, political commissar of Shenyang Military Region, was transferred out of the Guangzhou Military Region, where he had served as deputy chief of staff since 1993. Prior to that he was director of the Political Department of the Jinan Military Region.

Jiang Futang's experience of being transferred is an example of many similar moves among members of the top regional military leadership. The frequent reshuffling of regional officers, which was first adopted by Deng in the 1970s, has continued in the post-Deng era, especially among the new generation of high-ranking military officers.

## EDUCATIONAL BACKGROUND

### Level of Education and "Middle Career Training"

The most important change of leadership in China during the reform era is the dramatic increase in the number of political elites with higher education, especially those majoring in engineering and the natural sciences. Table 3.7 shows the distribution of educational levels of the fourth generation of leaders. This study counts only the highest level of education attained. For those who had a college/university education and also attended a Party school, this study counts only the college/university education. For those who did not have a college/university education but attended a Party school, this study includes them among Party school graduates.

Since the degree system was established in 1981, China has granted 35,000 Ph.D.s, 390,000 master's degrees, and 4,200,000 bachelor's degrees. In 1997, there

**Table 3.6    Reshuffle of Regional Top Military Officers in the Fourth Generation Leadership (1999 pool)**

| Name | Current Position | Since | Previous Position | Since |
|------|------------------|-------|-------------------|-------|
| Xu Caihou | Political commissar, Jinan Military Region | 1998 | Director, *PLA Daily* | 1994 |
| Guo Boxiong | Commander, Lanzhou Military Region | 1997 | Deputy commander, Beijing Military Region | 1993 |
| Chen Bingde | Commander, Nanjing Military Region | 1996 | Chief of staff, Nanjing Military Region | 1993 |
| Wu Yuqian | Deputy commander, Shenyan Military Region | 1996 | Chief of staff, Shenyan Military Region | 1995 |
| Jiang Futang | Political commissar, Shenyan Military Region | 1995 | Deputy chief of staff, Guangzhou Military Region | 1993 |
| Lei Mingqiu | Deputy political commissar, Nanjing Military Region | 1995 | Political Dept. director, Guangzhou Military Region | 1992 |
| Wang Tongzhuo | Deputy political commissar, Guangzhou Military Region | 1995 | Political Dept. director, Nanjing Military Region | 1993 |
| Li Qianyuan | Chief of staff, Lanzhou Military Region | 1994 | Deputy chief of staff, Guangzhou Military Region | 1990 |
| Pei Huailiang | Deputy commander, Jinan Military Region | 1994 | Deputy chief of staff, Nanjing Military Region | 1990 |

*Source:* Shen, *Zhonggong di shiwujie zhongyang weiyuanhui zhongyang jilü jiancha weiyuanhui weiyuan minglu.*

*Note:* The data were tabulated by the author.

were 176,000 registered graduate students, including 39,000 Ph.D. candidates. In addition, China established part-time graduate programs in 1985. By 1998, a total of 18,000 had completed their master's degrees and 460 had attained Ph.D. degrees. Today there are 7,000 studying in a master's degree program in business administration (MBA) and 1,600 majoring in the master's program in law.[54] Many members of the fourth generation of leaders included in this study are among the graduates of all these programs.

In the 1994 pool, approximately 90 percent of the leaders received a tertiary education or above; among them, 72.1 percent attended a university and 9.1 percent have postgraduate degrees. In the 1999 pool, over 98 percent of leaders received a tertiary education or above. The percentage of those who received postgraduate degrees increased to 17.4 percent, almost double that of the 1994 pool.

Table 3.7 Educational Levels of the Fourth Generation of Leaders in Comparison with the Third Generation of Leaders

| | 4th Generation | | | | 3d Generation | |
| | 1994 Pool | | 1999 Pool | | 1999 Pool | |
| Level | No. | % | No. | % | No. | % |
|---|---|---|---|---|---|---|
| Postgraduate (Ph.D./M.S./M.A.) | 27 | 9.1 | 39 | 17.4 | 24 | 10.3 |
| University | 215 | 72.1 | 132 | 58.9 | 112 | 48.3 |
| Two-year college or polytechnic | 9 | 3.0 | 22 | 9.8 | 40 | 17.2 |
| Military academy | 7 | 2.3 | 23 | 10.3 | 37 | 15.9 |
| Party school | 12 | 4.0 | 5 | 2.2 | 2 | 0.9 |
| High school or below | 25 | 8.4 | 2 | 0.9 | 16 | 6.9 |
| Unknown | 3 | 1.0 | 1 | 0.5 | 1 | 0.4 |
| Total | 298 | 99.9 | 224 | 100.0 | 232 | 99.9 |

Source: Liao and Fan, Zhongguo renming da cidian (1994); and Shen, Zhonggong di shiwujie zhongyang weiyuanhui zhongyang jilü jiancha weiyuanhui weiyuan minglu.

Note: The data were accumulated and tabulated by the author. Percentages do not add up to 100 due to rounding.

In addition, because the 1999 pool contains many military elites, the percentage of those who attended military academies in the 1999 pool is much higher than in the 1994 pool.

For comparison, table 3.7 also includes data about the level of education among the third generation of leaders. Although having completed a postsecondary degree or above is common to both generations, more leaders of the third generation attended two-year colleges, polytechnics, and military academies than those in the fourth generation. This study also found that those leaders with education from two-year colleges or polytechnics in both the third and fourth generations are more likely to have attended the Central Party School (CPS) during the late 1980s and the early 1990s. Although table 3.7 shows the low percentage of leaders who attended Party schools, the real number of elites who did so is much higher, since many of them attended Party schools as midcareer training. For example, Sun Chunlan, graduated from Lianning's Anshan Polytechnics in 1969 and worked as a factory director in Anshan for many years before being appointed deputy chair of Anshan Women's Association in 1988. After working as deputy chair of the Workers Union in Liaoning in 1991, Sun studied at the Central Party School in 1992. She now serves as deputy Party secretary of Liaoning and president of the Party school of the province. A similar example is Sun Gan, who graduated from Yunnan University in 1969. He worked successively as Party secretary of a commune, chair of the Scientists Association in a county, and deputy mayor of Kunming before attending an M.A. program at the Central Party School in 1986. He is now deputy Party secretary of Yunnan Province. In the 1999 pool, eighteen members of the fourth generation and ten members of the third generation attended the midcareer training program at the CPS. The Central Party School has become one of the main school networks producing provincial and ministerial elites during the reform era.

This study also found that a majority of high-ranking military officers received their midcareer training in military academies during the reform era, in many cases as recently as the late 1980s and the early 1990s. This is largely because a "mandatory link between military school education and officer appointment and promotion has been established."[55] According to a study of China's high-ranking military officers in the early 1990s, about four-fifths of the 45–57 age group received a tertiary education or above.[56] Junior military officers at the division and regiment levels are likely to include an even higher portion of college graduates. In 1990, for example, about three-fourths of warship captains and their immediate deputies in the PLA navy had received training in military academies. Dalian Warship Academy, Guangzhou Warship Academy, and the Navy Academy are characterized by *People's Daily* as "cradles of navy captains" in the PRC.[57]

For the new generation of high-ranking military officers, attending the National Defense University (NDU) is an important stepping-stone to higher military office in China.[58] The NDU did not exist until the early 1980s, when three elite PLA colleges—the Academies of Military Command, Logistics, and Political Education—merged to form the university.[59] The first president of the NDU was Zhang Zhen, who later became vice chairman of the Central Military Commission. During his presidency (1985–1992), Zhang claimed that the NDU would become the cradle of China's generals in the 1990s and the next century. To accelerate this process, Zhang established the Department of Defense Research in 1988. The candidates in this special department have to be major generals or bureau-level civilian cadres. After a one-year intensive program, the graduates are promoted to higher military posts or civilian leadership positions in defense industries. Most graduates of the first four classes became commanders of group armies or served in the headquarters of greater military regions, and they in turn sent more junior military officers from their units to the NDU, which has already become the center of a formidable informal political network.

Many military officers who are members of the fourth generation of leaders in both study pools attended the NDU, especially its Department of Defense Research, in the late 1980s and early 1990s. They include Sui Mingtai, political commissar of PLA Second Artillery Corps; Ge Dongsheng, chief of staff of PLA Second Artillery Corps; Xu Qiliang, chief of staff of PLA Air Force; Shen Binyi, deputy director of General Logistics Department; Zhang Dingfa, commander of North China Sea Fleet; Liu Zhenwu, commander of Military Force in Hong Kong; and Wang Huayuan, deputy Party secretary of Guangdong Province.

Zhang Zhen also promoted many of his protégés to higher military posts. Two Fourteen Central Committee members, Zhou Yushu and Zhang Meiyuan, for example, served at different times as commanders of the 24th Group Army, which

Zhang once served as commander. Earlier, very few commanders of group armies had been selected to the Central Committee of the CCP, and their association with Zhang explains the rapid promotion of these two young officers. Zhang's tenure as president of the country's most elite military academy has allowed him to cultivate ties with middle-ranking and senior officers. Since its founding in 1985, the NDU has graduated 5,000 military officers.[60] They now occupy some of the most important leadership positions in the PLA. According to one source, by 1992, about 65 percent of officers above the army level were graduates of the NDU and its predecessors.[61] In 1997, 90 percent of the commanders of group armies had been at the NDU.[62] Although the university has not existed long, it has already played, and will continue to play, a vital role in the formation of the PLA leadership.

The midcareer training program in both the CPS and the NDU serves various purposes for the new generation of leaders. For them, keeping abreast of modern science and technology is of secondary importance. These ambitious young leaders enroll in the program to receive necessary academic credentials for future career advancement and, most importantly, to be part of a powerful network. Chapter 4 elucidates this type of interconnection by discussing the role of Qinghua University in the recruitment of China's civilian technocrats.

## Academic Majors

Table 3.8 shows the distribution of academic majors in four elite groups: (1) 166 mayors; (2) 158 full members of the Fourteenth Central Committee of the CCP; (3) 273 members of the fourth generation of leaders in the 1994 study pool; and (4) 216 members of the fourth generation of leaders in the 1999 study pool. This includes only members having a tertiary education or above in these four pools. Data on the first two elite groups were based on the 1986 and 1989 sources, respectively.[63] This allows us to see both changes and continuities in the educational backgrounds of Chinese leaders during the reform era, although these four groups are not all at the same level of leadership.

A significant number of Chinese mayors in the 1986 survey were in their late thirties and early forties.[64] Some of them have since advanced their political careers and have become provincial and ministerial leaders—the same people in the two pools of the fourth generation of leaders. The members of the 14th Central Committee, however, consisted mainly of the third generation of leaders, although the second and fourth generations of leaders were represented to some extent. This provides an interesting perspective for comparison. The following three points identify some important trends in terms of educational backgrounds.

First, the predominance of those trained in engineering and natural sciences is evident in all four groups (the relatively low percentage on the Fourteenth Central Committee may be partly due to the fact that the academic majors of 36.7 percent of the study pool were unknown). As discussed in the previous chapter, these engineers or scientists turned politicians can be defined as technocrats—

Table 3.8    Comparison of the Distribution of Academic Majors of Three Elite
Groups: Mayors, Members of the 14th Central Committee of the CCP, and the
Fourth Generation of Leaders

|  | Mayors | | 14th CC | | 4th Generation | | | |
|---|---|---|---|---|---|---|---|---|
|  | (1986 Data) | | (1989 Data) | | (1994 Data) | | (1999 Data) | |
| Major | No. | % | No. | % | No. | % | No. | % |
| Engineering and natural sciences | | | | | | | | |
| Engineering | 107 | 64.4 | 46 | 29.1 | 109 | 39.9 | 75 | 34.7 |
| Geology | 0 | 0 | 3 | 1.9 | 2 | 0.7 | 2 | 0.9 |
| Agronomy | 7 | 4.2 | 2 | 1.3 | 6 | 2.2 | 9 | 4.2 |
| Biology | 0 | 0 | 1 | 0.6 | 2 | 0.7 | 1 | 0.5 |
| Physics | 4 | 2.4 | 3 | 1.9 | 15 | 5.5 | 8 | 3.7 |
| Chemistry | 3 | 1.8 | 2 | 1.3 | 10 | 3.7 | 3 | 1.3 |
| Medical science | 0 | 0 | 2 | 1.3 | 3 | 1.1 | 2 | 0.9 |
| Mathematics | 2 | 1.2 | 0 | 0 | 5 | 1.8 | 5 | 2.3 |
| Architecture | 1 | 0.6 | 0 | 0 | 1 | 0.4 | 2 | 0.9 |
| Subtotal | 124 | 74.7 | 59 | 37.3 | 153 | 56.0 | 107 | 49.4 |
| Economics and management | | | | | | | | |
| Economics and finance | 10 | 6.0 | 3 | 1.9 | 20 | 7.3 | 15 | 6.9 |
| Business administration | 4 | 2.4 | 1 | 0.6 | 2 | 0.7 | 0 | 0 |
| Statistics and accounting | 1 | 0.6 | 1 | 0.6 | 5 | 1.8 | 1 | 0.5 |
| Subtotal | 15 | 9.0 | 5 | 3.1 | 27 | 9.9 | 16 | 7.4 |
| Military science and engineering | 0 | 0 | 17 | 10.8 | 4 | 1.5 | 22 | 10.2 |
| Subtotal | 0 | 0 | 17 | 10.8 | 4 | 1.5 | 22 | 10.2 |
| Social sciences and law | | | | | | | | |
| Politics and party history | 5 | 3.0 | 9 | 5.7 | 22 | 8.0 | 14 | 6.5 |
| Political economy | 0 | 0 | 1 | 0.6 | 0 | 0 | 0 | |
| Journalism | 0 | 0 | 0 | 0 | 4 | 1.5 | 1 | 0.5 |
| Law | 1 | 0.6 | 1 | 0.6 | 15 | 5.5 | 7 | 3.2 |
| Subtotal | 6 | 3.6 | 11 | 6.9 | 41 | 15.0 | 22 | 10.2 |
| Humanities | | | | | | | | |
| Philosophy | 1 | 0.6 | 0 | 0 | 7 | 2.6 | 3 | 1.3 |
| History | 3 | 1.8 | 2 | 1.3 | 4 | 1.5 | 7 | 3.2 |
| Education | 10 | 6.0 | 1 | 0.6 | 6 | 2.2 | 4 | 1.9 |
| Chinese language/literature | 7 | 4.2 | 3 | 1.9 | 21 | 7.6 | 14 | 6.5 |
| Foreign language | 0 | 0 | 2 | 1.3 | 6 | 2.2 | 4 | 1.9 |
| Subtotal | 21 | 12.6 | 8 | 5.1 | 44 | 16.1 | 32 | 14.8 |
| Unknown | 0 | 0 | 58 | 36.7 | 4 | 1.5 | 17 | 7.9 |
| Total | 166 | 99.8 | 158 | 99.9 | 273 | 100.0 | 216 | 99.9 |

Source: Data on mayors are from Li and Bachman, "Localism, Elitism, and Immobilism," 71. Data on
the Fourteenth Central Committee are from Zang Xiaowei, "The Fourteenth Central Committee of the
CCP," 797; and Li and White, "The Fifteenth Central Committee of the Chinese Communist Party,"
250. Data on the fourth generation of leaders are from Liao and Fan, Zhongguo renming da cidian (1994);
and Shen, Zhonggong di shiwujie zhongyang weiyuanhui zhongyang jilü jiancha weiyuanhui weiyuan minglu.
    Note: The data were accumulated and tabulated by the author. Percentages do not add up to 100
due to rounding.

people who have three traits: technical education, professional experience, and high post. More inclusively, the category of technocrats also includes experts in economics and finance.[65] Using this definition, 180 out of the total of 273 college-educated fourth generation leaders in the 1994 pool and 123 out of the total 216 in the 1999 pool are technocrats (see table 3.8). They constitute 65.9 percent and 56.9 percent of these two pools, respectively. The real number of technocrats in the fourth generation of leaders is probably even higher because some who attended the military academy also studied engineering.[66]

Second, the training of the new generation of leaders also shows some important variations compared to the educational backgrounds of the third generation of leaders, although the latter has been known for being predominantly technocratic.[67] Table 3.8 shows that the percentage of the fourth generation of leaders who are trained in economics and management, including finance, accounting, and statistics, is about three times higher than that of the Fourteenth Central Committee.

Currently, young leaders who are in charge of China's financial system are usually economists by training. Dai Xianglong, governor of the People's Bank; Li Jinhua, auditor general of the State Council, Jin Renqing, vice minister of finance and director of the State Administration of Taxation, and Wang Chengming, Party secretary of the People's Bank, are all economists who graduated from China's Central Institute of Finance and Banking before the Cultural Revolution. Zhu Xiaohua, vice governor of People's Bank and director of the State Administration of Exchange Control, graduated from the Shanghai Institute of Finance and Economy in the early 1980s. Qian Guanlin, director of PRC General Administration of Customs, is a graduate of the Shanghai Institute of Foreign Trade. Liu Tinghuan, governor of the Industrial and Commercial Bank of China, graduated from the Liaoning Institute of Finance and Banking. Wang Xuebing, governor of the Bank of China, was a graduate of the Beijing Institute of Foreign Trade. He worked in London and New York for many years when the Bank of China first established its offices there and later served as general manager of the New York Branch of the Bank of China in 1988–1993. Many of these young economists and financial experts serve in the current Central Committee of the CCP.

Just a few years ago, the most important posts in China's financial system were usually occupied by the third generation leaders who were trained as engineers. Li Guixian, for example, a Soviet-trained engineer and a graduate of Mentzeliev Chemical Engineering Institute in Moscow, was governor of the People's Bank from 1988 to 1993.[68] During these five years, most bank loans and fixed asset investments went to the least productive part of the economy, causing many serious financial problems.[69] China's banking problems are not necessarily due to Li's poor handling of macroeconomic policy; nonetheless, his expertise in chemical engineering and his lack of experience in economic affairs did not prepare him for dealing with financial issues.

Another important change between the third and fourth generations is that the number of lawyers increased among the recently elected young leaders. The percentage of those trained in law among both the 1986 mayors and the Fourteenth

CC was extremely low (both 0.6 percent), but in the fourth generation of lead-ers, fifteen (5.5 percent) in the 1994 pool and seven (3.2 percent) in the 1999 pool are graduates of law schools such as the Beijing Institute of Political Science and Law and the East China College of Political Science and Law. Many of those in the 1994 pool serve as vice ministers in the Ministry of Justice, heads of provin-cial courts and provincial chief procurators. The youngest among them, Li Ke-qiang, was recently appointed governor of Henan Province. Li was born in 1955 in Anhui. He was sent to the same province during the CR and worked there as a farmer. He entered the Law Department at Beijing University in 1978. In addi-tion to his law degree, Li also received a Ph.D. in economics.

The 1999 study pool also includes many similar examples. Yuan Chunqing, newly appointed secretary-general of the CCDI, entered the department of law at Beijing University after the CR. He continued to study for a master's degree in Law at China's University of Political Science and Law in the late 1980s. Zhao Hong, deputy procurator general in the Supreme People's Procuratorate; Luo Feng, secretary of the Disciplinary Commission of the Ministry of Public Security, and Li Zhilun, vice minister of supervision, are all lawyers who graduated from the Beijing Institute of Political Science and Law. In contrast, among the third gen-eration of leaders with college education, very few majored in law.

These lawyer-turned-politicians follow the Party line in dealing with tough is-sues. However, the emergence of lawyers in China's provincial and ministerial leadership reflects efforts by the central authorities to establish and consolidate the Chinese legal system during the post-Deng era. China probably issued more laws and regulations during the 1990s than any other country during the same pe-riod. In the early 1980s there were only 3,000 lawyers in a country of over 1 bil-lion people. It is expected that by 2000 China will have 150,000 lawyers (the growth rate is even more rapid than in the United States, for better or worse!), and Chinese courts now hear over 3 million cases a year.[70] Since China sets such an ambitious target for the number of lawyers, many of them do not receive suffi-cient training. Nonetheless, the rapid development of the legal profession in China can be seen as a positive political change.

According to some theorists in studies of elites, the selection of elites by occu-pation is generally "determined by the types of problems confronting a society" and by the skills needed to solve those problems.[71] For example, when religion is highly valued, priests are the elite group; when political orthodoxy is valued, ide-ologues are given high status; when military prowess is essential, career officers rank highest.[72] The composition of elite groups changes over time as society de-mands new credentials for governing elites. A regime headed by technocrats, for example, can be expected to differ fundamentally from a state governed by lawyers. It remains to be seen whether the presence of this new group of lawyers will change the process of *how* to get to the top, challenge the technocratic dom-inance in the Chinese leadership, and, in the long run, contribute to the growing demand for the rule of law and political democracy.

The contrasts among these groups in terms of their educational experiences and occupational identities are important variables that may cause internal conflict within the fourth generation of leaders in the future. Engineers, economists, and lawyers are all professional experts, but variations in their expertise will likely lead to differences in their political perspectives and policy choices. For instance, a bridge engineer may favor building bridges, whether or not the place, time, and cost of building such bridges is justifiable. While engineers and economists tend to rely more on their own expertise in policy making, lawyers may be more concerned about decision-making procedures and the sociopolitical consequences of policies. This intra-generational tension is further intensified by heterogeneous political experiences during their formative years and their diversified career paths (discussed in chapter 6).

## Foreign Studies

China has been sending students abroad for over a century. Ever since the time of Yan Fu, who was one of the first Chinese students sent to Great Britain in 1876 and later became a leading reformer at the turn of the century, Chinese students who studied abroad and then returned to China with knowledge about the outside world "have played a pivotal role in changing the country."[73] Some of these students include Sun Yat-sen, a graduate of both a mission school in Hawaii and a medical school in Hong Kong, and the leader of the revolution that overthrew the Qing dynasty; Chiang Kai-shek, a graduate of a military academy in Japan and the leader of the Nationalist government; Zhou Enlai, a work-study student in France and a prominent leader of the Communist movement; and Deng Xiaoping, another work-study student in France and the architect of China's reform.

Table 3.9 shows foreign studies of the third and fourth generation of leaders in the 1999 pool. The category of foreign studies refers to both regular degree students and long-term (more than one year) visiting scholars. If a person studied in more than one country, all the countries attended are included on the table. There are more foreign studies in the third generation of leaders than the fourth generation. While some leaders in the third generation attended schools in both former Communist-bloc and Western countries, no one in the fourth generation of leaders studied in the former Soviet Union and Eastern European countries. This should not be surprising because between 1949 and the early 1960s, the period during which the third generation of leaders attended college, China sent about 11,000 students abroad, an overwhelming majority of whom went to the Soviet Union and Eastern European countries.[74] Now some of them have become top leaders in the country. Seven out of twenty-two current full Politburo members (32 percent) studied in the Soviet Union and other Eastern European countries, including four standing members of the Politburo: Jiang Zemin, Li Peng, Wei Jianxing, and Li Lanqing. Table 3.9 shows that eighteen out of the thirty-one members of the third generation (58.1 percent) who studied abroad went to the Soviet Union.

Table 3.9    Experience of Study Abroad (Student or Visiting Scholars) in the Third
and Fourth Generations of Leaders (1999 pool)

| Country | 3d Generation | | 4th Generation | |
|---|---|---|---|---|
| | No. | % | No. | % |
| United States | 3 | 9.7 | 7 | 43.8 |
| Great Britain | 3 | 9.7 | 4 | 25.0 |
| Australia | | | 1 | 6.3 |
| Sweden | 2 | 6.5 | | |
| West Germany | 1 | 3.2 | 1 | 6.3 |
| Norway | 1 | 3.2 | | |
| Japan | | | 2 | 12.5 |
| Soviet Union | 18 | 58.1 | | |
| East Germany | 1 | 3.2 | | |
| Czechoslovakia | 1 | 3.2 | | |
| Yugoslavia | 1 | 3.2 | | |
| North Korea | | | 1 | 6.3 |
| Total | 31 | 100.0 | 16 | 100.2 |

Source: Liao and Fan, Zhongguo renming da cidian (1994); and Shen, Zhonggong di shiwujie zhongyang
weiyuanhui zhongyang jilü jiancha weiynanhui weiyuan minglu.

Note: The data were accumulated and tabulated by the author. Percentages do not add up to 100
due to rounding.

During that period, members of the fourth generation leadership were in elementary school or middle school. For more than two decades since the mid-1960s,
China and the Soviet bloc of East Europe countries halted their educational exchange programs. China did not send any significant numbers of students abroad
until 1978, when Deng's reform began. Chinese scholars and students who have
studied abroad and then returned to China during the reform era will likely have
an even stronger impact on the political future of the country.

According to a recent report released from the official Xinhua News Agency,
from 1978 to 1998 China sent about 293,000 people to 103 countries as students
or visiting scholars.[75] Over half of the total (160,000) went to the United States.[76]
This is certainly the "greatest wave" of foreign studies in modern China.[77] Among
these 293,000 students and visiting scholars, 96,000 (32.8 percent) returned to
China.[78] From 1992 to 1998, the rate of those who returned increased by 13 percent each year, due to China's reform policy and rapid economic and social development.[79] In 1998, the total number of returning scholars exceeded the number of students who went abroad the same year. Altogether, 30,000 students and
scholars returned to China during the past five years.

This trend will likely continue, especially because of recent events in Sino-U.S.
relations such as the tragic bombing incident in Belgrade, the American media's

"demonization of China" after the Tiananmen incident, and allegations of tech-nological espionage. The Chinese authorities have recently established some ma-jor funds to attract more Chinese students and scholars who study or work abroad in order to encourage them to return to their native land. According to *Asia Week*, published in Hong Kong, those who have returned to China usually work in three main fields: academia, business, and government.[80]

Among the members of the Chinese Academy of Engineering, for example, 52 percent are students or scholars who have returned in the past decade. Approxi-mately 95 percent of the members of the Chinese Academy of Sciences are stu-dents or scholars who returned after 1949.[81] Lin Yifu, for example, a Taiwanese who received a Ph.D. in economics from the University of Chicago, established the Center of Economic Research at Beijing University. Among the first six re-search fellows with Ph.D. degrees at the Center, four were trained in the United States and two were trained in England. This center has become a major think tank in socioeconomic policies for the Chinese authorities.[82]

Fan Gang, another Ph.D. in economics and a visiting scholar at Harvard from 1985 to 1987, recently established an independent research institute with a 20 million yuan endowment from the private sector. This institute, which is called the Institute of National Economy, has over forty research staff members, ten of whom were trained in the United States. Fan claims that this research institute will someday become China's Brookings Institution.[83]

Returned scholars and students have also emerged in the fourth generation of leaders under study. In the 1994 pool, six leaders received their degrees from foreign universities (in France, Germany, England, Canada, the United States, and North Korea). Lu Yongxiang, the new president of the Chinese Academy of Sciences, re-ceived a Ph.D. in engineering science at Aachen Industrial University, Germany, in 1981. Hong Huasheng, vice chair of Fujian Provincial People's Congress, re-ceived her Ph.D. in oceanology from the University of Rhode Island in 1984.

Table 3.9 shows that some members of the Fifteenth CC and CCDI studied in Western countries and Japan. For example, Ma Qingsheng, deputy Party sec-retary of Guangxi, received his Ph.D. degree in molecular genetics in Great Britain, where he lived from 1980 to 1983. A few leaders had academic experi-ence in the United States as visiting scholars. For example, Chen Zhili worked as a visiting scholar at Pennsylvania State University from 1980 to 1982. Zhao Zhongxian, director of the Research Laboratory of Superconductors under the Chinese Academy of Sciences, studied at Cambridge University in England during the mid-1970s and worked as a visiting scholar at Iowa University in 1984–1986. Bai Chunli, vice president of the Chinese Academy of Sciences, worked at the California Institute of Technology as a postdoctoral fellow in 1985–1987 and guest professor at Northeast University in Japan in 1991–1992. Lü Feijie, president of the Chinese Academy of Agronomy, was a visiting scholar at MIT in 1982–1984. Jiang Enzhu, director of the Hong Kong Branch of the Xinhua News Agency, was a visiting senior research fellow in both the

Institute of International Affairs at Harvard University and the Brookings Institution in Washington, D.C.

The presence of Western-trained elites in China's top leadership, however, is
still marginal, although the number has increased in recent years. It remains to be
seen whether a large number of the coming fifth generation of leaders, the "reform
generation," will be those who have been trained in the United States, as China
has sent thousands of students to the United States during the reform era.[84] They
have already emerged as leaders of divisions or bureaus in the central government.
In the recently reshuffled Ministry of Finance, for example, the average age of its
division and bureau heads is forty-four. Over a quarter of them (sixteen out of
sixty-one) have master's or Ph.D. degrees, many from universities in the United
States.[85] In addition, two newly appointed vice ministers of foreign affairs, Wang
Guangya and Yang Jiechi, both studied at the London School of Economics. The
political implication of the increase in returned students in the Chinese leadership and the relationship between Western-trained and Chinese-trained elites are
issues that deserve further investigation in the years ahead.

## SUMMARY

At the turn of the century, a new kind of political elite, the technocrat-manager,
has completely replaced the old elite, the CCP's first and second generations of revolutionary mobilizers. The current Chinese leadership, however, is also composed
of two generations: the third generation of leaders who started to work during the
socialist transformation of the 1950s and the fourth generation who had their formative years during the Cultural Revolution. In 2000, the third generation of leaders occupied the most seats in the Politburo and the top posts in the state, but memberships of the Central Committee and the Central Commission for Discipline
Inspection of the CCP are rather evenly shared by two generations. More importantly, the tempo of elite turnover and upward mobility of the fourth generation of
leaders has been very fast. The fourth generation of leaders has already taken over
a majority of the posts of full ministers, full provincial Party secretaries, full governors, and especially top posts in greater military regions during the past few years.

In comparison, these two generations share similar biographical characteristics.
For the fourth generation of leaders, it is still an advantage to be a male of Han nationality who was born on the east coast, to have graduated from engineering
school, and to have attended a midcareer training program, such as the ones at the
Central Party School for civilian leaders and at the National Defense University
for officers. This is not surprising because the older generation of elites tends to use
social and political resources to shape the biographical profile of their successors.[86]

In terms of geographical distribution of elites, the three trends characteristic of
the third generation leadership continue to hold true for the fourth generation of
leaders. The first is the trend of a higher representation from East China provinces
such as Jiangsu and Shandong at the expense of South and Southwest China such

as Guangdong and Sichuan. The second is the higher percentage of provincial and mayoral leaders who serve in their native areas. This reflects the rise of localism in elite recruitment, which is reinforced by the erosion of the Chinese *nomenklatura* system and by the ongoing local elections. Yet in recent years, the central authorities have adopted more restrictive rules to limit the practice of selecting provincial Party secretaries and governors from their native province. And the third is the central authorities' tactic of frequently reshuffling top provincial leaders and especially senior officers of greater military regions in order to consolidate the power of the central government and/or to serve the interests of factional politics.

These trends in the geographical distribution of elites are closely related to some of the crucial political issues facing China at the beginning of the twenty-first century. Growing economic disparity between the coast and the interior, the tension between the demand for regional representation and restraints on the rise of localism, and social consciousness of the rights of women and ethnic minorities have been affected by, and will continue to exert an influence on, the formation of the new political leadership.

Comparing the educational backgrounds of the third and the fourth generations of leaders shows not only the shared characteristic of dominance of technocrats but also some important differences. There are more leaders of the fourth generation who attended postgraduate education than their predecessors who usually received undergraduate education (many attended only two-year colleges or polytechnics). Some members of the fourth generation of leaders studied in Western countries as Ph.D. students or visiting scholars in the 1980s, in contrast to the third generation of leaders who were predominantly trained in the Soviet Union and other Eastern European countries.

The fourth generation of leaders includes a growing number of lawyers, economists, and financial experts. They have been in charge of China's legal, economic, and financial reform during the past few years. This reflects recent efforts by the central authorities to establish and consolidate the legal and financial systems in the country. The long-term political implications of the increasing representation of lawyers in Chinese leadership should not be overlooked.

An aggregate analysis of biographical data, however, can take us only so far in our effort to understand the motivation of elites and their likely behavioral characteristics. While offering comprehensive quantitative data, this type of analytical research has its limits. It tells *who* governs but provides no clue on *how* they came to power. It may also give the wrong impression that this elite transformation has been achieved spontaneously and smoothly, without political infighting. A college education has become a prerequisite for elite recruitment during the reform era, but other factors also contribute to the career advancement of new elites.

In fact, Chinese technical elites came to power mainly because of their political connections and only partially because of their technical credentials. The full ramification of the rise of the fourth generation of leaders should be analyzed using other research methods in addition to a biographical analysis. The following chapter, a case study of Qinghua University, the cradle of Chinese technocrats, will show not only the long, arduous journey that technical elites have taken since the founding of the PRC but also the role of *guanxi*—connections and networks— in the rise of the new generation of leaders.

## NOTES

1. Liao Gailong and Fan Yuan, comps., *Zhongguo renming da cidian xiandai dangzhengjun lingdaorenwujuan* (Who's who in China: Current Party, government, and military Leaders) (Beijing: Foreign Languages Press, 1994).

2. Shen Xueming et al., comps., *Zhonggong di shiwujie zhongyang weiyuanhui zhongyang jilü jiancha weiyuanhui weiyuan minglu* (Who's who of the members of the Fifteenth Central Committee of the Chinese Communist Party and the Fifteenth Central Commission for Discipline Inspection) (Beijing: Zhonggong wenxian chubanshe, 1999).

3. Biographical information on the members of the Fifteenth Central Committee of the Chinese Communist Party and the Fifteenth Central Commission for Discipline Inspection, which formed in 1997, has been updated in the source. For example, the information that some members were promoted to new positions in 1998 is included.

4. The two pools of data have some overlaps. The first pool includes ninety-five members and alternates of the Fifteenth Central Committee of the Chinese Communist Party. In the second pool, four people—Wei Jianxin, Han Shubin, He Yong, and Zhou Ziyu—are members of both the Fifteenth CC and CCDI.

5. The data have been scrutinized using Microsoft Excel, which could not be reprinted with this book for technical reasons. It is available from the author on request.

6. For more information about the age distribution of the members of the Fifteenth Central Committee of the CCP, see Li and White, "The Fifteenth Central Committee of the Chinese Communist Party," 243–245.

7. For the formation of the military elite in the late 1980s and early 1990s, see, Cheng Li and Lynn White, "The Army in the Succession to Deng Xiaoping: Familiar Fealties and Technocratic Trends," *Asian Survey* 33, no. 8 (August 1993): 757–786.

8. Among the forty-two military members of the Fifteenth Central Committee, twenty-four have been newly elected and only five have been promoted from alternate status in the previous CC. Thus the turnover of military leaders is faster than that of civilian leaders. For a detailed discussion, see Li and White, "The Army in the Succession to Deng Xiaoping," 757–786; and Li and White, "The Fifteenth Central Committee of the Chinese Communist Party," 255–256.

9. Li and White, "The Army in the Succession to Deng Xiaoping," 757–786.

10. None of the longest-serving current CC members has ever had his or her tenure interrupted. All newly reelected members have served on each CC consecutively; see Li and White, "The Fifteenth Central Committee of the Chinese Communist Party," 254. The one among the fourth generation of leaders who has the longest tenure in the CC is Yang Yongliang, deputy Party secretary of Hubei, who was first elected when he was thirty-three years old as head of the Communist Youth League in Anhui Province.

11. Li and White, "The Fifteenth Central Committee of the Chinese Communist Party."

12. Zhang Yuqin is also included in the 1999 pool, since she was appointed as vice chair of the State Family Planning Commission in 1996 and now concurrently serves as a member of the CCDI.

13. James Kynge, "Reform Reaches Top Level," *Financial Times*, 16 November 1998, 6.

14. For the close relationship between Jiang and Chen, see Gao Xin, *Jiang Zemin de mu-liao* (Jiang Zemin's counselors), 4th ed. (Hong Kong: Mingjing chubanshe, 1997), 204–205; it is also widely known in Shanghai, where Jiang served as Party secretary and Chen served as his deputy in the late 1980s.

15. Li and White, "The Fifteenth Central Committee of the Chinese Communist Party," 243.

16. For an earlier discussion of the origins of the CCP leaders, see Franklin W. Houn, "The Eighth Central Committee of the Chinese Communist Party: A Study of Elites," *American Political Science Review* 51 (June 1957); Jurgen Domes, "The Nine CCP Central Committee in Statistical Perspective," *Current Scene* (Hong Kong) 9, no. 2 (1969); Robert Scalapino, ed., *Elites in the People's Republic of China* (Seattle: University of Washington Press, 1972); and Paul Wong, *China's Higher Leadership in the Socialist Transition* (New York: Free Press, 1976), 190–203.

17. Li and White, "The Thirteenth Central Committee of the Chinese Communist Party," 378.

18. Li and White, "The Army in the Succession to Deng Xiaoping," 766–767; Li and White, "The Fifteenth Central Committee of the Chinese Communist Party," 246–247.

19. *China News Analysis*, August 1–15, 1998, 15–19.

20. *China News Analysis*, April 1, 1998, 4–6.

21. Cheng Li and David Bachman, "Localism, Elitism, and Immobilism: Elite Formation and Social Change in Post-Mao China," *World Politics* 42, no. 1 (October 1989): 71.

22. Li and White, "The Fifteenth Central Committee of the Chinese Communist Party," 246–247; and Zang Xiaowei, "The Fourteenth Central Committee of the CCP: Technocracy or Political Technocracy," *Asian Survey* 33, no. 8 (August 1993): 795.

23. As Lyman Miller observes, "The coalition of leaders that governed China in the 1980s, consisted mainly of leaders who either were from or had had long career experience in China's southwestern province of Sichuan . . . or south China." See "Overlapping Transitions in China's Leadership," *SAIS Review* 16, no. 2 (Summer–Fall 1996): 24.

24. Ying-mao Kau, "The Urban Bureaucratic Elites in Communist China: A Case Study of Wuhan, 1949–1965," in *Communist Chinese Politics in Action*, ed. A. Doak Barnett (Seattle: University of Washington Press, 1972), 227.

25. Li and Bachman, "Localism, Elitism and Immobilism," 64–94.

26. The provincial and municipal leaders in the 1994 pool also include four military officers who are in charge of regional military districts.

27. John P. Burns, "China's Nomenklatura System," *Problems of Communism* 33 (September–October 1987): 36–51; and John P. Burns, "Strengthening Central CCP Control of Leadership Selection: The 1990 Nomenklatura," *China Quarterly* 138 (June 1994): 458–491.

28. Burns, "China's Nomenklatura System," 37–38, 40–41.

29. Wu Guoguang, *Zhulu shiwuda: Zhongguo quanli qiju* (Toward the Fifteenth Party Congress: Power game in China) (Hong Kong: Taipingyang shiji chubanshe, 1997), 215.

30. This discussion is based on Li and Bachman, "Localism, Elitism, and Immobilism," 87.

31. Li Cheng and Lynn White, "The Fifteenth Central Committee of the Chinese Communist Party: Full-Fledged Technocratic Leadership with Partial Control by Jiang Zemin" *Asian Survey* 38, no. 3 (March 1998): 254–255.

32. Quoted from Burns, "Strengthening Central CCP Control of Leadership Selection," 473.

33. For a discussion of the conflict between the central authorities and Cantonese offi-

cials regarding the selection of Guangdong's top leaders, see *Shijie ribao*, 17 September 1997, 2; also see Gao Xin, *Xiangfu Guangdong bang* (Taming the Guangdong gang) (Hong Kong: Mingjing chubanshe, 2000).

34. Burns, "Strengthening Central CCP Control of Leadership," 474.

35. It was also reported that in preliminary meetings before the congress, central authorities intended to appoint a non-Cantonese Politburo member as the new Party secretary of Guangdong (now China's richest province) to replace Xie Fei, a Cantonese Party secretary and the most important politician in his region. Local officials in Guangdong rejected that proposal. They had insisted that top officials in Guangdong should be Cantonese, even if they lost their representation in the Politburo. *Shijie ribao*, September 17, 1997, 2; and *South China Morning Post*, 16 September 1997, 1.

36. See Ellen Salem, "Things Fall Part, the Centre Cannot Hold," *Far Eastern Economic Review*, 27 October 1988, 38–40.

37. The origin of these two numbers is not identified, but they probably refer to the number of China's provinces and counties, respectively. Quoted from *Zhonggong wenti ziliao zhoukan* (Information weekly on problems of the Chinese Communist Party), 7 November 1988, 11. Also see *New York Times*, 11 December 1988, 1.

38. Edward S. Steinfeld, "The Asian Financial Crisis: Beijing's Year of Reckoning," *Washington Quarterly* 21, no. 3 (Summer 1998): 47.

39. *Liaowang*, 7 June 1999, 15–16.

40. *China News Analysis*, 1–15 July 1998, 15.

41. *Shijie ribao*, 4 November 1999, A9.

42. Wu, *Zhulu shiwuda: Zhongguo quanli qiju*, 56, 85.

43. For more discussion on Jiang's network in the propaganda circle in the central government, see Paul Cavey, "Building a Power Base: Jiang Zemin and the Post-Deng Succession," *Issues and Studies* 33, no. 11 (November 1997): 13.

44. See Burns, "Strengthening Central CCP Control of Leadership Selection," 472.

45. See Deng Xiaoping, "The Task of Consolidating the Army," in *Deng Xiaoping's Selected Works* (Beijing: Foreign Languages Press, 1984), 27; Yü Yü-lin, "The Role of the PLA in Mainland China's Power Transition," *Issues and Studies*, December 1985, 79–83; and Li and White, "The Army in the Succession to Deng Xiaoping," 757.

46. William Whitson, "The Field Army in Chinese Communist Military Politics," *China Quarterly* 37 (January–March 1969): 10–11; and William Parish, "Factions in Chinese Military Politics," *China Quarterly* 56 (October–December 1973): 667–699. On the evolutionary change of the field army system, also see Cheng Tzu-ming, "Evolution of the People's Liberation Army," *Issues and Studies* 15, no. 12 (December 1979).

47. For many years, even lower-ranking officers from the Fourth Field Army (lacking any direct association with Lin Biao) could not be promoted.

48. Ian Wilson and You Ji, "Leadership by 'Line': China's Unresolved Succession," *Problems of Communism* 39, no. 1 (January–February 1990): 38; and Michael D. Swaine, *The Military and Political Succession in China: Leadership, Institution, Beliefs* (Santa Monica, Calif.: Rand Corporation, 1992).

49. Li and White, "The Army in the Succession to Deng Xiaoping," 770–771.

50. In 1993, the PLA had over 10,000 enterprises with about 700,000 employees. The military-owned firms expanded rapidly during the mid-1990s. See Thomas J. Bickford, "The Chinese Military and Its Business Operations: The PLA as Entrepreneur," *Asian Survey* 34, no. 5 (May 1994): 461.

51. James Kynge, "Military to Quit Business," *Financial Times*, 16 November 1998, 8.

52. *Far Eastern Economic Review*, 29 April 1999, 22; and Kynge, "Reform Reaches Top Level," 6.

53. For a discussion of the organizational structure of the PLA's military regions in the recent decade, see Li Nan. "Organizational Changes of the PLA, 1985–1997." *China Quarterly* 158 (June 1999): 314–349.

54. *Shijie ribao*, 17 December 1998, A9.

55. Li, "Organizational Changes of the PLA, 1985–1997," 338.

56. Li and White, "The Army in the Succession to Deng Xiaoping," 776–780.

57. Li and White, "The Army in the Succession to Deng Xiaoping," 780.

58. For a detailed discussion of the role of the National Defense University in elite recruitment during the reform era, see Li and White, "The Army in the Succession to Deng Xiaoping," 779–781.

59. For a discussion of the PLA's military academies during the recent decade, see Li Nan, "Organizational Changes of the PLA, 1985–1997," 334–340.

60. Shu Zhan et al., "Guofang daxue, jiangjun de yaolan" (The National Defense University: The cradle of generals), *Zhonghua yingcai* (China talents) 171 (August 1997): 40–42.

61. *Nanbeiji* (North and south poles), November 1992, 59.

62. Shu, "Guofang daxue, jiangjun de yaolan," 40–42.

63. Dates on mayors are from Li and Bachman, "Localism, Elitism, and Immobilism," 71. They are originally based on Zhongguo chengshi jingji shehui nianjian lishihui (The council of the almanac of China's urban economy and society), comp., *Zhongguo chengshi jingji shehui nianjian 1986* (The almanac of China's urban economy and society) (Beijing: Zhongguo chengshi nianjian chubanshe, 1986). Data on the Fourteenth Central Committee are from Zang Xiaowei, "The Fourteenth Central Committee of the CCP," 797; and Li and White, "The Fifteenth Central Committee of the Chinese Communist Party," 250. They are originally based on Liao Gailong and Fan Yuan, comp., *Zhongguo renming da cidian* (Who's who in China), vol. 3 (Shanghai: Shanghai Dictionary Publishing House, 1989).

64. About 26 percent of these mayors were born after 1941. Li and Bachman, "Localism, Elitism, and Immobilism," 69.

65. Most studies of technocrats in Latin America and Asia have identified those trained economists as technocrats. See, for example, Patricio Silva, "Technocrats and Politics in Chile: From the Chicago Boys to the CIEPLAN Monks," *Journal of Latin American Studies* 23, no. 2 (May 1991): 385–410; Marshall Edward Dimock, *The Japanese Technocracy: Management and Government in Japan* (New York: Walker/Weatherhill, 1968); Laurence D. Stifel, "Technocrats and Modernization in Thailand," *Asian Survey*, December 1976, 1184–1196; and Peter Smith, "Leadership and Change, Intellectuals and Technocrats in Mexico," In *Mexico's Political Stability: The Next Ten Years*, ed. Roderic Camp (Boulder: Westview, 1986), 101–117.

66. Among the 116 military schools in the PRC at the end of the 1970s, for example, forty are command schools, five in political schools, fifty-four in engineering, medical, and other technical schools, and seventeen in flight schools. See Li, "Organizational Changes of the PLA, 1985–1997," 335.

67. Hong Yung Lee, "China's 12th Central Committee: Rehabilitated Cadres and Technocrats," *Asian Survey* 23, no. 6 (June, 1983): 673–691; and Richard Baum, *Burying Mao*:

*Chinese Politics in the Age of Deng Xiaoping* (Princeton: Princeton University Press, 1994), 365.

68. One of his predecessors, Chen Muhua, served as governor of the People's Bank of China in the mid-1980s. Without much knowledge and experience in banking, she did not acquire a good reputation during her tenure in that post. See Cheng Li, *Rediscovering China: Dynamics and Dilemmas of Reform* (Lanham, Md.: Rowman & Littlefield, 1997), 294–295.

69. Steinfeld, "The Asian Financial Crisis," 44.

70. Henry S. Rowen, "The Short March: China's Road to Democracy," *National Interest*, Fall 1996, 63.

71. Gaetano Mosca, *The Ruling Class* (New York: McGraw-Hill, 1939), 65.

72. For a full discussion of the functional need of elites in a society, see Fred Chwan Hong Lee, "The Recruitment of Elites in the Republic of China: A Case Study in the Social Utility of Education" (Ph.D. diss., University of Oregon, 1983), 1–2.

73. Quoted from John H. Jia and Kyna Rubin, "China's Brain Trust Abroad: Students Are Pivotal Players in China's Reform and in U.S. China Relations," *International Educator*, Spring 1997.

74. Jia and Rubin, "China's Brain Trust Abroad."

75. Among these 293,000 people, 47,000 were sent by the government and 92,000 were sent by universities or research institutes; 154,000 were "self-sponsored"—sponsored by relatives or foreign institutions. See *Shijie ribao*, 12 January 1999, A9. *China Daily*, however, gave somewhat different statistics. It reported that over the past twenty years, the country has sent 320,000 students and scholars to 103 countries. To date, more than 100,000 of them have returned to work in the country. See *China Daily*, 4 February 1999.

76. About 130,000 of them have remained in the United States. The Chinese Student Protection Act was passed after the events of 4 June 1989. It enabled roughly 50,000 PRC students and scholars to obtain permanent resident status. About 3,000 PRC students trained in the United States have now become faculty members in American universities and colleges. Among them, 2,400 teach natural sciences. See Liu Ningrong, "Niuzhuan guoyun de liumei xuesheng" (American-trained Chinese students are changing China) *Yazhou Zhoukan* (Asia week), 8 November 1998; and Jia and Rubin, "China's Brain Trust Abroad."

77. *Shijie ribao* (World journal), 7 December 1998, A9.

78. Of those sent by the government, 83 percent returned to China; by universities, 57 percent. Only 4 percent of self-sponsored students returned to China. *Shijie ribao*, 12 January 1999, A9.

79. *China Daily*, 4 February 1999, 1.

80. Liu, "Niuzhuan guoyun de liumei xuesheng."

81. *Shijie ribao*, 7 December 1998, A9.

82. Liu, "*Niuzhuan guoyun de liumei xuesheng.*"

83. Liu, "*Niuzhuan guoyun de liumei xuesheng.*"

84. For a discussion of the Chinese students in the West, see Jia Hao, "Dui dangqian woguo liuxue renyuan zhuangkuang de fenxi he jidian jianyi" (Analysis of Chinese study abroad and some recommendations), *Shehui kexue* (Social science) 6 (1997): 58–62.

85. *Mingbao*, 11 September 1998, 1; and *Shijie ribao*, 11 February 1998, A12.

86. Seweryn Bialer, *Stalin's Successors: Leadership, Stability, and Change in the Soviet Union* (Cambridge: Cambridge University Press, 1980), 101.

# 4

~

# The "Qinghua Clique": School Networks and Elite Recruitment

A Harvard degree may not be as important as belonging to the Harvard network.

—Miguel Angel Centeno

Education, whether ancient or modern, Chinese or Western, has always been closely interrelated with politics. It is most often perceived as a primary way to prepare elites in society. Confucius asserts that the principal purpose of education is "to study to become an official."[1] In the *Republic*, Plato gives an extraordinary amount of attention to the education of the "guardians." In addition to its other functions, education serves generally as a system of ideological legitimization. It not only legitimizes certain kinds of knowledge as authoritative and essential but also designates specific persons as carriers of that knowledge.[2] Therefore, education, and higher education in particular, plays an important role both in the process of elite political socialization and in the stabilization of the political system in a given society.

Because of these vital functions, higher education is one of the most potent political institutions. This is especially the case in our time, as both Robert Putnam and John Kenneth Galbraith observe, when "the school is replacing the family as an avenue to the top" for political elites, and technical institutions have become "preparatory academies for the technostructure."[3] Politicians often exert tremendous influence in an effort to mold the educational system and school networks to produce future political elites. The crucial role of college networks in elite re-

cruitment has been widely recognized in many countries. For example, Eton College in Great Britain, the Ecole Nationale d'Administration (ENA) in France,
the Law School of Tokyo University (Todai) in Japan, the Doon School in India,
and the Universidad Catolica of Santiago, Chile (graduates of this school later
became the well-known "Chicago Boys"), have all been famous for engendering
political networks.[4] Likewise, China now has one educational establishment that
surpasses the rest—Qinghua University. Indeed, there is no more telling example
of the role of a university network in the rise of technocratic elites in post-Mao
China than this institution.

Qinghua University (also spelled and pronounced "Tsinghua"), located in Beijing, is one of the most prestigious universities of science and engineering in the
nation and is often recognized as "China's MIT." Qinghua was destined to be the
most important educational and political institution when it was founded by
Americans in 1911, a time during which the imperial system collapsed and republican China was born. Chinese traditional elites, the scholar-gentry class
whose knowledge is almost entirely based on Confucian doctrine, were not able
to meet the needs of society and the economy at the turn of the twentieth century.[5] New public intellectuals and political elites from modern schools such as
Qinghua demanded political and social change.

Qinghua has played a pivotal role in PRC politics since the 1949 revolution,
repeatedly serving as a major battleground for conflicting viewpoints and rival political forces. Qinghua has experienced several "firsts" in major national political
events during the second half of the century. The dichotomy of "red" and "expert"
was *first* used in the context of Qinghua in the 1950s, with the Anti-Rightist campaign at the university, making this dichotomy a central ideological issue in the
country. Qinghua was a breeding ground for the Cultural Revolution in 1966,
when the Red Guards were *first* formed by students in the secondary school at-
tached to Qinghua University. Qinghua was the *first* institution entered by a
worker-soldier Mao Zedong thought propaganda team, whose purpose was to in-
augurate "proletarian leadership in the realm of superstructure."[6] Qinghua was
also hailed as "a typical case in the educational revolution personally nurtured by
Chairman Mao." The university was a pacesetter for the rest of the country when
it admitted the *first* class of "worker-peasant-soldier students" in 1970.[7] The power
struggle between Deng and the "Gang of Four" in China's top leadership in the
mid-1970s became evident when it was *first* exposed in the conflict among
Qinghua officials. To some extent, Qinghua is a microcosm of Chinese politics.

Qinghua University has become the most important cradle for Chinese technocrats during the reform era.[8]. The dominance of Qinghua graduates in Chinese
leadership was evident in the Fifteenth Party Congress and in the Ninth National
People's Congress, which were held in 1997 and 1998, respectively. Among the
twenty-two full members of the Politburo, five, including two standing members,
are Qinghua graduates (23 percent). Zhu Rongji, still dean of the Institute of Business Management at Qinghua, now serves as the premier of the State Council. Hu

Jintao, a political celebrity of Qinghua since his enrollment there in 1959, is the acknowledged "leader" of the fourth generation. Qinghua graduates in their forties and fifties constitute a formidable force in the fourth generation of leaders today. Dozens of ministers and governors, hundreds of mayors and county heads, and thousands of bureau heads and factory directors, are Qinghua graduates.

A study of Qinghua is revealing because it challenges two interrelated myths in studies of technocrats in general and Chinese technocrats in particular. The "technological imperative" myth posits that technological change has inevitably brought about sociopolitical transformation. This thesis is closely associated with the functional explanation for elite transformation.[9] According to this theory, the utilitarian needs of society determine the behavior and the rewards of the individuals within it. Many writers on technocracy rely on impersonal forces to account for the "technocratic turnover."[10] In other words, the rise of technocrats has resulted from the functional requirements of technological and economic change, not from the course of political events and social environments in a country.

But empirical evidence, whether based on historical or cross-national comparison, shows no neat correspondence between the stage of technological development and the attributes of a political system. For example, during the 1960s and 1970s, when technocrats became an important political elite in some other countries (including the Soviet Union), China moved in an opposite direction by diminishing the role of technical elites. Because of their vague notion of the technological imperative, scholars have devoted little attention to the analysis of how and under what political circumstances technical elites have succeeded or failed to construct a political system for which they seem indispensable.[11] This case study of Qinghua will present a dramatic story of the historical evolution of technocratic thinking and fighting at Qinghua throughout most of the twentieth century. Although technocrats assumed national leadership in the middle of the 1980s, their political demands underwent a long zigzag journey because of the sociopolitical environment of the country.

The second myth about technocrats is that some scholars believe technocratic elites lack close interpersonal ties or political networks[12] and that technocrats come to power mainly because of their technical expertise.[13] Yet a careful analysis of the social backgrounds of Qinghua technocrats shows that their political networks at Qinghua are more important than their technical expertise for explaining their success in acquiring leadership posts. As the epigraph of this chapter notes, belonging to an elite university network is far more essential for politicians than having an elite university degree. Intelligence and skills facilitate career advancement, but connections, or *guanxi*, are what really count.

At Qinghua, the network was initially fostered by Jiang Nanxiang. During his fourteen-year presidency, Jiang led a wholehearted effort to make Qinghua "the cradle of red engineers"—a key source of both political and technical power for the nation.[14] To reach this objective, Jiang created a "system of political counselors" (*zhengzhi fudaoyuan zhidu*) which was later adopted in all the tertiary institutions of China and still continues today. He developed the idea that Qinghua should train what Jiang dubbed "double-load cadres" (*shuangjian tiao ganbu*)—those who could heft technical supervision on one shoulder and political leadership on the other. The selection of political counselors reflected Jiang's intention to build a power network based on both patron-client relationships and the idea that a legitimate modern government needs technical knowledge.[15]

A great number of political counselors in the 1950s later became double-load cadres outside of Qinghua. Most of the fourth generation of leaders from Qinghua were political counselors during their college years. The Qinghua case shows the crucial role that institutional networks, particularly college ties, have played in the emergence of technocrats. In Chinese politics today, college ties seem to carry more weight in the elite selection process than other kinds of networks that were considered crucial for many decades in the past (e.g., those based on shared revolutionary experiences or field army affiliation).[16]

The Qinghua network has already emerged as a distinctive elite group. Its group identity may politicize the decision-making process in the new political spectrum and indicate future sources of elite conflict in Chinese politics. Technocrats produced by Jiang Nanxiang's "Qinghua system for cadres" have similar political outlooks and other characteristics originating in their shared experiences that, for better or worse, will have an impact on Chinese politics in the years to come.

## JIANG NANXIANG AND THE FORMATION OF THE "QINGHUA CLIQUE"

> [Qinghua] is under political control and is subordinating educational standards to those of politics. In about twelve years the school has had more than a half-dozen presidents. . . . The result has been the introduction of new staff and faculty members favored by the oft-changing presidents, the attempt to control faculty policy through appointments and intimidation.[17]

These words were not written about the debate on "red and expert" in the 1950s or the turmoil during the CR, but of the Nationalist era in 1923 by an American visiting professor at Qinghua. While the idea that higher education should be run by professors and experts was always strong in this elite university, political control over Qinghua did not start with the establishment of Communist rule. Among the twenty-four presidents in Qinghua's history, however, none exerted political control over the university more firmly and successfully than did Jiang Nanxiang.

Jiang headed Qinghua from 1952 to 1966 and was in charge of China's Ministry of Education for many years, both before and after the CR. He was second to President Mei Yiqi (1931–1948) in terms of longevity as president at Qinghua. Although Jiang did not hold any official position at Qinghua from the end of the Cultural Revolution to his death in 1988, he was perceived as the "overlord" (*tais-*

*hanghuang)* of the university. If any broad description of Chinese technocrats is not complete without a discussion of the institutional impact of Qinghua University, then any analysis of Qinghua under Communists is not conclusive without an examination of the role of Jiang. To understand his efforts in transforming Qinghua and his role in fostering PRC technocrats, we should first look at the history of the university and the political environment Jiang encountered when he arrived there in 1952.

## The History of Qinghua and American Influence

Qinghua was founded in 1911 by Americans with funds from the Boxer indemnity.[18] In its early days, it was merely a preparatory school (*Tsinghua xuetang)* for the students who were sent by the government to study in the United States. It later changed to Tsinghua School. Because of its background, Qinghua School strictly followed the American model of education in terms of school administration and curricula. British philosopher Bertrand Russell, after a visit to the campus in 1920, described Qinghua as a "school transplanted from the U.S. to China."[19]

Qinghua's principal mission, as stated by its tenth president, Cao Yunxiang, was to train the "future leaders of China."[20] In 1925 Qinghua School was reorganized into the National Qinghua University consisting of colleges of arts, sciences, and law. Three years later, however, the Nationalist government adopted a new educational policy, "emphasizing science and engineering and restricting humanities and law" (*tichang ligong, xianzhi wenfa)*. Mei Yiqi, a trained engineer from Worcester Polytechnic Institute in the United States, was appointed Qinghua's fifteenth president in 1931. Mei enhanced Qinghua's academic reputation not only by keeping a number of well-known professors at Qinghua but also by recruiting many promising young scholars into the faculty. They included Chen Xingsheng and Hua Luogeng in mathematics, Zhou Peiyuan in physics, Tao Baokai in engineering, Liang Sicheng in architecture, Chen Daisun in economics, Chen Yinke and Zhu Ziqing in literature, Feng Youlan in philosophy, Wu Han in history, and Pan Guangdan and Fei Xiaotong in sociology. Many of them are the scholars who introduced China to these modern disciplines.

Table 4.1 shows the educational background of Qinghua faculty members in 1946. The fact that approximately half of them held a Ph.D. degree is impressive because in the 1940s even some major universities in the United States did not have many Ph.D.s among their faculty. About 90 percent of these Qinghua professors had studied abroad, and 70 percent of these studied in the United States. Out of a total of 134 full and associate professors at Qinghua, seventeen (13 percent) had graduated from Harvard, fourteen (10 percent) from MIT, thirteen (10 percent) from Cornell, eleven (8 percent) from Chicago, and ten (7 percent) from Columbia. The department of civil engineering was dominated by MIT graduates, and the department of mechanical engineering by University of Michigan graduates.[21]

Table 4.1  Educational Background of Qinghua Professors and Associate Professors in 1946 (N = 134)

|  | Number | Percentage |
|---|---|---|
| Educational levels |  |  |
| B.A./B.S. | 17 | 12.6 |
| M.A./M.S. | 50 | 37.3 |
| Ph.D. | 64 | 47.7 |
| Unknown | 3 | 2.2 |
| Total | 134 | 99.8 |
| Foreign trained | 120 | 89.5 |
| United States | 84 | 70.0 |
| Great Britain | 13 | 10.8 |
| Germany | 12 | 10.0 |
| France | 5 | 4.1 |
| Japan | 2 | 1.6 |
| Soviet Union | 1 | 0.8 |
| Canada | 1 | 0.8 |
| Hong Kong | 1 | 0.8 |
| Austria | 1 | 0.8 |
| Domestic trained | 11 | 8.2 |
| Unknown background | 3 | 2.2 |
| Total | 134 | 99.9 |

*Source:* Guoli qinghua daxue yilan (A general survey of national Qinghua University), no. 2, Faculty and Staff (Beijing: Qinghua University, 1946).

*Note:* Both level and place count the highest degree only. The data were accumulated and tabulated by the author. Percentages do not add up to 100 due to rounding.

When the Chinese Communists seized national power in the late 1940s, a few professors, including President Mei, left for Taiwan or the United States. But a majority of the faculty members remained at Qinghua. It was a great challenge to the CCP to take over the administration of this predominantly American-influenced institution.

## The Reorganization of Higher Education and the Arrival of Jiang Nanxiang

For the new Communist regime, the first and most urgent goal was, of course, the consolidation of political power. To that end, they reorganized the higher educational institutions to "develop specialized schools and technical institutions."[22] The new government was unambiguously following the Soviet model, which also stressed science and engineering at the expense of humanities and social sciences. The CCP regarded social sciences, law, and the arts as bourgeois. What the newly established regime really needed were its own technical specialists. As a result, out of sixty-five liberal arts colleges in China in 1949, only seven remained open by the end of 1950. The percentage of students majoring in law and public administration nationwide declined from 6.3 percent in 1949 to 2 percent in 1952 and to 0.5 percent in 1962.[23] This is one of the reasons of why the fourth generation of leaders is dominated by trained engineers.

Most of Qinghua's colleges for arts, law, and sciences were further compressed and merged into Beijing University. Meanwhile, Qinghua absorbed all of the engineering departments of Beijing University and Yanjing (Yenching) University and became a multidisciplinary university of engineering. The reorganization of higher educational institutions aroused deep resentment among the faculties in China's colleges, particularly at Qinghua. When the CCP's decision was announced in early 1950, several famous Western-trained professors, including Fei Xiaotong and Qian Weichang, held a meeting at Qinghua to express their disapproval.

It was under these circumstances that Jiang Nanxiang was appointed the president and Party secretary of Qinghua. Jiang was only thirty-nine years old when he took over Qinghua's leadership in 1952. Like many faculty members at the university, Jiang was born in Jiangsu Province and did his undergraduate study at Qinghua. He entered the university in 1932. Unlike most of his junior colleagues, whose majors were science and engineering, Jiang majored in Chinese literature. He joined the CCP in 1933 and served as Party secretary of the CCP's Qinghua branch. In 1935, Jiang had become chief editor of the student journal *Qinghua Weekly* (another editor of the journal was Yao Yilin, who later became a standing member of the Politburo in the 1980s).

Jiang's formative years occurred during the Anti-Japanese War and the Civil War, which make him a member of the second generation of the CCP leadership. Jiang was one of the student leaders of the anti-Japanese December Ninth movement of 1935. In "The Open Letter by the Qinghua Salvation Committee to Fellow Citizens," Jiang wrote, "There is no room for a desk in the vast land of North China," which immediately became the slogan of student-led patriotic movements in the country.[24] During the movement, he became a close friend of Peng Zhen, then a leader of the CCP's Northern Bureau and later the Party boss of Beijing. In the late 1930s, Jiang assisted Liu Shaoqi in editing the CCP's internal journal *Douzheng* (Struggle). He also played a key role in establishing the New Democratic Youth League in Yan'an, the predecessor of the Chinese Communist Youth League. He moved to Beijing when the Communists seized national power in 1949 and headed the secretariat of the CCYL.

Jiang's association with Yao Yilin, Peng Zhen, Liu Shaoqi, and other prominent leaders may explain his 1952 appointment as president of Qinghua. When he arrived at Qinghua in December 1952, the reorganization of higher educational institutions was already completed. Although many Qinghua professors were newcomers who had been transferred from other institutions, senior faculty members remained generally homogeneous in terms of their Western educational back-

ground. Jiang quickly sensed that he could not run Qinghua without first building up his own power base. Table 4.2 shows the background of top officials, both
in the Party and administration, at Qinghua in the late 1950s. They formed the
core of Jiang's leadership.

Among these officials, vice secretaries Liu Bing, Gao Yi, and Hu Jian were "outsiders" whom Jiang brought with him to Qinghua. All three were high-ranking officials (rank 9) before they came to the university. They had no formal college education but were all graduates of the Party schools of the CCP. They had been
associated with Jiang when he was in charge of youth affairs at Yan'an in the early
1940s. Gao Yi had also worked with Jiang in northeastern China and Liu Bing had
been an assistant to Jiang in the secretariat of the CCYL in the early 1950s. Li
Shouci, like Jiang a native of Jiangsu, had become acquainted with Jiang in 1935
when both studied at Qinghua and were involved in the December Ninth movement. He Dongchang, Ai Zhisheng, and Chen Shunyao (wife of Song Ping, a
Qinghua graduate who later became a standing member of the Politburo) were underground Party members at Qinghua before the 1949 Communist revolution, and
they were selected by Jiang as representatives of young cadres in the university.

All of the three vice presidents—Liu Xianzhou, Zhang Wei, and Chen Shihua—were professors of engineering. None of them were Qinghua graduates, nor
had they studied in the United States. Both Liu and Zhang were introduced to
the CCP by Jiang himself in the mid-1950s. Although Chen was the only non-
CCP member in this core group at Qinghua, he served as chairman of the
Qinghua branch of the Democratic League, an organization of intellectuals sup-
porting the CCP. All of these vice secretaries and vice presidents had some kind
of political connection to Jiang. In public, Jiang claimed that his administration
respected all Qinghua professors, but he did not include any American-trained
professors—the mainstay of the previous administration of Qinghua—in the decision-making circle at the university. Instead, Jiang apparently cultivated a web
of personal ties centered on his connections and patron–client relationships.

Jiang not only established his core group in the leadership of Qinghua but also
started to develop a vertical political network at the university. As a former underground Party member at Qinghua, Jiang knew firsthand of the widespread enthusiasm for the new regime among Qinghua students. There had been as many as 200
student members of the underground CCP at Qinghua on the eve of the 1949 Communist revolution.[25] In 1952, Jiang appointed some of these to CCP leadership positions at Qinghua, particularly at the departmental level. They were only in their
twenties at the time of their appointment. The oldest, He Dongchang, who later became China's minister of education, was twenty-nine years old. Peng Peiyun, twenty-
three, was appointed departmental Party secretary. She later served as vice minister
of education and state counselor of the State Council; she is now chair of China's
Federation of Women. Ai Zhisheng, twenty-four, a graduate of civil engineering in
1950, was appointed as departmental Party secretary. Three decades later, Ai served
as deputy general of the State Council and minister of radio, film, and television.

**Table 4.2  Background of Top Officials at Qinghua University (1959)**

| Name | Position at Qinghua | Age | Educational Background | Political Association |
|---|---|---|---|---|
| Jiang Nanxiang | Party secretary and president | Mid-40s | Qinghua | Underground CCP member at Qinghua, associate of Peng Zhen at the Northeastern Bureau |
| Liu Bing | Executive deputy Party secretary | Early 40s | Middle school & Central Party University | Associate of Jiang Nanxiang in the secretariat of the CCYL |
| Gao Yi | Deputy Party secretary | Early 40s | Anti-Japanese University at Yan'an | Associate of Jiang Nanxiang in youth affairs in Yan'an, Guo Mingqiu's husband[a] |
| Hu Jian | Deputy Party secretary | Early 40s | Primary school and Anti-Japanese Univ. at Yan'an | Associate of Jiang Nanxiang in youth affairs in Yan'an |
| Li Shouci | Deputy Party secretary | Mid-40s | Qinghua | Political activist in the December 9th movement and a friend of Jiang Nanxiang |
| He Dongchang | Deputy Party secretary | Mid-30s | Qinghua (Associated Southwestern University) | Underground CCP member at Qinghua |
| Ai Zhisheng | Deputy Party secretary | Late 20s | Qinghua | Underground CCP member at Qinghua |
| Chen Shunyao | Deputy Party secretary | Mid-30s | Qinghua | Underground CCP member at Qinghua and Song Ping's wife |
| Liu Xianzhou | Executive vice president | Late 60s | Hong Kong University | Teacher of Liu Shaoqi, Li Fuchun, and Li Weihan; introduced to the CCP by Jiang Nanxiang and He Dongchang |
| Zhang Wei | Vice president | Mid-40s | Tangshan Jiaotong University Berlin Polytechnic Institute | Introduced to the CCP by Jiang Nanxiang |
| Chen Shihua | Vice president | Mid-50s | Munich Polytechnic Institute | Chair of the Democratic League in Qinghua |

*Sources*: The data are collected from various sources, including interviews and documents at Qinghua. *Qinghua Daxue yilan* (General survey of Qinghua University) (1959), 263–264; *Qinghua daxue jiang nanxiang jinian wenji bianji xiaozu* (Editorial group of commemorative collection of Jiang Nanxiang at Qinghua University), *Jiang nanxiang jinian wenji* (A Commemorative collection of Jiang Nanxiang) (Beijing: Qinghua University Press, 1990); Qinghua daxue xiaoshi zu (Writing group of history of Qinghua University). *Renwu zhi* (Personage) (Beijing: Qinghua University Press, 1983), 1–23. Xu Zhichun et al, *Zhongguo kexuejia cidian* (Dictionary of Chinese scientists), vols. 1–4, (Jinan: Shandong Science and Technology Press, 1982–85); and *Qinghua xiaoyou tongxun* (Newsletter of Qinghua alumni) Taiwan, 1966–79.

[a] Guo was an associate of Jiang in the December Ninth Movement, and was later in charge of China's Women's Federation.

## Political Counselors and the Double-Load Cadres

In his presidential inaugural speech, Jiang declared that the "CCP's leadership is the key to educational reforms."[26] The first priority in Jiang's agenda was to establish the System of Political Counselors (SPC). The idea of the SPC originated in the organizational structure of the Soviet army, and Qinghua was the first institution of higher learning in China to adapt this system for educational use. In early 1953, the Bureau of Political Counselors was set up at Qinghua to select students from the junior and senior classes who "excelled both politically and academically."[27] Their schooling was extended for one more year so they could develop their political skills as political counselors. The first group comprised twenty-five people, almost all of them secretaries of the CCYL in their respective departments. According to Teng Teng, then a midlevel cadre at Qinghua and later vice minister of education, Jiang himself examined the profile of each candidate and made the final decision.[28] The first meeting of political counselors was even held at Jiang's home.

The main function of the SPC, as the official explanation indicates, was to strengthen political and ideological education among college students and others affiliated with the school. Jiang used this system to control the distribution of career chances and to award the best opportunities to those who were associated with his political network. For a Qinghua student, to remain in the university as an assistant instructor (*zhujiao*) after graduation had always been a mark of tremendous prestige.[29] The SPC downplayed academic credentials and encouraged some academically mediocre students to seek political means through which they could "surpass" their fellow students. Although a few political counselors distinguished themselves in both curricular studies and political activities (e.g., Hu Jintao and Teng Teng), many of them, as some Qinghua officials admitted, were academically below average.[30]

Mao Zedong's famous article on being "red and expert" was published in 1958, but the discussion of this dichotomy had started earlier at Qinghua. Jiang had his own explanation of "red and expert." In his view, in a country in which only a minute percentage of the population could receive education above the middle school level, students at Qinghua were destined to become "experts"—and it was therefore essential that they become "red" as well, in their support of the leadership of the Party and adherence to the Party's politics.[31]

Since the mid-1950s, all Qinghua officials have been familiar with a motto, *tinghua chuhuo* (be obedient and productive), that reflected Jiang's expectations of his subordinates. It originated at Qinghua and was used only among Qinghua members and alumni. It was not clear whether *chuhuo* (productive) referred to academic or political work, but no one at Qinghua would fail to understand what *tinghua* implied. Because "obedience" and "redness" were generally subjective standards, people were inclined to flatter officials and form patron–client relations. Within a few years after his arrival at Qinghua, Jiang firmly controlled the university, which was run through the System of Political Counselors and the patronage network.

A major task for political counselors was to recruit new CCP and CCYL members. Table 4.3 shows the change in the percentage of the CCP and CCYL members in the 1950s. The percentage of faculty who were members of one or the other of these two organizations increased from 22 percent in 1952 to 83 percent in 1959. The data do not specify how many of the academics were specifically CCP members, but it was reported that Qinghua as a whole had 1,300 CCP members in 1956—out of a total of 6,400 students and 833 faculty.[32] An overwhelming majority of these Party members were students and assistant instructors; from 1949 to 1955, only seventeen faculty members with the rank of professor and associate professor at Qinghua joined the CCP. Therefore, an overwhelming majority of faculty who joined the CCP were young assistant instructors.

By recruiting young assistant instructors rather than those in the higher academic ranks, Jiang made political counselors and other assistant instructors the most important political force on campus in the 1950s. In an article published in 1971, a member of the Workers Propaganda Team at Qinghua wrote that before the 1949 revolution the CCP organization at Qinghua was a "Party of students" (*xuesheng dang*); in the 1950s it was a "Party of assistant instructors" (*zhujiao dang*); and it would have become a "Party of professors" (*jiaoshou dang*) if the Cultural Revolution had not erupted.[33] The author probably never expected that several years after the CR, it would indeed be a "Party of professors" that ran Qinghua University. In 1988, over 63 percent of the professors and associate professors at Qinghua, most of whom had been assistant instructors in the 1950s, were CCP members.[34]

It was Jiang's strategy that in time the "Party of assistant instructors" would naturally become a "Party of professors." To fulfill this goal, he helped political counselors become double-load cadres. He sent some political counselors abroad to study in new branches of learning such as aerospace engineering; they later became leading scholars in new research fields when they returned to China. For example, Zhang Haoruo, an underground Party member before the Communist victory in 1949 and a 1952 Qinghua graduate, was sent to the Soviet Union in 1954. He later served as governor of Sichuan, minister of domestic trade, and in the later 1990s, deputy chair of the State Commission for Restructuring Economy. At the same time, Jiang also recruited political counselors to the graduate program at Qinghua. For example, Wu Guanzheng, who joined the CCP at Qinghua in 1962 and graduated in 1964, entered the graduate program in the following year. Now he is member of the Politburo

Table 4.3    Change in the Percentage of CCP and CCYL Members among the Faculty and Students at Qinghua University (1952–1959)

|                  | 1952 | 1957 | 1959 |
|------------------|------|------|------|
| Faculty members  | 22%  | 67%  | 83%  |
| Students         | 55%  | 78%  | 84%  |

Source: *Qinghua daxue xiaowu bangongshi* (General office of Qinghua University) *Qinghua daxue yilan* (General survey of Qinghua University), (Beijing: Qinghua University Press, 1959), 4.

and Party secretary of Shandong Province. Song Baorui entered Qinghua in 1957 and joined the CCP in 1958. After an undergraduate education, he continued with graduate studies at Qinghua. He later served as governor of Sichuan Province.

During the 1950s, Jiang appointed many Party officials to key academic administrative posts at both university and departmental levels. For example, in the late 1950s, He Dongchang, the deputy Party secretary of Qinghua, was appointed chairman of the department of engineering physics. For Jiang, these young Qinghua cadres were key sources from which to strengthen his power base; and in the long run, some would become leaders of the PRC.

## QINGHUA UNIVERSITY AS A BATTLEGROUND FOR ELITE CONFLICT

Jiang Nanxiang's grand plan to make Qinghua the cradle of red engineers in China and to form the Qinghua clique were not achieved without resistance. On the contrary, throughout the entire Mao era, Qinghua was a major battleground of elite conflict. Jiang and his Qinghua cliques engaged in a tough fight against both the rightists in the 1950s and the Maoists during the CR. Indeed, both the Anti-Rightist campaign and the Cultural Revolution originated at Qinghua.

### Qian Weichang and the Anti-Rightist Campaign at Qinghua

The SPC and Jiang's network were strongly opposed by some professors at Qinghua in early 1953. The leading opponent of Jiang's policy was Qian Weichang, a professor in mechanical engineering and provost at Qinghua. Qian was born in Wuxi in 1912. He studied physics at Qinghua in the 1930s. Like Jiang, Qian participated in the December Ninth movement, although he was never a member of the CCP. While Jiang was involved in Communist activities after his graduation, Qian went to Canada and continued graduate study at the University of Toronto. After receiving his Ph.D. in applied mathematics, he worked as a senior fellow at the California Institute of Technology. Because of his exceptional academic credentials, he was appointed full professor at Qinghua when he started teaching at the age of thirty-three. A man of great ability with an arrogant personality, Qian once held twenty-six academic and administrative positions both within and outside of Qinghua. He successively served as associate provost, provost, and, briefly, vice president at Qinghua between the 1949 revolution and the Anti-Rightist campaign.

Qian criticized Jiang on two major issues. First, during the Hundred Flowers movement of 1957, Qian accused Jiang and Party officials of controlling everything at Qinghua: "All important courses are taught by Party members, regardless of their qualifications. Genuine experts are always put aside."[35] In the provost's report on teaching and research at Qinghua, Qian pointed out that many of the new young teachers, Jiang's hand-picked assistant instructors, were not qualified for teaching and research.[36] Qian particularly resented political counselors because "these Party members keep watch on professors and students and report others' 'incorrect words and deeds' to the Party committee, who will organize political campaigns against intellectuals."[37] Qian's most important statement, which later led to a major accusation against him, was that "those outside the profession cannot lead those inside." Qian argued that Qinghua should honor professionalism in education and respect academic hierarchy.

Second, Qian denounced Jiang and the Party for rigidly following the Soviet model in educational reform at Qinghua.[38] During the 1950s, "learning from the Soviet Union" was in political vogue throughout China. At Qinghua, the pre-1949 curricula were completely replaced by their Soviet equivalents. All instructors and students were required to take an intensive course in the Russian language, and teachers of English had to teach Russian instead. From 1952 to 1960, Qinghua had fifty-six Soviet instructors offering 108 courses. These instructors were treated as authorities in various fields. In the second issue of the university academic journal, *Xin Qinghua yuebao* (New Qinghua monthly), for example, six out of seven articles were written by Soviet advisers.[39] Although there were a few genuine experts in scientific-technical areas among these Soviet instructors, most were academically far less competent than their Chinese colleagues. Nevertheless, the latter had to follow the former's "expert guidance."

This awkward situation aroused discontent on the Qinghua campus, especially among the Western-trained Chinese professors. In the spring of 1957, Qian Weichang collected the signatures of 6,000 people at Qinghua (the number of students at the university was 6,400), demanding that more theoretical science be taught at the university. He argued that many courses taught by assistant instructors or "Soviet experts" were merely technological training without a solid foundation in science and were not worthy to be university courses. In May 1957, Qian claimed that leaders of China's higher education needed to "listen to real academic experts, not these ignorant people." Other Qinghua professors referred to Liu Bing and Hu Jian—two vice Party secretaries who had not received a formal college education—as "country bumpkins" (*tubaozi*) and asserted that they should be thrown out of Qinghua.[40]

Months later, the CCP launched the Anti-Rightist campaign and Qian was labeled the "top rightist professor in China" and an "active member of the nationwide anti-Party clique." He was accused of using science as a tool to attack the Party and was criticized for his endeavor to run Qinghua using the MIT model. In the following year, Qian was dismissed from most of his twenty-six posts. During the Anti-Rightist campaign, 572 people were labeled rightists at Qinghua.[41] In 1959, a total of 210 people were further criticized for spreading "rightist" and technocratic views.[42] Almost all of the American-trained professors were subjected to criticism.

After the Anti-Rightist campaign, Jiang further strengthened his dominant role at Qinghua. The number of CCP members at the university increased from 1,300 in 1956 to 2,300 in 1959.[43] Most of these new CCP members were again students and assistant instructors. The SPC became a standard means of producing the new faculty members at Qinghua. They were usually chosen from among Qinghua's own graduates, while many "outsiders"—instructors who were not Qinghua's own graduates—were forced to leave the university. For example, from 1957 to 1966, among twenty-seven faculty members in the teaching and research group of the physics department who were transferred to other universities, twenty-six were "outsiders."

The Party committee at Qinghua remained the core of Jiang's network. Jiang was appointed vice minister of education in 1960 and then minister of higher education in 1965 while he concurrently held his posts at Qinghua. He promoted his assistant Gao Yi to be vice president of Qinghua and vice minister of higher education. Jiang's control over the leadership of China's Ministry of Higher Education, allowed Qinghua graduates, beginning in the early 1950s, to take over important leadership positions at other universities, research institutions, and large enterprises all over China in the early 1960s. For example, Peng Peiyun, Zhou Guangzhao, and Zhang Haoruo, three early 1950s graduates of Qinghua, respectively served as deputy Party secretary of Beijing University, director of a major research institute in nuclear physics, and director of a large enterprise in the oil industry in the early 1960s.

Paradoxically, although Jiang denounced Qian Weichang's "technocratic" views, he himself, as already noted, consistently adhered to the hope that Qinghua would become an elite technical university producing the future leaders of the country. Jiang's SPC system had its "trilogy": (1) to make his second-rate academic staff "red," (2) to provide them with the best opportunities to become "experts," and (3) to offer them both professorships and leadership positions. In the 1950s Jiang was "anti-expert" in response to the fact that well-known academics at Qinghua did not obey his leadership, but in the early 1960s he became a "pro-red expert" because his "own men" had gained academic titles. He asserted that the CCP committee could not successfully lead the university unless it became a "Party of professors." Just prior to the CR, among fifteen standing members of the Party committee at Qinghua seven (46.7 percent) were professors. In the university council, professors occupied 75 percent of the seats. All twelve department chairs were professors, and among forty vice chairs, professors accounted for 77 percent. Most of these academic administrators were Party members.

From the Anti-Rightist campaign to the eve of the CR, Jiang made a "great leap forward" toward the realization of his goal. But he had probably never imagined that his "cradle of red engineers" would turn into a center of forces against technocracy in China for the next ten years or that his Qinghua clique would come under severe attack.

## Qinghua under Maoists during the CR

Although Jiang Nanxiang and Qian Weichang had a ferocious political fight at Qinghua in the late 1950s, they shared similar technocratic views and educational elitism. But in the Mao era, tensions frequently arose between educational egalitarianism and educational elitism over the issues of who should run the university and whom education should serve. Mao supported Jiang during the Anti-Rightist campaign but was always uneasy about the way in which Jiang ran this most important engineering school in the country. This was partly due to Jiang's close relationship with Liu Shaoqi and Peng Zhen—Mao's political rival and partly to the technocratic orientation of the university.

In the middle of the 1960s, as Mao slowly gained the upper hand over policy in the cultural and educational realm, class labels and political behavior became more essential than academic credentials. As some scholars have noted, class labels assumed paramount importance with ironic results: "children of cadres were favored more than the children of ordinary workers and peasants."[44] At the beginning of the CR, Kuai Dafu, a student in the department of chemical engineering who had a peasant family background, joined with others to launch an open offensive against Jiang Nanxiang and the Party committee of Qinghua.[45] With Mao's backing, Kuai soon became the most famous Red Guard in the country. All administrative officials and Party cadres, including political counselors, came under attack. Many older "bourgeois academic authorities" and young double-load cadres were persecuted and some committed suicide.[46]

A work team of 500 members led by Wang Guangmei, Liu Shaoqi's wife, tried to protect the top Party officials of the university, such as Jiang Nanxiang and He Dongchang. The work team labeled Kuai "counterrevolutionary" and intimidated many other students. But Kuai and other rebels, supported by Mao's wife Jiang Qing, counterattacked and expelled the work team from the university.[47] A provisional committee was established in an attempt to take over the leadership at Qinghua after the withdrawal of the work team. This committee was led by Liu Tao (Liu Shaoqi's daughter), He Pengfei (Marshal He Long's son), and other children of top government leaders.[48] However, Kuai and his faction, the "Jinggangshan Regiment," were able to disband the provisional committee and subsequently became engaged in a violent conflict with another major Red Guard organization in the university.

When Mao decided in 1968 to disband the Red Guards, he sent Chi Qun and Xie Jingyi to take charge of Qinghua. Chi had served as deputy head of the Propaganda Department of the 8341 Regiment, which provided the squad of bodyguards for Mao and other top leaders. An experienced ideologue with a middle school education, Chi was only in his late thirties when he was appointed chair of the Revolutionary Committee of Qinghua. Xie Jingyi was several years older. Before she came to Qinghua, she had worked in a junior position for a decade in the confidential department of Mao's personal office. Chi and Xie identified themselves as "two soldiers at Chairman Mao's side." Their connection with Mao bolstered their power at Qinghua.

The toughest challenge for Chi and Xie in the late 1960s came from the Qinghua-trained double-load cadres. Chi and Xie repeatedly stated that middle-aged Party intellectuals were the "most dangerous people" because they were the

core force of Jiang's technocratic educational system. Chi and Xie particularly denounced Jiang's effort to promote "technocratic leadership in education" (*zhuanjia zhixiao*). They sent 3,000 faculty and staff members, including many of Jiang's
double-load cadres, to the labor camps of Jiangxi Province.

When the Party committee of Qinghua was reestablished in 1970, most of the
members came from worker or poor peasant families and had only a middle school
level education. In fact, Chi assigned two old cadres to be vice secretaries of the
Party committee largely because they did not have formal college education. In
the same year, Qinghua admitted its first class of worker-peasant-soldier students.
Maoist "educational egalitarianism" did not truly bring historically less privileged
social classes to higher education, as they claimed it would. In fact, because political evaluation of students replaced the entrance examination for admission,
nepotism and favoritism were prevalent in their recruitment. Many of them were
children of high-ranking leaders, like the daughter of Ji Dengkui, Politburo member and vice premier. It was unknown how many others came from high-ranking
officials' families, but it was evident that the campus was crowded with Red Flag
sedans, the luxurious cars provided for Chinese top leaders, when entering classes
of students arrived at Qinghua.[49] Chi brought many of these new students into
the university and departmental leadership at Qinghua. Like his predecessor
Jiang, Chi not only had absolute power at Qinghua as the top official, but also
served as one of the most important figures in making national educational policies. He was appointed deputy head of the State Council's Science and Education
Group when it was established in 1970 to replace the Ministry of Education.[50]

From 1971 to 1975, Mao attempted to cement his succession by creating a balance of power among the factions in China's leadership. On the one hand, Mao
encouraged Chi Qun and other radicals to launch political campaigns against
"rightist tendencies" in education and other areas and, on the other hand, reas-
signed many old "rightist" cadres, including Deng Xiaoping, to leadership positions. In September 1974, Jiang Nanxiang's name was placed on the list of people who would attend the banquet for the celebration of National Day. That list
was drawn up by Zhou Enlai and approved by Mao. Under these circumstances,
Chi and Xie had to "liberate" Jiang. Jiang returned to Beijing after doing manual
labor in a remote province for many years. Although some members of Jiang's network such as He Dongchang and Ai Zhisheng resumed some middle level leadership positions at Qinghua, Chi refused to give Jiang a post.[51] Meanwhile, Chi ordered that Qinghua work out a list of its own cadres who would be ready to take
over power at the national level.[52]

The biggest victory for Chi came at the end of 1975 when he received Mao's
endorsement in his conflict with some old Qinghua officials. Mao urged people at
Qinghua and elsewhere to "debate" the issues raised by some Qinghua officials
who wrote Mao two letters in the care of Deng. Mao made comments on the letters: some Qinghua officials "have lodged a complaint against Chi Qun and Lit-

tle Xie, but their real target is me." Radicals claimed that the most important task was to ferret out the top leaders behind these Qinghua officials. On March 26, 1976, the Politburo invited eight Qinghua officials, including Chi and Xie, to attend a Politburo meeting to confront Deng Xiaoping. The meeting lasted more than three hours and Deng did not say one word.[53] As He Dongchang later noted, this was the first time in the history of the CCP that the Politburo had a joint meeting with a grassroots committee. After that meeting, Chi and Xie, supported by Mao, launched a nationwide campaign against Deng and the rightist resurgence in higher education. About two weeks later, Deng was purged again.

Although Chi Qun and radicals won these battles against "rightist forces," they lost the war. Within a month after Mao's death, Chi, Xie, and about thirty Qinghua officials under them, including all those who attended the Politburo meeting that confronted Deng, were taken into custody. Their radical policies in education would be completely revised in the years that followed.

What do all of these fights at Qinghua during the ten years of the Cultural Revolution tell us? Chi Qun claimed that the conflict between Maoists and Jiang Nanxiang's revisionists reflected the tension between educational egalitarianism and educational elitism. This explanation was only valid to the extent that Maoists adopted some radical policies such as admission based on political background rather than academic merit, and curricular reform that favored practical skills over rigorous disciplinary training. Maoist policies were not really meant to fight for educational egalitarianism, and Maoists' claims that Jiang Nanxiang's policies favored only the children of bourgeois class backgrounds were groundless. The percentage of students with worker-peasant family backgrounds increased from 12.8 percent in 1952 to 22 percent in 1957 and to 36 percent in 1959.[54] By 1966, on the eve of the CR, students with worker or peasant designations accounted for 65 percent of the college students and those from exploiting-class families only 9 percent.[55] As already noted, nepotism and favoritism were prevalent in the recruitment of the worker-peasant-soldier students. Chi and other radical leaders were employing these students to fill their own network of future elites.

The real struggle between Jiang and Chi concerned political power. Jiang's political counselors and double-load cadres and Chi's worker-peasant-soldier students differed significantly in their educational credentials. But they were all created for political rather than educational purposes. Education policies and education institutions like Qinghua were battlegrounds on which factional politics were fought out among elite groups. Whether it was Qinghua officials such as Chi Qun, Xie Jingyi, and Jiang Nanxiang, or top leaders like Mao Zedong, Liu Shaoqi, and Deng Xiaoping, all realized the importance of institutions of higher learning in Chinese politics. This explains why they were so intensively engaged in the power struggle at Qinghua. They fought against each other in order to seize or maintain their personal dominance over Qinghua and the entire country.

## HU JINTAO AND QINGHUA GRADUATES IN
## THE FOURTH GENERATION LEADERSHIP

For Jiang Nanxiang and his Qinghua clique, the reform era is the time of harvest. In the 1980s, Jiang's double-load cadres not only occupied virtually all leadership posts at both university and department levels at Qinghua but also became a major source of technocratic elites throughout China. By the end of the 1990s, Qinghua graduates held some of the most important posts in the country. Jiang's vision of Qinghua as the cradle of PRC technocrats had remarkably been realized at the turn of the century. Meanwhile, Jiang's baton for fostering the Qinghua clique, which was first handed over to He Dongchang, Ai Zhisheng, and Peng Peiyun, the third generation of leaders, passed to Hu Jintao's generation. The process by which Jiang and the Qinghua clique were able to accomplish this further demonstrates their political acumen and the crucial role of school networks in elite recruitment.

### The Revival of the Qinghua Network

Jiang's Qinghua network was revived almost immediately after the fall of Chi Qun in October 1976, but it required three years for it to firmly control the university. Jiang did not return to Qinghua to resume his leadership posts after Chi and Xie were purged. A long-time friend of Jiang, Liu Da, was initially appointed to take over the posts of Party secretary and chairman of the Revolutionary Committee. About 120 cadres from other educational institutions were sent to Qinghua with Liu Da to take over all leadership posts at both university and department levels. But within a few years, almost all of these "outsiders" except Liu Da left Qinghua after they had rehabilitated Jiang's double-load cadres.[56]

For members of Jiang's Qinghua network, no outsider was able to run the university better than they were. He Dongchang, Ai Zhisheng, and Teng Teng, three top double-load cadres, soon resumed their posts as vice secretaries of the Party committee and vice presidents of the university. Hu Qili, who used to be Jiang Nanxiang's assistant in the CCYL, was transferred to Qinghua and appointed vice president in 1978. He later became a standing member of the Politburo. Jia Chunwang, a double-load cadre and a leader of the conservative Red Guards faction that had protected Jiang in the earlier period of the CR, was made secretary of the CCYL Committee at Qinghua. Jia now serves as minister of public security.

The Qinghua officials had Deng Xiaoping's endorsement. Deng, who in 1978 had just been rehabilitated and was in charge of educational, science, and technology affairs in the State Council, wrote, "Qinghua used to select senior students and young faculty members to work concurrently in the realm of political affairs. These people, after several years of work experience, became a 'red and expert' political force. This was a good model."[57]

While many universities in China such as Beijing University allowed more political liberalization on campus in the 1980s, the Qinghua administration did not lose its political control over faculty members and students. The SPC continued to serve as a means of political control. In the late 1980s, before the Tiananmen student movement, Fang Huijian, Party secretary of Qinghua, claimed that the SPC would not be abolished in the future but should be strengthened.[58] While the leadership of Beijing University was reshuffled in 1990 because of its "incompetence" in dealing with the student movement in the spring of 1989, the Qinghua administration was praised by the central government for its continued emphasis on both "red and expert." Earlier, when the administration of China's University of Science and Technology supported student protests in 1986, two prominent Qinghua network members, Peng Peiyun and Teng Teng, were transferred there to replace Guan Weiyan and Fang Lizhi as the top officials of the university. Both Peng and Teng also served concurrently as vice ministers of education.

Qinghua officials attribute the firm political control at Qinghua to the "legacy of Nanxiang" *(Nanxiang jingshen)*.[59] When political counselors and double-load cadres graduated or were transferred from Qinghua, they continued this legacy. For example, in the late 1980s Qinghua graduates won all of the three national awards for political and ideological work as Party secretaries in large enterprises. One winner wrote an article entitled "To Be a Qualified Political Engineer," describing how his Qinghua political experience helped him, as Party secretary, to run one of the largest enterprises in China.[60]

The important role of the SPC in both the formation of school networks and the selection of future political elites is certainly not unique to Qinghua. Chapter 6 will show that in general, a majority of the fourth generation of leaders joined the Party prior to college graduation. The SPC continues to exist in all colleges in the country today. The Shanghai municipal government, for example, ruled in 1998 that political counselors should receive priority in terms of salary raises, academic promotion, and study abroad.[61]

From 1978 to 1984, Qinghua also transferred 1,757 officials, faculty, and staff members to other educational institutions.[62] Two kinds of people were transferred out. The first group included mainly those who had arrived at Qinghua during the Cultural Revolution, for example, worker-peasant-soldier students who had remained at Qinghua after graduation. They were actually forced to leave. The second group included members of Jiang's network, political counselors and/or double-load cadres. The nature of their transfer differed greatly from that of the first group. They were mostly assigned to leadership positions at other universities, thus extending Qinghua's influence. It was reported that about a hundred of these Qinghua faculty members took posts as top officials in other institutions.[63]

Two points should be noted, however. First, not all of the Qinghua-trained leaders have been associated with Jiang's Qinghua network. For example, Qian Weichang and Fei Xiaotong, who are now vice chair of the CPPCC and vice chair of the NPC, respectively, were targets of Jiang's Qinghua network during the Anti-Rightist campaign. Their political rise was due to Deng Xiaoping's policy of conciliation toward well-known public intellectuals. Second, membership in the Qinghua network, which is based on institutional support of a member's career advancement, does not always guarantee a member's political consistency. A few in the network later became leading political dissidents; Luo Zhengqi, Ruan Ming, and Wan Run-nan are three examples. All three used to be political counselors at Qinghua and all had been picked by Jiang Nanxiang at different times to be top officials in the Qinghua Committee of the CCYL, but all three later opposed the Party leadership during the 1989 Tiananmen protests.[64] Yet these three Qinghua-trained cadres are exceptional, considering that most officials at Qinghua have been *tinghua chuhuo* (obedient and productive).

## Passing the Baton: Qinghua Graduates in the National Leadership

Qinghua graduates have constituted a significant proportion of the Chinese technocrats at high levels of leadership in the post-Mao era. Table 4.4 lists the universities from which top political elites of the late 1980s graduated.[65] Universities whose graduates account for less than five leaders are omitted. Qinghua stands far ahead of the second on the list, Beijing University. Some other studies of China's national and mayoral leadership had similar findings. For example, Qinghua ranked the highest among the universities that educated China's mayors in the 1980s.[66] Data on high levels of leadership in the 1990s show a similar pattern of overrepresentation of Qinghua graduates.[67] At the Fourteenth Party Congress, held in 1992, twenty-nine Qinghua graduates and faculty were selected for the Central Committee of the CCP, which has 319 members.[68] At the Fifteenth Party Congress, held in 1997, Qinghua again dominated the roster (24 seats), although the presence of other major schools was also evident: the Central Party School (12 seats), Beijing University (11 seats), People's University (11 seats), and Harbin Military Institute of Engineering (8 seats).[69]

Table 4.4 also shows that the Chinese leadership during the late 1980s included a large number of officials who graduated from Qinghua prior to the Communist revolution in 1949. As members of the Anti-Japanese War generation, many of them held top leadership posts during the first decade of the reform. Table 4.5 lists some prominent CCP leaders with Qinghua backgrounds in the late 1980s. They were the main participants in the two student movements prior to the Communist victory: Jiang Nanxiang, Yao Yilin, Song Ping, Kang Shi'en, and Hu Qiaomu were student leaders of the Anti-Japanese December Ninth movement; Hu Qili, Li Ximing, He Dongchang, and others were members of the Democratic Youth League, a pro-Communist student organization in the 1940s. Almost a half century later, in the mid-1980s, they were in top leadership positions in the country. Seven leaders in the list served in the Politburo in the 1980s, including three standing members (Song, Yao and Hu). In the late 1980s, they played a crucial role in passing the baton of the Qinghua network to their junior alumni.

In terms of distribution by decade of graduation, Qinghua graduates rank the

**Table 4.4  Distribution of College Graduates in High Level Leadership Positions (1989), (Top 22 Schools)**

| University | Pre 1949 | 1950s | 1960s | 1970s | 1980s | Total |
|---|---|---|---|---|---|---|
| | | | Year of Graduation | | | |
| Qinghua University | 41 | 29 | 20 | 3 | | 93 |
| Beijing University | 24 | 15 | 5 | | 1 | 45 |
| Anti-Japanese University | 45 | | | | | 45 |
| People's University | | 27 | 13 | | | 40 |
| Central University | 32 | | | | | 32 |
| Shanghai Jiaotong University | 17 | 11 | 2 | | | 30 |
| Yanjing University | 28 | | | | | 28 |
| Fudan University | 16 | 4 | 3 | | 1 | 24 |
| Central Party School | 18 | | 2 | | | 20 |
| Associated Southwestern University | 15 | | | | | 15 |
| St. John's University (Shanghai) | 13 | 2 | | | | 15 |
| Zhongshan University | 11 | 2 | | | | 13 |
| Nankai University | 4 | 5 | 4 | | | 13 |
| Zhejiang University | 11 | | 1 | | | 12 |
| Dalian Institute of Engineering | | 6 | 4 | | | 10 |
| Wuhan University | 8 | 2 | | | | 10 |
| Harbin  Military Institute of Engineering | | 3 | 7 | | | 10 |
| Nanjing University | 2 | 5 | 2 | | | 9 |
| Tangshan Institute of Engineering | 8 | | | | | 8 |
| Beijing Normal University | 2 | | 3 | 1 | | 6 |
| Furen University | 6 | 1 | | | | 6 |
| Xiamen University | 4 | | 1 | 1 | | 6 |

Source: *Liao Gailong and Fan Yuan, (comps.), Zhongguo renming da cidian* (Who's who in China) vol. 3 (Shanghai: Shanghai Dictionary Publishing House, 1989).

Note: The distribution of universities in providing graduates at high-level leadership was accumulated and tabulated by the author.

highest in number among the elites who graduated in the 1950s and 1960s (see table 4.4). They even exceed graduates of the People's University, which was established in the 1950s primarily to train political leaders in the country. A majority of these Qinghua graduates in the 1950s and the 1960s were political counselors during their student years on campus. Out of a total of 682 political counselors on campus from 1953 to 1966, two-thirds were later transferred out of Qinghua and rose to be governors, ministers, managers of large industrial enterprises, and presidents of other universities.[70]

Using the two study pools for the previous chapter, table 4.6 lists some prominent figures in both the third and fourth generation leadership who are Qinghua graduates or associates. Among forty-two leaders listed here, three of them—Zhu Rongji, Peng Peiyun, and Zhou Guangzhao—enrolled at Qinghua prior to the

Table 4.5  Qinghua Graduates and Associates with Pre-1949 Revolutionary Background in the CCP Leadership during the 1980s

| Name | Birth | Grad. | CCP | Positions in the 1980s | Revolutionary Experience | Experience at Qinghua |
|---|---|---|---|---|---|---|
| Jiang Nanxiang | 1913 | 1937[a] | 1933 | Minister of Education; executive vice president of Central Party School | Participant, December 19 movement | Underground secretary of the CCP's Qinghua branch; president and Party secretary |
| Song Ping | 1917 | 1937[a] | 1936 | Standing member of Politburo; Head, CCP Organization Dept | Participant, December 19 movement; Zhou Enlai's personal secretary | Underground CCP member |
| Yao Yilin | 1917 | 1937[a] | 1935 | Standing member of Politburo; Vice premier; chair, State Planning Com. | Participant, December 19 Movement | Underground CCP member |
| Hu Qiaomu | 1912 | 1935[a] | 1932 | Member of Politburo | Participant, December 19 Movement; Mao's personal secretary | Underground CCP member |
| Kang Shi'en | 1915 | 1937[a] | 1936 | Vice premier; chair, State Econ. Com. | Participant, December 19 movement | Underground CCP member |
| Hu Qili | 1929 | — | 1948 | Standing member, Politburo | Member, Democratic Youth League | Vice president |
| Li Ximing | 1926 | 1949[a] | 1948 | Mem. of Politburo; Party sec. Beijing | Member, Democratic Youth League | Underground CCP member |
| He Dongchang | 1923 | 1945 | 1947 | Minister of Education | Founder, Democratic Youth League | Underground CCP member; Deputy Party secretary and vice president |

| Name | | | | | | |
|---|---|---|---|---|---|---|
| Peng Peiyun | 1929 | 1949 | 1946 | Vice minister of Education; Chair, State Family Planning Com. | Member, Democratic Youth League | Underground CCP member, political counselor; Party branch secretary |
| Wang Hangbin | 1925 | 1946 | 1941 | Alternate of Politburo; sec.-general, National People's Congress | Member, Democratic Youth League | CCP member at Associated Southwestern University |
| Ai Zhisheng | 1928 | 1950 | 1948 | Deputy sec. general, State Council | Member, Democratic Youth League | Underground CCP member; vice president |
| Zhu Rongji | 1928 | 1951 | 1949 | Mayor, Shanghai | Member, Democratic Youth League | Chair, Student Union; dean |
| Wang Jialiu | 1929 | — | 1946 | Deputy Party secretary, Beijing | Member, Democratic Youth League | Deputy Party secretary |
| Teng Teng | 1930 | 1951 | 1948 | Vice minister of Education; Deputy head, CCP Organization Dept. | Member, Democratic Youth League | Underground CCP member; vice president |

Source: Liao and Fan, (comp.) Zhongguo renming da cidian (1994); Gao Xin and He Pin, Zhu Rongji zhuan: Cong fandang youpai dao Deng Xiaoping jichengren (Biography of Zhu Rongji: From anti-party rightist to Deng's successor) (Taibei: Xinxinwen wenhua chubanshe, 1992); and China News Analysis, no. 1613–1614, 14–20.

[a]Attended Qinghua but did not graduate because of the Anti-Japanese War and their Communist revolutionary activities.

1949 revolution. Only two, Xi Jingping, son of former Politburo member Xi
Zhongxun and governor of Fujian, and Xie Zhenhua, director of the State Environment Bureau, were graduates of the late 1970s (they were therefore worker-
peasant-soldier students). Two took the midcareer training program in the early
1980s. A large majority of them (79 percent) entered Qinghua between the late
1950s and the mid-1960s (most of the programs at Qinghua then lasted six years).
These Qinghua-trained technocrats usually joined the CCP prior to their graduation. Among the forty-six Qinghua graduates who are CCP members on table
4.6, thirty-six (78 percent) had joined the Party before graduating from the university. Among forty-one who entered Qinghua before the CR, thirty-two (78
percent) had been political counselors and/or leaders of the CCYL during their
school years. Most of them, therefore, were Jiang Nanxiang's political counselors
and double-load cadres.

Although not all Qinghua-graduated leaders attained high positions because of
their political network, the Qinghua connection helps to explain some rapid career
advances. During the late 1980s and the 1990s, for example, three governors of
Sichuan Province—Zhang Haoruo, Xiao Yang and Song Baorui—were Qinghua
graduates. The quick rise of Zhu Rongji during the post-Mao era was particularly revealing. Zhu was chair of the Student Union at Qinghua in the early 1950s. After
graduation, he worked first as a deputy chief of Production Planning Section of Industrial Department under the Northeast China government and then deputy division chief in the State Planning Commission but was removed from this position after being labeled a rightist. When he was rehabilitated in 1979, Zhu was appointed
deputy bureau chief in the Ministry of Petroleum Industry by Minister Kang Shi'en,
himself a Qinghua graduate. A few years later, Zhu was promoted to the position of
vice chairman of the State Economic Commission, which Kang at that time chaired.

The large number of Qinghua graduates in positions of power during the reform
era has been attributed not only to the political network that Jiang Nanxiang and
his associates have established, but also to their efforts to seize power in the following three strategically important areas.

### The Central Party School and Organizational Department

Jiang ended his career at the Central Party School, where he served as executive
vice president under Wang Zhen. Jiang's choice was no surprise when one considers the critical role that the CPS played in the transformation of China's political elite during the reform era. As noted in chapter 3, a large number of the
technical elite attended the CPS before their appointments to important leadership posts. It is unknown how many Qinghua graduates went to the CPS during
the 1980s to advance their political careers, but the close connection between the
CPS and Qinghua is evident. Lin Feng, a former president of the CPS, was a leader
of the December Ninth movement and a close friend of Jiang. Lin and Jiang had
promoted faculty and cadre exchanges between Qinghua and the CPS when they

**Table 4.6  Some Qinghua University Graduates in the Third and Fourth Generation Leaders (1999)**

| Name | Birth | Grad. | CCP | Current Position | Experience at Qinghua |
|---|---|---|---|---|---|
| 3d Generation | | | | | |
| Zhu Rongji | 1928 | 1951 | 1949 | Standing mem. Politburo, premier | Chair, Student Union, dean |
| Huang Ju | 1938 | 1963 | 1966 | Mem. Politburo, Party secretary of Shanghai | |
| Wu Guanzheng | 1938 | 1964 | 1962 | Mem. Politburo, Party secretary of Shandong | Political counselor |
| Wu Shaozu | 1939 | 1964 | 1958 | Head, National Sports Commission | Political counselor, CCYL sec. |
| Peng Peiyun | 1929 | 1949 | 1946 | Chair, Federation of Women | Pol. counselor, party branch sec. |
| Zhou Guangzhao | 1929 | 1951 | 1950 | President, Academy of Sciences | Dean |
| Jia Chunwang | 1938 | 1964 | 1962 | Minister, Public Security | Political counselor, CCYL sec. |
| Song Baorui | 1937 | 1962 | 1958 | Governor, Sichuan | Political counselor |
| Zeng Peiyan | 1938 | 1962 | 1978 | Vice chair, State Planning Com. | |
| Zhang Fusen | 1940 | 1958 | 1965 | Deputy Party secretary, Beijing | Political counselor |
| Zhang Delin | 1939 | 1964 | 1964 | Party secretary, Chongqing | Political counselor |
| Luan Enjie | 1940 | 1968 | 1966 | Head, State Aerospace Bureau | Political counselor |
| Huang Yinkui | 1940 | 1964 | 1977 | Deputy secretary, Sichuan | |
| Shen Guojun | 1939 | 1982 | 1965 | Deputy secretary, Sichuan | Cadre middle career program |
| He Meiying | 1937 | 1963 | 1958 | Party secretary, Qinghua University | Pol. counselor, CCYL sec. |
| Zhang Xiaowen | 1935 | 1957 | 1955 | Gen. secretary, Academic Degree Com. | Political counselor, president |
| Chen Shineng | 1938 | 1964 | 1962 | Director, State Light Industry Bureau | Political counselor |
| Zhang Haoruo | 1932 | 1952 | 1949 | Member, National People's Congress | CCYL secretary |
| Teng Teng | 1930 | 1951 | 1948 | Member, National People's Congress | Pol. counselor; vice president |
| Zhu Senlin | 1930 | 1952 | 1952 | Chair, Guangdong People's Congress | Political counselor |
| Ye Rutang | 1940 | 1965 | 1965 | Vice minister, Construction | Political counselor |

*continued*

**Table 4.6    Continued**

| Name | Birth | Grad. | CCP | Current Position | Experience at Qinghua |
|---|---|---|---|---|---|
| 4th Generation | | | | | |
| Hu Jintao | 1942 | 1965 | 1965 | Stand. mem, Politburo; vice president | Political counselor, CCYL sec. |
| Wu Bangguo | 1941 | 1967 | 1964 | Mem. Politburo, vice premier | Political counselor |
| Tian Chengping | 1945 | 1968 | 1964 | Party secretary of Shanxi | Political counselor |
| Li Jiating | 1944 | 1968 | 1964 | Governor, Yunnan | Political counselor |
| Liu Yandong | 1945 | 1970 | 1964 | Exe. vice head, Dept. of United Front, CCP | Political counselor |
| Xi Jinping | 1953 | 1979 | 1974 | Deputy Party secretary, Fujian | During CR |
| Zhang Huazhu | 1945 | 1963 | 1965 | Vice chair, State Com. of Defense S&T Ind. | |
| Xie Qihua | 1943 | 1968 | 1980 | General manager, Banshan Steel Co. | |
| Wang Weizhong | 1945 | 1970 | 1973 | Deputy Party secretary of Liaoning | During CR |
| Yang Jianqiang | 1948 | 1984 | 1975 | Vice governor, Yunnan | Cadre middle career program |
| Xie Zhenhua | 1949 | 1977 | 1969 | Director, State Environmental Adm. | Pol. counselor, CCYL sec. |
| Chen Yuan | 1945 | 1970 | 1975 | Vice governor, People's Bank of China | During CR |
| Du Yuzhou | 1942 | 1966 | 1965 | Vice chair, Nat. Assoc. Textile Industry | Political counselor |
| He Pengfei | 1944 | 1970 | 1965 | Deputy commander, navy | Political counselor |
| Jiang Yiren | 1942 | 1966 | 1970 | Vice mayor, Shanghai | |
| Li Tielin | 1943 | 1968 | 1980 | Vice head, Org. Dept. CCP | During CR |
| Liu Zepeng | 1946 | 1970 | 1974 | Deputy head, Overseas Chinese Affairs | During CR |
| Liu Zhizhong | 1942 | 1967 | 1965 | Deputy Party secretary, Chongqing | Political counselor |
| Sun Changji | 1942 | 1966 | 1964 | Vice minister, Machinery Industry | Political counselor |
| Wang Hanmin | 1943 | 1968 | 1961 | Vice governor, Qinghai | Political counselor |
| Wang Shucheng | 1941 | 1968 | 1965 | Minister, Electric Power Industry | Political counselor |

*continued*

**Table 4.6   Continued**

| Name | Birth | Grad. | CCP | Current Position | Experience at Qinghua |
|------|-------|-------|-----|------------------|----------------------|
| Xu Bingsong | 1942 | 1968 | 1965 | Vice governor, Guangxi | Political counselor |
| Xu Rongkai | 1942 | 1966 | 1960 | Vice minister, Light Ind. Association | Political counselor |
| Zhao Baojiang | 1941 | 1966 | 1966 | Mayor, Wuhan | Political counselor |
| Zhao Xizheng | 1942 | 1966 | 1965 | Vice minister, Electric Power Industry | Political counselor |
| Bai Dahua | 1942 | 1967 | No | Mem. CPPCC | |

*Source:* Liao and Fan, *Zhongguo renming da cidian,* (1994); Gao Xin and He Pin, *Zhu Rongji zhuan: Cong fandang youpai dao Deng Xiaoping jichengren* (Biography of Zhu Rongji: From anti-Party rightist to Deng's successor) (Taibei: Xinxinwen wenhua chubanshe, 1992); and *China News Analysis,* no. 1613–1614, 14–20.

headed these two schools. After Jiang took the post at the CPS in 1982, he brought several Qinghua cadres with him. Other Qinghua cadres occupied many of the top administrative posts at the CPS. For example, Xing Jiali, who had been a vice head of the provost's office at Qinghua for several decades, was appointed provost of the CPS. The Qinghua clique's control over the CPS has continued in the 1990s. Hu Jintao and Wang Jialiu have held two top positions of the CPS, president and executive vice president, since 1993.

Equally important, among the ten top posts in the two most important departments of the Central Committee of the CCP, the Organization and Propaganda Departments, Qinghua graduates occupied five of the top ten posts in the late 1980s. Song Ping, Zhao Zongnai, and Liu Zepeng, three Qinghua graduates, served as head and vice heads of the Organization Department. Liu was concurrently director of the training center for China's high-ranking cadres. In the 1990s, the presence of Qinghua graduates in the Organization Department is still evident. Li Tielin, a 1996 Qinghua graduate, has held the post of deputy head since 1993. Another deputy head, Song Defu, though not a Qinghua graduate, is a close friend of Hu Jintao, who nominated Song for that position. By occupying these key institutions of personnel development in China, the Qinghua network has been able to promote alumni to still other leadership posts.

## Educational and Academic Administration

Since the late 1950s, China's top educational administration has usually been led by the people from Qinghua. Before the CR, Jiang Nanxiang even supervised national educational affairs through his Qinghua office. In 1979, Jiang resumed his post as minister of education. Before he left for the CPS in 1982, Jiang passed on his post as minister to He Dongchang, his long-time assistant. Peng Peiyun and Teng Teng, two other officials handpicked by Jiang, also served as vice minister of education during the 1980s. For the PRC's first four decades, except the CR, people in educational institutions called the Ministry of Higher Education *Jiang guanqu* (district under Jiang's control).[71] Since the mid-1990s, the Qinghua clique's dominance over the ministry has been challenged by other forces. Yet Zhang Xiaowen, then president of Qinghua and alternate of the Fourteenth Central Committee of the CCP, also concurrently held the post of vice minister of education.

Many members of the Qinghua network occupy top posts in the science and technology administrations. Soon after Deng Xiaoping regained power in 1978, he asked Jiang to assist him in organizing a national science conference. Jiang served as general secretary of the conference and thereafter as executive vice chair of the State Science and Technology Commission. In the mid-1980s, his protégés, Zhou Guangzhao and Teng Teng, became president and vice president of the Chinese Academy of Sciences, the most prestigious academic institution in the country. In addition, He Dongchang assumed the chair of the national academic degree committee. In the 1990s, China's high-tech and nuclear research centers were often headed by Qinghua graduates. For example, Zhang Huazhu, a 1969 Qinghua graduate and alternate of the Fifteenth Central Committee of the CCP, serves as head of the Research Center of Nuclear Energy and vice chair of the Commission of Science, Technology, and Industry for National Defense. Another vice chair of the commission is Luan Enjie, who did his graduate study at Qinghua in the early 1960s and now serves as head of the newly established Bureau of Space Technology under the State Council.

## The CCYL and All-China Students Federation

The Chinese Communist Youth League has long been a major channel of elite recruitment in the PRC. Many technocrats have advanced their political careers not through fields of industry or scientific research but through the administration of youth affairs. As a founder of the CCYL and a top leader in its earlier years, Jiang Nanxiang claimed that CCYL officials would naturally succeed to leadership positions of the CCP and the government. He first brought CCYL officials to Qinghua with him, and then he appointed Qinghua graduates to lead the CCYL. The top officials of the CCYL as well as the All-China Students Federation (ACSF) were usually from Qinghua. In the 1980s, for example, Hu Jintao, Jia Chunwang, Wu Shaozu, Lin Yanzhi (son of Lin Feng), and Liu Yandong were, at the different times, in charge of youth affairs in Beijing and in the entire country. In the early 1990s, both the first secretary of the CCYL and the chair of the ACSF were from Qinghua.

All the evidence above reflects the strategies of Jiang and his associates. By occupying leadership posts in these three areas, the Qinghua network not only controlled the recruitment and promotion of technocratic elites through the CCP's organizational department and the CPS but also had the authority to determine the academic degrees and ranks that these elites might need in order to advance. In this way Qinghua's double-load cadres in the 1950s and the 1960s became national double-load leaders in the 1980s and the 1990s. The Qinghua graduates in the CCYL leadership today will likely become leaders of the Party and government tomorrow.

In the 1980s, Qinghua resumed its tradition of having a graduate reunion every April. Qinghua graduates among China's top leadership (e.g., Yao Yilin, Song Ping, Li Ximing, Kang Shi'en, and Hu Qiaomu in the 1980s, and Zhu Rongji, Hu Jintao, Wu Bangguo, Jia Chunwang in the 1990s) often attended the reunions. During the reform era, especially in the 1990s, Qinghua has worked to form an active network of alumni associations. For example, alumni association members exceeded 2,000 in Shanghai and 1,000 in Guangzhou during the mid-1980s, a period in which Qinghua graduates occupied many top leadership posts in these two cities.[72] Jiang Yiren, vice mayor of Shanghai, who serves as president of Qinghua's Shanghai Alumni Association, is one example. In 1990, Qinghua graduates occupied the four top positions in the Party and municipal government in Shanghai.[73] Every province has a Qinghua alumni association in its capital. Alumni associations have now been established in 111 cities in the country, and information about these associations is available at Qinghua University's Web site.[74]

As China approaches a new century, Qinghua seems to be well situated academically. Qinghua now consists of six schools, thirty-one departments, forty-four research institutes, nine engineering research centers, and 163 laboratories, including fifteen key national laboratories. The university offers 37 bachelor's degree programs, 107 master's degree programs, and 64 doctorate degree programs. There are sixteen postdoctoral research centers. According to the statistics released by Qinghua in 2000, since the establishment of China's academic degree system in the early 1980s, Qinghua has granted over 15,000 master's and doctorate degrees.[75] No other university in the country has produced more advanced degree holders than Qinghua. In 1999, Qinghua admitted about 3,600 graduate students, and this number exceeded that of undergraduate students admitted.[76]

In addition, of the 879 members of the Chinese Academy of Science, 274 are Qinghua alumni (31 percent of the total). Of the 312 members of the Chinese Academy of Engineering, 64 are Qinghua alumni (21 percent of the total).[77] Since the reform began in 1978, Qinghua has sent more students abroad than any other higher education institution in the country.[78] Qinghua has recently decided to resume its law school, which was abolished in 1952.[79] This will likely prove to be an important move as the country has now called for establishing and consolidating its legal system. Politically and more importantly, Hu Jintao and others Qinghua graduates like him are well situated in China's fourth generation leadership.

## Hu Jintao: The Golden Boy of the Qinghua Network

Hu Jintao was regarded twice by China watchers as a dark horse during the 1990s. The first time was when he was promoted from one of the 300-plus members of the Central Committee of the CCP to standing member of the Politburo in the Fourteenth Party Congress in 1992. Prior to this promotion, Hu served as provincial Party secretary of Guizhou and Tibet consecutively. Guizhou has long been one of the poorest provinces in the country. Hu Jintao's three-year tenure there did not seem to make many changes. Tibet, probably the most troubled region in the PRC in terms of ethnic tensions, has remained so (if not getting worse) during Hu Jintao's three-year "supervisorship" in the region. In fact, Hu spent most of these three years in Beijing rather than in Lhasa. There were quite a number of capable provincial top leaders whose local achievements were far more impressive than Hu's, as some China watchers have noted.[80]

The second surprise occurred when Hu was elected vice president of the PRC during the Ninth National People's Congress in 1998. For almost his entire career until then, Hu had been in charge of Party affairs. He did not have much experience in state administration. This appointment, along with his posts of standing member of the Politburo and vice chair of the Central Military Commission, has made Hu a recognized successor to Jiang Zemin.

The rise of Hu Jintao, however, should not be a surprise if we understand the powerful Qinghua connections that Hu has established over the past three decades and the political acumen that he has developed since his student years. To a certain extent, Hu Jintao is a man whose political career and behavior exemplify the Qinghua-trained leaders. Hu was born in 1942. His ancestral home is in Jixi, located in southern part of Anhui Province. His ancestors left Jixi and moved to Taizhou, the northern part of Jiangsu Province where the family opened a small store selling teas and other local products. The family business boomed during the time of Hu's great-grandfather who opened several similar stores in Shanghai and Zhejiang. Hu's father, Hu Jingzhi, often worked in the family store in Shanghai. Hu Jingzhi married in Shanghai and had three children, one boy and two girls; the oldest is Hu Jintao.[81] His two sisters still live in Taixian, a county in the Taizhou prefectural region where they are engaged in small business. Hu was born in Taizhou, which is not far away from Yangzhou, Jiang Zemin's birthplace.[82] Hu's mother died before the founding of the PRC and left three small children for her husband and her mother-in-law to raise. Hu was brought up mostly by his grandmother. While Hu Jintao attended elementary and high school in Taizhou, his father, who was not rich, worked in a local company as an accountant. His father died when the Cultural Revolution was about to end.

Hu was seventeen years old when he was admitted to Qinghua in 1959. At Qinghua, he majored in water conservancy and power in the department of hydraulic engineering. This field was understandably very popular at the time of the Great Leap Forward. Hu was the youngest student in his class but also one of the brightest. He earned almost straight As in his six-year course work.[83] Meanwhile, Hu was fond of social and recreational activities on campus. He was secretary of the CCYL of the students' dance troupe. At Qinghua, Hu met his future wife, Liu Yongqing, who was his classmate in the same field.

During his sophomore year, Hu was considered a "prospective Party member" (fazhan duixian) by the Party branch of his department. Hu was an activist of political movements such as "Anti-Rightist Tendency campaign" and "Socialist Educational movement." In the spring of 1964, he was recruited as a probationary Party member and started to work as a political counselor offering political and ideological supervision to students of lower classes. Becoming a political counselor later proved to be an important step in his political career. As already noted, being appointed a political counselor at Qinghua was comparable to gaining membership in a very exclusive club at an American Ivy League university.

One year later, in 1965, Hu became a full Party member and graduated from Qinghua. Like many other double-load cadres, Hu remained at Qinghua after graduation and continued to work as a political counselor and assistant instructor. Everything seemed to be perfect for Hu: he was a Party member, he met his future wife, and he held a double-load job that signified a rosy political and professional career. But the Cultural Revolution took place in the following year. Hu's association with Jiang's network turned him from a promising double-load cadre into a target of the revolution.[84] This dramatic change certainly taught him a lesson about power politics.

When the Cultural Revolution cooled down in 1968, Hu was sent to Gansu, a remote interior province, where he worked as a construction worker in the Liujiaxia hydroelectric power station. After one year of manual work, he was appointed technician, office secretary, and deputy division Party secretary in the power station consecutively. These jobs were no challenge for a Qinghua-trained double-load cadre. During the catastrophic Tangshan earthquake in 1976, Hu led the Gansu construction team to help relief efforts, thus demonstrating his dedication to the Party. Often during his early career, he had answered the Party's call at times of great need.

In 1980, Hu met Song Ping, a Qinghua graduate who was then Party secretary of the province. Song Ping's wife, Chen Shunyao, was deputy Party secretary of Qinghua when Hu was a student there. Meeting with Song was another important step for Hu's political career. Song soon promoted Hu to deputy director of the Gansu Provincial Construction Committee. Song also sent Hu to study at the CPS. Song then appointed Hu as secretary of the CCYL in Gansu. In 1981, at the recommendation of Yao Yilin, Song's comrade in arms at Qinghua during the December Ninth movement, Song returned to Beijing and worked as executive chair of the State Planning Commission under Yao. Song recommended his protégé Hu Jintao to Hu Yaobang, who appointed Hu Jintao as secretary of the national CCYL in 1982. Hu Jintao then worked in Guizhou and Tibet as provincial Party secretary. In 1992, Song recalled Hu to be president of the CPS, the position that Song had once held. When Song retired from his post as standing member of the Politburo in 1992, he lobbied among revolutionary veterans to offer the post to Hu Jintao.

This review of Hu Jintao's career highlights three points. First, Hu's major career advancement clearly reflects the importance of the Qinghua network. Hu may not have known Song Ping's wife, Chen Shunyao, when he was a political counselor at Qinghua, but his identity with Qinghua's SPC and his experience as a double-load cadre were enough to get help from Song and his wife in his career later.

Second, Hu Jintao has not had any major "achievements" in his career thus far, nor has he pursued any direct confrontation with other leaders or political forces. But he is certainly the kind of Qinghua-trained double-load cadre who is both "obedient and productive." (He remembers Jiang Nanxiang's motto very well.) He was willing to take on some dirty work—for example, working in the remote province for over a decade, participating in earthquake relief in Tangshan, and accepting tough posts in Guizhou and Tibet.

And third, Hu has occupied some of the most critical leadership posts, such as heads of the CCYL and the CPS. Between 1980 and 1985, when he was in charge of the CCYL, thirty-four people from the CCYL system entered the Central Committee of the CCP. Since he was appointed president of the CPS in 1993, the school has trained 820 leaders at provincial and ministerial levels and a total of 8,300 at all levels of cadres.[85] The 1997 class of provincial and ministerial leaders included Xu Kuangdi, mayor of Shanghai, Wu Yi, then minister of foreign trade, and Xiang Huaicheng, minister of finance.[86]

The fact that Hu Jintao has kept a low profile may continue to help him in factional politics in the future. When Hu was Party chief in Guizhou, he told journalists in the province that he did not want the media to provide too much coverage of him. In his words, "too much praise for a young provincial Party secretary can only lead to his quick fall from power."[87] In addition, the fact that Hu was born into an ordinary family may also give him an advantage in the competition with *taizi* in the fourth generation of leadership.[88]

Until now, Hu's political views and policy orientations have been largely unknown to public. This, of course, should not be a surprise to students of elite studies. Even in democratic countries, some fast-rising political figures are "known for their mysteriousness." For instance, how much do we really know Vladimir Putin, recently elected president of Russia? Has George W. Bush, the presidential candidate of the Republican Party, clearly explained his domestic and foreign policies to the American public? Understandably, candidates for top leadership posts usually do not publicly express their views until they obtain power. The front-runners in China's fourth generation leadership, such as Hu Jintao, have certainly done the same.

Nonetheless, a close look at Hu's life experience and his recent speeches suggests a couple of points about his political future and his policy orientation. First, Hu Jintao's ability to succeed Jiang in the years ahead should not be underestimated. No one, of course, can eliminate the possibility that Hu will have a tough fight against other top contenders in his generation such as Zeng Qinghong, Wen

Jiabao, and Li Changchun, or a dark horse candidate. Yet the strong political network that Hu has established, his intelligence and personality, and the fact that no other faction has been able to change the balance of competing forces all indicate Hu's political potential. One interesting comparison between Hu and many other appointed successors in the PRC history is that the general public has often made fun of "helicopter-style" leaders, for example, Wang Hongwen and Hua Guofeng (and to a certain extent Jiang Zemin as well), but surprisingly there has been a lack of political jokes about Hu Jintao.

Second, in recent years, especially since his appointment as vice president of the state, there has been a consistent theme in Hu Jintao's speeches, emphasizing nationalism and patriotism. In 1999, for example, Hu Jintao delivered major speeches on four occasions: (1) the event to commemorate Li Dazhao's 110th birthday, (2) the award ceremony of the National Social Sciences Fund, (3) the opening ceremony unveiling the monument that commemorates the handover of Hong Kong, and (4) the remark on television regarding the bombing of the Chinese embassy in Belgrade.[89] In all four of these speeches, Hu expressed a strong nationalistic sentiment. In his commemorative speech for Li Dazhao, a founder of the Chinese Communist Party, Hu claimed that Li should be best remembered for his role as a great patriot, and for his contribution to China's national liberation. In Hu's view, Li left an important legacy for China at this time as the country faces the destructive undercurrents of westernization (xihua) and disintegration (fenghua).[90] In his speech at the award ceremony of the National Social Sciences Fund, Hu also appealed to Chinese social scientists, especially those in the younger generation, to be alert to hostile foreign forces that intend to Westernize China and cause it to disintegrate.[91] His remarks on television demonstrated strong nationalistic sentiment in the wake of the embassy bombing and certainly left a lasting image on millions of Chinese viewers.

This does not necessarily mean that Hu Jintao is more nationalistic than most other top Chinese leaders. But his political experience, especially his training as a double-load cadre at Qinghua and his long-term association with the CCYL, has fostered his ability to make eloquent nationalistic rhetoric. This suggests that Hu may well use nationalistic appeal as the dominant theme of his platform as he consolidates power. Fortunately for Hu, his nationalistic appeal seems to correspond with the current public view in China. It remains to be seen whether Hu Jintao can succeed Jiang Zeming and defeat his rivals of the same generation in the next decade, but the political acumen and potential of this "golden boy" of the Qinghua network is obvious to all.[92]

## SUMMARY

In the classic writings on technocracy, technocrats are usually portrayed as people who are not interested in power but only in technical matters. They are selected not because of their political associations but because of their technical expertise. This case study of the role of the university network challenges these assumptions. There can be little doubt that the technical skills and administrative knowledge of Chinese technocrats help them claim and consolidate their governing power. One important question, however, has rarely been asked in the study of China's technocrats: do technical knowledge and skills account for success, or are these ancillary to other aspects of their experience?

An analysis of the political history of Qinghua since the 1950s shows that President Jiang Nanxiang made a great effort to establish political networks based on patronage at Qinghua during his fourteen-year presidency and beyond. He first created the system of political counselors, encouraging politically ambitious students (some of whom were academically mediocre) to seek nonacademic means through which they were able to "surpass" their fellow students. Jiang used this system to control the distribution of career chances and to award the best opportunities to those who were associated with his political network. He then initiated the idea of the double-load cadres and provided favorable conditions to help his political counselors become both "top officials and leading scholars." Although Jiang denounced Qian Weichang's technocratic views, he himself shared much of Qian's idea that Qinghua should become an elite technical university producing the future leaders of the country.

Jiang's "grand plan," however, was interrupted by Mao's CR. Sweeping changes in the educational system during that period should be understood against a broad background of power struggles among political leaders and not as a controversy over educational policy. Maoists' accusations against Jiang during the CR, just like Jiang Nanxiang's charges against Qian Weichang in the 1950s, were intended not just to demean the previous educational system but to undermine the elites created by it.

After the CR, Jiang's double-load cadres, endorsed by Deng Xiaoping, resumed leadership posts at Qinghua at the end of 1970s. Jiang's political network developed beyond the university and the realm of education. Members of the Qinghua network first seized power in some strategically important places such as the CCP's organizational department and the CPS and then promoted Qinghua graduates to leadership positions in all parts of the country. During the two decades of the reform, the baton of the Qinghua network has been passed from Jiang and his December Ninth movement generation to the generation that graduated from Qinghua in the 1950s and now to Hu Jintao's generation, who started to work before or during the CR. Hu's appointment to standing member of the Politburo and vice president highlights the presence of Qinghua graduates in the fourth generation leadership. His career path and political acumen reflect both the crucial role of the Qinghua network and the characteristics of the Qinghua-style leaders.

The selection of Chinese technocrats, therefore, is not based on criteria that are universal, scientific-technical, or impersonal. Instead, these leaders are conditioned by the political and institutional network through which they have been promoted. China is entering a new era in its century-long modernization process. A new generation of leadership, a technocratic elite, is moving toward the center stage of Chinese politics. In the process, the Qinghua network has emerged as a distinctive elite group. Their group identity may politicize the decision-making process in the new political spectrum and indicate future sources of elite conflict in Chinese politics.

This does not mean that all the Qinghua graduates in China's high-level leadership have been associated with the Qinghua network, nor does it suggest that membership in the Qinghau clique is permanent. Some Qinghua graduates in the top leadership (e.g., Huang Ju) seem to be closer to Jiang Zemin than to his fellow Qinghua graduates. Jiang Zemin's relationship with the Qinghua clique, especially with Hu Jintao, is not entirely clear. Group identities, for example, the "Shanghai gang" and the "Qinghua clique" are often overlapping. Politicians have more information about processes and factors of succession and elite promotion than distant academics can garner. And the technocratic leaders in China use this better information—and can change it by shifting their loyalties—to affect the outcome of the power struggle. Yet life histories and political associations tell a great deal concerning actors' notions about rule and about the networks available to them.

Every society has its networks: "groups of people who help each other along in life, in ways that mystify and infuriate those excluded."[93] Political elites often establish networks on the basis of common backgrounds, either contemporary ones such as revolutionary experiences or traditional ones such as family-like fealties. Technocratic identity, tied to group loyalty fostered at universities, has now become a generalized basis for claims to legitimate rule in China. Without measures to constrain favoritism and particularism in this elite recruitment, Hu Jintao and other Qinghua technocrats like him, who now hold the baton of the Qinghua clique, can be expected to further increase their power and influence in the years to come.

## NOTES

1. "Xue er you ze shi" in Chinese.

2. John Meyer, "The Effects of Education as an Institution," *American Journal of Sociology* 83, no. 1 (1977): 55–77; and C. Montgomery Broaded, "Higher Educational Charters in Mainland China," *Issues and Studies* 21, no. 2 (February 1985): 53.

3. Robert Putnam, *The Comparative Study of Political Elites* (Englewood Cliffs, N.J.: Prentice-Hall, 1976), 205; and John Kenneth Galbraith, *The New Industrial State* (Harmondsworth, U.K.: Penguin, 1969), 370. Michel Young asserted in the middle of the twentieth century that education superseded more traditional channels of circulation of elites. See *The Rise of the Meritocracy, 1870 to 2033* (London: Thames & Hudson, 1958).

4. In Britain, three successive prime ministers in the postwar period were graduates of the same public school—Eton College. Old Etonians have dominated government circles such as the parliament and cabinet and also controlled major private sectors. According to one study, 35 percent of the directors of the banks and insurance companies are from Eton College. See Jane Marceau, *A Family Business? The Making of an International Business Elite* (London: Cambridge University Press, 1989), 180; also see Rupert Wilkinson, *Gentlemanly*

*Power: British Leadership and the Public School Tradition* (London: Oxford University Press, 1964). In France, 43 percent of the chairmen and directors of the most important public and private organizations are ENA Graduates. See J-L. Bodiguel, "Political and Administrative Traditions and the French Senior Civil Service," *International Journal of Public Administration* 13, no. 5 (1990): 735. In Japan, graduates from universities other than Tokyo University face difficulty in rising to the very highest posts. *Tokyo Business Today*, August 1988, 14. For the important role of school ties in Chile, see Patricio Silva, "Technocrats and Politics in Chile: From the Chicago Boys to the CIEPLAN Monks," *Journal of Latin American Studies* 23, no. 2 (May 1991): 385–410. For an excellent general survey of school ties in elite recruitment worldwide, see *Economist*, "The Good Network Guide: Being One of Us," 26 December 1992–8 January 1993, 20–22.

5. The classical examinations for the civil service, which lasted for a thousand years, were completely eliminated by 1905.

6. See William Hinton, *Hundred Day War: The CR at Tsinghua University* (New York: Monthly Review Press, 1972).

7. Quoted from Theodore Hsi-en Chen, *The Maoist Educational Revolution* (New York: Praeger, 1974), 142–143.

8. For a detailed discussion of the history and recent development of Qinghua University, especially its role as the cradle of Chinese technocrats, see Li Cheng, "University Networks and the Rise of Qinghua Graduates in China's Leadership," *Australian Journal of Chinese Affairs* 32 (July 1994): 1–32.

9. For further discussion of functionalism or neofunctionalism, see Ernst B. Haas, *Beyond the Nation-State: Functionalism and International Organization* (Stanford: Stanford University Press, 1964); and David Mitrany, *A Working Peace System* (London: Royal Institute of International Affairs, 1943).

10. For example, Thorstein Veblen's "engineers" emerge largely as a result of the "force of circumstances." Similarly, James Burham's "managers" ascend because of social structural changes caused by technological development. Thorstein Veblen, *Imperial Germany and the Industrial Revolution* (New York: Viking, 1915); and James Burnham, *The Managerial Revolution* (New York: John Day, 1941).

11. For a few exceptions, see Guillermo A. O'Donnell, *Modernization and Bureaucratic-Authoritarianism: Studies in South American Politics* (Berkeley: University of California Press, 1973); Ezra N. Suleiman, *Politics, Power, and Bureaucracy in France: The Administrative Elite* (Princeton: Princeton University Press, 1974); and Miguel Angel Centeno Gutierrez, "The New Cientificos: Technocratic Politics in Mexico 1970–1990" (Ph.D. diss., Yale University, 1990).

12. Hong Yung Lee made this point in his book on China's elite transformation. Hong Yung Lee, *From Revolutionary Cadres to Party Technocrats in Socialist China* (Berkeley: University of California Press, 1991), 406–407.

13. Daniel Bell, *The Coming of the Post-Industrial Society* (New York: Basic, 1973), 348.

14. Jiang initiated the notion of "red engineers." *Renmin ribao*, 7 May 1998, 11. Jiang Nanxiang was also the first to refer to Qinghua as "the cradle of red engineers." See *Xin Qinghua* (New Qinghua), 30 April 1989, 4. However, the term originated in the Soviet Union.

15. See Teng Teng and Huang Shenglun, "Yi nanxiang tongzhi changdao zhengzhi zhidaoyuan zhidu" (Recollections of Comrade Nanxiang's efforts to promote the system of political counselors), in *Jiang nanxiang jinian wenji* (A commemorative collection about Jiang

Nanxiang), ed. *Qinghua daxue Jiang Nanxiang jinian wenji bianji xiaozu* (Editorial group for the commemorative collection of Jiang Nanxiang at Qinghua) (Beijing: Qinghua University Press, 1990), 148–151.

16. Similarly, Andrew J. Nathan has noted that Chinese political elites are no longer an ideologically disciplined cadre. Instead, they have become a "network of the 'best and the brightest'—those with the training and connections to get things done." See Andrew J. Nathan, "China's Path from Communism," *Journal of Democracy* 4, no. 2 (April 1993): 38. For more than four decades the field-army identity of Chinese leaders has provided a focus for personal and group loyalties not only in the People's Liberation Army but also in the government and the Party. See William Whitson, "The Field Army in Chinese Communist Military Politics," *China Quarterly* 37 (January-March 1969): 1–30.

17. Harold Scott Quigley, "Politics vs. Education," *Tsing Hua Alumni Association Year Book 1923* 2 (1923): 23.

18. In 1900, the allied armies of eight powers occupied Beijing after suppressing the Boxer Rebellion. It forced the government of the Qing dynasty to sign a treaty known as the Protocol of 1901, under which China was required to pay these countries a large sum called the Boxer Indemnity. The U.S. government later decided to use the $11 million that it received to train Chinese students.

19. *Qinghua Niankan* (Qinghua yearbook, 1927). Cited from *Qinghua daxue xiaoshi bianxie zu* (Writing Group of Qinghua University history), *Qinghua daxue xiaoshi gao* (A draft of Qinghua University history) (Beijing: Zhonghua Press, 1981), 27.

20. *Qinghua Zhoukan* (Qinghua weekly), 17 April 1925, 4.

21. *Guoli qinghua daxue yilan* (A general survey of national Qinghua University), no. 2 (Beijing: Qinghua University, 1946).

22. *Renmin ribao*, 24 September, 1952, 1.

23. See Chung Shih, *Higher Education in Communist China* (Hong Kong: Union Research Institute), 46–47; also Suzanne Pepper, "Education and Political Development in Communist China," *Study of Comparative Communism* 3, no. 3–4 (July 1970): 142.

24. *Jiang Nanxiang jinian wenji*, 429.

25. *Xin Qinghua*, 26 April 1981, 4.

26. *Jiang Nanxiang jinian wenji*, 435.

27. By the late 1950s, political counselors were also recruited from among young faculty members.

28. *Jiang Nanxiang jinian wenji*, 148–149.

29. Faculty members at higher educational institutions in China are divided into four academic ranks: assistant instructor (*zhujiao*), instructor (*jiangshi*), associate professor (*fujiaoshou*), and professor (*jiaoshou*).

30. This was particularly the case at Qinghua after the Great Leap Forward. Political counselors were largely recruited from "political activists" who showed relatively little interest in academic studies. See *Jiang Nanxiang jinian wenji*, 150.

31. *Jiang Nanxiang jinian wenji*, 206; and *Qinghua daxue jiaoyu yanjiu* (Educational research at Qinghua University) 2 (1989): 2–4.

32. *Qinghua daxue yilan* (General survey of Qinghua), 1959, 33.

33. *Qinghua zhanbao* (Qinghua battlefield report), 14 September 1971, 4.

34. *Xin Qinghua*, 24 September 1988, 2.

35. *Guangming ribao* (Enlightenment daily), 22 May 1957; and Wang Hsueh-wen, "Peking and Tsinghua Universities," *Issues and Studies* 13, no. 6 (June 1977): 79.

36. *Xin Qinghua yuebao* (New Qinghua monthly) 16 (January 1956): 4.

37. *Guangming ribao*, 22 May 1957.

38. *Xin Qinghua yuebao* 1 (1954): 5.

39. *Xin Qinghua yuebao*, 30 November 1954.

40. *Qinghua zhanbao*, 21 February 1974, 5.

41. Among these 572 rightists, 569 were rehabilitated in 1980. *Xin Qinghua*, 14 October 1980, 1.

42. *Xin Qinghua*, 6 June 1980, 1.

43. *Qinghua Daxue yilan*, 1959, 33.

44. Quoted from Suzanne Ogden, *China's Unresolved Issues: Politics, Development, and Culture*, 2d ed. (Englewood Cliffs, N.J.: Prentice-Hall, 1992), 303. For a detailed discussion of egalitarianism versus elitism in education, see Anita Chan, Stanley Rosen, and Jonathan Unger, "Students and Class Warfare: The Social Roots of the Red Guard Conflict in Guangzhou," *China Quarterly*, September 1980; Stanley Rosen, *Red Guard Factionalism and the CR in Guangzhou* (Boulder: Westview, 1982); Jonathan Urger, *Education under Mao: Class and Competition in Canton Schools, 1960–1980* (New York: Columbia University Press, 1982); and Anita Chan, *Children of Mao: Personality Development and Political Activism in the Red Guard Generation* (Seattle: University of Washington Press, 1985).

45. For a detailed study of Kuai Dafu and his conflict with the Party Committee of Qinghua and the work team, see Hinton, *Hundred Day War.*

46. During the Cultural Revolution, forty faculty and staff members at Qinghua either were beaten to death or committed suicide. See *Qinghua daxue* (Qinghua University), 30 May 1978, 1.

47. For the connection between Kuai and Jiang Qing, see Lin Qingshan, *Jiang Qing chenfu lu* (The rise and fall of Jiang Qing) (Beijing: China News Agency, 1988), 1:344–367.

48. The children of high Party leaders were involved in violent activities against "bourgeois academic authorities" at Qinghua, especially American-trained professors. But after the Cultural Revolution, they claimed they had been major victims of the Cultural Revolution. In the late 1980s, many of them became high-ranking technocrats and some became wealthy entrepreneurs. In a recent article, Anita Chan comments on these children of the revolution's leadership: "Twenty-five years ago they claimed themselves the legitimate 'revolutionary successors,' today they are surely succeeding." Anita Chan, "Dispelling Misconceptions about the Red Guard Movement: The Necessity to Re-examine Cultural Revolution Factionalism and Periodization," *Journal of Contemporary China* 1, no. 1 (September 1992): 76.

49. This phenomenon was prevalent at many other universities too. In May 1972, the Central Committee had to issue a regulation to limit the "backdoor" admission of such students.

50. The formal head of the State Council's Science and Education Group was Liu Xiyao, but Chi was actually in charge of China's educational system then.

51. After Jiang was "liberated," he returned to Qinghua to see Chi Qun, who reportedly asked him, "Now that you are back, what do you want to do at Qinghua?" Jiang replied, "I can do some manual labor." "Good idea. Why don't you go to work in the automobile workshop." See *Jiang Nanxiang jinian wenji*, 55.

52. *Qinghua zhanbao*, 10 September 1977, 2.

53. *Qinghua zhanbao*, 13 April 1976, 1.

54. *Qinghua zhanbao*, 26 September 1971, 3; and *Qinghua daxue yilan*, 1959, 4ff.

55. *Peking Review,* 16 December 1977; and *Qinghua daxue xuebao* (Journal of Qinghua University) 4, no. 1 (March 1958): 18.

56. Liu later became the honorary president of Qinghua after serving as president for five years. What enabled him to survive at Qinghua was his association with Jiang and his willingness to be led by Jiang's network, instead of leading the university. *Qinghua xiaoyou tongxun* (Newsletter of Qinghua alumni) 23 (1991): 43.

57. *Qinghua daxue,* 12 September 1978, 1.

58. *Yanjiusheng tongxun* (Graduate students newsletter), 5 December 1988, 1–2.

59. "Editor's words," *Qinghua daxue jiaoyu yanjiu* (Research on education, Qinghua University) 2 (1989): 1.

60. *Qinghua xiaoyou tongxun* 13 (April 1986): 42.

61. Wenhuibao (Wenhui daily), 8 September 1998, 1.

62. Among them, 779 were faculty members, accounting for 20 percent of Qinghua faculty during that period. This number does not include the members of the workers' and soldiers' propaganda teams who were transferred back to where they had come from soon after Mao's death. *Xin Qinghua,* 28 April 1985, 1.

63. *Xin Qinghua,* 28 April 1985, 1.

64. Luo served as deputy Party secretary of Qinghua after the Cultural Revolution and later was transferred to Shenzhen University as its Party secretary. In 1989, when students in Beijing were on a hunger strike, Luo wrote a letter to Deng and asked for Deng's resignation. Luo lost his post soon afterward. Ruan Ming left Qinghua in the late 1950s, worked at the CPS, and occasionally served as Hu Yaobang's speechwriter. After Hu's death, Ruan became an articulate dissident leader. Wan Runnan did not serve as secretary of the CCYL at Qinghua (Luo and Ruan did), but he was closely associated with the Qinghua network. Wan married twice, first to a daughter of Liu Shaoqi's and then to a daughter of Li Chang's, a Qinghua graduate who was on the Central Committee. In the late 1980s, Wan was president of the Stone Company, the wealthiest private company in China, specializing in advanced electronics and computers. He was involved in the antigovernment movement in 1989 and escaped the country after the crackdown.

65. The data are accumulated from Liao Gailong and Fan Yuan, comps., *Zhongguo renming da cidian* (Who's who in China), vol. 3 (Shanghai: Shanghai Dictionary Publishing House, 1989).

66. *Zhongguo chengshi jingji shehui nianjian lishihui* (The council of the almanac of China's urban economy and society), comp., *Zhongguo chengshi jingji shehui nianjian* (The almanac of China's urban economy and society) (Beijing: Zhongguo chengshi nianjian chubanshe, 1986).

67. In the 1994 edition of Liao and Fan's reference book, Qinghua again has the largest number of graduates (108) among China's political elites, much higher than the second largest, People's University (68). See *Zhongguo renming da cidian* (Who's who in China) (Beijing: Foreign Languages Press, 1994). Data were accumulated by the author.

68. Qinghua xiaoyou tongxun (Newsletter of Qinghua alumni) 27 (April 1993): 8.

69. Shen, *Zhonggong di shiwujie zhongyang weiyuanhui zhongyang jilü jiancha weiyuanhui weiyuan minglu.* The data were accumulated by the author.

70. *Jiang nanxiang jinian wenji,* 148–151.

71. Ren Zhichu, *Hu Jintao: Zhongguo kuashiji jiebanren* (Hu Jintao: China's first man in the twenty-first century) (Hong Kong: Mirror Books, 1997), 57.

72. See Qinghua Shanghai xiaoyou tongxun lu (address book of Qinghua alumni in

Shanghai), 1986, and Qinghua daxue Guangzhou diqu xiaoyou tongxun lu (address book of Qinghua alumni in the Guangzhou area), April 1988.

73.  They were Zhu Rongji (mayor and Party secretary), Huang Ju (executive vice mayor and deputy Party secretary), Wu Bangguo (deputy Party secretary), and Yi Tianzeng (vice mayor).

74.  On the Internet at the following address: http://www.tsinghua.edu.cn. Last accessed on 15 May 2000.

75.  *Shijie ribao*, 9 February 2000, A9.

76.  Ibid.

77.  http://www.tsinghua.edu.cn/docse/qhdxjk. Last accessed on 2 September 2000.

78.  In 1998, for example, 379 (15.4 percent) Qinghua undergraduates continued their graduate study abroad. *Shijie ribao*, 23 April 1999, A9.

79.  Qinghua reinstated the Law Department in 1995. *Shijie ribao*, 26 April 1999, A8.

80.  Ren, *Hu Jintao: Zhongguo kuashiji jiebanren*, 16; and Yang Zhongmei, *Zhonggong kuashiji jiebanren: Hu Jintao* (Hu Jintao: The cross-century successor of China) (Taibei: Shibao chubanshe, 1999), 144–156.

81.  For a detailed discussion of Hu's family origin, see Ren, *Hu Jintao*, 31–44.

82.  According to some sources, Hu was born in Shanghai and then moved to Taizhou. See Ren, *Hu Jintao*, 38–39. In the official biography of Hu Jintao, his birthplace is Jixi, Anhui. In China it is not unusual for people to use their ancestral home (*zuji*) as their home town (*jiguan*).

83.  This discussion is based on interviews and Ren, *Hu Jintao*.

84.  Lie Xing, "Zhonggong disidai hexi daremen Hu Jintao" (Hu Jintao: A front-runner of the fourth generation of leaders), in *Zhong gong disidai mengren* (The fourth generation of leaders of the CCP), ed. Xiao Chong (Hong Kong: Xiafeier guoji chubangongsi, 1998), 7–17.

85.  Ren, *Hu Jintao*, 152, 247. For a list of Hu Jintao's friends, see Yang, *Zhonggong kuashiji jiebanren*, 192–193.

86.  Ren, *Hu Jintao*, 152.

87.  Yang, *Zhonggong kuashiji jiebanren*, 183.

88.  Hu reportedly has had problems with members of *taizi* in the fourth generation leadership. For example, he did not get along well with He Guangwei, a *taizi*, when both worked in the secretariat of the CCYL. However, Hu's association with Zhang Hong, Deng's son-in-law, who came from the same hometown, may have helped Hu obtain a seat on the Standing Committee of the Politburo. Yang, *Zhonggong kuashiji jiebanren*, 111, 164.

89.  The on-line database of *People's Daily* includes these four speeches. See http://www.peopledaily.com.cn/item/ldhd/hujint/2000/huiyi.html. Last accessed 12 May 2000.

90.  *Renmin ribao*, 30 October 1999, 1.

91.  *Renmin ribao*, 25 October 1999, 1.

92.  This term is from "Hu Jintao: Communist Party 'Golden Boy,'" *Agence France Presse*, 15 March 1998.

93.  *Economist*, 26 December 1992, 20.

# 5

~

# *Taizi* and *Mishu:*
# Informal Networks and
# Institutional Restraints

It's easier to climb to the penthouse from the fiftieth floor than from the basement.

—Ronald Brownstein

China's new leaders have advanced their political careers not only through administrative channels and educational credentials but also through personal networks or connections *(guanxi)*. The case study of Qinghua University presented in chapter 4 shows the important role that school ties played in the promotion of the fourth generation of leaders. School networks are not the only form of nepotism in elite recruitment during the reform era. In addition to school ties, blood ties, such as having a parent who is a high-ranking official (these children are called princelings, *taizi* or *taizidang* in Chinese) or being chosen to serve a senior leader as *mishu* (personal secretary) are currently two other major informal channels for the career advancement of leaders, including technocrats.

Nepotism and patron–client relations are not new in PRC history. *Taizi* and *mishu* were also prevalent among the third generation of leaders. Studies of the Thirteenth and Fourteenth Party Congresses show that many third generation leaders were children of high-ranking officials and/or protégés of veteran patrons.[1] Jiang Zemin and Li Peng, the two top leaders, both came from the families of Communist martyrs; their deceased fathers' comrades in arms were surely helpful to their political careers.

It is also not new in the PRC that the post of *mishu* has served as a stepping-stone for political elites. Song Ping, standing member of the Politburo in the 1980s, was Zhou Enlai's *mishu* in the late 1940s. Hu Qiaomu, also a member of the Politburo in the 1980s, served as Mao's *mishu* in the 1940s. During the Cultural Revolution, Chen Boda, a veteran Communist theoretician and standing member of the Politburo, also served as Mao's *mishu* earlier in his career. Chen Xitong, Party secretary of Beijing before being purged in the mid-1990s, started his political career as *mishu* for Beijing municipal leaders in the 1950s. Another example is Wang Ruilin, currently deputy director of the General Political Department of the PLA. Wang served as Deng Xiaoping's *mishu* for over three decades prior to serving in his current post.

The advantage of family background and work association with senior leaders is certainly not unique to the elite formation in China. Nepotism and favoritism are also widespread in democratic countries. India, for example, was led by "three generations of Nehrus" during the most part of the twentieth century—India's first prime minister, Jawaharlal Nehru, his daughter Indira, and her son Rajiv.[2] In Japan, according to a recent study conducted by Gerald Curtis, "between 40 and 50 percent of the incumbent Diet members in the ruling Liberal Democratic Party are the sons or sons-in-law of former Diet members."[3] In predemocratic Taiwan, the island was ruled by two Chiangs, father and son, for about four decades. Two leading contenders in the ruling party for the 2000 presidential election before the party split, Lian Chan, vice president of Taiwan, and Soong Ch'u-yu (James Soong), former secretary-general of the Nationalist Party, are both from high-ranking official families. Lian's father, Lian Chen-tung, was an adviser to the president, and Soong's father, Soong Ta, was a prominent army general. Soong Ch'u-yu also served as President Chiang Ching-kuo's *mishu*, as did Ma Ying-jeou, now mayor of Taibei and another rising political star in Taiwan.[4]

Princelings and spouses of political leaders dominate the 2000 elections in the United States too, although Americans often criticize the "Byzantine network of family ties" in third world countries.[5] The presidential race between Al Gore, the son of a senator, and George W. Bush, the son of a president who was himself the son of a senator, as Ronald Brownstein observed, "speaks volumes about the enduring power of pedigree."[6] All these examples echo Robert Putnam's argument that "achievement and ascription are blended in almost every elite recruitment system, from Confucian China to contemporary America, and some credentials, such as formal education, seem in themselves to link inheritance and performance inextricably."[7]

In China nepotism and favoritism in elite recruitment have become prevalent at a time when educational criteria and technical expertise are more important than class background and revolutionary experience. There are two seemingly contradictory developments that highlight both the persistence of and the resistance to *taizi* and *mishu* in the third and fourth generations of PRC leaders. According to a survey on the children of more than 1,700 PRC central and provincial leaders conducted in the early 1990s, about 3,100 hold official positions above the government bureau or military division level. Another 900 are the principal leaders of large and middle-sized state enterprises.[8] During the 1980s, a large number of *taizi* seized the medium-level leadership posts (both civilian and military) in China as part of the compensation for the retirement of their parents. This study also shows that a significant portion of the fourth generation of leaders come from high-ranking cadre families and/or have served as *mishu* in their careers.

But this does not mean that nepotism and favoritism can go without opposition in today's China. Paradoxically, public resistance to, and the institutional restraints on, *taizi*, *mishu*, and other personal networks have been stronger than ever during the past few years. Deputies in both the Party congress and the National People's Congress regularly have used their votes to prevent some well-known *taizi* and *mishu* from being elected to the Central Committee of the CCP or posts in the central and provincial governments. The same phenomenon can be found in many Party congresses and people's congresses at the provincial level or below. These recent developments reflect the growing tension between nepotism in elite recruitment and the call for a more representative government, and certainly deserve more scholarly attention.

## TAIZI IN THE NEW LEADERSHIP: ORIGINS AND CHARACTERISTICS

The prevalence of *taizi* in the fourth generation leadership reflects the deficiency of Chinese political institutions and is caused by two situational factors. First, as discussed in previous chapters, during the Deng era, China was ruled mainly by elderly revolutionary veterans who, like Deng, resumed their leadership posts after the Cultural Revolution. Those who had advanced their careers during CR were largely demoted or even purged. Although those Long March veterans were already in their late sixties and early seventies in the early years of the reform era, they were hesitant to give up the leadership posts that they had just taken back from the so-called Cultural Revolution beneficiaries.

But Communist veteran leaders also understood that it was just a matter of years until they would have to pass on the baton of power to young leaders because many of them were in failing health in the 1980s. As a result, it became a common practice for veteran leaders to retire with the "compensation" of having their children appointed to leadership posts. Understandably, old revolutionaries felt no one was more politically trustworthy than *taizi*. What had happened in the former Soviet Union and other East European countries in the late 1980s and early 1990s, in Chinese leaders' view, would not be repeated in China if Communist veteran leaders passed the batons to their children. Besides, elderly leaders could continue their privileged lifestyles if their children succeeded them in official positions. In fact, official status has become particularly important over the past decade because political power can often lead to tremendous economic wealth as official corruption becomes rampant.

The second situational factor is that the princelings' advantages began literally at birth. They were "born red," a large number of them being born during the 1940s and the 1950s as their parents' generation won the victories of the Anti-Japanese War and the Civil War and became the new rulers under the Communist regime. These princelings grew up under the "red flag of the PRC" and usually received the best education available for becoming "red engineers" prior to the Cultural Revolution. A couple of decades later, educational credentials, especially professional backgrounds as engineers, have become an important criterion for elite recruitment in the reform era. Meanwhile, these princelings usually grew up in the Communist inner circle and learned a great deal about political survival in an authoritarian system. Thus they understood power politics from an early age. It is no coincidence that many of the princelings received their high-level leadership posts at a remarkably young age.

### Formation of Informal Networks of Taizidang

In China, children of high-ranking officials are usually called taizidang (the party of princes) instead of taizi. This can be misleading in English translation because those who are princelings do not necessarily form a monolithic organization or a formal network. Although they have a shared political identity, the political interests of members of taizi are not always identical. They often have to fight each other for power and wealth. As a result, children of high-ranking officials usually form various factions of taizidang and informal political networks.

### Family Ties

In their breakthrough study of princelings, He Pin and Gao Xin observed that there are seven major taizidang, which are largely based on the families of individual senior leaders. They are the Ye Jianying family headed by Ye Xuanning, the Hu Yaobang family headed by Hu Deping, the Deng Xiaoping family headed by Deng Pufang, the Wang Zhen family headed by Wang Jun, the Chen Yun family headed by Chen Yuan, the Tao Zhu family headed by Tao Shiliang, and the Yang Shangkun family headed by Yang Shaoming.[9] Family ties are clearly the most important basis for the formation of taizidang, but some family-based factions are far more powerful than others. The Tao Zhu family headed by Tao Shiliang does not have much political influence or real power. The Hu Yaobang family and the Yang Shangkun family no longer enjoy the kind of tremendous political power that they used to have before they lost Deng Xiaoping's support.

The study by He and Gao provides detailed information about how children of high-ranking officials carved up power vacancies that developed because their fathers, Communist veterans, were about to retire. These taizidang sometimes mutually used one another and sometimes fought against each other. The children of the Deng family and the Chen family, for example, hardly ever contacted each other. The Deng family and the Yang family used to be very close, especially during the 1989 Tiananmen crisis, but grew apart when the Yang family lost the power struggle in the early 1990s.[10]

But *taizi* and their parents have been seriously concerned about how to maintain their political power during a time of rapid changes in Chinese society. It was reported in the Hong Kong media that prior to the Fourteenth Party Congress in 1992, several princelings who were born in the 1940s (e.g., Chen Yuan and Yu Zhengsheng) were on the ballot for membership in the Central Committee, but not one of them was elected.[11] Consequently, many veteran leaders and princelings made greater efforts to seize leadership posts. Bo Yibo, who was in charge of the personnel affairs of the Fourteenth Party Congress, did not hide his disappointment with the result of the election. He proposed that each senior-ranking revolutionary veteran (e.g., Politburo members, state leaders, and PLA marshals) could have one child promoted to a high-ranking official post (vice provincial governor, vice minister level, or above).[12]

The fourth generation of leaders listed on table 5.1 seems to echo what Bo proposed. Sons of senior-ranking revolutionary veterans (e.g., Deng Xiaoping, Chen Yun, Bo Yibo, Yao Yilin, Hu Yaobang, Peng Zhen, Wan Li, Li Xiannian, Liao Chengzhi, Chen Yi, Li Weihan, Lin Boqu, and Xi Zhongxun) all hold high-ranking official positions in the Party or the government. Deng Xiaoping's family, as Bo Yibo proposed, could have two children in high-ranking official posts because Deng Pufang, who heads the Chinese Federation for the Disabled, was unusual. Therefore, Deng Nan, Deng Xiaoping's daughter, was also appointed as vice minister of the Science and Technology Commission.[13]

A number of *taizi* hold important posts in the military. Many of them have the military rank of major general or above (see table 5.1). He Pengfei, He Long's son, is now vice commander of the PLA navy, and Dong Liangju, Dong Biwu's son, is general director of the General Office of the powerful Central Military Commission of the CCP. He Ping, Deng's son-in-law, is in charge of the PLA's Armament Department. Because of the conventions of the PLA, *taizi* usually could advance more quickly in the military than in the Party or governmental hierarchies.

The CCP Organization Department may have set a quota for the "family representation of *taizi*" in political and military leadership, but high-ranking official families are not limited as to the number of *taizi* who participate in corporate firms. Actually, many high-ranking official families have created an "internal division of labor" for *taizi* within the family—one member pursues a political or military career while others serve as CEOs or general managers of large corporate firms, including joint ventures and private enterprises (see table 5.1). For example, in the late 1980s, three children of Bo Yibo served as governmental officials: Bo Xiyong was vice president of China's Association of the Auto Industry, Bo Xilai was vice mayor of Dalian, and Bo Xicheng was director of the Tourism Bureau of the Beijing municipal government. Following Bo Yibo's "one high-ranking official fam-

**Table 5.1    Some Members of the Fourth Generation of Leaders Having High-Ranking Cadre Family Background**

| Name | Current Position | Family Background |
|---|---|---|
| Party and Government | | |
| Deng Pufang | CC alternate, president, Chinese Federation for the Disabled | Father: Deng Xiaoping, fmr. secretary-general CCP |
| Deng Nan | Vice minister, Science and Technology | Father: Deng Xiaoping (see above) |
| Chen Yuan | President, State Development Bank | Father: Chen Yun, fmr. Politburo standing member |
| Xi Jinping | CC alternate, acting governor of Fujian | Father: Xi Zhongxun, fmr. Politburo member |
| Bo Xilai | Mayor of Dalian | Father: Bo Yibo, fmr. Politburo member |
| Yao Mingwei | Deputy director, State Machine-Building Industry Bureau, State Council | Father: Yao Yilin, fmr. Politburo standing member |
| Hu Deping | Vice chair, All-China Federation of Industry & Commerce | Father: Hu Yaobang, fmr. secretary-general of CCP |
| Fu Rui | Vice president, China National Nuclear Corporation | Father: Peng Zhen, fmr. chair of NPC |
| Wan Jifei | Deputy director, Economic Reconstructing | Father: Wan Li, fmr. chair of NPC |
| Li Xiaolin | Vice president, China Friendship Association | Father: Li Xiannian, fmr. president of the PRC |
| Liao Hui | CC Member, director, Hong Kong and Macao Affairs Office, State Council | Father: Liao Chengzhi, fmr. vice chair of NPC |
| Chen Haosu | Vice president, China Friendship Association | Father: Chen Yi, marshal, fmr. Politburo member |
| Li Tielin | Vice head, CCP Organization Department | Father: Li Weihan, Communist veteran leader |
| Lin Yongsan | Vice minister of Labor and Social Security | Father: Lin Boqu, fmr. vice chair, NPC |
| He Guangwei | Director, China National Tourism Administration, State Council | Father: He Changgong, Communist veteran leader |
| Zhou Xiaochuan | President, China Construction Bank | Father: Zhou Jiannan: fmr. minister, Construction |
| Military | | |
| He Pengfei | Vice admiral, vice commander, navy | Father: He Long, marshal, fmr. Politburo member |

*continued*

**Table 5.1   Continued**

| Name | Current Position | Family Background |
|---|---|---|
| Dong Liangju | Lt. general, director, General Office Central Military Commission | Father: Dong Biwu, fmr. vice president of PRC |
| Ye Xuanning | Lt. general, director, Liaison Department of the PLA General Political Department | Father: Ye Jianying, fmr. PLA marshal |
| He Ping | Major general, director, Armament Dept. | Father-in-law: Deng Xiaoping, (see above) |
| Tan Dongsheng | Major general, deputy commander, Guangzhou Military Region | Father: Tan Zhenlin, fmr. Politburo member |
| Su Rongsheng | Major general, commander of PLA's No. 24 Group Army | Father: Su Yu, fmr. PLA general |
| Qin Tian | Major general, deputy commander of army | Father: Qin Jiwei, fmr. Politburo member |
| Zhang Xiang | Major general, deputy chief of staff | Father: Zhang Aiping, fmr. minister of Defense |
| Wang Suming | Major general, deputy director, Bodyguards Bureau | Father: Wang Zheng, fmr. deputy chief of staff |
| Liu Yuan | Major general, political commissar Hydropower Control Department, PLA | Father: Liu Shaoqi, fmr. president of PRC |
| Corporate | | |
| Wang Jun | China International Trust & Investment Co. | Father: Wang Zhen, fmr. vice president, PRC |
| Rong Zhijian | President, CITIC Securities Corporation Ltd. | Father: Rong Yiren, fmr. vice president, PRC |
| Kong Dan | President, China Everbright International Trust and Investment Corporation | Father: Kong Yuan, fmr. head, CCP Investigation Department |
| Song Kehuan | CEO, Beijing Landmark Ltd. | Father: Song Renqiong, fmr. Politburo member |
| Deng Zhifang | CEO, Shifang Group Ltd. | Father: Deng Xiaoping (see above) |
| Chen Weili | CEO, China Venturetech Investment Corp. | Father: Chen Yun (see above) |
| Bo Xicheng | Chair, board of directors, Beijing Liuhe Hotel | Father: Bo Yibo (see above) |

*continued*

Table 5.1    Continued

| Name | Current Position | Family Background |
| --- | --- | --- |
| Fu Yan | Chair, board of directors, Beijing Fuli Ltd. | Father: Peng Zhen (see above) |
| Wang Xiaochao | General manager, Poly Group Ltd. | Father-in-law: Yang Shangkun, fmr. PRC president |

Source: Liao and Fan, *Zhongguo renming da cidian*, (1994); Shen, *Zhonggong di shiwujie zhongyang weiyuanhui zhongyang jilü jiancha weiyuanhui weiyuan minglu*; He Pin and Gao Xin, *Zhonggong "Taizidang"* (China's communist "princelings") (Taibei: Shih-pao Ch'u-pan Kung-ssu, 1992); and *China Directory 1999*. (Tokyo: Radiopress, 1999).

Note: The data were tabulated by the author.

ily, one official seat for its offspring" proposal, Bo Xiyong and Bo Xicheng quit their government posts and began business careers. Bo Xilai has become the sole candidate for political power from the Bo family. Similarly, the Deng family, the Chen Yun family, the Peng Zhen family, the Ye Jianying family, and the Yang Shangkun family have all developed their own "internal division of labor."

Some princelings, however, have multiple identities. They are simultaneously CEOs of business firms, officials of the Party/government, and officers of the PLA. They have frequently moved into business, government, the military, or the intelligence community. For example, Wang Jun simultaneously held the posts of chair of the China International Trust and Investment Corporation (CITIC), China's largest investment firm, and chair of the China Poly Group, the largest and most profitable PLA company before the "decommercialization" of China's army.[14] Similarly, Wang Xiaochao (Yang Shangkun's son-in-law) holds both military and civilian leadership positions. Ye Xuanning (Ye Jianying's son), director of the Liaison Department of the PLA General Political Department, is also the CEO of the Carrier Group, the army-run company that has primarily been engaged in sales and purchases of armaments overseas.[15] Interestingly, Ye Xuanning has another name, Yue Feng, the name he used as a member of the Chinese People's Political Consultative Conference. Because of his firm's involvement in arms sales and military intelligence, Ye Xuanning has become an important figure in Chinese politics. Jiang Zemin, Li Ruihuan, and other top leaders called him "boss" *(laoban)*. As a result of his power and influence, many *taizi* called Ye the "spiritual leader of the new generation of *taizidang*."[16]

In addition to family ties, three other forms of affiliation serve as major channels for the formation and political association of *taizidang*: attending the same school, working for the same business firms, or marrying into one of the high-ranking cadre families. Outsiders and children of lower levels of cadres often have to attach themselves to these *taizidang* bigwigs in order to advance their political careers. A brief review of these three forms of affiliation reveals how informal networks of *taizi* are established.

*School Affiliation*

When Communists entered Beijing after the 1949 revolution, they immediately set up (or in some cases strengthened) special elite schools at all levels—elementary school, high school, and university—primarily for children of high-ranking officials. The Yuecai Elementary School, which originated from the School for Children of Cadres in Yan'an during the mid-1940s, became an elite school that mainly admitted children of civilian cadres above the level of bureau heads. The Bayi Elementary School, which was originally based on the Rongzhen School of the Beijing Military Region, turned into a school that exclusively admitted children of military officers above the division commander level (*shiji*).[17] Many of these children's families often lived in the same residential compounds; Zhongnanhai, for instance, was the residential compound for top leaders. The other important residential compounds include the compound for senior officers of the PLA air force, and the compound for senior officers of the Beijing Military Region. The offspring of high-ranking officials made friends in the same residential compounds during their childhood years and have maintained these bonds ever since. Many childhood friends and/or former classmates later formed informal political networks during the post-Mao era. The study by He Pin and Cao Xin shows that a large number of Deng Pufang's classmates in the Bayi Elementary School actually worked under Deng Pufang in the 1980s. These former classmates advanced their political careers partially because of the connection established during their early school years.[18]

Another example is the Beijing No. 4 Boys High School, one of the best high schools in the country and the one attended by a large number of children of PRC top leaders during the 1950s and the early 1960s. For instance, Chen Yuan, Bo Xiyong, Bo Xicheng, He Pengfei, Liu Yuan, Fu Rui, Lin Yongsan, Yang Shaoming, and Qiao Zhonghuai (Qiao Guanhua's son) all attended the Beijing No. 4 Boys High School. Bo Xicheng once recalled that in his class, thirteen out of forty-five students were children of high-ranking officials.[19]

A majority of these princelings continued their college education at elite universities, such as the Harbin Military Institute of Engineering or Qinghua University. The Harbin Military Institute of Engineering was established in 1953, a few years after the PRC was founded. Chen Geng, a PLA general and the first president of the institute, planned to turn the institute into the largest military academy in the Far East and a cradle of China's top military officers suitable for modern high-tech warfare. Not surprisingly, children of high-ranking officials were a major source of students for this elite military academy. Each year, the institute recruited a certain number of high school graduates who did not need to take regular national entrance exams for higher education. This policy allowed many princelings, especially those who might not be able to pass national exams, to enter this elite university. Mao Yuanxin (Mao's nephew), Chen Danhuai (Chen Yi's son), Wang Zhi (Wang Zhen's son), Zuo Taibei (Peng Dehuai's adopted daughter), Fu Ping (Peng Zhen's son), Su Rongsheng (Su Yu's son), Jiang Zhuping (Jiang Nanxiang's son), Liao Hui (Liao Chengzhi's son), Dai Qing (Ye Jianying's adopted daughter), and Lin Yongsan (Lin Boqu's son) all attended the institute, usually majoring in the technology of ballistic missiles.[20] The Harbin Military Institute of Engineering was called by some the "base of *taizijun*" (the army of the princelings).[21] Some of them indeed hold important military posts at present; for example, Su Rongsheng is commander of PLA's Twenty-Fourth Group Army.

Meanwhile, many other princelings, including Chen Yuan, Bo Xiyong, He Pengfei, Qiao Zhonghuai, Fu Rui, Li Tielin, Liu Tao (Liu Shaoqi's daughter), Lin Doudou (Lin Biao's daughter), Lin Yanzhi, and Liu Hu (Hu Yaobang's second son), attended Qinghua University, China's most prestigious civilian engineering schools, prior to the beginning of the Cultural Revolution.

The shared sense of superiority in terms of revolutionary family backgrounds actually led these princelings to organize informal political networks even during their school years. For example, during the beginning of the Cultural Revolution, those who were in elite high schools, such as the Beijing No. 4 Boys High School and the Beijing No. 101 School, formed the United Action Committee of the Red Guards in the Capital (*liandong*). This organization, almost exclusively composed of children of high-ranking officials, was one of the most radical Red Guard factions in the country. It not only advocated the use of violence and "red terror"[22] but also tortured and murdered numerous innocent people in Beijing and many other cities at the beginning of the Cultural Revolution. Some members of the *liandong*, as shown in the following pages, have reemerged as prominent members of the fourth generation of leaders.

*Corporate Affiliation*

Some of the school ties that existed prior to the Cultural Revolution have extended to business connections during the reform era. Probably the best example is the Kanghua Development Corporation, which was founded by Deng Pufang in 1984. Many members of *taizi*, including some of Deng Pufang's classmates in elementary school and high school, joined the Kanghua, which was supposed to be a business firm run by and for China's disabled people. At its peak, the Kanghua was believed to include over 200 members of *taizidang* as its managers and representatives.[23] Various provincial branches of the Kanghua were often headed by the *taizi* of provincial top leaders. The high profile of the Kanghua could also be seen from the composition of its management team. In 1987, Tang Ke, former minister of petroleum industry, served as chair of the Kanghua's board of directors, Gao Yangwen, former minister of coal industry, served as vice chair of the board;

and Han Boping, former executive vice mayor of Beijing, served as general manager of the Kanghua. The appointments of these high-profile cadres to the management team of the Kanghua suggest the powerful political connections of this particular corporation.

Some *taizi* in the Kanghua later moved up to higher leadership posts. For example, Lin Yongsan, son of Lin Boqu, later served as vice governor of Inner Mongolia and now is vice minister of labor and social security. Liu Jing, another member of the *taizi*, later served as vice governor of Yunnan and now is deputy director of General Administration of Customs under the State Council. Deng Pufang also recruited Yu Zhengsheng (whose brother was Deng Pufang's elementary school classmate) to administer daily affairs of both the Kanghua and the China Welfare Fund for Handicapped. Yu is now minister of construction and a member of the Central Committee of the CCP.

During the 1980s, when China accelerated its market reform by adopting some new economic incentives such as joint ventures, a stock market, and land lease to foreigners, many members of *taizidang* rushed to the business sector in order to make huge personal gains. For *taizi*, one of the quickest ways to make a fortune was to take advantage of the two-track pricing system, which allowed these well-connected *taizi* to buy raw materials or commodities at a fixed price and then sell them on the private market, thus reaping huge profits. In addition, corrupt officials and *taizi* made fortunes by issuing certificates, business permits, tax breaks, land leases, and quotas.[24] It came as no surprise when the State Council had to issue an order in 1988 to dismantle the Kanghua Development Corporation because of its rampant corruption and other illegal business activities.

The Kanghua was not the only business firm through which *taizi* made huge fortunes and/or advanced their political careers. Two other large corporations in the country, CITIC and the China Everbright Group, Ltd., have also been headed by *taizi*. For example, Kong Dan, president of the China Everbright International Trust and Investment Corporation, is a son of Kong Yuan, former head of the CCP Investigation Department. Wang Jun, son of Wang Zhen, controls CITIC while his two brothers run two other large state-backed business firms. With the political power of their families and the economic resources that they now control, informal political networks of princelings, such as the ones based in the Wang family and the Deng family, have become a new formidable force of bureaucratic capitalists in the country.

*Career Advancement through Marriage*

Intermarriage among high-ranking cadre families (*gaogan lianyin*) is the third major channel of the formation of *taizidang*. Table 5.2 provides some examples of the marriages between children of high-ranking officials. Intermarriage among high-ranking cadre families was common during the 1950s and the early 1960s. Many PLA marshals and generals like Chen Yi, He Long, Ye Jianying, and Su Yu often encouraged their children to marry people with similar family backgrounds. Chen Yi's son, Chen Xiaolu, for example, married Su Yu's daughter, Su Huining. Chen Xiaolu is now president of the Beijing Standard International Investment Corporation and his wife serves in the PLA's Second Artillery Corps.

Hu Yaobang was often praised for the integrity of his family at the time of rampant official corruption. Though his children have never engaged in business activities, his elder son married An Li, daughter of An Ziwen, former director of the CCP Organization Department, Hu Yaobang's predecessor. His second son married a daughter of the vice minister of foreign affairs. These marriages do not necessarily suggest nepotism or any wrongdoing. The Hu family, however, clearly used its power and influence to advance An Li's political career. After graduating from Qinghua University, An Li worked as an assistant instructor at Beijing Normal University. In 1984, the CCP Organization Department recruited her directly into the Party and then almost immediately transferred her to the position of vice mayor of Xiamen, a major city in Fujian, which has the status of a special economic zone. During the student protest movement in 1985, the student representatives from Beijing Normal University used this case to criticize the nepotism practiced by Hu Yaobang, then the secretary general of the CCP. The Central Commission for Discipline Inspection led by Hu's political rival, Bo Yibo, investigated this case and removed An Li from her post in Xiamen.[25]

Political advancement through *marriage among* high-ranking official families or through *marriage into* high-ranking official families has continued to be an important channel for elite recruitment during the 1990s. It has become a norm in the PLA that a junior officer who marries a senior officer's daughter can be promoted very quickly. In both the military and civilian leaderships, a number of sons-in-law of prominent political leaders have quickly risen to power in the post-Mao era. Some well-known examples are Zou Jiahua, vice chair of the NPC (son-in-law of Ye Jianying), Ding Henggao, standing member of the CPPCC (son-in-law of Nei Rongzhen), Dai Bingguo, head of CCP International Liaison Department (son-in-law of Huang Zhen), Pan Yue, deputy head of State Property Bureau of the State Council (son-in-law of Liu Huaqing), and Wang Guangya, vice minister of foreign affairs (son-in-law of Chen Yi).

The rapid rise of Deng Xiaoping's three sons-in-law, He Ping, Wu Jianchang and Zhang Hong, is particularly revealing. He Ping comes from a high-ranking official family while the other two are from nonofficial families. All of them married Deng's daughters during the Cultural Revolution. Soon after Deng Xiaoping returned to power in 1978, all three sons-in-law of the paramount leader changed their professional identities from technicians to governmental officials. He Ping serves as head of PLA's Armament Department, Wu Jianchang is concurrently deputy director of State Metallurgical Industry Bureau of the State Council and president of China's Nonferrous Metals Corporation. Zhang Hong is director of the Research and Development Bureau of the Chinese Academy of Sciences. In terms of official rank, He Ping and Wu Jianchang are now minister-level leaders

**Table 5.2  Intermarriage among *Taizi***

| Names (Couple) | Current Position | Father's Name | Father's Position |
|---|---|---|---|
| Hu Deping & | Vice chair, All-China Federation of Industry & Commerce | Hu Yaobang | Former secretary-general of the CCP |
| An Li | Former mayor of Ximen | An Ziwen | Former head of CCP Organization Dept. |
| Liu Hu & | Director, Dept. of Scientific & Technological Development, Ministry of Foreign Trade and Economic Cooperation | Hu Yaobang | Former secretary-general of the CCP |
| Wang Yangzi | — | Wang Youping | Former vice minister of Foreign Affairs |
| He Ping & | Director, Armament Dept., PLA General Staff Headquarters | He Biao | Former member of Central Advisory Committee of the CCP |
| Deng Rong | Vice president, China Association for Int'l Friendly Contacts | Deng Xiaoping | Former secretary-general of the CCP |
| He Pengfei & | Deputy commander, PLA navy | He Long | Former PLA marshal |
| Feng Lu | Director, Taiwan Dept., Office of Overseas Chinese Affairs | Feng Jiping | Former vice mayor of Beijing |
| Ye Xuanping & | Vice chair, Chinese People's Political Consultative Com. | Ye Jianying | Former PLA marshal |
| Wu Xiaolan | Vice chair, Shenzhen People's Congress | Wu Yuzhang | CCP veteran leader |
| Zou Jiahua & | Former vice premier | Zou Taofen | CCP veteran martyr |
| Ye Zhumei | Former vice chair, Commission of Science, Technology, and Industry for National Defense | Ye Jianying | Former PLA marshal |
| Chen Xiaolu & | President of the Beijing Standard Int'l. Investment Corp. | Chen Yi | Former PLA marshal and minister of Foreign Affairs |
| Su Huining | PLA senior officer, Second Artillery Corps | Su Yu | PLA veteran general |
| Yu Zhengsheng & | Minister of Construction | Huang Jing | Former mayor of Tianjin |
| Zhang Zhikai | Former chair, Economic Commission of Yantai | Zhang Aiping | Former minister of Defense |
| Bo Xiyong & | Former vice chair of China's Auto Industry | Bo Yibo | CCP veteran leader |
| Zhang Yu | | | Former vice commander of Beijing Military Region |
| Wang Xiaochao & | General manager, the Poly Co., PLA chief-of-staff | | CCP veteran leader |
| Yang Li | Assistant president, China Association for Int'l Friendly Contacts | Yang Shangkun | Former president of the PRC |

*Source*: He Pin and Gao Xin, *Zhonggong "Taizidang"* ("China's Communist "princelings""), (rev. ed.) (Taibei: Shibao chubanshe, 1999). The data were tabulated by the author.

*Note*: Wu Yuzhang is grandfather of Wu Xiaolan.

and Zhang Hong is also a bureau-level cadre. He Ping is responsible for China's weaponry business, Wu Jianchang is in charge of China's gold business in the world market, and Zhang Hong handles matters concerning China's high technology. It is not surprising that Hong Kong media reported that Deng's sons-in-law manage the "three most lucrative businesses in the country."[26]

Over a half century ago, Chinese Communists claimed that their 1949 revolution destroyed the so-called Four Big Families *(sidajiazu)*, the wealthiest bureaucratic-capitalist families in the country, and liberated millions of poor, jobless, and homeless people. Ironically, the Four New Big Families, which refers to the families of Deng Xiaoping, Wang Zhen, Rong Yiren, and Chen Yun, seem to be far wealthier now than the old ones in the Nationalist government a half century ago. Meanwhile, China's unemployment has risen to its highest level since the founding of the PRC in 1949.[27]

### Comparing the Third and Fourth Generations of *Taizi*

Cross-generational comparisons are useful in assessing the distinctive characteristics of *taizi* in the fourth generation of leaders. The prevalence of *taizi* is common phenomenon among both the third and fourth generations of leaders. Yet there are some important differences between these two generations of *taizi*. Table 5.3, based on the two study pools used in chapter 3, lists some of the most prominent *taizi* in the third and fourth generation leadership. The fourth generation of *taizi* differs profoundly from the third generation in terms of revolutionary background, work experience, and current power status. The fourth generation leaders usually cannot depend on their own political credentials and are politically less secure than *taizi* in the previous generation.

*Orphans of Communist Martyrs versus Privileged Children of the PRC Rulers*

A number of distinguished members of *taizi* in the third generation leadership are the orphans of Communist martyrs. For example, Jiang Zemin, Li Peng, Zou Jiahua (former vice premier and currently vice chair of the NPC), and Guo Shuyan (vice chair of the State Planning Commission) all lost their fathers during the Communist revolution when they were young boys. In addition, Jiang, Zou, and Li all participated in the Communist revolution themselves. They all joined the CCP at a young age. Li Peng, for example, joined the Party when he was only seventeen years old.

In contrast, *taizi* in the fourth generation leadership cannot claim much revolutionary experience or political credentials from the early years of their careers. Partly because of their privileged family backgrounds in the newly established Communist regime, they usually attended elite high schools and key universities, as already noted. Unlike many third generation leaders who were educated in the

**Table 5.3** Comparison of the Third and Fourth Generations of Leaders Having High-Ranking Cadre Family Background

| Name | Born | CCP | Education | Position | Main Early Experience | Family Background |
|------|------|-----|-----------|----------|----------------------|-------------------|
| **3rd Generation** | | | | | | |
| Jiang Zemin | 1926 | 1946 | Jiaotong Univ. and Soviet Union | Secretary-general | Factory/research administration | Uncle and Adoptive father: Jiang Shangqing, Communist martyr |
| Zou Jiahua | 1926 | 1945 | Soviet Union | Vice chair, NPC, former Politburo member | Factory/research administration | Father: Communist martyr, adoptive father: Ye Jianying, former chair, NPC |
| Li Peng | 1928 | 1945 | Soviet Union | Chair, NPC; Politburo standing member | Factory/bureau administration | Father: Communist martyr, adoptive father: Zhou Enlai, former premier |
| Ding Henggao | 1931 | 1953 | Soviet Union | Member, CPPCC, former minister of industry of national defense | Research administration | Father-in-law: Nie Rongzhen, former Politburo member |
| Guo Shuyan | 1935 | 1957 | Soviet Union | Vice chair, State Planning Commission | Research administration | Father: Guo Liusheng, Communist martyr |
| Li Tieying | 1936 | 1961 | Czechoslovakia | Member of Politburo | Research administration | Father: Li Weihan, former director of Dept. of United Front |
| Jiang Zhuping | 1937 | 1960 | Harbin Mil. Ins. of Engineering | Governor of Hubei | Missile research | Father: Jiang Nanxiang, former minister of education |

continued

Table 5.3  Comparison of the Third and Fourth Generations of Leaders Having High-Ranking Cadre Family Background

| Name | Born | CCP | Education | Position | Main Early Experience | Family Background |
|------|------|-----|-----------|----------|----------------------|-------------------|
| 4th Generation | | | | | | |
| Chen Haosu | 1942 | 1963 | China's Univ. of S&T | Vice president, China Friendship Assoc. former vice mayor of Beijing | CCYL, Beijing municipal gov't | Father: Chen Yi, former member of Politburo |
| He Pengfei | 1944 | 1965 | Qinghua Univ. | Deputy commander, navy | PLA | Father: He Long, former member of Politburo |
| Deng Pufang | 1944 | 1965 | Beijing Univ. | CC alternate, president, Chinese Federation for the Disabled | Chinese Federation for the Disabled | Father: Deng Xiaoping, former secretary-general of CCP |
| Chen Yuan | 1945 | 1975 | Qinghua Univ. & CASS | President, State Development Bank | Beijing municipal government | Father: Chen Yun, former standing member of Politburo |
| Liu Yandong | 1945 | 1964 | Qinghua Univ. | CC alternate, deputy head, United Front Dept. of CCP | CCYL | Father: Liu Ruilong, former vice minister of agriculture |

| | | | | | | |
|---|---|---|---|---|---|---|
| Yu Zhengsheng | 1945 | 1964 | Harbin Mil. Ins. of Engineering | CC member, minister of construction, former mayor of Qingdao | Qingdao municipal government | Father: Yu Qiwei (Huang Jing), former mayor of Tianjin |
| Wang Qishan | 1948 | 1983 | Northwestern Univ. | CC alternate, executive vice governor of Guangdong | Office under the State Council | Father-in-law: Yao Yiling, former member of Politburo |
| Bo Xilai | 1949 | 1980 | Beijing Univ. & CASS | Mayor of Dalian | General Office of Central Committee of CCP | Father: Bo Yibo, former member of Politburo |
| Xi Jinping | 1953 | 1974 | Qinghua Univ. | CC alternate, deputy Party secretary, acting governor of Fujian, former Party Secretary of Fuzhou | *Mishu* to Geng Biao, minister | Father: Xi Zhongxun, former member of Polibuto |

*Source:* Liao and Fan, *Zhongguo renming da cidian*, (1994); Shen, *Zhonggong di shiwujie zhongyang weiyuanhui zhongyang jilü jiancha weiyuanhui weiyuan minglu*; and He Pin and Gao Xin, *Zhonggong "Taizidang"* ("China's communist "princelings"") (Taibei: Shih-pao Ch'u-pan Kung-ssu, 1992). The data were tabulated by the author. CASS stands for Chinese Academy of Social Sciences.

Soviet Union, the fourth generation of leaders studied at home due to the deterioration of Sino-Soviet relations in the 1960s.

Some prominent members of the fourth generation leadership actually joined the CCP when they were in their thirties. For example, Bo Xilai joined the Party in 1980 when he was thirty-one. Wang Qishan, executive vice governor of Guangdong, joined the Party when he was thirty-five. Wang was born in Beijing in 1948 into the family of a professor at Qinghua University. During CR, Wang was sent to do manual labor in the countryside of Yan'an county, Shaanxi Province, where he met his future wife, the daughter of Yao Yilin, who later became vice premier and standing member of the Politburo. During his years in Shaanxi, Wang also worked in the Shaanxi Museum and studied history at China's Northwestern University. In 1982, soon after his father-in-law became vice premier under Deng Xiaoping, Wang was transferred to work for both the Research Center of Rural Development in the State Council and the Research Center of Rural Policies of the secretariat of the Central Committee of the CCP. Ironically, Wang, who was then not even a Party member, worked in these two supreme think tanks of the government and the Party. He joined the Party in 1983, and four years later he was named director of the Development Research Institute under the State Council.[28] In 1988, he joined other members of *taizidang* in establishing trust and investment corporations. He established China's Rural Development Trust and Investment Corp. A year later he became vice president of China's Construction Bank. In 1997, Zhu Rongji closed the investment firm that Wang established because of its poor management; it had 3 billion yuan in bad loans. Wang's case reaffirms that the lack of political achievements among the fourth generation leaders with *taizi* backgrounds prevents them from standing on their own.

Some princelings may have suffered during the CR when their fathers were labeled "capitalist roaders." This was certainly true in the case of Deng Pufang, who became disabled as a result of political persecution. The children of Bo Yibo were in jail for years during the CR. But their suffering was usually less severe than children of some other social groups (e.g., landlords, rightists, and capitalists). Some *taizi* were actually radical Red Guards of the CR. For example, Tan Lifu, son of revolutionary veteran Tan Zhenlin, was the man who invented the "blood theory," which claims that "the son of a revolutionary must be a revolutionary, and the son of a counterrevolutionary must be a bad egg." This theory caused a horrible "red terror" during the CR, nationwide political persecution of children from "bad class" family backgrounds (e.g., landlords, rich peasants, capitalists, rightists). But later Tan Lifu claimed to be a victim of the CR because he also suffered under the "Gang of Four." Now Tan is a bureau-level official in Beijing.[29] As a matter of fact, Bo Xilai was also an advocate of the blood theory and an active member of *liandong*, a brutal Red Guard organization.[30]

Another example is He Pengfei, who always identified himself as a victim of the CR. But during the beginning of the CR, he led his group of Red Guards at Qinghua University in brutally beating up many "class enemies" and their children.[31] Later, however, He Pengfei was also persecuted by Red Guards of other factions. Soon after the CR, He joined the PLA and entered the postgraduate program at the University of Science and Technology for National Defense, where he studied missile technology. After graduation, he worked as bureau-level officer in the PLA General Staff Headquarters. In 1984, he was appointed director of the Armament Department in the General Staff Headquarters. In 1988, after having served in the army for only about ten years, he became the youngest major general in the PLA.

Although He was appointed to his leadership post when his father passed away, a large number of *taizi* in the fourth generation leadership were promoted to high positions when their fathers or fathers-in-law were still alive. This was in a sharp contrast to the third generation of leaders with *taizi* backgrounds whose parents were often Communist martyrs. Deng Pufang, Chen Yuan, Wang Qishan, Bo Xilai, and Xi Jinping, for example, were all appointed to high-ranking official posts when their fathers or fathers-in-law were still alive and very powerful.

*"Step-by-Step" Promotion versus "Helicopter-Style" Elevation Taizi*

Third generation leaders usually had significant work experience at the grassroots level during their early careers and were promoted step-by-step to their current high leadership posts. For example, Jiang Zemin, Li Peng, and Zou Jiahua all worked as factory directors, bureau directors, and heads of research institutions for about two decades before being appointed to ministerial-level positions. In the case of Jiang Zemin, after he graduated from college in 1947, he worked as factory director and head of a research institution in Shanghai, Changchun, and Wuhan for twenty-seven years except for one year of study in the Soviet Union. He was first appointed to the vice minister–level position in 1982. Other third generation leaders with *taizi* background, such as Ding Henggao, Guo Shuyan, Li Tieying, and Jiang Zhuping, worked in the field of science and technology over a couple of decades.

In contrast, *taizi* in the fourth generation leadership usually did not have much administrative experience at the grassroots level. They often came to power through some form of shortcut, although some of them were sent to the countryside during CR; for example, Xi Jinping was sent to Yanchuan County, Shaanxi Province, where he worked as a farmer. But a few years later, he was selected to be a worker-peasant-soldier student at Qinghua University. After graduation, he immediately worked in the State Council, where he was *mishu* to his father's comrade in arms, Geng Biao, then minister of defense. Similarly, soon after graduating from college, Wang Qishan and Bo Xilai worked for the offices of the State Council and the Central Committee of the CCP, respectively. Serving as *mishu* in offices of the central government seems to have been a shortcut in career mobility for members of the fourth generation of leaders, and with their family connections, *taizi* seem to have used this shortcut most effectively.

The "helicopter style" of advancement also includes serving on the Central Committee of the CCYL or studying under well-known scholars in postgraduate programs. Chen Haosu and Liu Yandong, for example, worked at research institutions or factories for only a short period of time. Their political careers were mainly in the CCYL, where both served as secretaries of the Central Committee of the CCYL before receiving their vice minister-level appointments. Many *taizi* enrolled in some prestigious graduate programs after the Cultural Revolution. Both Chen Yuan and Bo Xilai attended the Chinese Academy of Social Sciences soon after China reestablished its postgraduate program in 1978. Chen Yuan majored in industrial economy under Ma Hong and Yu Guangyuan, two celebrated economists who were also close friends of Chen's father. Bo Xilai, who had not yet even finished his sophomore year at Beijing University, enrolled in the master's program in International Journalism at CASS. After graduation, Bo worked under the supervision of Du Runsheng, a leading expert of China's rural reform and a close friend of his father. These experiences seemed to add "expert credentials" to both Chen and Bo, as they were soon appointed to head a district in Beijing and a county in Liaoning Province, respectively.

The helicopter style of advancement has often elevated *taizi* to some crucial leadership posts that have a good chance for further career advancement. Table 5.3 also shows that Yu Zhengsheng, Bo Xilai, and Xi Jinping have served as either mayor or Party secretary of Qingdao, Dalian, and Fuzhou, cities whose economic planning is under direct supervision of the State Council (*danlieshi*) or cities with the status of special economic zones (*jingjitequ*). There are three main reasons why these princelings have become top municipal leaders of these cities. First, these are the coastal cities designated special economic zones, where economic growth rates are high and the future potential even greater. Municipal leaders, therefore, can receive credit for economic achievements in these rich coastal cities much more easily than those leaders who work in other cities. Second, top municipal leaders in these cities automatically receive the administrative rank of vice provincial governor or deputy provincial Party secretary. And third, these posts do not need approval from the provincial people's congress, unlike most posts of vice governor and deputy Party secretary at the provincial level.

*Solid Power Position versus Uncertain Political Status*

Princelings in the third generation leadership hold some of the most important posts in the center, including the two top posts in the country at present. But no *taizi* in the fourth generation leadership has been elected as a full member of the Politburo. This indicates that few *taizi* in the fourth generation of leaders have entered the circle of central power. Although some *taizi* in the fourth generation, for example, Wang Zhen's sons and Deng Xiaoping's sons-in-law, currently hold some of the most lucrative posts in the country, their political future is uncertain. Chen Haoshu, vice president of the Chinese People's Association for Friendship with Foreign Countries, and Deng Pufang, president of the Chinese Federation for the

Disabled, are largely ceremonial figures, and they do not hold much real power in the policy-making process. Chen Yuan, Yu Zhengsheng, and Xi Jinping certainly hold very important posts, but the overall presence of *taizi* in the top leadership is still limited. Many *taizi* in the fourth generation hold deputy positions in their respective organizations, such as vice governor, deputy head, and deputy commander. This is largely because deputy positions at the provincial and ministerial levels do not need to get confirmation from the NPC, as discussed earlier. The NPC often prevents the nominees by the CCP Organization Department with *taizi* backgrounds from being appointed. Furthermore, as will be elaborated later in this chapter, Chen, Yu, and Bo all experienced strong resistance and even public humiliation as they advanced to high leadership posts.

All these generational differences in terms of *taizi's* own political credentials are the main reasons for public resentment and institutional resistance toward the leaders of the fourth generation with *taizi* backgrounds. The princelings of the fourth generation usually have had a privileged life (though in some cases it was interrupted briefly during the first few years of the CR). Because of this privileged life, they are less secure than leaders of the third generation, who could stand on their own. The weaknesses in terms of political credentials and grassroots-level leadership experience further undermine their chances of reaching the top position of political power. Before discussing the institutional opposition to, and public resentment against, *taizi*, we will look at the *mishu* as another informal channel for political career advancement among the fourth generation of leaders.

## MISHU IN THE NEW LEADERSHIP: PATRON–CLIENT RELATIONSHIPS AND BEYOND

In their seminal study of the *mishu* in Chinese leadership, Wei Li and Lucian W. Pye argue that the ubiquitous role of the *mishu* reflects Confucian political culture, especially the "intensely personalized element in Chinese politics."[32] This patron–client relationship, as Li and Pye characterize it, is based on the fact that "*shouzhang* [masters] depend on *mishu* for shelter, comfort and convenience in life and work; and *mishu* depend on *shouzhang* for status, prestige and career advancement."[33] Consequently, with the large presence of *mishu* in leadership, the Chinese political process has become even less institutionalized.

Although Li and Pye's argument has some validity, it overlooks some positive impacts that *mishu* can make on China's political institutionalization.[34] *Shouzhang's* dependence on *mishu* is not just limited to the need of "shelter, comfort and convenience." *Mishu*, especially those who have *taizi* and other important political and administrative backgrounds, may contribute to negotiation and interdependence of various factions, coalition building, and more political consultation and compromising in the Chinese political process. *Mishu's* managerial experiences can be very useful as they later become *shouzhang* themselves. This section examines situational factors, variations, and functions of *mishu* in the post-Mao China. The emphasis is to reveal the distinctive role of *mishu*, which goes beyond patron-client ties. The case studies of Wen Jiabao and Zeng Qing-hong, the two most prominent *mishu* during the reform era, reveal their crucial role as coalition builders in Chinese politics.

### Situational Factors That Contribute to the Prevalence of *Mishu*

The prevalence of *mishu* in Chinese leadership during the reform era, similar to the pervasive role of *taizi*, can be better understood if placed in a historical con-text. Several situational factors contributed to the rapid rise of *mishu* in post-Mao China. First, between the late 1970s and the mid-1990s, gerontocratic leaders (e.g., Deng Xiaoping, Chen Yun, Wang Zhen and Yang Shangkun) still held the real power in the country although they were retired or semiretired; most of them often exerted their power and influence "behind the scenes." The well-established role of *mishu*, as Wei Li and Lucian Pye noted, made it possible for "nearly senile leaders to continue to perform as major political figures."[35]

Second, some *taizi* serve as *mishu*, as already noted. Both Deng Xiaoping's daughter and Yang Shangkun's daughter, for example, served as *mishu* to their own fathers. In fact, even during the final years of the Mao era, Mao Yuanxin and Wang Hairong, Mao's nephew and niece, served as Mao's *mishu*. These cases might be exceptional because only top leaders are able to hire their children as *mishu* officially.[36] A large number of *taizi*, however, have served as *mishu* to the se-nior leaders who are their fathers' old comrades in arms. Xi Jinping, for example, served as *mishu* to his father's long-time friend Geng Biao, minister of defense from 1979 to 1981. Zeng Qinghong served as *mishu* to Yu Qiuli, chair of the State Plan-ning Commission in the same period. These experiences as *mishu* certainly accel-erated their political careers.

Third, the growing power of *mishu* during the past decade is also related to the rampancy of official corruption as a result of market reform. A good example is the corruption case in the Beijing municipal government, which involved Chen Xitong, Party secretary; Wang Baosheng, vice mayor; Huang Chao, vice mayor; and Tie Ying, deputy chair of the people's congress in Beijing. All of them had a *mishu* who played a direct role in helping them receive bribes and embezzle bank loans. These senior leaders in Beijing and their *mishu* were later sentenced to five to sixteen years in prison.[37] Wang Baosheng, who had served as *mishu* to Chen Xi-tong before he held the post of vice mayor, committed suicide when he and his boss, Chen, were under investigation by Jiang Zemin's people. The corruption scandal of the Beijing municipal government that involved the conspiracy be-tween leaders and their *mishu* is by no means unique in today's China. Wu Shaozu, a ministerial-level leader who used to be a *mishu* to Vice President Wang Zhen, said honestly that a *mishu* can easily use his master's position "to promote his pri-vate interests, if a *mishu* is so minded."[38]

The main difference between the Beijing municipal government and their counterparts in some other government bodies is that the corruption in the former was exposed to the public because Chen Xitong lost the power struggle with his political rivals. According to a recent study conducted by Chinese scholars, a shared characteristic of corruption cases in China since 1995 is that chiefs of staff, office directors, and *mishu* often played a major role in assisting illegal activities of their bosses.[39] In other cases, some *mishu* turned leaders committed crimes. For example, Wang Xinming, a *mishu* turned mayor (Jinjiang, Jiangsu Province), received a lifelong prison sentence because of his involvement in a serious corruption scandal.[40]

Fourth, throughout the PRC history, especially during the post-Mao era, China's top leaders have been concerned about region-based factionalism. To avoid this potential threat to the central leadership, Mao, Deng, and Jiang constantly arranged large-scale reshuffles of top provincial leaders and, especially, top officers in China's greater military regions.[41] This policy has been aimed at weakening the power bases of local leaders. When regional top leaders, both civilian and military elites, moved to new regions, they could not take any of their old subordinates with them. Yet they were often allowed to bring their personal *mishu* to their new posts.[42]

This common practice was also true of Deng Xiaoping during the Cultural Revolution, although in his case, Deng was exiled, not reshuffled, to a new place. When Deng was purged for the first time in 1967, he was allowed to take an assistant with him to Jiangxi. Deng chose Wang Ruilin, who had begun serving as Deng's *mishu* soon after the the PRC was founded. They survived the physical hardship and political uncertainty together. When Deng returned to power in the late 1970s, Wang became the director of Deng's office and a major political figure who later was in charge of personnel in the PLA. Ironically, the policy that is supposed to limit factional politics actually leads to close bonds between high-ranking leaders and their aides, contributing to an even stronger role of *mishu* in the Chinese leadership.

The final situational factor is the increasing complicity of the government administration, especially during the time of rapid technological change and globalization. When the reform started in 1978, senior leaders in both the central and provincial governments, most of whom were not well educated, often hired *mishu* with good educational backgrounds. As a result, people with technical backgrounds constituted a large portion of *mishu*. They are often seen as their leaders' "brain trust," and many of them later become technocratic leaders themselves.[43] Zeng Qinghong, Wu Shaozu, and Xi Jinping, who served as *mishu* for senior leaders in the late 1970s and early 1980s, as already noted, are all engineers by training.

Starting in the early 1990s, many economists in their late forties and early fifties have held some important *mishu* posts. Zhu Rongji's chief assistants in economic and financial affairs, known as "four top aides" (*sida tianwang*), Lou Jiwei, Zhou Xiaochuan, Li Jiange, and Guo Shuqing, all hold doctoral degrees in economics.[44] Lou Jiwei was born into a high-ranking official family in Shanghai in 1951 (his father was a vice minister in the 1950s). After the CR, he entered Qinghua University, where he received a bachelor's degree in economic management in 1982 and a master's degree in automation in 1984. Like Chen Yuan, Lou then studied under Yu Guangyuan for his Ph.D. in economics. After graduation, Lou worked as a fellow at the Research Center of Economic Development under the State Council. In 1988, at the recommendation of his brother-in-law, Chen Qingtai, also a Qinghua graduate and then head of China's No. 2 Motor Vehicle Plant, Lou started to work for Zhu in Shanghai as his aide in economic affairs. In 1991, when Zhu was appointed vice premier, Lou followed him to Beijing as his personal *mishu*. One year later, he gave his *mishu* post to his classmate, Li Jiange, and served as director of the Department of Comprehensive Plans under the State Commission for Reconstructing Economy. In 1994, Lou passed this post to Guo Shuqing, another classmate of his, and became vice governor of Guizhou. He is currently executive vice minister of finance.

Zhu's other three aides also currently hold important posts: Zhou Xiaochuan is governor of China Construction Bank, Li Jiange is executive vice chair of China Securities Regulatory Commission under the State Council, and Guo Shuqing is chief of staff of Economic Restructuring Office under the State Council. In the mid-1980s, Guo was a Ph.D. student of Su Shaozhi, a well-known dissident intellectual.[45] Economists turned *mishu* have also increased their presence in the ministerial- and provincial-level leadership. For example, in 1999, the provincial Party committee of Helongjiang selected a large number of young cadres with advanced degrees (mainly in economics) to serve as assistants to top municipal leaders in the province.[46] These members of the fourth generation leadership, who are trained economists and have broad administrative experience, including serving as *mishu* for top leaders, will likely play an even more important role in the future.

### Prevalence and Promotion of *Mishu* in the Post-Mao Era

There are many considerable variations in the broad category of *mishu*. There are important distinctions between organizational (*jiguan*) and personal (*geren*) *mishu*, between chiefs of staff (*mishuzhang*) and office directors (*bangongchu zhuren*), between aides with high official status (*zhuli*) and clerks who do nothing but type and answer phones (*banshi yuan*).[47] *Mishu* also differ greatly from one another in terms of the level of the leadership body they serve.

This study codes the work experience of *mishu* and office directors (including chiefs of staff) in the two data pools primarily used in chapter 3. If a leader has work experiences as both *mishu* and office director/chief of staff, only that of office director/chief of staff is coded. Table 5.4 shows that among the members of the Fifteenth CC and the Fifteenth CCDI, a significant number of them have worked as *mishu* or office directors. In this respect, there is not much difference between the third and fourth generations of leaders. Approximately 41 percent of the fourth generation leaders have had work experience either as *mishu* or as office directors; the percentage for the third generation is 43 percent. In both generations of leaders, almost half of them have served as office director or chief of staff.

Table 5.4  Members of the Third and Fourth Generations of Leaders with *Mishu* and/or Office Director/Chief of Staff Experience in the Fifteenth CC and CCDI`

|  | 3d Generation (N=232) | | 4th Generation (N=224) | |
|---|---|---|---|---|
|  | No. | % | No. | % |
| Work experience as *mishu* | 47 | 20.3 | 45 | 20.1 |
| Work experience as office director or chief of staff | 53 | 22.8 | 46 | 20.5 |

*Source:* Shen, *Zhonggong di shiwujie zhongyang weiyuanhui zhongyang jilü jiancha weiyuanhui weiyuan minglu.*

*Note:*The data were accumulated and tabulated by the author. Percentages do not add up to 100 due to rounding.

Table 5.5 presents a partial list of members of the fourth generation of leaders who have worked as chief of staff or *mishu*. A majority of these leaders are members or alternates of the Fifteenth Central Committee of the CCP and most of them hold top ministerial and provincial top posts or above. Hu Jintao, for example, served as *mishu* in the early stage of his political career. The twenty-two leaders with *mishu* experience listed in the table all used to work directly for high-ranking leaders, including mainly ministers of the State Council and top provincial leaders.[48] Some even directly served as *mishu* for a Politburo standing member or vice premier. Most of them had their high-level *mishu* experience after the CR.[49] The average tenure of their career as *mishu* to high-ranking officials is about four or five years.

In many cases, the *mishu* experience served as a career turning point. For example, Wang Chengming spent most of his career as a journalist on economic affairs after graduating from China's Central Institute of Finance and Banking in 1964. About twenty years later, in 1985, he started to work as *mishu* to a vice premier in the State Council. A few years later he was transferred to the People's Bank of China, where he has worked as office director, assistant governor, and now Party secretary of the bank.

In order to form their political networks, some leading members of the third generation leadership have worked particularly hard to ensure that their *mishu* and chiefs of staff advance to top posts in the provinces that these leaders used to head. For example, Li Tieying, currently a Politburo member, served as Party secretary of Liaoning Province during the mid-1980s and established a personal network there. Some *mishu* and assistants in the provincial administration of Liaoning during that period now hold the top posts in Liaoning or other important leadership positions elsewhere. They include Wen Shizhen, now Party secretary of Liaoning; Wang Zhan, deputy Party secretary of Neimenggu; and Bai Lichen, vice chair of CPPCC (all three are also in the Fifteenth Central Committee of the CCP).

**Table 5.5  A Partial List of Members of the Fourth Generation of Leaders Having Worked as *Mishu* or Chiefs of Staff**

| Name | Born | Current Position | Chief of Staff or Mishu Experience | Period |
|---|---|---|---|---|
| Mishu | | | | |
| Wang Zhan | 1941 | Deputy secretary of Neimenggu | *Mishu* to Party secretary of Liaoning | 1980–81 |
| Bai Lichen | 1941 | Vice chair of CPPCC | *Mishu* to governor of Liaoning | 1984–85 |
| Cai Changsong | 1941 | Deputy Party secretary, Hainan | Assistant to governor, Hainan | 1992–93 |
| Wang Chengming | 1941 | Party secretary, People's Bank | *Mishu* to vice premier | 1985–90 |
| Chen Fujin | 1941 | Member, CCDI | *Mishu* to minister of Coal Industry | 1975–79 |
| Wang Gang | 1942 | Deputy director, General Office of CCP Central Committee | *Mishu* to Party secretary of Xingjiang, *mishu* to director of Taiwan Office of the CCP | 1977–85 |
| Ren Qixing | 1942 | Deputy secretary of Ningxia | *Mishu* to Party secretary of Ningxia | 1972–83 |
| Xu Yongyue | 1942 | Minister of state security | *Mishu* to Chen Yun, Politburo standing mem. | 1983–88 |
| Huang Zhiquan | 1942 | Deputy Party secretary, Jiangxi | Assistant to Wu Guangzheng, governor, Jiangxi | 1991–93 |
| Zhang Bailin | 1942 | Vice head, CCP Organization Dept. | *Mishu* to minister of No. 6 Machine Building | 1978–81 |
| Fan Xinde | 1942 | Member, CCDI | *Mishu* to president of Chinese Aca. of Sciences | 1970–75 |
| Hu Jintao | 1942 | Vice president | *Mishu* to chair, Gansu Construction Com. | 1974–75 |
| Zhao Hong | 1942 | Deputy procurator general | *Mishu* to Party secretary of Jiangsu | 1981–83 |
| Tian Congming | 1943 | Vice minister, radio and TV | *Mishu* to Party secretary of Neimengguo | 1980–81 |
| Zhang Dingfa | 1943 | Commander, North Fleet, navy | Assistant to chief of staff, North Fleet, navy | 1985–86 |
| Zhang Li | 1943 | Head, Political Dept. Chief of Staff | *Mishu* to Central Military Commission | 1984–89 |

*continued*

**Table 5.5   Continued**

| Name | Born | Current Position | Chief of Staff or Mishu Experience | Period |
|---|---|---|---|---|
| Lu Feng | 1944 | Member, CCDI | Assistant to minister of public security | 1993–95 |
| Li Jiating | 1944 | Governor, Yunnan | Assistant to governor of Helongjiang | 1992 |
| Jia Zhibang | 1946 | Deputy Party secretary, Shaanxi | *Mishu* to governor, Shaanxi | 1985–87 |
| Lu Hao | 1947 | Mayor, Lanzhou | *Mishu* to Party secretary of Gansu | 1982–85 |
| Bai Zhijian | 1948 | Vice minister, agriculture | *Mishu* to minister of agriculture | 1977–83 |
| Xi Jinping | 1953 | Deputy secretary of Fujian | *Mishu* to Geng Biao, minister of defense | 1979–81 |
| **Chief of Staff** | | | | |
| Wang Zhaoguo | 1941 | Head, United Front Dept., CCP | Chief of staff, Central Committee of CCP | 1984–87 |
| Wang Yunkun | 1942 | Party secretary, Jilin | Chief of staff, Jilin CCP Committee | 1988–89 |
| Chen Yujie | 1941 | Deputy Party secretary, Jilin | Chief of staff, Hebei CCP Committee | 1990–94 |
| Fang Fengyou | 1941 | Deputy Party secretary, Tianjin | Chief of staff, Tianjin municipal government | 1989–91 |
| Zheng Wantong | 1941 | Chief of staff, CPPCC | Chief of staff, Tianjin CCP Committee | 1983–88 |
| Wen Jiabao | 1942 | Vice premier | Chief of staff, CCP General Office | 1986–88 |
| Li Tielin | 1943 | Vice head, CCP Organization Dept. | Deputy chief of staff, Organization Dept. | 1989–90 |
| Gao Siren | 1944 | Deputy Party secretary, Guangdong | Chief of staff, Guangdong CCP Committee | 1991 |
| Zhang Zuoji | 1945 | Minister, labor & social welfare | Deputy chief of staff, State Council | 1994–98 |
| Huang Huahua | 1946 | Deputy Party secretary, Guangdong | Chief of staff, Guangdong CCP Committee | 1992–95 |
| Li Jianguo | 1946 | Party secretary, Shaanxi | Chief of staff, Tianjin CCP Committee | 1989–92 |
| Li Shenglin | 1946 | Mayor, Tianjin | Deputy chief of staff, Tianjin CCP Committee | 1983–86 |

*continued*

Table 5.5    Continued

| Name | Born | Current Position | Chief of Staff or Mishu Experience | Period |
|------|------|------------------|-------------------------------------|--------|
| Chen Liangyu | 1946 | Deputy Party secretary, Shanghai | Deputy chief of staff, Shanghai CCP Com. | 1992 |
| Meng Jianzhu | 1947 | Deputy Party secretary, Shanghai | Deputy chief of staff, Shanghai CCP Com. | 1992–93 |
| Zhao Hongzhu | 1947 | Vice minister of supervision | Deputy chief of staff, CCDI | 1996–98 |
| Quan Zhezhu | 1952 | Vice governor, Jilin | Deputy chief of staff, Jilin CCP Committee | 1990–91 |
| Yuan Chunqing | 1952 | Chief of staff, CCDI | Chief of staff, National Student Union | 1985–87 |
| Jin Daoming | 1953 | Member, CCDI | Office director, minister of supervision | 1987–89 |

Source: Liao and Fan, *Zhongguo renming da cidian* (1994); Shen, *Zhonggong di shiwujie zhongyang weiyuanhui zhongyang jilü jiancha weiyuanhui weiyuan minglu*; He Pin and Gao Xin, *Zhonggong "Taizidang"* (China's communist "princelings") (Taibei: Shih-pao Ch'u-pan Kung-ssu, 1992); and *China Directory 1999* (Tokyo: Radiopress, 1999)
Note: The data were tabulated by the author.

Wu Guanzheng, another Politburo member and a native of Jiangxi, worked in his native province from 1986 to 1997, serving consecutively as deputy Party secretary, governor, and Party secretary. Jiangxi's current governor, Shu Shengyou; Party secretary, Shu Huiguo; and deputy Party secretary, Huang Zhiquan; as well as current governor of Shaanxi, Cheng Andong, all served as assistants or chiefs of staff to Wu when he was the "boss of Jiangxi." All of these four former *mishu* now also hold full memberships in the Fifteenth Central Committee of the CCP. The political connections that they formed in Jiangxi during Wu's tenure there seem to have played an important role in the promotion of these four provincial leaders.

Serving as an office director, or especially as a chief of staff, is a crucial career stepping-stone. Table 5.5 shows that such an experience among the members of the fourth generation leadership usually occurred in the late 1980s and the early 1990s (in most cases either immediately or a few years prior to their current appointments). Their average tenure as chief of staff is two or three years. The importance of chief of staff certainly did not begin in the fourth generation of leadership. This is true for both provincial and central leaders. For example, Huang Ju, currently Party secretary of Shanghai and a Politburo member, served as chief of staff to Jiang Zemin in Shanghai during the mid-1980s, when Jiang was the Party boss of the city. Now Huang's two former deputy chiefs of staff, Chen Liangyu and Meng Jianzhu, both in their early fifties, have been promoted to deputy Party secretary in Shanghai and CC alternate. Because of their political connection with top leaders and their relatively young age, Chen and Meng are on a fast track for further promotion.

At the national level of leadership, the most important chief of staff is the director of the General Office of the Central Committee of the CCP, which functions primarily as a chief of staff to the head of the Party. Table 5.6 lists all the directors of this general office in PRC history. All of the previous directors later moved to supreme leadership posts. Yang Shangkun, the first director, held that post for over two decades until he was fired by Mao at the beginning of the CR. He was charged with "establishing another headquarters" within the Party against Mao. Yang later became a standing member of the Politburo and president of the PRC. At a certain period in the Deng era, Yang almost succeeded Deng as the "new paramount leader" in the country. Wang Dongxing, previously Mao's bodyguard, held that post throughout the CR. The great importance of this post was also evident when Wang helped his new boss, Hua Guofeng, arrest Mao's wife and other political rivals. Wang served as vice chair of the Party under Hua. The following three directors, Yao Yilin, Hu Qili, and Qiao Shi, all served under Hu for a couple of years and then moved to higher leadership posts. All of them later became standing members of the Politburo, the supreme decision-making body in the country.

Probably the most "unusual" director of the general office is Wen Jiabao, since he served as a chief of staff to three top leaders in the Party: Hu Yaobang, Zhao Ziyang, and Jiang Zemin, consecutively. Although Hu and Zhao were purged at different times as a result of a power struggle, Wen not only survived but was promoted after each purge, showing Wen's political shrewdness and extraordinary intelligence. More importantly, Wen's distinctive career as a chief of staff suggests that the ubiquitous role of *mishu* in today's China goes beyond patron–client relations. The "indispensability" of Wen Jiabao cannot be attributed to his factional affiliation or personal loyalty to any head of the Party, since he switched bosses three times. In addition, Wen never publicly criticized a boss who had been purged when he started to serve his new boss. Both his talent as a superb administrator and his role as a coalition builder seem to explain his legendary survival and success.

## MISHU AS COALITION BUILDERS:
## WEN JIABAO AND ZENG QINGHONG

Most studies on *mishu* tend to emphasize the aspect of how *mishu* can benefit from this career experience to foster their upward mobility.[50] In most cases *shouzhang* provide their *mishu* with the "rope" that they can climb. But meanwhile, some *mishu*, with both their political wisdom and their own connections, can play a

Table 5.6   Tenure and Promotion of Directors of the General Office of the Central Committee of the CCP

| Name | Tenure | Head of the CCP During Tenure | Highest Party and/or Government Posts Thereafter |
|------|--------|-------------------------------|--------------------------------------------------|
| Yang Shangkun | 1945–66 | Mao Zedong | Standing member of Politburo, president of the PRC |
| Wang Dongxing | 1967–78 | Mao Zedong Hua Guofeng | Vice chair of CCP |
| Yao Yilin | 1978–82 | (Hua Guofeng) Hu Yaobang | Standing member of Politburo |
| Hu Qili | 1982–83 | Hu Yaobang | Standing member of Politburo |
| Qiao Shi | 1983–84 | Hu Yaobang | Standing member of Politburo, vice chair of NPC |
| Wang Zhaoguo | 1984–86 | Hu Yaobang | Member of secretariat |
| Wen Jiabao | 1986–93 | Hu Yaobang Zhao Ziyang Jiang Zemin | Member of Politburo, vice premier |
| Zeng Qinghong | 1993–99 | Jiang Zemin | Alternate member of Politburo |
| Wang Gang | 1999– | Jiang Zemin | N/A |

Source: Wei Li and Lucian W. Pye, "The Ubiquitous Role of the Mishu in Chinese Politics," China Quarterly 132 (December 1992): 930; China Directory 1999 (Tokyo: Radiopress, various years). The data were tabulated by the author.

crucial role in consolidating the power of their shouzhang. In other words, shouzhang can benefit substantially from their mishu in terms of consensus making and coalition building. A crucial factor in Jiang Zemin's effective rule is the remarkable assistance supplied by his two chiefs of staff, Wen Jiabao and especially Zeng Qinghong.

In 1989, when Deng Xiaoping transferred Jiang Zemin from Shanghai to Beijing to replace Zhao Ziyang as secretary-general of the Party, Jiang was no more than a figurehead. Jiang had no charisma, no common touch, no solid basis of power in Party hierarchy, no contacts in the military, no respect from other leaders in his own generation, especially Chen Xitong, Party secretary of Beijing and Jiang's principal rival. To make his situation even more vulnerable, Jiang had no clue whether or not he would face the same fate as his two predecessors Hu and Zhao, as a result of the order of the paramount leader Deng Xiaoping. Not surprisingly, observers in both China and abroad often considered Jiang a Hua Guofeng–like figure,[51] but Jiang surely had the will to succeed power from Deng. Jiang quickly learned two lessons from the fall of his two predecessors. First, neither Hu nor Zhao paid much attention to coalition building in the Party establishment, especially the necessary close contact with veteran leaders and the military. Second, some top personal aides of Hu and Zhao were very arrogant. Bao Tong, Zhao Ziyang's political secretary, claimed to be "China's Henry Kissinger."[52]

Bao seemed to do more harm than good for his boss. As Li and Pye observed, a "large portion of the factional fighting between Zhao Ziyang and the conservative" revolved around Bao Tong.[53]

To avoid making the same mistakes, Jiang paid particular attention to the personality and capacity of his top aides in terms of coalition building within the Party establishment. To many people's surprise, Jiang asked Wen Jiabao to remain as director of the General Office of the Central Committee of the CCP. In retrospect, Jiang's decision to keep Wen proved to be a marvelous political move. As a new Party boss who just moved to the capital from Shanghai, Jiang knew that he could not survive without his own power base in the Beijing Party hierarchy. But it was politically too sensitive and too late to build his own personal network from scratch. The best choice for Jiang was to play around with some existing factions. Wen Jiabao, intelligent but not arrogant, energetic but not intimidating, well-connected but not really faction-oriented, seemed to be a great asset for Jiang.[54] More importantly, by keeping Wen in the same post, Jiang actually sent the message that a majority of subordinates of Hu and Zhao could remain in power as long as they did not challenge Jiang. In the process, Jiang inherited from his fallen predecessor a capable staff without much effort.

Meanwhile, Jiang appointed Zeng Qinghong as deputy director of the office. Zeng served as Jiang's chief of staff in Shanghai when Jiang was the Party boss there. Zeng, like Wen, is a humble, competent, and well-rounded administrator. But probably differing from Wen, Zeng is also a marvelous tactician in power politics. Because of his family background and personal experience, he had some important connections in both the circles of veteran leaders and senior military officers. For over a decade, Zeng has served as Jiang's "hand, ear, and brain." Zeng played a crucial role in Jiang's victories over the Yang brothers, Chen Xitong and Qiao Shi.[55] Zeng has also been actively involved in forging China's foreign policies, especially dealing with the Taiwan Strait crisis.[56] A widely circulated rumor in Hong Kong and Taiwan stated that Zeng met Su Zhicheng, the chief of staff to the president of Taiwan, in Zhuhai, Guangdong, in 1995, initiating a dialogue on the relations across the Taiwan Strait.[57]

Both Wen and Zeng have emerged as two primary figures in the post-Jiang leadership. A closer look at the personalities and career paths of these two figures is essential to an understanding of the characteristics of Chinese politics in the post-Deng era and beyond.

### Wen Jiabao: A Versatile Political Coordinator

Wen was born in Tianjin in 1942. Between 1960 and 1965, he studied at the Beijing Geology Institute. Like Hu Jintao and many other members of the fourth generation of leaders, Wen was a political councilor at college. During his senior year, he was recruited into the CCP. He continued his postgraduate study at the same Institute, majoring in structural geography. But his postgraduate study was interrupted by the CR. In 1968, he was sent to the backward province of Gansu. During the following decade, he served as a technician, a clerk of political affairs, and head of the Political Department of the Gansu Geomechanics Zone Survey Team, consecutively. In 1978, as soon as Deng Xiaoping and other reformers controlled power throughout the country, Wen was appointed deputy director of the Geomechanics Zone Survey Team and, three years later, deputy director of the Gansu Provincial Geology Bureau.[58]

The turning point of Wen's political career occurred in 1982, when Sun Daguang, then minister of China's geology and mineral resources, came to Gansu to inspect work there. According to one source, both the director and the Party secretary of the bureau were *caobao* (blockheads) who did not know how to report their work to the minister. Consequently, they asked Wen Jiabao to handle the minister's inspection.[59] This proved to be an excellent opportunity for the thirty-nine-year old deputy director to display his talent and capacity. Minister Sun was very impressed by the eloquence of Wen's oral presentation and his knowledge about Gansu. During his inspection, Sun praised Wen as someone who was like "a walking map of Gansu."[60] When Sun returned to Beijing, he nominated Wen, whom he saw as a prime candidate among the third echelon of leaders, for the post of vice minister. This "helicopter-style" promotion, however, met much resistance in the Ministry of Geology and Mineral Resources. Instead of immediately obtaining the post of vice minister, Wen first held the directorship of the Policy and Regulations Research Office of the ministry. One year later, at the age of forty-one, he was appointed vice minister and was in charge of daily administrative affairs of the ministry. He became one of the youngest ministerial-level leaders in the country—a front-runner among the third echelon.

In 1985, Wen was appointed deputy director of the General Office of the Central Committee of the CCP. One year later, he replaced Wang Zhaoguo as full director of the General Office, serving as chief of staff to Hu Yaobang, then secretary-general of the CCP. In contrast to his predecessor, Wang Zhaoguo, who was known for his arrogance and his authoritarian personality, Wen was often seen as a very accessible and low-profile leader with a common touch.[61] His "lack of a distinct faction affiliation" also helped Wen remain in this critically important post while his two former bosses were purged.[62]

Wen's common touch was exemplified by two incidents, which were widely reported throughout the country. First, Wen accompanied Zhao Ziyang to talk to student protesters at Tiananmen Square on the eve of the military crackdown. This incident, which showed the sympathy toward students that the liberal leaders in the Party establishment felt, left the whole nation with a lasting positive image of both Zhao and Wen.[63] This action was appropriate for Wen because he assisted his boss at a time of crisis. This also earned Wen great respect from other political leaders, including Jiang Zemin.

The second incident occurred in the summer of 1998, when China experienced one of the most severe floods of the twentieth century. Much of China was under water that summer; more than fifty days and nights of rain and consequent flooding resulted in the death of over 3,000 people. As many people as live in the United States—233 million—were directly affected by the floods. Six million were left homeless and 3 million lived in shacks on dikes along the Yangtze for a few months. The government launched the largest request for donations in the PRC history, appealing to the people, including overseas Chinese, to contribute medicine and clothes. Wen was appointed by Jiang Zemin and Zhu Rongji to be in charge of the coordination on all fronts of antiflood measures in the country. During this difficult situation, which attracted great public attention within China, Wen had plenty of exposure to the media: Wen stood next to President Jiang when the latter spoke of the strength and unity of the Chinese people and their heroic spirit in fighting the floods. Wen was also there when Premier Zhu expressed his outrage about the improper construction of the dike in Jiujiang, Jiangxi Province, which was washed away by the flood. Zhu called it the "dike made of tofu" and fired the corrupt local officials who had used reinforced concrete intended for the dike to build their own houses instead. But more often, Wen was seen in the emergency area commanding antiflood measures. Wen's unremitting presence in flood-stricken areas and his leadership role in coordinating with various regions and bureaucratic institutions, including the army, who responded to the disaster, left the Chinese public with an exceptionally good impression of him.[64]

His common touch made him a popular grassroots politician, but it was his versatility and leadership ability that led Jiang and Zhu to give Wen a greater role to play. As already noted, Wen's undergraduate and graduate education were in the field of geography. After graduation, he spent most of his early career as a Party functionary engaged in organizational and propaganda affairs. Wen's role as a Party functionary was most evident when he served as a chief of staff in the General Office of the Central Committee. But Wen certainly did not want to limit his role to only that of a Party functionary. He made his first move in 1993 when he served as secretary-general of the Central Financial and Economic Leading Group, which was headed by Jiang Zemin. While holding this important post in China's financial affairs, Wen has also served as head of the Central Rural Work Leading Group. As the youngest vice premier in the State Council, Wen has assisted Zhu in agricultural and financial affairs—two major sectors of the Chinese economy. Wen seems to be a fast learner, for he has assumed these important leadership posts one after another in the past few years. Wen's personality, experience, capability, public image, and age all suggest that he will be a major figure in the generation succeeding Jiang and Zhu.

## Zeng Qinghong: A Well-Rounded Tactician

Similar to the generational ambiguity of Deng Xiaoping and Hu Yaobang, who participated in the Long March but were usually seen as the second generation of leaders, Zeng Qinghong's generational identity is also two-edged. Zeng was born in 1939 and graduated from college in 1963. He was too young to participate in the Socialist Transformation but was a few years older than the eldest cohort group of the so-called Cultural Revolution generation. Most studies of the Chinese leadership consider Zeng as a leader of the fourth generation rather than the third generation.[65] Along with Hu Jintao and Wen Jiabao, Zeng is generally seen as one of the three leading figures in the post-Jiang era. This study used the year 1941 as a dividing line between the third and fourth generations of leaders. In reality there is hardly any difference between those who were born in 1939, 1940, or 1941. As noted in chapter 1, designating a certain year as the beginning of a political generation is always arbitrary. Although the quantitative analysis of this book does not include Zeng as a member of the fourth generation leadership, the qualitative analysis of this chapter treats him as an exception.

Zeng has a double identity as both a *taizi* and a *mishu*. His father, Zeng Shan, was a veteran Communist and a member of the Seventh, Eighth, and Ninth Central Committees of the CCP. Zeng Shan was born into a family that was deeply involved in revolutionary activities, especially the peasant riots of 1927–1928 in Xingguo County, Jiangxi Province. Jiangxi, especially its Xingguo and Jian Counties, was known for the intense fighting between Communists and Nationalists during some of the "annihilation campaigns" waged by the Nationalists in an attempt to destroy the Communists in the early 1930s. The well-known Jinggang Mountain, which served as the headquarters of Mao's Red Army, is located in this area. Zeng Shan's father, Zeng Caiqin, died in a Nationalist prison. In addition, two of Zeng Shan's brothers and their wives died at the hands of the Nationalists.[66] Zeng Shan was a prominent Communist leader in the region. He was named chair of the Jiangxi Provincial Soviet in 1932 and served as a member of a nine-person Central Bureau of the Soviet Areas headed by Zhou Enlai.[67] While the main forces led by Zhu De and Mao Zedong escaped from the Nationalist campaign and started the Long March in 1934, Zhou Enlai ordered the forces led by Zeng Shan, Chen Yi, and Qu Qiubai to remain at their guerilla bases. This actually meant that Zhou, Mao, and Zhu planned to sacrifice these branches of the Red Army. A majority of the forces led by Zeng, Chen, and Qu were indeed killed during the Nationalist campaigns.[68] It is highly likely that Zeng Shan later described all these historical incidents to young Zeng Qinghong, who must have learned about the cruelty of politics from an early age. According to some people close to Zeng Qinghong, he was awed by the manipulative skills of Zhou Enlai.[69]

Zeng Shan, however, survived and later joined the New Fourth Army in 1938. In the same year, he married Deng Liujin, one of a small number of women who participated in the Long March. One year later, Zeng Qinghong, their eldest child, was born in northern Jiangsu. Almost immediately after his birth, Zeng was sent to Jiangxi's Jian County, where he was raised by his grandmother. When the Communists seized power in 1949, Zeng Shan first worked in Shanghai and held the post of vice mayor. A few years later, Zeng moved to Beijing to serve as minister of textile industry, minister of commerce, director of the CCP Communication and Transportation Department, and minister of interior affairs, consecutively.[70] During their years in Shanghai, Zeng's mother established a kindergarten exclusively for orphans of revolutionary martyrs and children of high-ranking officials. According to some sources, many of these children are now holding senior political and military posts.[71] Although Zeng Qinghong's power does not rely on them, they will give Zeng their support when needed.

After attending an elementary school in Shanghai for two years, Zeng Qinghong moved to Beijing with his parents. He enrolled in the Beijing No. 101 School, which was for children of high-ranking officials. In 1959, Zeng entered the Beijing Institute of Engineering, majoring in automatic control. He joined the Party during his sophomore year in college. After graduation, he worked as a technician in the PLA's No. 743 Army, a troop that specialized in ground-to-air missiles. Two years later, the military research unit with which he was affiliated changed to a civilian institute for missile technology research. Zeng was not a radical activist during the CR. In 1969, Zeng was sent first to a military base in Guangdong and then to a collective farm in Hunan where he worked as a manual laborer. One year later, he returned to the same research institute in Beijing. The Zeng family did not suffer much during the CR. Zeng Shan continuously held his membership in the Ninth Central Committee in 1969. He died from a heart attack in 1972.[72]

Zeng Qinghong made his first important career move in 1979, when he began to work as a *mishu* to Yu Qiuli, then chair of the powerful State Planning Commission. Yu, a native of Jiangxi, was Zeng Shan's protégé. It was Zeng Shan who invited Yu, who was then just a teenager, to join the Communist movement in the late 1920s. About a half century later, Zeng's son became Yu's protégé. By the late 1970s and early 1980s, Yu became one of the most powerful veteran leaders in the country. In addition to promoting many of his junior colleagues in the petroleum industry, which he headed for many years, Yu was particularly interested in helping *taizi* expedite their political careers. In a few Party meetings held in the 1980s, Yu Qiuli, along with Wang Zhen, straightforwardly called for "promoting children of senior leaders" (*tixie laoshouzhang de haizi*).[73] Just as Wang Zhen selected Wu Shaozu as his personal secretary, Yu chose Zeng as his *mishu*, hoping that the *mishu* experience would be a "springboard" for his protégé's quick rise in the Chinese leadership. When Yu moved to the State Energy Commission in 1981, he brought Zeng with him and appointed him as deputy chief of staff in the General Office of the commission. One year later, when Yu took the post of director of the General Political Department of the PLA, he helped Zeng move to his power base, the Ministry of the Petroleum Industry, where Zeng assumed, first, the post of deputy director of the Liaison Department of Offshore Petroleum Corporation and then deputy director of the Foreign Liaison Department.

In 1984, Zeng moved to Shanghai, the city in which his father had served as vice mayor soon after the Communist takeover. About a half century later, three of his father's junior colleagues, Chen Guodong, Hu Lijiao and Wang Daohan, occupied three top posts in the city. Zeng was appointed deputy director of the Organization Department of the Shanghai CCP Committee. One year later, when Jiang Zemin arrived in Shanghai as mayor, Zeng was promoted to director of the Organization Department. Jiang and Zeng share similar family backgrounds: both are from high-ranking Communist families, both their fathers were associated with the New Fourth Army during the Anti-Japanese War, and both lost family members during the Communist fighting with the Nationalists. In 1986, Zeng became chief of staff to Jiang in the Shanghai municipal administration and began their "long-term mutually beneficial cooperation."[74]

Zeng Qinghong's rise to the power center clearly reflects the advantage of *taizi* and the importance of political networks. His appointment as Yu Qiuli's *mishu* and his transfer to Shanghai should be attributed to nepotism and favoritism, without which Zeng could not have advanced so rapidly. But Zeng Qinghong differs from most members of *taizidang* in an important aspect: he is a well-rounded tactician with exceptional intelligence and vision about the future while other *taizi* do not have these characteristics. Many episodes and choices that he made during his career demonstrate Zeng's unconventional wisdom. For example, in the early 1980s, when he was the head of the Organization Department in Shanghai, Zeng selected five bright young college graduates in the city and sent them to the United States to study political science instead of the then fashionable academic disciplines such as physics and engineering. One of these five young fellows, Wang Huning, after having received his training as a visiting scholar in political science at both the University of Michigan at Ann Arbor and the University of Iowa, returned to Shanghai in the late 1980s and became chair of the department of international politics and subsequently dean of the law school at Fudan University. In 1998, Wang became deputy director of the Policy Research Center under the CCP Central Committee, a vice minister–level aide to Jiang Zemin. Wang has been a key figure in designing legal and administrative reforms in the country.

For Zeng Qinghong, probably the first important personal decision (demonstrating his uniqueness) was to attend the Beijing Institute of Engineering instead of elite universities where *taizi* assembled, such as the Harbin Military Institute of Engineering and Qinghua University. From a young age, Zeng Qinghong was already reluctant to be too close to other princelings. In the early 1980s, when a majority of *taizi* rushed to the business sector, especially those institutions closely linked to foreign trade, Zeng quit his post as deputy director of the Foreign Liaison Department under the Ministry of the Petroleum Industry. This post would certainly have made him wealthy. Even more surprising to many observers, Zeng did not join the military when his mentor, Yu Qiuli, was appointed as director of the PLA's General Political Department, a top military post. One sound explanation was that Zeng did not want to advance his political career through the military. Furthermore, China's military during the reform era, similar to the business sector, has been known for rampant corruption. Zeng would not allow any short-term material gain to jeopardize his great political ambition.

Unlike many *taizi* who are eager for quick promotion and instant profits, Zeng has a great sense of timing; he knows *when* he should move on to the next higher post. When he moved to Beijing along with Jiang Zemin, he took only the post of deputy director of the General Office of the CCP Central Committee. He waited for four years to assume the post of full director of that office. In the Fourteenth Party Congress held in 1992, Zeng's name was not even on the ballot for an alternate seat on the Central Committee, although he was well-known for his role as Jiang's "hand, ear, and brain." There were two possible reasons that Zeng did not want to place his name on the ballot. First, he sensed the strong resistance from the deputies of the Party congress against princelings. In the election of the previous Thirteenth Party Congress, Deng Pufang failed to be elected. Many candidates with *taizi* backgrounds (e.g., Chen Yuan and Yu Zhengsheng) also were not elected to the Fourteenth Party Congress. Second, in 1992, Jiang's power was not solid. Zeng was more interested in helping Jiang defeat their political rivals in the central leadership than in getting a seat on the Central Committee. One year after the Fourteenth Party Congress, Zeng was appointed director of the General Office of the CC, the only director in CCP history who was not a member of the CC. This meant that, with his continuing effort in networking and coalition building, his membership in the next congress would be ensured.

During the 1990s, with his family connections among civilian veteran leaders such as Chen Yun and Yao Yilin and top military officers such as Yu Qiuli and Zhang Zhen, Zeng Qinghong played a crucial role in helping Jiang overcome his opponents one at a time. The Yang brothers, Chen Xitong, and Qiao Shi were all defeated, in different ways, by the seemingly incompetent Hua Guofeng–like figure Jiang Zemin. After all these victories, Zeng moved to the forefront. During the Fifteenth Party Congress in 1997, despite some resistance from the deputies, Zeng made his "triple jump" from not even being an alternate to the previous Central Committee to becoming an alternate in the Politburo.

Since 1999, he has been head of the Organization Department of the Central Committee. This position is "one of the most coveted positions among political factions and was once held by such political heavyweights" as Chen Yun, Peng Zhen, Deng Xiaoping, Hu Yaobang, Qiao Shi, Wei Jianxing, and Song Ping.[75] As a foreign journalist observed, this post is "particularly crucial as it is the key to all future personnel appointments by the 16th CCP Congress in 2002."[76]

What makes Zeng Qinghong differ even more from other *mishu* is the manner in which he handles his relationship with his boss and presents himself to the public. Partly because Zeng can stand on his own, he has never left the public any impression that he is the kind of *mishu* who curries favor with the boss. Instead, he has earned his boss's respect. Zeng has always attempted to keep a distance from any single veteran leader or even his boss, Jiang. In addition, Zeng has been noticeably distant from other *taizi*. Zeng's role model, as he told his associates and friends, is Zhou Enlai, a tactician who was known for his gracious interpersonal skills and his capacity for political manipulation.[77] Zeng's relationships with his main political competitors, such as Hu Jintao and Wen Jiabao, are unknown at

present. Each step of Zeng's advancement in the central leadership, however, often occurred after the promotion of Hu and Wen. Undoubtedly, Zeng has been
very cautious about avoiding premature or unnecessary conflicts with other political "heavyweights" who are of similar age.

The remarkable political careers of both Wen and Zeng can be only partially attributed to their *mishu* experience or *taizi* background (or both in the case of Zeng).
Their other characteristics—administrative competence, sense of timing for career
moves, extraordinary capacity to remain both loyal and independent, and their
mastery of interpersonal relationships—all contributed to their successes. The
*mishu* or *taizi* background can actually be a hurdle to the supreme level of leadership; this is especially true now that new election methods are being introduced.

## INSTITUTIONAL OPPOSITION TO NEPOTISM

Although many princelings gained leadership posts during the reform era, institutional restraints on them and public resentment against them are also evident.
The institutional restraints have occurred as a result of pressure from the top leadership to deal with the problem of nepotism in elite recruitment and demands
from the political establishment (e.g., deputies of the Party congress and the
NPC) for more representative government.

### "Voting Power of Deputies": New Institutional Mechanism to Restrain *Taizi*

As early as in the mid-1980s, especially during Hu Yaobang's tenure as secretary-
general of the CCP, the Organization Department of the CC issued orders to restrain the appointment of *taizi*, particularly those *taizi* whose revolutionary veteran
fathers were still alive.[78] In general, approval of the county, bureau, and prefecture
levels of leaders is made on the provincial and ministerial levels (previously approval was needed by the Organization Department of the CC); however, the appointment of children of high-ranking officials to these levels of leadership or above
should be confirmed by the Organization Department of the CC. In addition, the
central authorities have recently made some efforts to limit the nepotism and corruption resulting from the growing power of *mishu* on the provincial and ministerial levels, especially after the scandals associated with Chen Xitong and other top
leaders of the Beijing municipal government, as well as with their *mishu*.[79]

Another important institutional development during the reform era is the
change in voting within the establishment such as the Party congress and the National People's Congress. For understandable reasons, many China watchers are
cynical about any high-level "election" in the PRC. Personnel authorities allow
only candidates whom they prefer on the ballot. But this does not mean the hierarchy can absolutely control everyone's vote. For example, in 1982, one year after Chen Yuan finished his postgraduate study, he was appointed deputy head of
Xicheng District in Beijing and standing member of the Beijing Party Commit-

tee. Five years later, the CCP Organization Department and the Beijing Party Committee wanted to appoint him as deputy Party secretary of Beijing. But this year, the Beijing Party Congress, like all other provincial and municipal Party congresses, adopted the "election with more candidates than posts." Chen Yuan could not just be reappointed to his seat on the Beijing Party Committee; instead, he needed to be elected by the congress, which had over 700 deputies. Chen was listed among fifty-five candidates for the fifty membership seats for the new Beijing Party Committee. The deputies would continue to select eleven of these fifty members for seats on the standing committee. After these two elections, the CCP Organization Department could appoint, among these eleven elected standing members, the Party secretary and deputy secretaries. Ironically, Chen Yuan, "Beijing deputy Party secretary-designate," was defeated in the first round of the election; he was one of the five candidates who lost the election.[80]

Election has also been used in the formation of the Central Committee and the Politburo during the past three Party congresses. Some candidates earmarked by top authorities to important positions could not even get elected to the CC. For example, during the Thirteenth Party Congress, Deng Liqun, a conservative hardliner and Twelfth Politburo member, lost a reelection bid to the Thirteenth CC. Xiao Yang, former governor of Sichuan Province, who was reportedly chosen by Deng and other veteran leaders to be a Politburo member on the Fourteenth CC, did not get enough votes even for full membership on the CC.

The strongest evidence of opposition to nepotism in the selection of CC members is that many candidates on the ballot for the CC did not get elected despite (or perhaps because of) their high-ranking family backgrounds. The Fifteenth Congress, like the two previous congresses, formed its CC by an "election with more candidates than posts." Many princelings were among the 5 percent of candidates who were defeated. They included Chen Yuan, Wang Jun, and Bo Xilai. Among the ten elected alternate members receiving the lowest votes, five were princelings, including Deng Pufang (who was next to last in terms of votes received), Wang Qishan, Liu Yandong, and Xi Jinping (who received the lowest number of votes).[81]

The opposition to the election of Bo Xilai is particularly revealing. When his father, Bo Yibo, proposed that each high-ranking official family could "contribute one child" to become a high-ranking official, the Bo family must have had an "internal division of labor" and chosen Bo Xilai instead of Bo Xicheng as their "family representative."[82] As discussed earlier in this chapter, the Bo family's decision was a rational one, partly because Bo Xicheng had more business connections than his younger brother and partly because Bo Xicheng had only a degree from a television university while his younger brother attended Beijing University and received a master's degree from the CASS.

Bo Yibo's desire to make his youngest son a major political figure was well-known. Prior to the Fifteenth Party Congress in 1997, in order to publicize Bo Xilai's "achievements" in Dalian, the Bo family launched a nationwide campaign that included frequent TV appearances and extensive articles about him written by well-known novelists. For example, Chen Zufeng, a celebrity writer and a family friend of Bo's, wrote a report entitled "Dalian's Mayor Bo Xilai," portraying Bo Xilai as a man who is as statesman-like as Henry Kissinger, as environmentally conscious as Al Gore, and almost as beloved by the public as Princess Diana.[83] Chen Zufeng portrayed Dalian as the most beautiful city in China, especially for the many grass parkways, or what she calls "Xilai grass," the grass named after Bo Xilai.[84]

Despite the fact that his high-placed father and friends had designated him to be a member of the Fifteenth Central Committee of the CCP, ironically, Bo Xilai failed to even get a deputy seat in Liaoning Province's delegation to attend the Fifteenth Party Congress. Bo may have been popular in Dalian because he used his family connections to get Dalian some favorable policies, especially its free trade zone status, but his colleagues in other cities and counties of Liaoning resented the special favor that Bo brought to Dalian. As discussed earlier, Li Tieying, a Politburo member who formerly worked in Lianning, has more influence in the province than Bo's father. Furthermore, Li's brother, Li Tielin, served as deputy head of the CCP Organization Department and may have created more obstacles to Bo's promotion. In a way, factional politics among *taizi* may have also restricted their own career advancement. Eventually, Bo's father helped Bo Xilai to be a member of the delegation of Shanxi, his native province, but his name was still not placed on the ballot of the CC during the preliminary election.

### Restraints on Other Forms of Nepotism

In recent years, deputies of the Party congress and the NPC not only opposed the selection of *taizi* to the leadership, but also resented other forms of nepotism such as the "Qinghua clique" and the "Shanghai gang." The Qinghua faction in the Fifteenth Party Congress, though it remains as strong as in the previous Congress, has met similar difficulties: Qinghua people failed to gain more seats. Zhang Xiaowen, a former Qinghua president and alternate in the Fourteenth Central Committee, was not even placed on the ballot for the Fifteenth Party Congress.

Deputies at the Fifteenth Party Congress used their newly obtained voting power to block some candidates chosen by Jiang Zemin, especially those from Shanghai, despite the fact that Jiang and his associates tried to ensure that their people would win. Prior to the Fifteenth Party Congress, it was widely speculated that Shanghai Party Secretary Huang Ju and Mayor Xu Kuangdi would move to Beijing to take over important offices, while other Shanghai notables would enter the CC. A few days before the congress, Jiang promoted Chen Zhili, deputy Party secretary of Shanghai, to be the Party secretary of the State Education Commission. This could have meant that Chen's membership on the CC would not count as part of the Shanghai delegation. But in the preliminary election, three men from Shanghai (including two vice mayors and You Guixi, head of Jiang's bodyguards originally from Shanghai) had to be dropped from full to alternate membership as a result of not receiving enough votes.[85] Huang and Xu, therefore, had to remain in Shanghai because it would have been inappropriate to let mere alternate members of the CC run China's largest city. Other candidates from Shanghai, including Bao Qifan, a model engineer and long-time protégé of Jiang, and Xu Guangchun, the spokesperson for the Fifteenth Congress and former head of the Shanghai Branch of Xinhua News Agency, could not obtain even alternate membership. While Huang Ju, Xu Kuangdi, and Chen Zhili were elected to the CC, their vote tallies were remarkably low. Out of a total of 2,074 votes, Huang received only 1,455 (the lowest among all candidates who were elected to the Politburo). Xu and Chen received 1,374 and 1,315 votes, respectively, which meant that more than one-third of the deputies did not vote for them.[86]

When the 344 members of the Fifteenth CC elected the Politburo, Jiang's "Shanghai gang" again fared badly. They could add just one person, Zeng Qing-hong, to the Politburo, but Zeng's votes (231 out of 344) were among the lowest. This again meant that approximately one-third of the members of the CC did not vote for him. It was a further embarrassment for Jiang personally that seventeen members of the CC did not vote for him as a Politburo member.[87]

The election of members to the State Council and other State positions in the Ninth NPC held in 1998 was similar to the fate of Jiang's "Shanghai gang." For example, Chen Zhili, minister of education, received the fewest votes among twenty-nine ministers. About 35 percent of the deputies opposed the appointment of Han Zhubin, Jiang's long-time associate in Shanghai, to procurator-general of the state.[88] All these examples suggest that political nepotism in its various forms has received growing opposition and criticism, not only from Chinese society but also from deputies of both the Party congress and the NPC, who blocked the election of some *taizi*, *mishu*, and other nominees favored by Jiang.

As noted in chapter 3, in the reform era, especially during the 1990s, the strong growth of regionalism is reflected in the formation of the political elite. Some institutional arrangements have been made to curtail overrepresentation of certain regions in the central leadership. In the Fifteenth CC, all but one of the thirty-one province-level administrations has two full members (the exception is Yunnan, which has one seat). These two seats are usually occupied by the Party secretary and governor (or mayor or chairman) of the province.[89] No province as such has more than two full seats in the Fifteenth CC. This further explains why Jiang appointed his close friend Chen Zhili to be Party secretary of the State Education Commission just a few days before the congress. Otherwise, she too would probably not have been elected to full membership in the CC. Similarly, the transfer of Jia Qinglin, Jiang's long-time friend, from Fujian to Beijing prior to the Fifteenth Congress was also part of Jiang's plan to later promote Jia to Party chief of Beijing and member of the Politburo.[90]

This pattern of distribution can also be found in China's seven greater military regions, each of which has two representatives to the Central Committee. This study also shows that each province and ministry has one representative on the CCDI. Hu Angang, a prominent member of a think tank in the Chinese leadership even proposed a "one-province, one-vote" system for membership to the Politburo. His plan would give every province a voice in Party policy and narrow the disparity between coastal and interior provinces.[91]

This does not necessarily mean that political nepotism is unimportant in Chinese elite recruitment today. The number of *taizi* and the "Shanghai gang" in the central leadership, for instance, may not be high, but numbers alone are not indicative of where the true power lies. Some of the most important leadership posts are often occupied by Jiang's confidants. The most recent example is the above mentioned appointment of Zeng Qinghong as head of the CCP Organization Department. But Zeng's prominence in the Chinese leadership, as previously discussed, is only partially due to his *taizi* background and *mishu* experience. Talent, competence, vision, and interpersonal skills have become increasingly important while institutional restraints on all sorts of nepotism have been implemented.

Jiang, Zeng, and their associates have apparently cultivated a web of personal ties based on Shanghai connections and various other forms of nepotism, and so have other factions in Chinese leadership. Every new leader, however, has strengths and weaknesses and needs to deal with elections, public opinion, and coalition building.

## SUMMARY

What is fascinating about sociopolitical life in China during the reform era is its seemingly contradictory trends and paradoxical developments. This is particularly evident in the realm of the political leadership. Nepotism and favoritism in elite recruitment have become prevalent at a time when educational criteria and technical expertise are more important than class background and political identity. The ubiquitous role of informal networks has accompanied the growing demand for a more representative leadership. New idiosyncratic leaders have often expedited their political careers through *guanxi*, yet they are far more interested in seeking their legitimacy through institutional channels than their predecessors were.

A significant number of the fourth generation of leaders have *taizi* background and/or *mishu* experience. Several situational factors have contributed to this phenomenon. In the 1980s, many veteran leaders retired with the "compensation" that their offspring and loyal *mishu* would be appointed to leadership posts. Some senile leaders, after their official retirement, continued to exert their power and influence "behind the scenes," often through their *taizi* or *mishu* or both. As China's market reform accelerated in the past decade, many *taizi* and *mishu* have actually expanded their interests to the corporate world (some work in the PLA and are in charge of arms sales businesses). They have made huge profits for their families, bosses, and, of course, for themselves. In addition, *taizi* and *mishu* in the fourth generation leadership often received the best possible education in science, engineering, and economics, which has become an important criterion for elite recruitment of the reform era. During the mid-1990s, for example, each and every one of four top aides to Zhu Rongji holds a Ph.D. in economics or business management.

*Taizi* usually form their own factions of *taizidang*, which are based on informal networks, such as associating with individual senior leaders' families (e.g., the Deng family or the Chen Yun family), attending the same school (e.g., Beijing No. 4 Boys High School or the Harbin Military Institute of Engineering), working for the same business firms (e.g., the Kanghua Development Corporation or the CITIC), and marrying into high-ranking cadre families (e.g., the offspring of Chen Yi, Su Yu, and Hu Yaobang).

The fourth generation of leaders with *taizi* background differs profoundly from those of the third generation. *Taizi* in the third generation leadership usually participated in the Communist revolution themselves; some of them were the orphans of Communist martyrs. Most had long-time work experience at the grassroots level in their earlier careers and were promoted step-by-step to their current high leadership posts. Their political legitimacy seems solid and they could stand on their own. In contrast, *taizi* of the fourth generation usually grew up in the newly established Communist regime and have had a privileged life (though in some cases it was interrupted briefly during the first few years of the CR). Both *taizi* and *mishu* in the fourth generation usually did not have much administrative experience at the grassroots or lower levels of leadership. Many often obtain ministerial and provincial leadership posts through some sort of "shortcut" (e.g., working as a *mishu* to a top leader, studying in a postgraduate economics program under a well-known economist, working in the Central Committee of the CCYL, serving in a junior but crucially important or highly visible leadership post). In addition, most *taizi* in the fourth generation were appointed to high-ranking official posts when their fathers or fathers-in-law were still alive and very powerful.

Because of these differences, *taizi* as well as *mishu* in the fourth generation often feel less secure than their counterparts in the previous generation. Their lack of political credentials and grassroots-level leadership experience further undermines their capacity to reach the top of political power. Consequently, despite the prevalence of *taizi* and *mishu* in the bureau/county and ministry/province levels of leadership, the overall presence of the *taizi* through helicopter-style elevation to the top leadership is still limited.

Exceptions, however, do exist. The cases of two idiosyncratic leaders in the new generation, Wen Jiabao and Zeng Qinghong, show the complexities of elite formation and some emerging characteristics in Chinese politics today. Wen's political career advancement is largely attributed to his *mishu* experience. Similarly, Zeng Qinghong's rise to the power center clearly reflects the advantage of *taizi* and the importance of political networks. Yet as they move to the center of power, both of them seem to quickly understand that *guanxi* and patron–client ties from which they greatly benefited could become the source of their weakness rather than their strength. Their legitimacy, therefore, should rely on something beyond their political networks.

Wen Jiabao's experience is remarkable, not only because he worked as a chief of staff for three bosses and the first two were purged while he survived, but also because he gained broad administrative experience during the past decade—handling political crises, coordinating power transitions, commanding the antiflood troops, supervising the nation's agricultural affairs, and overseeing ongoing financial and banking reform. Wen's talent as a superb administrator and his role as a coalition builder seem to explain his legendary survival and success.

Zeng's idiosyncratic personality and performance are even more revealing. As a *taizi*, Zeng differs from most members of *taizidang* in an important aspect: while many other *taizi* tend to seize the "last opportunity" to rush for quick promotion and instant profits, Zeng is a well-rounded tactician with a long-term vision and a great sense of timing. As a *mishu*, Zeng differs from other *mishu* in the manner in which he handles his relationship with his boss and presents himself to the public. Zeng does not have a reputation for fawning over his boss.[92] Instead, he has earned respect from Jiang, who needs Zeng as his "hand, ear, and brain."

These characteristics of Wen and Zeng are better understood against the institutional development in the political establishment and the growing demand by the Chinese people for a more representative and more accountable government. In fact, the experiences of Wen and Zeng reflect the broader changes in the Chinese political system and the increasing importance of public opinion. During the past decade, genuine elections (with some limits) have been adopted at various levels of Party congresses and people's congresses, from the grassroots to the top. Deputies of these congresses have used their voting power to effectively block the election of *taizi* and other kinds of beneficiaries of nepotism and favoritism. The CCP Central Committee now includes two full members per province and two per military region. Such norms are not, however, already democratic. They do not mean that all representatives are equally powerful—except perhaps in the actual process of balloting, which takes place only after many prior conditions regarding who may vote have been met. Yet elections, the distribution of seats based on geographical region, and other policies that restrain nepotism are all available now. It is likely that these institutional measures will be further implemented in the years to come.

*Taizi* background, *mishu* experience, school and business affiliations, birthplace ties, and other bases of nepotism in elite formation are likely to continue in the future. But what is most evident in Chinese politics at present is the broad trend of movement from an all-powerful single leader, such as Mao and Deng, to greater collective leadership, as is now characteristic of the Jiang era. It remains to be seen whether post-Jiang leaders, because of their restraints and limitations, will depart from their predecessors and rely more on power sharing, negotiation, consultation, and consensus building. The cases of Wen Jiabao and Zeng Qinghong seem to point in that direction.

## NOTES

1. See Li and White, "The Thirteenth Central Committee of the Chinese Communist Party," "The Army in the Succession to Deng Xiaoping," and "The Fifteenth Central Committee of the Chinese Communist Party," passim, for many points and tables about technocrats' nontechnocratic connections.

2. This discussion is based on Ronald Brownstein, "The Successor Generation: American Politics as a Family Business," *American Prospect*, November-December 1998, 38–44.

3. Gerald L. Curtis, *The Logic of Japanese Politics* (New York: Columbia University Press, 1999). Quoted from Brownstein, "The Successor Generation," 43.

4. For a comparative study of technocrats and their family backgrounds, see Li Cheng and Lynn White, "Elite Transformation and Modern Change in Mainland China and Taiwan: Empirical Data and the Theory of Technocracy," *China Quarterly* 121 (March 1990): 21–25. In addition, *mishu* played an important role in the Nationalist era. See Lo Chiungkuang, *Jiang Jieshi shouxi mishu Chen Bulei* (Chen Bulei: Jiang Jieshi's chief *mishu*) (Changchun: Qilin wenshi chubanshe, 1994).

5. Murray Scott Tanner and Michael J. Feder, "Family Politics, Elite Recruitment, and Succession in Post-Mao China," *Australian Journal of Chinese Affairs* 30 (July 1993): 90.

6. Brownstein, "The Successor Generation," 39.

7. Robert D. Putnam, *The Comparative Study of Political Elites* (Englewood Cliffs, N.J.: Prentice-Hall, 1976), 57.

8. He Pin and Gao Xin, "Taizidang jieban de shishi yu kenengxing" (The succession of the "party of princes": Reality and possibility), *Dangdai* (Contemporary monthly), April 1992, 51. For a long list of *taizi* in Chinese leadership, see He Pin and Gao Xin, *Zhonggong "Taizidang"* (China's Communist "princelings"), rev. ed. (Taibei: Shibao chubanshe, 1999), 671–682.

9. He and Gao, *Zhonggong "Taizidang,"* 19.

10. Xiao, *Zhong gong disidai mengren* (The fourth generation of leaders of the Chinese Communist Party) (Hong Kong: Xiafeier guoji chubangongsi, 1998), 194.

11. Ibid., 337.

12. Ibid., 337–339.

13. Ibid., 339.

14. James Kynge, "Military to Quit Business," *Financial Times*, 16 November 1998, 8.

15. Xiao, *Zhong gong disidai mengren*, 221.

16. For a detailed discussion of Ye Xuanning, see Xiao, *Zhong gong disidai mengren*, 193–224; and He and Gao, *Zhonggong "Taizidang,"* 402–404.

17. For more information about the school affiliation of *taizidang*, see He and Gao, *Zhonggong "Taizidang,"* 16–17.

18. Ibid., 520.

19. Ibid., 630.

20. Lin Biao later ordered that the Harbin Military Institute of Engineering move to Changsha and change its name to University of Science and Technology for National Defense. Since then, the institute has lost its prominent role as the cradle of China's top military officers.

21. He and Gao, *Zhonggong "Taizidang,"* 330.

22. Ibid., 271.

23. For a detailed discussion of *taizi* at the Kanghua, see He and Gao, *Zhonggong "Taizidang,"* 520–549.

24. For further discussion of informal political networks and corruption, see He Qinglian, *Xiandaihua de xianjing: Dangdai Zhongguo de jingji shehui wenti* (The Pitfall of modernization: Economic and social problems of contemporary China) (Beijing: Jinri zhongguo chubanshe, 1998), 120–124.

25. This information is based on He and Gao, *Zhonggong "Taizidang,"* 111–112.

26. Ibid., 515.

27. Hu Angang, *Zhongguo fazhan qianjing* (Prospects of China's development) (Hangzhou: Zhejiang remin chubanshe, 1999), 35–36.

28. This discussion is based on Li Xiaozhuang, *Zhu Rongji renma* (Zhu Rongji's men) (Taibei: Dujia chubanshe, 1998), 188–204.

29. Based on interviews that I conducted in Beijing in 1996. Also see Anita Chan, "Dispelling Misconceptions about the Red Guard Movement: The Necessity of Re-Examining Cultural Revolution, Factionalism, and Periodization," *Journal of Contemporary China* 1, no. 1 (September 1992): 62–85.

30. Because of his role in the liandong, Bo Xilai spent five years in jail. See He and Gao, *Zhonggong "Taizidang,"* 623.

31. Ibid., 348.

32. Wei Li and Lucian W. Pye, "The Ubiquitous Role of the *Mishu* in Chinese Politics," *China Quarterly* 132 (December 1992): 915.

33. Ibid., 930.

34. For a more comprehensive study of *mishu*, see Wei Li, "The Role of the *Mishu* (Staff) Institution in Chinese Politics" (Ph.D. diss., Massachusetts Institute of Technology, 1994).

35. Li and Pye, "The Ubiquitous Role of the *Mishu* in Chinese Politics," 926.

36. According to Wei Li and Lucian W. Pye, only "leaders with the rank of minister, vice-minister, governor, deputy governor and their equivalents are entitled to have one personal *mishu*; state councilors, vice-premiers, members of the Secretariat or their equivalents are entitled to have two or more; and the key national leaders, such as general secretary, premier, chairman of the Central Military Commission and state president, are entitled to have their personal mishu offices, which are simply named after the leaders" ("The Ubiquitous Role of the *Mishu* in Chinese Politics," 917). As a norm, only the leaders in the last category can have their children or other relatives serve as their personal *mishu*.

37. *Mishu* 7 (July 1998): 11–12.

38 Wu Shaozu, "Shouzhang mishu gongzuo zongsheng tan" (Extensive observation on a *mishu*'s work for a leader), in *Lingdao tongzhi tan mishu gongzuo* (The remarks by leading officials on *mishu* work) (Beijing: Xiandai chubanshe, 1989), 118. Quoted in Li and Pye, "The Ubiquitous Role of the *Mishu* in Chinese Politics," 927.

39. Ibid., 12.

40. *Mishu* 7 (July 1998): 12.

41. Li and White, "The Army in the Succession to Deng Xiaoping," 757–786; and Li and White, "The Fifteenth Central Committee of the Chinese Communist Party," 255–256.

42. For the policy concerning the reshuffling of military officers along with their mishus, see Li and Pye, "The Ubiquitous Role of the *Mishu* in Chinese Politics," 925.

43. Ibid., 918.

44. Li, *Zhu Rongji renma*, 207.

45. Xiao Chong, ed., *Beijing zhinangqun* (Beijing's think tanks) (Hong Kong: Xiafeier Guoji Chubangongsi, 1999), 208.

46. *Baokan Wenzhai* (Newspaper digest), 29 July 1999, 1.

47. For a further discussion of the distinctions between various types of *mishu*, see Li and Pye, "The Ubiquitous Role of the *Mishu* in Chinese Politics," 916–925.

48. Not all the members of the fourth generation of leaders with a *mishu* background served in high offices as the leaders listed in the table. The remaining twenty-three members usually worked for leaders at the bureau or county level.

49. They may also have served as *mishu* at lower levels of leadership earlier in their careers.

50. Li and Pye, "The Ubiquitous Role of the *Mishu* in Chinese Politics."

51. Li and White, "The Fifteenth Central Committee of the Chinese Communist Party," 236.

52. Officially Bao Tong was the *mishu* to the Politburo Standing Committee, but in practice he was responsible only for Zhao Ziyang, then secretary-general of the Party. *New York Times,* July 21, 1992, 3. Quoted from Li and Pye, "The Ubiquitous Role of the *Mishu* in Chinese Politics," 914.

53. Li and Pye, "The Ubiquitous Role of the *Mishu* in Chinese Politics," 914.

54. Some Hong Kong sources reported that Wen owed his elevation mainly to his "lack of a distinct faction affiliation." Willy Wo-Lap Lam, "Promotion to Set Wen on Leadership Path," *South China Morning Post,* 6 March 1998, 10.

55. For more discussion on the power struggle between Jiang and his rivals, see Li and White, "The Fifteenth Central Committee of the Chinese Communist Party," 236–239.

56. This is based on an interview in China in 1999. Zeng's name, however, is not listed in the Central Leading Group for Taiwan Affairs in the Central Committee of the CCP in Chinese publications.

57. See Xiao, *Zhong gong disidai mengren,* 26; and Li, *Zhu Rongji renma,* 142.

58. The information is based on various sources, especially Liao and Fan, *Zhongguo renming da cidian* (1994); Shen, *Zhonggong di shiwujie zhongyang weiyuanhui zhongyang jilü jiancha weiyuanhui weiyuan minglu;* and Xiao, *Zhong gong disidai mengren,* 54–61.

59. Xiao, *Zhong gong disidai mengren,* 56.

60. Ibid.

61. For Wang Zhaoguo's arrogance among his associates and subordinates, see Ren Zhichu, *Hu Jintao: Zhongguo kuashiji jiebanren* (Hong Kong: Mirror Books, 1997), 127–132; for Wen's humble personality, see Mary Kwang, "'Capable and Pragmatic' Vice-Premier Wen Draws Wide Interest," *Straits Times* (Singapore), 19 March 1998, 22.

62. Lam, "Promotion to Set Wen on Leadership Path," 10.

63. Kwang, "'Capable and pragmatic' Vice-Premier Wen Draws Wide Interest," 22.

64. Ibid.

65. He and Gao, *Zhonggong "Taizidang,"* 303–316; Xiao, *Zhong gong disidai mengren,* 18–27; and Oliver Chou, "Key Jiang Protégé Being Groomed," *Straits Times* (Singapore), 15 April 1999, 42.

66. This discussion is based on Donald W. Klein and Anne B. Clark, *Biographic Dictionary of Chinese Communism, 1921–1965* (Cambridge: Harvard University Press, 1971), 862–866; and *Who's Who in Communist China* (Hong Kong: Union Research Institute, 1970), 2:642–643.

67. Other members included Mao Zedong, Xiang Ying, Zhu De, Ren Bishi, and Ye Fei. See Hsiao Tsuo-liang, *Power Relations within the Chinese Communist Movement, 1930–1934* (Seattle: University of Washington Press, 1961), 150–151. Quoted from Klein and Clark, *Biographical Dictionary of Chinese Communism 1921–1965,* 863.

68. The author thanks Dai Qing for providing this information, which is also confirmed by other sources, e.g., Klein and Clark, *Biographical Dictionary of Chinese Communism, 1921–1965*, 863.

69. This is based on my interview with Dai Qing, March 1999.

70. The Ministry of Internal Affairs in the PRC, unlike the situation in many communist countries, is not "a euphemism for secret policy; its main tasks are related to veterans' affairs, the census, and emergency relief measures when natural calamities strike." Klein and Clark, *Biographic Dictionary of Chinese Communism, 1921–1965*, 865.

71. Xiao, *Zhong gong disidai mengren*, 18; and Chou, "Key Jiang Protégé Being Groomed," 42.

72. According to the author's interview in 1999 with a *taizi*, Zeng Shan died because of overwhelming joy when he learned of the fall of Lin Biao and Lin's associates.

73. This is based on an interview in Shanghai in August 1999.

74. Xiao, *Zhong gong disidai mengren*, 23.

75. Chou, "Key Jiang Protégé being Groomed," 42.

76. Ibid.

77. This is based on an interview in Shanghai, August 1999.

78. Xiao, *Zhong gong disidai mengren*, 335.

79. *Mishu* 7 (July 1998): 11–12.

80. For more discussion on Chen Yuan and the Beijing Party Congress election in 1987, see He and Gao, *Zhonggong "Taizidang,"* 171–178.

81. For more discussion on the election, see Li and White, "The Fifteenth Central Committee of the Chinese Communist Party," 231–264.

82. This discussion is based on Xiao Chong, *Zhong gong disidai mengren*, 332–348.

83. Chen Zufeng, "Dalian shizhang Bo Xilai" (Dalian's mayor Bo Xilai), *Caifu* (Fortune) 15 (1998): 6–36. The report was originally published in *Zhongguo zuojia* (Chinese writers) 2 (1997).

84. Chen, "Dailian shizhang Bo Xilai," 21.

85. *Qianshao yuekan* (Advance guard monthly), October 1997, 16–17.

86. *Zhengming* (Contend), October 1997, 9.

87. *Zhengming,* October 1997, 9.

88. Willy Wo-Lap Lam, "All the President's Men," *South China Morning Post,* 18 March 1998, 1; Vivien Pik-Kwan Chan, "Strong Opposition as Jiang Man Gets Top Law Job," *South China Morning Post,* 18 March 1998, 1; and *Shijie ribao,* 20 March 1998, A9.

89. In the municipalities where one full CC member concurrently holds the positions of both Party secretary and mayor, for example, Jia Qinglin in Beijing or Zhang Lichang in Tianjin, usually a deputy Party secretary in the city also holds a full membership in the Fifteenth CC.

90. Xiao, *Zhong gong disidai mengren*, 43.

91. Wu An-chia, "Leadership Changes at the Fourth Plenum," *Issues and Studies* 30, no. 10 (October 1994): 134. Hu Angang also argues that the Financial Committee of the National People's Congress, which is responsible for deciding budgetary matters, should consist of thirty members (each province has one representative in the committee). Hu, *Zhongguo fazhan qianjing*, 312.

92. This observation is based on the author's conversations with several scholars of Chinese studies, including Douglas Paal and Dai Qing.

# 6

# Collective Characteristics: Attitudes and Outlooks of the New Generation of Elites

That which seems the height of absurdity in one generation often becomes the height of wisdom in the next.

—John Stuart Mill

The greatest discovery of my generation is that a human being can alter his life by altering his attitudes of mind.

—William James

What do the following people have in common: Zhang Yimou, Wei Jingsheng, Li Xiaohua, He Qinglian, Jing Yidan, and Li Hongzhi? Very little, except that they are all well-known Chinese.

- Zhang Yimou, a film director whose numerous international award-winning movies such as *Red Sorghum*, *To Live*, *Old Well*, *Judou*, *Raise the Red Lantern*, and *Not One Less* have placed his achievements next to those of Akira Kurosawa
- Wei Jingsheng, a legendary fighter for Chinese democracy whose vision of the "fifth modernization" has inspired people in China and elsewhere for over two decades
- Li Xiaohua, a self-made billionaire whose wealth and entrepreneurship com-

175

pelled the Chinese government to designate a newly found star in the galaxy in his honor

- He Qinglian, a previously obscure economist whose 1998 book *China's Pitfall* launched probably the most provocative criticism of China's reform to date
- Jing Yidan, an anchorwoman (known as "China's Diane Sawyer" among those who are familiar with American news programs), whose call for social justice has changed the image of the CCTV and made her a household name to 300 million prime-time viewers
- Li Hongzhi, a founder of Falun Gong, the newly emergent quasi-religious *qigong* movement, who claims to have gained tens of millions of followers in only a few years and whose growing influence has terrified the Chinese government

These six people differ profoundly from one another in terms of occupational identities, political spectra, and philosophical views. However, they all grew up during the Cultural Revolution and belong to the so-called CR generation. This generation was previously known as China's "lost generation," for an overwhelming majority of them lost the opportunity to pursue an education during the CR. Yet some distinctive members of this generation, as exemplified by the six mentioned above, have now become a formidable force in all walks of life in the country. Despite enormous differences among them, they are all very much aware of their CR identities and often attribute their careers to the lessons learned, the hardships endured, and the wisdom acquired during the CR.[1]

He Qinglian, for example, claims that her generation of public intellectuals is a generation that is "unprecedented and unrepeatable" *(kongqian juehou)*.[2] It is "unprecedented" because the dramatic change in their lives, especially the sense of social responsibility and humanitarianism in the wake of the decade-long national madness and fanatic violence, makes this generation unique. It is "unrepeatable," she argues, because the "hardship environment that fostered her generation will never occur again in China."[3] Consequently, no matter how different members of this generation might be, this "unparalleled revolution in the history of mankind" (borrowing Mao's words) and dramatic changes thereafter had an everlasting impact on the group consciousness and collective characteristics of this generation. He Qinglian's emphasis on the uniqueness of this generation represents the views of others in her age-group. Probably no other generation in contemporary China has a shared identity and group consciousness stronger than that of the CR generation.[4]

Both commonality and diversity are evident among the members of the fourth generation leadership, an important subgroup of the CR generation on which this study focuses. The fourth generation of leaders is neither a monolithic group of people with the same views and values nor a cluster of individuals without any commonality other than that of the same age cohort. The contrast among the members of the fourth generation leadership may be as striking as the difference between Wei Jingsheng and Li Xiaohua, or between He Qinglian and Jing Yidan. Yet all of them have certain shared characteristics fostered by the historical environment in which they grew up. Members of the fourth generation leadership are distinguished from their predecessors by their backgrounds and experiences, as well as by their attitudes and worldviews. For example, Robert Putnam and other theorists in elite studies argue that an elite is not a collection of isolated individuals, not a mere statistical artifact. Its individuals "have similar backgrounds and (though they may have occasional differences of opinion) share similar values."[5] James Meisel, another expert on elite studies, summed up this proposition as the "three Cs—group consciousness, coherency and conspiracy."[6] An analysis of the common traits of the new generation of Chinese elites will help us assess the political trends and tensions of the country in the future.

This chapter first surveys the views and values of new leaders, which have become more accessible in recent years. It also considers the new wave of studies of the CR generation by Chinese scholars, many of whom are also members of this generation. It attempts to highlight collective characteristics of the CR generation in general and members of the fourth generation leadership in particular— their shared idealism, difficult life experiences, disillusionment during their formative years, and eventual maturing thereafter. Although these CR legacies are very important to an understanding of the views and behaviors of the fourth generation of leaders, this chapter also analyzes some other factors, including their experiences during the reform era and the impact of global technological and geopolitical changes that have undoubtedly affected these new leaders.

## RECENT ACCESSIBILITY OF LEADERS' VIEWS AND THE NEW WAVE OF STUDIES OF THE CULTURAL REVOLUTION GENERATION

One of the remarkable political developments in the late 1990s, which itself reflects a new trait of the fourth generation of leaders, is the fact that Chinese leaders seem more accessible and more open about their views and policies than their predecessors were. In 1998, for example, almost all newly appointed cabinet ministers appeared, one at a time, on *Xinwen lianbo,* a prime-time national news program on China's CCTV.[7] In 1999, all provincial governors and Party secretaries did the same. The Internet version of *Renmin ribao* now routinely provides links to the writings and speeches of China's ministerial and provincial leaders. High-ranking leaders' public activities, including their domestic and foreign trips, meetings, and interviews, are made readily available on the *Renmin ribao* Web site.

Meanwhile, numerous books written by or about new leaders have been recently published in the PRC.[8] Leaders at both the minister/province level and the bureau/municipal level have now become a main group of participants in public discourse on reform policies. In 1998, Guo Shuqing, secretary-general of the State Commission for Restructuring Economy, published a book entitled *Integral Grad-*

*ualism,* in which he presented his proposal for China's reform strategy at the turn of the century.[9] As discussed in chapter 5, Guo has been seen as one of Zhu Rongji's four top aides.[10] Guo was born in 1956 and spent many years in Neimenggu, where he worked as a farmer. He studied at Nankai University, received his Ph.D. in political economy from the Chinese Academy of Social Sciences, and also studied at Oxford University as a visiting scholar in the mid-1980s. Prior to assuming his current position, Guo served as vice governor of Guizhou Province. The book, based on both his academic studies and personal experiences, discusses how China should handle the issues of regional disparity and coordination of banking reform with reforms in other areas.

In 1999, Wu Yi, former vice mayor of Beijing and current alternate of the Politburo, edited a book entitled *Woman Mayors,* which includes profiles and interviews of fifty-two woman mayors.[11] About 83 percent of these woman mayors are members of the fourth generation leadership.[12] In addition, a few official periodicals regularly offer comprehensive profiles about new leaders. For example, *Zhonghua yingcai* (China's talents) routinely publishes interview reports about distinctive members of the fourth generation leadership, such as Minister of Education Chen Zhili, Deputy Minister of Foreign Affairs Yang Jiechi, and Auditor General of the State Council Li Jinhua.[13]

In addition, the 1990s also witnessed a new wave of public discourse on the legacies of the CR, including an intellectual search for the group consciousness of the CR generation in general and the so-called three old classes (*laosanjie*) in particular.[14] The three old classes refer to those who graduated from both junior and senior high schools in 1966, 1967, and 1968. They constitute a large part of the CR generation. Most were among the 30 million young men and women who were sent to the countryside in connection with the so-called sent-down movement in the late 1960s and early 1970s.[15] The origins of this new wave can be traced back to 1990, when the Chinese Museum of History in Beijing organized a multiformat exhibition called *Spirit Bound on the Black Earth: The Great Northern Wilderness in Retrospect.* This two-week long exhibition attracted 150,000 visitors.[16] Throughout the 1990s, many other cities organized similar exhibitions, concerts, gatherings, and other events.[17]

Numerous books on the CR generation, especially the "old three classes," were published during the 1990s.[18] Jin Dalu's 1998 book, *Time and Fate: Survival and Development of Three Old Classes,* for example, was one of the first questionnaire surveys of a large number of members (a total of 1,666) of the three old classes, which was conducted in Shanghai in 1995–1996.[19] This survey examined five aspects of the members of the three old classes: (1) biographical information (e.g., their experiences during the CR), (2) current economic conditions (e.g., employment and income distribution), (3) political outlooks (e.g., views about the reform and political participation), (4) group identities, and (5) contrasts with other generations. In the same year, Xu Youyu, a research fellow at CASS, published a collection of memoirs by witnesses of the CR entitled *1966: The Remi-*

*niscences of Our Generation.*[20] Both books explored in detail the lessons and legacies of the CR.

Many of these studies elicit painful memories and serious self-examination of the CR. For example, Chen Kaige, a former member of the three old classes and now an internationally known film director, writes pointedly,[21]

> After a socio-political calamity, there are always many who previously had kneeled but now would stand up and say: "I denounce!" and very few who would kneel and say "I confess!" But when the calamity comes again, there are always many who would kneel and say: "I confess" and very few who would stand up and say "I denounce."

According to Chen and many others, the time has come for the Chinese people to undertake a thorough soul-searching in regard to the causes and meaning of the calamities such as the CR that occurred in the history of the PRC.

Also in 1998, CCTV and many provincial stations aired a twenty-part documentary series entitled *The Three Old Classes: Journey Along with the People's Republic,* which examined how CR experiences fostered some of the basic characteristics of this generation.[22] The production team spent two years traveling in Yunnan, Shaanxi, Hainan, Heilongjiang, and many other provinces, shooting this emotionally powerful and intellectually stimulating documentary series. The producers of the film claimed that it was one of the largest social surveys ever conducted in contemporary China.[23] A significant number of the people who were interviewed in this film were leaders of the fourth generation at various levels, although the film attempted to interview people in all walks of life.

Most studies of the CR generation reveal the continuing misfortunes of some members of this generation—those approaching middle age who were barred from education during the Mao era and are now often unemployed. Their misfortunes during the CR, as Chen Yixin observes, "caused their present disadvantages."[24] In Chen's view, no generation in the PRC suffered more misfortunes than the CR generation. This generation benefited from neither Maoist revolution nor Dengist reform:[25]

> In childhood they experienced the great famine of 1959–1961; in adolescence they endured the CR (1966–1976), which closed schools and sent them to the countryside; in their twenties they were told to defer marrying and to have only one child when they did marry; in their thirties they were denied opportunities of career promotion because they lacked the college diplomas recently required; in their forties many of them were suddenly laid off by their employers. . . . Mao's revolution abandoned them, sweeping them out of urban centers; Deng's reform left them on the sidelines when China moved to embrace the market.

Other books, in contrast, focus on the "tip of the iceberg" of this generation—those who were fortunate enough to return to college after the CR to complete their education, especially those who were later promoted to leadership posts or emerged as distinguished public intellectuals.[26] Zhong Yan's book *China's Three New Classes of Scholars*, for example, focuses on the classes of 1977, 1978, and 1979, those who entered college during these three years as Deng Xiaoping reinstituted entrance examinations for higher education.[27] These so-called three new classes included a great number of the most talented and intellectually mature students in PRC history who had been denied education during the CR. Despite all the odds against them during earlier years of their adult lives, they managed to get their careers back on track. Two recently published books, *Recollections of China's New Generation of Thinkers* and *The Question of the Century: Voices from the Intellectual Community*, present extensive interviews with political leaders and public intellectuals of this generation.[28]

All these exhibitions, television programs, documentary films, books, and interviews have contributed a great deal of useful evidence for scholarly analysis, especially evidence about the collective characteristics of the CR generation, including those who have become political leaders. In addition, the increasing transparency of individual leaders' views and ideas provides important information about policy preferences in dealing with domestic issues and their perceptions of China's strategic interests in a changing world.

## SHARED IDENTITIES AND COLLECTIVE CHARACTERISTICS: THE LEGACIES OF THE CULTURAL REVOLUTION

Just as World War II and the Vietnam War are often seen as defining generational watersheds for Americans, the CR, arguably the most extraordinary event in contemporary China, fostered some very distinctive traits for PRC's fourth generation leadership. Trying to analyze this generation of leaders without studying the effect of the CR on their views, values, and behaviors is akin to examining the baby boom generation in the United States without discussing the roles of economic prosperity and the Vietnam War or studying postwar Jewish communities in Europe without looking at the impact of the Holocaust.

A strong consensus in almost all recent writings about the characteristics of the CR generation is the perception that virtually all members of this generation went through enormous mental trauma and physical hardship. As a result of their CR experiences, they are ideologically less dogmatic, intellectually more sophisticated, and more down-to-earth and capable than their predecessors. These traits have reinforced one another, making this generation of leaders particularly remarkable.

### The Lessons Learned: The End of Ideological Commitments

As already noted, this study defines the fourth generation of leaders as the people who were born between 1941 and 1956. Although there is a fifteen-year span between the oldest and youngest members of the fourth generation of leaders, they usually acquired their first political experiences over the course of the CR. When the CR began, the members of the oldest group were twenty-five years old and the youngest were ten years old. Because an overwhelming majority of them were in elementary school, high school, or college in 1966, many served as Mao's Red Guards and were the most enthusiastic participants at the beginning of the CR.

It is understandable that Mao's most active supporters were China's high school and college students.[29] In addition to being energetic, rebellious, naïve, and pro-violence, like youth elsewhere, the young Chinese students in the 1960s grew up in a "political and cultural environment characterized by idealism, collectivism, moralism, and radicalism," as described by a member of the fourth generation.[30] For years the young students were taught to lead lives of personal sacrifice, blind obedience to Mao and Communism, and revolutionary sadism against class ene-mies.[31] Min Weifang, executive vice president of Beijing University, said in an in-terview that the CR generation had received a "truly unique education" that "aimed to purify people's spirit." The result of this quasi-religious education, ac-cording to Min, was that the young people were very "sincere about their faith in the revolutionary cause."[32]

This faith and this kind of idealism indoctrinated the entire generation that grew up during the CR. They were educated to "value patriotism, heroism, altru-ism, and idealism, and to sacrifice themselves for socialism."[33] Meanwhile, vio-lence, torture, vandalism, and other kinds of brutality were all justified in the name of revolution. Some distinguished members of the fourth generation leadership were radical Red Guards at the beginning of the CR. Information about the be-haviors of members of the fourth generation leadership during the CR is unavail-able, except for some with *taizi* backgrounds. For example, He Pengfei, Bo Xilai, Qiao Zhonghuai, Tan Lifu, and Chen Xiaolu were all famous for their radicalism and their advocacy of the "blood theory."[34] According to an official source, during the two months of August and September 1966, the Red Guards in Beijing (mainly the radical Red Guard group called *liandong*, as discussed in chapter 5) killed 1,700 people, searched 33,600 households, and forced 85,000 people out of the city.[35]

In the spring of 2000, the CCTV program *Commentary* (*shishi luntan*) aired a story about a former Red Guard who confessed his brutality and animalistic behavior to-ward his teacher. The man, now forty-four years old, made a heartfelt request for the teacher's forgiveness for what he did over thirty years ago. This story attracted over 50 million television viewers and caused a "new wave of victimizers' search for for-giveness from victims of the Cultural Revolution."[36] A majority of fourth genera-tion leaders may not have been so radically involved, but idealism and fanaticism were norms and common phenomena during the first two years of the CR.

Their faith was shattered as time passed. Those Red Guards with *taizi* back-grounds, including He, Bo, Qiao, Tan, and Chen mentioned above, were soon persecuted by other factions of the Red Guard movement. A majority of the three old classes were sent to the countryside during the sent-down movement. If ide-alism and devotion to the revolutionary cause inspired many of these teenagers when they left the cities, they felt completely betrayed by the time they were settled in some of the most backward rural areas in the country. Ren Zhiqiang, currently CEO of the Beijing Huayuan International Corporation, probably speaks for all members of his generation who participated in the sent-down movement: "Our dream was broken, energy wasted, education lost, and careers interrupted."[37]

Tens of thousands of young people lost their lives in the countryside because of accidents or other tragic causes. Almost all who participated in the sent-down movement, including those who pledged that they would permanently settle in the country, returned to their home cities after the CR.[38] The contrast between these two large-scale migrations is astonishing: they left for the countryside with "big bangs and big red flowers" in the late 1960s, and a decade later they returned to cities in what they called "the 1979 great escape" *(shengli dataowang)* with a "broken heart and a lost soul."[39]

Many prominent members of the fourth generation leadership were among the 30 million youths who were sent to the countryside. For example, Xi Jinping and Wang Qishan went to Yan'an; Ma Qizhi (governor of Ningxia), Xie Zhenhua (director of the State Administration of Environmental Protection under the State Council), and Zhu Xiaohua (former chair of Everbright Bank of China) spent years in the "great northern wilderness." Ma Wen (secretary of the Discipline Inspection Committee for Central Government Organs) was sent to Neimenggu; Li Keqiang (governor of Henan), Zhang Dejiang (Party secretary of Zhejiang), Shen Guofang (China's ambassador to the United Nations), Ma Kai (deputy secretary-general of the State Council), and Li Ke (Party secretary of Nanning) worked as farmers in rural areas near their native cities.

Older members of the fourth generation leadership had already graduated from college in 1966, but many of them were also sent to remote areas during the CR. Hu Jintao and Wen Jiabao, for example, were sent from Beijing to Gansu Province, where both worked for over a decade. Similarly, both Dai Xianglong, governor of People's Bank, and Jin Renqing, director of the State Administration of Taxation, were sent to Yunnan Province after they graduated from China's Central Institute of Finance and Banking in the early years of the CR. Both worked in Yunnan for over a decade. Tian Chengping (Party secretary of Shanxi) spent a few years on a collective farm in Anhui. As a matter of fact, a majority of those who had recently graduated from college spent some time in the so-called May Seventh schools—what people in the West call "China's labor camps."

The CR certainly affected this generation of leaders in ways that were remarkably different from other generations. Despite some important differences among members of this generation, especially in terms of class and family background, virtually all of its members were idealistic and believed in Mao and Maoism (at least in the early stages of the CR). As Chen Yixin observes, "Such idealism inspired many of them to behave violently in the Red Guards movement because they honestly believed that what they were doing served a great revolution, or to go down to villages because they saw themselves as engaged in a radical transformation of the backward countryside."[40] Later, however, they were all disillusioned and felt manipulated. In the documentary film *Three Old Classes*, for example, many participants of the sent-down movement claimed that their generation was betrayed by Mao, by socialist ideals, by cities, and by the whole society.[41]

As a generation that first went through intensive Communist indoctrination, suffered all kinds of mental and physical trauma, and then woke up with disillusionment, they are doomed to be cynical about ideology and isms. Members of this generation learned lessons from their own mistakes. For example, Yin Hongbiao, a former Red Guard and currently professor of international politics at Beijing University, compared the CR to the Japanese invasion of China during World War II. He believed that participants of both events should draw lessons from their mistakes and crimes.[42] According to Yin and others who studied the CR, fanaticism, violence, blind obedience, ultranationalism, and totalistic ideologies should be vigorously rejected in a healthy society. Yin believes that the lessons learned from the CR directly led to the initiation of reform.[43] This generation, in Yin's words, transformed from the "generation of sloganeers" (*xuanyan de yidai*) to the "generation of down-to-earth practitioners" (*wushi de yidai*).[44]

Liang Heping, deputy secretary-general of a provincial government of Shaanxi, believes that his idealism during the early years of the CR and his disillusionment thereafter have had a positive impact on his life, as he is now a high-ranking government official.[45] This experience helped him realize that any government policy should be based on actual conditions in the country. At present, what China needs the most are, in his words, "down-to-earth practitioners" instead of ideologues.[46]

Many fourth generation leaders are outspoken about how the CR shaped their political attitudes. For example, Chen Zhili wrote in 1999 that "the great calamity that the CR inflicted upon my family and myself made me first wander and wonder, and then wake up to reality, becoming politically and intellectually mature."[47] The CR experience, in Chen's view, also influenced the way in which she handles her leadership job now. "I want to constantly deal with imminent work and issues instead of thinking too much about the long-term future."[48]

Members of the CR generation learned hard lessons about the failure of a planned economy and the problems of a Communist political system. As a result of abandoning their idealism, this generation is characteristically more concerned about today than tomorrow. An aphorism reflects this mentality: "Yesterday has already gone, tomorrow is far away, we should focus on today."[49] Xu Bing, CEO of the Nanjing Xingye Corporation, criticizes socialism for being "obsessed with tomorrow and neglecting today."[50] For Xu, the empty promise that "under socialism, tomorrow will be even better" illustrates nothing but irony.

Members of the fourth generation leadership reaffirm through speeches and interviews that they are more interested in specific issues than ideological debate.[51] For example, during the interviews with ministers in the twenty-six-part television series telecast in 1998, none of the ministers talked about isms, Party leadership, or other slogans, which were typical topics for Chinese leaders in previous generations.[52] Instead, all of these newly appointed ministers addressed the main challenges facing their respective ministries and how they would respond to them. For example, for the minister of education, the challenge was the low investment in education (China's 2.49 percent of GDP in contrast to 4 percent among developing countries on average); for the minister of state ethnic affairs, poverty relief in minority regions; for the minister of supervision, anticorruption measures in the financial sector; for the minister of labor and social security, unemployment, reemployment, medical care, and elderly care; for the minister of construction, the availability of the low-income housing. When asked what should be done to reform civil services, Song Defu, fifty-two-year-old minister of personnel, replied that "Chinese officials should establish the concept that they owe their responsibility to tax payers. They should be subject to the supervision of tax payers."[53] His remarks sound more like the rhetoric of Western politicians than the words of a minister of the Chinese government.

When reform began in 1978, it clearly had the "mandate" of the Chinese people. Turning away from an emphasis on revolutionary campaigns against "class enemies" of the Mao era, Deng Xiaoping and his associates stressed economic development and social stability. Except for a small number of people who were beneficiaries of the CR, most of this generation, especially the 30 million youths who had been sent to the countryside, were enthusiastic about the advent of a new era. The group that benefited the most included those members of the three old classes who returned to college through reinstituted national entrance examinations for college. Their support for the reform was best reflected by the poster "Hello, Xiaoping" that several students of the 1977 class from Beijing University exhibited during the thirty-fifth anniversary parade at Tiananmen.[54] Of 11.6 million who took the examinations in 1977 and 1978, about 674,000 (5.8 percent) were admitted.[55] Some members of the fourth generation leadership and prominent public intellectuals were among this 5.8 percent of the "lucky exceptions" of the "lost generation." Li Keqiang, Ma Wen, Bo Xilai, Guo Shuqing, Lu Zhangong (deputy Party secretary of Hebei), and Lu Hao (Party secretary of Lanzhou) were all students of these two classes, and so were Liu Wei and Hu Angang, two leading Chinese economists who have done occasional consulting work for top leaders.

Sang Xinmin, professor of philosophy at Beijing University and research fellow at the Central Research Institute of Education, states straightforwardly, "Without the reestablishment of the national entrance examination for college, this generation of scholars would not exist. Our fate is so closely tied with the reform."[56] In the early years of the reform, both public intellectuals and political leaders of this generation were heavily influenced by Western ideas and values and were enthusiastic about a market economy. A favorable view of the United States, especially its economic and political systems, was prevalent among them.

The experiences of some leaders with *taizi* backgrounds were particularly revealing. Bo Xilai majored in international journalism in postgraduate school. When he became mayor of Dalian, one of his proudest accomplishments was initiating the annual fashion festival in the city, which was inspired by fashion shows in Paris and other European cities.[57] Chen Yuan, Wang Qishan, Chen Haosu, and Deng's children were all very open-minded in the 1980s, many actively participating in the so-called bourgeois liberal movement. Wang Qishan, for example, was very close to those who later became political dissidents in exile, such as Chen Yizhi and Zhu Jiaming,[58] who vigorously called for more political reform. Similarly, Chen Haosu, then deputy minister of radio, film, and television, introduced many Western films and television programs into China and encouraged young talented film directors such as Zhang Yimou to pursue artistic freedom.[59] In the spring of 1989, prior to the government crackdown at Tiananmen, Chen stated in a conference hosted by CASS that "the Chinese people's demand for democracy is reasonable and justified."[60]

Another example is Chen Yuan, who in the early 1980s was far more interested in Western liberal economic theories than in his father's "bird cage model" for China's economic reform.[61] Almost a decade later, however, Chen became one of the leading proponents of neoconservative economic thought. Also in the 1980s, Hu Deping helped establish a liberal journal in Wuhan called *Youth Forum*. In the first issue, Hu wrote a now widely read essay entitled "Saluting Freedom," in which he argued that Chinese scholars should not avoid using the term "freedom."[62] It was also widely believed that Deng's children were instrumental in accelerating China's economic reform during the early 1990s, when they accompanied Deng on his famous "southern journey."[63]

But many important events in the 1990s—the difficulties and dilemmas of China's market reform, Russia's shock therapy that led to only shock and no therapy, the East Asian financial crisis, and American political scandals—had an impact on them. After two decades of remarkable socioeconomic changes, many solutions to the old problems of socialism have themselves turned into new problems, and the undesirable side effects of the rush to capitalism have become acute. As a result, this generation of Chinese leaders is also suspicious of the "great ideas" suggested by "Harvard economic geniuses" like Jeffrey Sachs. Some have wondered if Adam Smith might be as wrong as Karl Marx, although the results of their errors have been profoundly different. For the new generation of political leaders and public intellectuals, both "the capitalist market economy" and "socialist public ownership" are myths; neither system exists in a pure form.[64] Hu Angang, for example, argues that the "market is by no means omnipotent and one should not idealize it."[65] A young provincial leader recently wrote that "for China the real issue is about the tension between economic efficiency and social justice. The real challenge for policy-makers, therefore, is to achieve the best possible equilibrium."[66]

A favorable view of the United States among Chinese elites in the early years of the reform was shattered during the mid-1990s. Members of the new generation of scholars and political leaders now have "dual attitudes" toward Western ideas, as described by Xu Jilin, a seasoned Chinese scholar. While they continue to be influenced and inspired by some Western values and ideas, new elites have become cynical about the moral superiority of the West and resentful of Western arrogance. The political leaders of the new generation, like public intellectuals in the same generation, are no longer passive recipients of Western ideas but have become "independent thinkers."[67]

Compared with college students of the Tiananmen movement in 1989, public intellectuals of the CR generation are generally far more sophisticated about notions of democracy, freedom, and capitalism. Ren Zhiquang observes that the public intellectuals and political leaders of the CR generation are certainly influenced by Western ideas, but they do not blindly endorse Western values and the Western political system.[68] Zhu Xueqin, another sent-down youth and now professor of history at Shanghai University, explains that in the 1980s Chinese students and intellectuals used the theories of others to express their views, but in the 1990s, public intellectuals do not need such theories because they have developed their own.[69]

## The Hardships Endured: Greater Political Capacity

Enormous physical hardship, imminent needs for survival, and an ever changing sociopolitical environment have also made the CR generation much more enterprising and capable than previous generations in contemporary China. A common expression found in all the recent writings, exhibitions, and documentary films about the CR is that this event was a catastrophe for the nation but could be an asset for an individual's growth.[70]

Wang Yizhou, deputy director of the Institute of World Economy and Politics of CASS, argues that those cultural and political elites who suffered from hunger, poverty, chaos, hardship, and discrimination usually have a better understanding of politics and society than those who have not had such experiences.[71] Wang used the example of leading American scholars and practitioners in political science and international relations. Many of them were born and grew up in foreign countries: Henry Kissinger (Germany), Stanley Hoffmann (Austria), Ernst Haas (Germany), Karl Deutsch (Czechoslovakia), and Zbigniew Brzezinski (Poland). At a young age, many of them witnessed catastrophes inflicted on European nations by Hitler and fascism and therefore vigorously searched for the causes and lessons of the tragedies. In Wang's words, "because of the hardship, discrimination, and war that they experienced during their formative years, they later laid the philosophical and theoretical foundations for the field of international politics in the United States."[72] Not surprisingly, most of them subscribe to the realist school of thought.

Bai Miao, deputy director of China's Center of International Exchanges, used natural disasters as a metaphor to illustrate a similar point. Earthquakes, floods, and hurricanes are catastrophes to the survivors, but the human strength and spirit gained from fighting these disasters, in Bai's words, "is something precious and truly admirable."[73]

Throughout the 1990s, members of the three old classes in Beijing, Shanghai, Chengdu, Xi'an, Guangzhou, and many other major cities in the country organized commemorative gatherings about the sent-down movement. They often named these activities "Have No Regret for One's Youth" (qingchun wuhui).[74] These activities, as some participants explained, did not mean that people were nostalgic about the hard times they faced during their younger years.[75] Bai Miao argued that one should make a distinction between the destruction caused by the sent-down movement and the unyielding spirit nurtured among the young participants of the movement.[76] Rather than celebrate the suffering that they experienced, they saluted the spirit and strength that enabled them to overcome hardship and suffering. This spirit continues to help them deal with new challenges that they face now.

In fact, it is the CR generation that has shouldered the heaviest economic burden during the reform era. They need to support the elderly family members and raise their often spoiled children, while they themselves face the threat of unemployment. In 1997, for example, 60 percent of unemployed people in urban China were members of the three old classes.[77] Liang Xiaosheng, a well-known Chinese novelist who recently wrote a great deal about social stratification and economic disparity, believes that it is fortunate for China to have this "weather-beaten generation" take the burden of structural changes in the Chinese economy.[78] Those laid-off workers often quickly found a new way to make a living. Their adaptability and unyielding spirit, which were nurtured during the CR, also helped them survive the privatization of the state-owned enterprises, another earthshaking change in the socioeconomic life of the country. Their previous experience of *xiaxiang* (down to the countryside) helped them adjust to *xiagang* (off-post or unemployment).[79] If it weren't for the endurance and resilience of this weather-beaten generation that bears the "burden of the reform," as Liang hypothesized, China would probably have collapsed.[80]

Adaptability and strength are even more evident among fourth generation leaders who managed to get their professional and/or political careers back on track after the CR. Wu Hongguang, deputy bureau director in the State Commission for Restructuring Economy, stated that nothing can really intimidate or upset the fourth generation of leaders because they have already experienced all kinds of difficulties.[81] Largely because of their difficult life experiences, some prominent members of the fourth generation leadership did not mind taking challenging jobs. Hu Jintao's tenure in Guizhou and Tibet and Wen Jiabao's leadership role in commanding antiflood measures in 1998 are examples.[82] Similarly, both Lou Jiwei and Guo Shuqing, two top aides to Zhu Rongji, served as vice governors in Guizhou, one of the poorest provinces in the country.[83]

This, of course, does not mean that all members of the fourth generation leadership are competent and experienced. As discussed in chapter 5, some fourth generation leaders lack grassroots-level leadership experience and have risen very quickly, often because of networks, patron–client ties, and *taizi* backgrounds. Some have not put in their time at the grassroots level as the third generation leaders did. These two images about the grassroots experience of the fourth generation are both true. Fourth generation leaders did temper themselves through the CR but rose very quickly after that event.[84] Yet many other members of the fourth generation, especially those who were sent to remote areas after completing their college edu-

cation in the early years of the CR or became sent-down youth, are quite competent. They are able to stand on their own, perhaps more so than third generation
leaders. More importantly, the lack of political credentials and grassroots experience on the part of some new leaders, especially those *taizi*, may undermine their
capacity to reach the top rungs of the political ladder in the future.

Many fourth generation leaders were members of the three new classes of college students. They were already in their late twenties and early thirties when they
took the entrance examinations for college in the last three years of the 1970s.
These three classes of college students are known for their determination, self-reliance, vision, and intelligence. During the Mao era, when anti-intellectualism
was the dominant social mode, it required vision to believe that knowledge and
educated people would be greatly needed in the years ahead and to therefore ed-
ucate oneself for the coming of a new era.

Because of their previous experience, scholars and political leaders of the CR
usually have a strong sense of self-reliance. Li Xiaobing, professor and deputy dean
of the graduate school of the Central Party School, states that "our generation is
a lonely one. No preceding generation ever showed us the way to advance in terms
of either intellectual or political growth. We have to learn everything by ourselves
the hard way."[85] When they were suddenly thrown into the countryside by Mao,
they had no idea what they were going to go through. Only after their disillusionment did they come to realize the need to pursue their own interests.

Lin Yanzhi, a member of the 1977 class at Qinghua University and currently a
standing member of the Henan Provincial Party Committee, likens the students
of the three new classes to the "seeds once buried in the desert," which survived
drought and ultimately excelled over all odds against them.[86] Lin argues that students of these three new classes are tougher, more independent, and more capable than other classes of college graduates in the PRC, either those before or after the CR.[87] Yang Wei, another member of the 1977 class and currently chair of
the department of mechanical engineering at Qinghua University, argues that the
CR enriched the life experience of this generation of leaders and public intellectuals. As a result, according to Yang, they have developed two seemingly contradictory traits: they are "more strong-willed" on one hand and "more tolerant of
different views and values" on the other.[88]

All these characterizations included in recent Chinese intellectual discourse
about the CR generation seem to echo the observations made earlier by some
China watchers in the West. Michael Yahuda, for example, argued that as a result
of the CR, this generation also "acquired a variety of political skills and . . . the
habit of independent thinking."[89]

## The Wisdom Derived: The "Grassroots Consciousness"

The hardship that the sent-down youths experienced has not only enhanced their
problem-solving ability but has also developed their wisdom and knowledge about

the "real China," the vast backward rural areas of the country. The CR threw those privileged urban youths to the bottom of Chinese society. As a result, they have firsthand knowledge of how 85 percent of the Chinese population live. Those sent-down youths who later returned to college often felt that, prior to receiving academic degrees, they also obtained their "degree in social experience" (shehui jingli de zhengshu) during their tenure in rural China.[90]

Yang Fan believes that, despite all the tragedies and difficulties that the CR generation experienced, those who have now become political leaders should be grateful for the "grassroots consciousness" (caogen yishi) that they derived through their extraordinary life experience in rural China.[91] Yang argues that the gentry class that ruled China for centuries prior to the beginning of this century consisted primarily of scholar-landlords who were deeply rooted in the countryside. According to Yang, the way in which the gentry class ruled the country was certainly not democratic (minzhu zhuyi), but it was populist (minben zhuyi).[92] The populist thinking centered around the conviction that the gentry class and bureaucrats should not be out of touch with commoners (laobaixin), especially the vast number of Chinese peasants.

This grassroots consciousness, however, declined at the turn of the century as a result of Western invasions and the collapse of the Chinese imperial system. Urban prosperity was achieved at the expense of rural decay. Later, the victorious Chinese Communist revolution, in Yang's view, further reflected the great importance of the grassroots consciousness. But, for a large part of the twentieth century, this grassroots consciousness has been neglected. The sent-down youths, however, gained this consciousness through years of hard experience in poverty-stricken rural China. This grassroots consciousness is particularly invaluable, as Yang asserts, for those who later become political leaders and public intellectuals because it can better integrate the elites with the masses at times of crisis, such as the crises of unemployment and economic disparity that China is currently experiencing.[93]

The sent-down experience has also led many distinguished public intellectuals of the CR generation to become interested in what Fei Xiaotong called "rural China" (xiangtu zhongguo) or what some young scholars call the "real China."[94] In 1980, artist Luo Zhongli, a member of the three old classes, painted Father, probably the most famous painting in contemporary China. It portrays an old peasant who has a wrinkled, weather-beaten face. These deep wrinkles symbolize both the Chinese nation, which experienced hardship throughout the century, and the yellow earth, which is rough and dry. "Chinese peasants," Luo Zhongli recently explained, "were and still are the spine of China. I would have never understood them if I had not grown up in the countryside. Because of my close ties with Chinese peasants, I would devote my whole life to painting them and telling their stories."[95]

Similarly, Qin Hui, professor of history at Qinghua University, has devoted his professional career to studying Chinese peasants as a result of his nine-year-long work in a poor village in Guangxi Province. His research focuses on the process of marketization and social justice, especially with regard to peasants.[96] Liu Wei, associate dean of Institute of Economics at Beijing University and a consultant of the Beijing municipal government, states that the great northern wilderness, in which he spent almost a decade as a sent-down youth, fostered his character, his worldview, and his approach to economics.[97] He argues that the real objective of China's economic reform and the criterion for its success is not the rapid growth of some major coastal cities, but the structural transition of China's rural economy and the termination of dualism in the Chinese economy.[98]

Fan Gang and Hu Angang, two leading economists who are actively engaged in the current political and intellectual discourse, also spent much of their youth in rural China. Fan worked as a farmer, first in Heilongjiang and then in Hebei, before enrolling at Hebei University in 1977. He received his Ph.D. in Western economics at CASS and worked at Harvard University as a visiting scholar. He is currently secretary-general of the Foundation of China's Economic Reform and director of the Institute of the National Economy. He and his research team have completed fifty projects during the past two years. Fan claims that the defining moment of his career as an economist was his experience as a sent-down youth in Heilongjiang.[99] Interviewed by a Chinese journalist, Fan said, "When I now make policy proposals, I always think of poor farmers who have worked on the barren mountains for generations."[100] In contrast to some economists in both China and the West who are only interested in proving economic theories and constructing analytical models, Fan Gang is more concerned about economic problems in the real world and always uses nonacademic language to explain these problems to ordinary people. "Genuine Buddhists," Fan Gang explains, "give only small talks."[101]

Similarly, Hu Angang spent seven years at a collective farm in Heilongjiang during the CR. Hu is known for his remark that "one who has no knowledge of rural China does not know about China; one who does not understand China's poverty-stricken regions does not have a real understanding of China."[102] After working at Yale University as a visiting economist for a few years, he returned to Beijing. Hu frequently visits the rural areas in poor remote provinces such as Guangxi and Guizhou. As already noted, Hu has also boldly proposed a "one-province, one-vote" system for membership in the Politburo. In his view, this would not only give every province a voice in party policy but would also lead to a more genuine effort to ease local dissatisfaction with the central government and the increasing disparity between coastal and interior provinces.[103] Hu was one of a few scholars who first appealed for the reallocation of resources to China's interior region. He recently claimed that the difference in GDP per capita between Shanghai and Guizhou has increased from 7.3 times in 1990 to 12 times in 2000.[104] In his view, the government should adopt some measures to seriously deal with this growing regional disparity. He also calls for political reform in China, but he believes that the priority of political reform should be technocratic decision making in social-welfare policy, which involves more open discussion and consultation among independent think tanks instead of adoption of the Western multiparty system.[105]

As a prominent young economist consulted by government leaders, Hu has always identified himself as an independent scholar rather than as an aide to a top leader. In his own words, his role model is U.S. economist and Nobel laureate Paul Samuelson, who refused to serve as an adviser to the White House. During the past few years, many distinguished economists, such as Fan Gang and Hu Angang, have begun working for nongovernmental research institutes sponsored by the private sector in China or by foreign charitable foundations. "To speak on behalf of poor people," as Hu recently claims, is the "supreme principle of my professional career."[106]

Hu Angang's sympathetic position toward less privileged and less fortunate people is shared by many well-known public intellectuals in the CR generation. While many intellectuals like Hu Angang and Liu Wei work in influential think tanks, others are influential in the mass media. Jing Yidan, the anchorwoman mentioned at the beginning of the chapter, attributed her distinctive "human touch" on the TV screen to her life experience during the CR. Jing explained that she made her transition from adolescence to adulthood almost overnight when her parents were attacked and their house was searched by the Red Guards.[107] As a thirteen-year-old girl, Jing was responsible for taking care of her two younger brothers. She later spent five years at a collective farm in Heilongjiang. As both a member of the CPPCC and anchorwoman of the most popular television commentary program in the country, Jing believes that she has an obligation to "speak for those who have no means to express their views and their grievances."[108]

In a recently published book on the new generation of public intellectuals and political leaders, Yang Dongping, a senior fellow in the study of higher education at the Beijing Institute of Science and Technology, used the title "From Red to Green" for the chapter that highlights the dramatic change in political values and behavior of the CR generation.[109] Although they were fanatic Red Guards in the 1960s, thirty years later some of them, including Yang Dongping, became advocates for the "Green movement" of environmental protection. In the early 1990s, Yang and his associates established a nongovernmental organization called Friends of Nature, which focused on environmental issues. Yang argues that China must learn lessons from both the tragedies in PRC history and the mistakes made by other industrialized nations. According to Yang, China's current leadership should work to ensure that today's progress does not come at tomorrow's expense.

In addition to participating in the Green movement, Yang has also worked as a chief producer for China's first talk show, *Shihua shishuo* (To speak honestly). More than 300 hours have aired since the program started in April 1996. It has become one of the most popular CCTV programs in the country, similar to the feature news program *Jiaodian fangtan* (Focus), which has approximately 300,000,000 daily viewers.[110] The talk show provides an entirely new forum for the Chinese people to learn, in Yang's words, "how to express your feelings honestly, how to be a good listener, how to care about others, and how to exchange ideas and values."[111] As Yang implies, the emergence of this new forum for dialogue may have profound implications for sociopolitical developments in the country. Like many other public intellectuals in the CR generation, Yang attributes his maturity to his experience as a Shanghai youth who was sent down to the great northern wilderness. "My life in the great northern wilderness," Yang explained, "served a double purpose: to come to understand China's countryside and to know my fellow Shanghaiese."[112] As a son of the former vice mayor of Shanghai, Yang lived an isolated and privileged life in the city prior to being sent down to the countryside.

One of the main challenges that China has faced during the reform era is internal migration, or the so-called floating population (liudong renkou). Gu Shengzu, a former sent-down youth, has been widely recognized as both a leading scholar in the study of China's internal migration and a "spokesperson for millions of Chinese migrants."[113] Born to a peasant family in Huangpuo, Hubei Province, in 1956, Gu returned to his home village after finishing his high school education during the Cultural Revolution. He worked as a farmer, a construction worker, a teacher at a village school, and a newspaper correspondent before enrolling at Wuhan University in 1977, majoring in economics. Gu also studied as a visiting scholar in Japan in 1989 and taught at Wuhan University for many years. In the early 1990s, Gu was among a small number of scholars who were the first to argue that the positive impact of China's tidal wave of migration far outweighs its negative implications.[114] Gu argued that it was inappropriate, or even offensive, to regard China's floating population as the "blind migration" (mangliu). According to Gu, no major economic projects, such as the establishment of the Pudong development zone in Shanghai, the construction for the Asian Games in Beijing, the Three Gorges Dam on the Yangtze River, or the economic "miracle" of the Zhujiang delta, could have been achieved without the contribution of migrant laborers. He attributes this view to his humble experience during his formative years in the rural area. In 1998, Gu was appointed as both dean of the Institute of Strategic Management at Wuan University and vice mayor of Wuhan. Since 1993, Gu has served as a member of the Chinese People's Political Consultative Conference. He has repeatedly urged the adoption of basic rights and more favorable policies for China's millions of migrant workers.

The above examples, however, are mainly based on the views and attitudes of public intellectuals and members of think tanks. Yet, as some Western China watchers observe, there are many indications that China's top leadership, especially the new generation of leaders, is aware of and intensely concerned about China's socioeconomic problems and their political implications.[115] In fact, problems such as rural poverty, income disparity, environmental degradation, social grievances, and high unemployment rates are frequently and fervently discussed by public intellectuals and the general public in today's China, especially by members of government think tanks. This fact alone may be one of the most encouraging indications that the Chinese leaders have tried to adjust themselves to the new socioeconomic environment in the country.

A good example comes from a recent incident concerning Zhang Yimou's film Not One Less, which won the top award at Italy's Venice Film Festival in September 1999. The film tells a story of a very young teacher from a poverty-stricken village who travels to a city to find a dropout from her class. The film was also a great success in China, where the government made it required viewing for students across the country. The movie also inspired the so-called Hope Project, a governmental charity program for rural primary schools, which received donations from the private sector. At first glance, there seems nothing unusual about this incident. Zhang Yimou previously received a handful of prestigious awards from international festivals. It was a common practice for the government to require people to watch certain films (those who lived during the Mao era are surely very familiar with this). Also, it was certainly not new for the Chinese government to campaign for donations from society.

But all these interpretations are superficial, and they miss a number of important new phenomena. Zhang Yimou, as a public intellectual, is known for his critical views, and many of his previous films were banned by the Chinese authorities. Recently, however, Zhang has been more critical of the Western media than of the Chinese government. A few months before the Venice Film Festival, he withdrew *Not One Less* from competition in the Cannes Film Festival. He told journalists both in China and abroad that "the West has for a long time politicized Chinese films. If they are not anti-government, they are considered just pro-government propaganda."[116]

In fact, Zhang's film is critical of present-day China. He makes the point that fifty years after the founding of the PRC and twenty years after the reform, the government is still unable to guarantee a primary school education. Compared with revolutionary veterans, current technocratic leaders in post-Deng China seem to be more tolerant of criticism from public intellectuals, more willing to admit problems, more concerned about the coordination with various sectors and different regions, and more enterprising in allocating resources. Most of the government officials who are in charge of the Hope Project are members of the CR generation. In a number of interviews with Chinese journalists, newly appointed minister of education, Chen Zhili, mentioned the improvement of elementary education in poor rural areas as the top priority of the Ministry of Education.[117] Min Weifang, a former member of the three old classes who is now in charge of Beijing University, says that as an administrator of China's educational system, what he cares about the most is the Hope Project. Throughout the 1990s, he traveled to poor, remote areas and helped these regions establish more elementary schools. It was his experience during the sent-down movement that led him to make a lifelong commitment to education for poor rural children.[118]

Meanwhile, entrepreneurs responded to the government's Hope Project very positively. All the profits from *Not One Less* go to the Hope Project. Li Xiaohua, who is mentioned at the beginning of the chapter, recently donated over 100 million yuan (or about US$12 million) to both educational and sports programs in the country.[119] With his support, a few rural schools were established (many were named after Li Xiaohua). Entrepreneurs now seem to be concerned about their reputations, and they do not want to be seen just as "big-money bugs."

It is no coincidence that the Hope Project received enormous support from people like Zhang Yimou, Chen Zhili, Min Weifang, and Li Xiaohua, who are all members of the CR generation. It is reasonable to believe that, because of their difficult life experiences during their formative years and their "grassroots consciousness," the members of the fourth generation leadership may have a better understanding of issues concerning rural poverty, disparity, and especially the high unemployment rate. Urban unemployment has affected their nonelite generational peers more than anyone else. This partly explains why these issues have received so much attention in today's China. Reaffirming this point, the fourth plenum of the Fifteenth Party Congress, held in September 1999, decided to give greater support to economic development in the interior areas.[120]

## TECHNOCRATIC ORIENTATION AND THE WORLDVIEWS OF THE NEW LEADERSHIP

The legacies of the CR have fostered some of the basic characteristics of the fourth generation of leaders. Yet their personal backgrounds and events after the CR have also affected new leaders. As noted in chapter 3, a majority of the fourth generation of leaders are technocrats, although the number of those who are trained in law and other fields has increased in the Chinese leadership during the past few years. Partly because of their educational training and partly because of the socioeconomic environment in which they grew up, these engineers-turned-politicians often tend to develop technocratic worldviews and policy preferences. In the following section the concept of technocratic orientation and its evolution during the reform era is reviewed.

### Technocratic Orientation: Concept and Context in China

Technocratic orientation is displayed in technocratic leaders' attitudes and policies in both the domestic and international arenas. Domestically, technocratic leaders tend to see scientific and technological developments as determinant of socioeconomic changes in a given society. They generally emphasize the role of technical expertise in the decision-making process, including the role of think tanks. From a technocratic perspective, in a given country, economic growth is more closely linked to technological innovations than to sociopolitical factors.[121] Some socioeconomic problems may have been caused by technological development, but they can be solved only by more technological innovation. To a certain extent, the legitimacy of technocratic leadership is based on rapid economic growth. Technocrats often favor major technological projects at the expense of large-scale dislocation of people. Technocracy, as some scholars observe, is characterized by elite decision-making procedures, hierarchical power structures, unfavorable attitude toward public participation, and sets of regulations that are of a nondebatable character.[122]

In terms of foreign policies, technocrats tend to ascribe to what U.S. economist Robert B. Reich calls "techno-nationalism."[123] Techno-nationalism emphasizes competitiveness among nation-states as the result of scientific and technological development. Technological strength is seen as one of the most important determinants of the rise and fall of major powers. Technology has increasingly become an important economic resource that can increase industrial productivity and create exports. Because of the decisive role that it plays in the modern world, technology is viewed as a body of essential knowledge, a precious commodity that people in one country should save for themselves rather than share with foreigners.[124] National governments, according to techno-nationalists, can shape and reshape the structure of domestic and global industry to the benefit of national welfare. States that have the most advanced technology always offer the best jobs and the highest incomes. Techno-nationalists tend to restrict the transfer of technology, especially high technology, among states.[125] They assume that the economic power generated by technological advances can also be converted into military power. When military conflict occurs, victory is likely to go to the most advanced states.[126]

In China, the technocratic orientation in the reform era certainly departs from the Mao era, when the Chinese Communist regime was preoccupied with constant political campaigns and "mass line" politics. Technocratic thinking was condemned under Mao. Meanwhile, technical experts, along with humanitarian intellectuals, were repeatedly attacked during the first three decades of the PRC, especially during the CR. The notion of "technology in command" (*jishu diyi*) was one of the main revisionist views that Maoists denounced. To a certain extent, ideological indoctrination and political movements characterized the entire Mao era.

Under Deng Xiaoping, there was a correlation between rapid economic reform and the rise of technocrats to leadership. Of course, not all leaders who are trained in the same field have the same outlooks and policies. In the "mixed bag of technocrats," one can find "juicy apples" along with "fuzzy peaches."[127] While acknowledging differences among technocrats (chapter 7 elaborates on differences within the fourth generation of leaders), one can reasonably argue that political elites' attitudes and behaviors may be developed or constrained by their educational and occupational backgrounds, and these may lead them to certain policy preferences. For instance, a bridge engineer may favor building bridges, whether or not the particular place, time, and cost of the bridge are justifiable.[128] Pharaohs built pyramids, but technocrats such as Li Peng, a hydraulic engineer, vociferously favor the Three Gorges Dam.[129] Despite all the controversies surrounding this dam project, the government decided to build it, largely because technocrats in power wanted to do so.[130] In addition, China's "construction fever" in the 1990s and the large-scale dislocation of urban residents in major cities such as Shanghai and Beijing also reflect technocratic attitudes and policy preferences.[131]

Technocratic orientation is also evident in China's foreign policy during the post-Deng era, which has adopted the strategy of "state building through technological strength" (*jishu liguo*). When Deng returned to power in the late 1970s, he proclaimed that science and technology are "productive forces." As a result, Frederick Taylor's "scientific management," Alvin Toffler's "third wave" and his notion of the "information age," and so-called soft science (operational research) all found their way into China during the late 1970s and early 1980s.[132] In 1989, Deng went a step farther to argue that science and technology are "the most important productive forces."

While Deng's statements and the Chinese craze about Taylor, Toffler, and soft science primarily concerned domestic politics, Deng's approval of the so-called 863 Project clearly aimed to increase China's technological competitiveness in a global setting. The 863 Project was initiated in a letter addressed to Deng Xiaoping by four prominent Chinese scientists in March 1986.[133] In the letter, they argued that China should establish its long-term plan for scientific and high-tech research in response to President Ronald Reagan's Star Wars II. They believed that China could not survive among the major powers of the twenty-first century if it did not pursue "state building through technological strength." They requested a total of 200 million yuan for research in seven areas: biology, aerospace, computer and information technology, laser, automation, energy, and material science. The letter was carried to Deng through Zhang Hong, Deng's son-in-law, and Deng immediately approved the plan. Instead of giving 200 million yuan, the Chinese government decided to give 10 billion yuan for the 863 Project.[134] China's recent launch of its first unmanned spacecraft is one of many results of this project.[135] Since 1991, China's State Council has ordered construction of twenty-seven "high-tech development zones" in cities across the country.

When Jiang Zemin became secretary-general of the CCP in 1989, he also strongly advocated the strategy of state building through technological strength. In 1991, Jiang stated, "International competition is actually the competition of comprehensive national power, the key is scientific and technological competition."[136] During the post-Deng era, Jiang Zemin and Zhu Rongji have paid even more attention to the importance of technological innovation and the role of think tanks in the policy-making process. In 1999, Jiang convened the National Conference for Technological Innovation, making technological development the country's top priority.[137] The greatly improved economic conditions in the country during the past two decades have led to China's increasing prestige and power in the world. As the world's fastest growing country, China has attempted to transform its economic wealth to political influence and military might in global affairs.

One of the main differences between Deng's leadership and Jiang-Zhu's leadership is the fact that the latter has placed much more emphasis on think tanks. Both Jiang and Zhu appointed many scholars-turned-politicians as their personal assistants.[138] For example, Wang Huning, a former dean of the law school at Fudan University and a prominent member of Jiang's think tanks, recently accompanied Jiang on his travels, both at home and abroad. As noted in chapter 5, many young economists now assist Zhu Rongji and are actively involved in the policy-making process, especially in the areas of socioeconomic policies. Members of think tanks have responded actively to the recent presidential election in Taiwan. For example, during the recent Taiwan Strait crisis, think tank members such as Xing Qi (fellow at the Research Center of Peace and Development in Beijing), Yu Keli (deputy director of the Taiwan Research Institute of CASS), and Li Ji-aquan (fellow at the Taiwan Research Institute of CASS), frequently appeared in the national and international media, acting as informal spokespersons for the Chinese government.

During the past few years, China hosted a number of international conferences on economic and technological development. For example, the 1999 Fortune Forum Meeting in Shanghai attracted not only CEOs of major corporations but also leading world economists and futurists. In November 1999, Shenzhen hosted the Global Think Tank Forum, at which about 200 representatives of over thirty think tanks in the United States, Japan, Great Britain, and elsewhere attended. The theme of the forum was the role of think tanks in the twenty-first century.[139] One Chinese scholar argues that a nation's degree of modernization depends largely on the extent to which the government uses its think tanks.[140]

Meanwhile, the decision making in China's national defense plan displays a growing attraction to techno-nationalism among Chinese military and political elites. The rapid increase in military expenditures in the PRC, especially in the R&D of the national defense industry, reflects this tendency. As some Western observers noted, China's enthusiasm over high-tech weapons has apparently stemmed from the decisive role of "smart" weapons, which were used by the United States in the Gulf War.[141] Top Chinese leaders urged the PLA to accelerate its research and development program and to obtain sophisticated military equipment. Just after the first Gulf War in 1991, the Chinese government spent several billion dollars to upgrade computer equipment in its military facilities. In addition, the Chinese government has accelerated its Blue Sea Plan, an ambitious long-term project for the modernization of the Chinese navy.[142]

## A New Generation of Leaders and a New Phase of Technocratic Development

In many ways, the technocratic orientation of new generation leaders is the continuation of worldviews and policies adopted by Deng's and Jiang's generations of leaders. Three reasons, however, suggest that the fourth generation of leaders has even stronger technocratic worldviews.

### Convictions Based on Life Experience

Educational credentials carried heavier weight in the recruitment of this generation of leaders than in any previous generation. Their life experiences, especially among those who entered college after the CR, have instilled in them three convictions. First, members of the fourth generation leadership know that their lives were not shaped only by the social and economic status they inherited from their

parents. The nation's ups and downs, its political and economic system, would become the dominant force in their lives. As some members of the CR generation
said, the turning point in their lives occurred in 1978, when the country experienced a turning point.[143] This led them to develop deep concerns about the country's direction and well-being. The whole generation could have been completely
wasted if the CR had continued for another ten years.

Second, as noted in previous chapters, educational credentials often serve as an
important criterion for the advancement of political careers of the fourth generation leaders. They characteristically value education and knowledge, especially
in science and technology. They often hold a technocratic, elitist view. In fact,
the idea of technocracy first spread among the members of the CR generation in
academia, and then became a base of legitimacy for Chinese technocrats. In 1978,
Wen Yuankai, then a thirty-two-year-old professor of chemistry at China's University of Science and Technology, attended a symposium on science and education convened by Deng Xiaoping. Wen proposed that universities recruit students
on the basis of talent rather than family background. This proposal, which was approved by Deng and went into effect the same year, gave members of the lost generation the opportunity to attend college.

In 1982, as a close aide to Wan Li and Zhao Ziyang, Wen asserted that "science
and technology are knocking at the door of China's reform."[144] Because of the
growing importance of science and technology, Wen argued that what China
most urgently needed was a managerial class—"leaders with modern scientific and
managerial knowledge."[145] Wen was also one of the scholars who, in 1986, first
advocated political reforms. In a lecture he delivered in Hong Kong that year,
Wen used a Rubik's Cube metaphor to describe China's reforms.[146] He said that
economic reform could not go forward unless accompanied by political changes.
Believing that all aspects of China, like the small parts of a Rubik's Cube, are interrelated, Wen implied that only intelligent people, those with high IQs, can
solve the Rubik's Cube puzzle.[147] Wen Yuankai later lost his chance to solve
"China's Rubik's Cube" because of his association with Zhao Ziyang. However, his
technocratic views have been shared by his generation of technocrats.

And finally, although the fourth generation leaders are probably more aware of the
need for political reforms than their predecessors, they want to "manage" political
reforms in a controlled way. This is understandable because the chaos of the CR led
them to be suspicious about any mass movement for economic and political changes.
Their life experiences, as well as the PRC history, demonstrate a certain irony—the
more often mass movements occur, the less things change.[148] Social stability, which
they often see as a precondition for other developments, ranks at the top of their
agenda. For example, in 1997 and 1998, the Central Party School conducted two
survey studies among about 100 officials at department and bureau levels who were
attending the school (see table 6.1). In both surveys, over half of the leaders considered social stability the most important factor affecting the process of China's reform.
The surveys also show differing attitudes among leaders in terms of geographical

Table 6.1    Assessment of the Factors That Affect the Process of China's Reform
(percentage)

| Factors | Degree of Importance | | | | | |
| | No. 1 | | No. 2 | | No. 3 | |
| | 1998 | 1999 | 1998 | 1999 | 1998 | 1999 |
| --- | --- | --- | --- | --- | --- | --- |
| Social stability | 50.0 | 53.7 | 9.1 | 9.9 | 14.5 | 11.6 |
| Democratic and scientific policy-making | 12.7 | 14.9 | 11.8 | 11.6 | 10.5 | 8.3 |
| Continuation of reform and Policies of openness | 16.8 | 7.4 | 14.5 | 21.5 | 12.3 | 9.9 |
| Openness of economic environment | 3.2 | 7.4 | 8.2 | 9.9 | 9.1 | 5.3 |
| Central government's authority | 1.8 | 5.4 | 6.4 | 10.7 | 4.5 | 5.8 |
| Controlling inflation, unemployment rate, crime rate, and corruption | 3.6 | 4.1 | 23.2 | 14.9 | 22.7 | 22.3 |
| Stability of financial system | — | 2.5 | — | 8.3 | — | 15.7 |
| Consolidation of legal system | 3.2 | 2.5 | 9.1 | 4.1 | 10.5 | 9.1 |
| Macro-economic control | 3.2 | 1.7 | 10.0 | 7.4 | 7.7 | 4.1 |
| Public opinion | — | 0.8 | 0.5 | 1.7 | 0.5 | 3.3 |
| International relations | — | — | 1.8 | — | 1.4 | 2.5 |
| Others | 5.5 | — | 5.5 | — | 6.4 | 2.5 |
| Total | 100.0 | 100.4 | 100.1 | 100.0 | 100.1 | 100.4 |

*Source and Note: Jingji cankao bao* (Economic reference), 27 January 1999, 6.

regions. A higher percentage of leaders from China's west region (64.3 percent) chose "social stability" as the most important factor, compared with those from the central region (52.2 percent) and the east region (45.5 percent).[149] This difference is likely related to policy difficulties in dealing with tough problems of state-owned enterprises and surplus rural laborers in China's west and central regions. Also understandably, "democratic and scientific policy making" (the Chinese euphemism for technocratic decision making) was ranked second highest in importance among these high-ranking officials because most of them are engineers and economists by training.

*Perceptions Derived from Recent International Events*

The fourth generation of leaders, like their predecessors, are nationalistic. While there is no fundamental difference between this generation and previous generations of leaders in terms of nationalistic sentiments, some recent incidents in China's relations with foreign countries, especially with the United States, as well as events in world politics, have had profound impacts on China's fourth generation of leaders.

Many members of the new generation of leaders have been actively involved in the 863 Project since its beginning. Zhu Lilan, then director of the Chemistry Institute of the Chinese Academy of Sciences, was appointed to direct the 863 Project.[150] She is currently minister of science and technology. Luan Enjie and Zhang Huazhu, both Qinghua graduates and both alternates to the Fifteenth Central Committee of the CCP, are now in charge of China's aerospace and atomic energy programs, respectively. Many prominent leaders on the national, provincial, and municipal levels studied in the West as visiting scholars or degree candidates during the reform era. Lu Yongxiang, who received a Ph.D. in engineering science from Aachen Industrial University in Germany in 1981, is now president of the Chinese Academy of Science. Minister of Education Chen Zhili, Shanghai Mayor Xu Kuangdi, President and Vice Presidents of the Beijing University Chen Jiaer, Chen Zhangliang, and Min Weifang all had promising academic careers in the West. Some (e.g., Xu Kuangdi and Chen Zhangliang) gave up attractive offers from foreign companies or research universities and returned to China at the time of the political uncertainty and economic difficulties. Patriotism and nationalism seemed to play an important role in their decision to return to China. Fan Gang made a generalization when he returned to China after studying at Harvard graduate school: "Those Chinese who lived in foreign countries are usually more patriotic than those who have never been abroad."[151]

A number of disturbing incidents during the past decade, at least from the Chinese perspective, reenforced nationalistic sentiment and technocratic worldviews among Chinese leaders. These incidents included the demonization of China by Western media after the Tiananmen tragedy; a coercive U.S. inspection of a Chinese ship, the *Yin He*, which was believed to be carrying chemical weapons to Iran (though nothing was found); Western opposition to China's bid to host the 2000 summer Olympics (ironically the U.S. Olympic Committee was later found guilty of bribery and other wrongdoing); the accusation of Chinese espionage against U.S. nuclear technology; concerns about the Taiwan Strait; difficulties in both renewing MFN (most favored nation) status and entering the WTO; and, most recently, NATO bombing of the Chinese embassy in Belgrade.

In his recent article "China's America Watchers: Changing Attitudes towards the United States," Phillip C. Saunders echoes a point made by many Chinese scholars that anti-American sentiment in the late 1990s was a "broad-based public reaction to specific events, not the product of government propaganda."[152] After Lee Tenghui's visit to the United States was announced, for example, over 57 percent of Chinese youth polled named the United States as the country they disliked most.[153] Within a decade, the popular image of the Unite States has shifted from "the U.S. as a source of help for China's modernization to the U.S. as a source of trouble."[154]

Joseph Fewsmith, a U.S. China expert, recently observed that some of the incidents reflected an American "sensitivity to certain opinion groups in the United States and an insensitivity to their impact on opinion in China."[155] Meanwhile, the "Nintendo-like" warfare conducted over the Persian Gulf by the United States, the continuing misfortunes in Russia, and NATO air campaigns over the former Yugoslavia all provided important lessons for Chinese technocratic leaders. In the wake of the bombing of the Chinese embassy in Belgrade and the subsequent mass protest against the United States and NATO, China is undergoing a momentous rethinking of its foreign policy.

In addition, both cultural and political elites in China were dismayed with some Western scholarly and journalist writings about the nature of the post–Cold War world and China's role in it. Samuel Huntington's "crash of civilizations," Francis Fukuyama's "end of history," Lester Brown's book *Who Will Feed China?*, and Richard Bernstein and Ross H. Munro's *The Coming Conflict with China* have all provoked resentment in the country. In 1999, for example, two middle-aged senior officers who are faculty members at the National Defense University, Hu Fan and Li Daguang, wrote a book entitled *The Dignity of a Big Country: Building the Firm Fortress of National Security for the Twenty-First Century,* in which they are particularly critical of these Western views.[156]

Some Chinese scholars believe that the military-industry complex in the United States intends to start a new Cold War targeting China. In an article entitled "Arms Sale: A Continuing Source of American Wealth," the author observes that U.S. companies made fortunes through weapon sales during the two World Wars and the Cold War. While many Western countries such as Great Britain have reduced military expenditures, the United States has budgeted an increase in its military budget of $112 billion for the next six years.[157] The author observes that the United States has produced half of the world's weaponry and that in recent years Taiwan has been its biggest customer.[158]

In such an international environment, it is no surprise that techno-nationalism is particularly popular among the new generation of Chinese elites. In an article published in the influential Chinese journal *Outlook,* Wang Yizhou argued that some of these incidents in both the real world and the academic studies of international politics should be seen as a wake-up call for China.[159] Wang was suspicious of NATO's claim for humanitarian intervention in the former Yugoslavia. For him, the disturbing statistics produced by the NATO bombing (10,000 tons of bombs, 3,000 missiles, 1,200 deaths, and 5,000 severe wounds among people in the region, the destruction of 20 hospitals and 250 schools, and thousands of refugees) did not justify their claim. In Wang's view, China needs to learn lessons from this incident and establish its long-term strategy in world affairs. This does not mean that China should take an isolationist foreign policy or emphasize only military buildup. Instead, according to Wang, the Chinese government should pay more attention to domestic problems such as corruption, disparity, unemployment, and ethnic tensions. Meanwhile, the government should establish a "multidimensional safety net" in dealing with any potential foreign threat, including areas such as national defense, information technology, finance and economy, ecology and environment.[160]

Wang's view is representative of the new generation of Chinese elites at present. In his recent article entitled "The Impact of the Information Revolution on Contemporary International Relations," Zhao Xiaochun argues that information technology has three profound impacts: (1) it determines economic strength and military might in a given country; (2) it determines the way and direction in which cultural values and ideas are spread; and (3) it causes the transformation of political and social structures.[161] The technological competition, according to Zhao, is deterministic and crucial for a developing country such as China. The key competition, as many middle-level military officers argue, is in the military. An expert in warfare argues that "the nineteenth century was known for sea wars, the twentieth century for air wars and the twenty-first century will be known for electronic wars."[162]

Not surprisingly, these perceptions have led to two policy recommendations. One is that the government should increase its military expenditures.[163] The other is that more military officers should receive advanced professional training.[164] In fact, the number of technocrats has grown even more rapidly in the military leadership than the civilian leadership in the country. By 1997, for example, about 90 percent of officers at the regiment level (tuanji) held four-year college degrees in military academies. Twenty thousand officers who hold master's and doctorate degrees currently serve in high-level leadership positions in the PLA.[165]

*Notions about the "Knowledge Economy"*

The emphasis on the necessity of technocratic leadership in the information age is most evident recently in the heated discussion of the so-called knowledge economy (zhishi jingji). The term "knowledge economy" is entirely new; it did not exist in the Chinese language before 1998.[166] But since 1998, this term has become one of the most frequently used new terms in the Chinese media. A Chinese news magazine listed it as one of the top ten most popular terms in China in the final years of the 1990s.[167] Several dozen books on the knowledge economy have been published in the past two years.[168] China's top leaders have strongly endorsed this new concept. For example, Jiang Zemin states that "knowledge economy and technological innovation are extremely crucial for China's development in the next century."[169] Jiang also argues that "innovation is the spirit of the development of the Chinese nation."[170]

The concept of knowledge economy is derived from "knowledge-based economy," which was first used by the Organization of Economic Cooperation and Development (OECD) under the United Nations, although similar concepts exist in writings by Daniel Bell, Zbigniew Brzezinski, Alvin Toffler, and John Naisbitt.[171] Yang Fujia, a nuclear physicist and president of Fudan University in Shanghai, identifies a "knowledge economy" as the third form of economy after "labor economy" *(laoli jingji)* and "natural resource economy" *(ziran ziyuan jingji)*.[172] A labor economy, which is also called an agricultural economy, is based on land and labor. A natural resource economy, also called an industrial economy, depends on natural resources from which people develop industries. In contrast, a knowledge economy relies on intellect and information. It is therefore also called an intellect economy or an information economy. According to Yang, as a result of rapid technological development, the world is moving toward "an era in which knowledge can be used as capital for promoting economic growth."[173] In the words of Wu Jisong, director general of the Research Department of the Environment and the Resources Committee of the NPC, "A knowledge economy is characterized by the possession, production, distribution, application and consumption of knowledge that centers around scientific and technological development."[174] In today's world, the linkage between knowledge and economy is closer than ever before.

The knowledge that those Chinese elites refer to does not include all kinds of knowledge. In their view, in an era of a knowledge economy, knowledge can be either extremely valuable or completely worthless.[175] The difference lies in whether the knowledge is innovative and links to recent developments in the high-tech world and the "information highway." Wu Mingyu, professor at the Institute of Asian Pacific Economics and Technological Research, used the following example: "A blank computer disk may cost only a half yuan, but a disk that contains a software can cost several thousand yuan. This is the value of knowledge."[176] According to Wu, there is a fundamental difference between industry economy and knowledge economy: in the former, knowledge serves only as an additional input, which may increase the productivity, while in the latter, knowledge becomes an asset and a product.

Some believe that the current technological revolution is unprecedented. As one study indicates, more than 90 percent of the R&D undertaken since the beginning of recorded history has been accomplished in just the last few decades. Approximately three-quarters of all scientists who have ever lived are still alive.[177] Some even predict that 80 percent of occupations in the twentieth century will disappear within the twenty-first century.[178] The economic consequences of scientific discovery and technological advance have never influenced the fortunes of particular countries and the entire world as much as they do today. Many Chinese writings on the subject have used similar examples and data to illustrate the importance of technological innovation:[179]

- Over 50 percent of the gross national product in advanced industrial nations can be attributed to a knowledge economy.
- In 1980, high-tech industry contributed only 15 percent toward the economic growth of the United States, but in the mid-1990s, it increased to 27 percent, and it is expected to reach 42 percent in 2005.
- In 1982, eight of the top ten richest people in the United States were mag-

nates in the oil industry, but in 1997, six are from the computer and telecommunication industries.

- Among 17,800 employees of Microsoft in the United States in 1998, 3,000 (17 percent) are millionaires.
- In 1998, Bill Gates's Microsoft invested $80 million in the Microsoft China Research Institute in Zhongguancun—the so-called silicon valley of China.
- The assets of the Legend Company (Lianxiang) increased from 200,000 yuan in 1988 to 2 billion yuan in 1998 largely because of its emphasis on technological innovation; the Beida Fangzheng Company increased its assets 7,000-fold within a decade for the same reason.

What do all these references to knowledge economy really mean? What, if any, political agendas lie behind the emphasis on technological innovation and economic development? The heated discussion of knowledge economy parallels the rapid political advance of the new generation of technocrats and economic experts. It also echoes the conventional argument of technocracy—the modern economy has become so complicated that only technical and economic experts can understand the implications of policy decisions, and therefore power should go to these technocrats.[180]

To a certain extent, the notion of knowledge economy serves to consolidate the legitimacy of technocratic rule. Wang Jianzeng, director of the Department of Resources Conservation and Comprehensive Utilization under the State Economic and Trade Commission, argues that in an era of knowledge economy, officials who do not have technical and managerial expertise and cannot adjust to the new economic environment should be replaced.[181] In 1998, about 100 high-ranking officials in the Beijing municipal government went to Qinghua University to study science and technology. At the same time, the same number of professors at Qinghua University went to the city government to inspect and supervise officials in various departments. Jia Qinglin, Party secretary of Beijing, stated that whoever controls state-of-the-art technology and updated information could occupy a vantage point in economic competition in today's world.[182]

The notion of knowledge economy has also led technocratic leaders to increase budgets for high-tech research projects, especially for recruiting talented people at home and abroad. Yang Fujai compares Fudan University in Shanghai with Cambridge University in England. In 1997, the research funding at Cambridge University was equivalent to 1.3 billion yuan, of which 10 percent was spent on equipment and 90 percent on faculty salaries. In contrast, at Fudan University, the grant from the government (100 million yuan) was spent entirely on equipment. Even if Fudan has the same advanced equipment as Cambridge, Fudan does not have any resources to attract talented people.[183]

Yang Fujia's concerns are shared by many university presidents and officials in the field of science and technology. According to Shi Qingqi, director of the Institute of Industrial Research and Development under the State Planning Commission, a majority of the young scientists who were involved in the 863 Project in its initial stages have now gone abroad or joined foreign joint ventures.[184] A 1997 survey also showed that 57–59 percent of Chinese students who were in Ph.D. programs in the United States planed to remain in the States while the percentages for students from South Korea and Taiwan were 24 percent and 28 percent, respectively.[185] According to Chen Zhangliang, about 95 percent of the graduates of Beijing University who are currently studying in Ph.D. programs in top schools in the United States and Europe do not plan to return to China. Chen said, "China's most precious assets have been lost. However, that does not concern the Chinese media, who are interested only in how much foreign capital China can attract."[186] Zhou Guangzhao, former president of the Chinese Academy of Sciences and currently vice chair of the NPC, argues that this "brain drain" problem should be fixed if China really wants to achieve rapid development in science and technology.[187]

There are some indications that during the past few years the Chinese government has made more vigorous efforts to keep and recruit young and middle-aged scientists. Jiang Zemin recently inspected the Research Institute of Chemistry and Physics in Dalian, where the average age of senior administrators was forty-one.[188] The Changjiang Plan, which intends to attract young and middle-aged scientists and technical experts, has been effective. The Chinese government recently committed 1.8 billion yuan each to Beijing University and Qinghua University for the coming three years.[189] Bai Chunli, vice president of the Chinese Academy of Sciences, predicts that in the coming five to ten years, many top-notch Chinese scholars and students who have studied abroad will return to China.[190] Bai's prediction is based on several factors: the improved political and economic conditions in the country, the government's aggressive program to recruit talented people, and China bashing in the United States, especially the recent espionage charge.

## SUMMARY

Among the factors that determine the attitudes and outlooks of political leaders in a given country, experiences they had during their formative years and the sociopolitical environment in which they grew up are the most important ones. China's fourth generation of leaders grew up during the CR. The CR, arguably one of the most extraordinary events in contemporary China, and the dramatic changes thereafter, have had an everlasting impact on the views and values of the fourth generation leaders. This chapter, largely based on recent Chinese publications, interviews, documentary films, and television programs about the CR generation, reveals some collective characteristics of the new generation of Chinese leaders:

- Because of disillusionment experienced during their formative years, fourth generation leaders are, in general, ideologically less dogmatic, intellectually more sophisticated, and practically more open-minded than their predecessors. They are more concerned about issues than isms. The recent difficulties in China's reform, the failure of Russia's shock therapy, and the East Asian financial crisis, along with other events, have also made them realize that a market economy is by no means perfect.

- Because of all kinds of hardships suffered at a young age, they are much more prepared and probably more capable than their predecessors to deal with tough challenges that the country faces. They are also more accessible and more open about their views and policies than their predecessors were.

- Because many of the members of the fourth generation of leaders were sent to the countryside, where they worked as farmers for years during the CR, they have a deep understanding of China, particularly its rural problems. They have developed a "grassroots consciousness," and they are more down-to-earth than their predecessors. They are also more likely than their predecessors to be sympathetic toward the needs of those less fortunate. New leaders are also more likely to be concerned about coordination with various sectors and different regions and more enterprising in allocating resources.

- Because of their common technical educational backgrounds, the fourth generation leaders' domestic and foreign policies are likely to be technocratic. Their convictions regarding the deterministic role of science and technology and their techno-nationalism have been reinforced by their life experiences, by recent international events such as the NATO action in the former Yugoslavia and the Chinese embassy bombing in Belgrade, and by fascinating developments in the high-tech world and on the information superhighway. They tend to overemphasize technical expertise in decision making and are interested in large-scale technological projects.

- Because of the chaos and violence they witnessed during the CR (and the lessons they learned from it), the fourth generation of leaders is deeply concerned about social stability and suspicious about any mass movement for economic and political change. Although members of the fourth generation are probably more aware of the need for political reform than their predecessors, they want to "manage" political reform in a controlled way.

These attitudes and outlooks have often reinforced one another. For example, an understanding of the backwardness of rural China derived from their experiences as sent-down youths may remind new leaders of the importance of the role of technology.[191] Meanwhile, resentment against Western arrogance has not led the new generation of leaders to take an isolationist foreign policy because they understand the need for cooperation and interdependence in what they call "the era of knowledge economy." There is no fundamental difference between this generation and previous generations of leaders in terms of nationalistic sentiments. Nor does the techno-nationalism of Chinese technocratic leaders differ fundamentally from similar ideas in other countries, including the United States.

The preceding generalizations are not free of contradiction or paradox. For example, the overconfidence of technocrats regarding their technical expertise and their inclination toward large-scale technological projects seem to contradict their "grassroots consciousness" and the "common touch" derived during their earlier life experiences. As always, their worldviews and values are also subject to change. Political leaders need to adjust to new socioeconomic environments. This is even more essential in today's China, where other social forces, especially entrepreneurs and public intellectuals, have become increasingly influential.

Most importantly, as noted at the beginning of the chapter, the fourth generation of leaders is not a monolithic group of people with completely identical views and values. Intra-generational differences may have existed in every generation of Chinese leadership, but they are particularly prevalent among the fourth generation of leaders, as the next chapter will show. A balanced analysis of the fourth generation leadership should address both its collective characteristics and its intra-generational diversity.

## NOTES

1. For further discussion of their experiences during the CR and the consequent impact on their worldviews, see Chen Jinsong, *Minzhu doushi Wei Jingsheng zhuan* (A fight for democracy: Biography of Wei Jingsheng) (Los Angeles: Pacific International Publishing, 1998); Wei Jingsheng, *The Courage to Stand Alone: Letters from Prison and Other Writings* (New York: Viking, 1997); Lu Weiyan, "Li Xiaohua zouxiang shijie" (Li Xiaohua: Marching to the world stage) *Caifu* (Fortune) 15 (1998): 84–93; and Xin Hong, "Jing Yidan de zhiqingwei" (The youth character of Jing Yidan), *Mingren* (Celebrities) 3 (March 1999): 4–6.

2. He Qinglian, *Xiandaihua de xianjing: Dangdai Zhongguo de jingji shehui wenti* (The pitfall of modernization: Economic and social problems of contemporary China) (Beijing: Jinri zhongguo chubanshe, 1998), 585–386.

3. Ibid., 386.

4. "Laosanjie: yu gongheguo tongxin," pt. 1; and Qu Taifeng, *Qingjie laosanjie* (The complex of the three old classes) (Xian: Shaanxi renmin chubanshe, 1996), 244.

5. Robert D. Putnam, *The Comparative Study of Political Elites* (Englewood Cliffs N.J.: Prentice-Hall, 1976), 4.

6. James H. Meisel, *The Myth of the Ruling Class: Gaetano Mosca and the "Elite"* (Ann Arbor: University of Michigan Press, 1962), 4.

7. Li, *Buzhang fangtan lu.*

8. For example, Xing Junfang, *Zhongguo ershiyi shiji jingji zouxiang: busheng ji lingdao ganbu fangtanglu* (The direction of China's economy in the twenty-first century: Interviews with ministerial and provincial leaders) (Beijing: Central Party School Publishers, 1997); Zhang Yuan, *Chongsu zhengfu: '98 zhengfu jigou gaige jiaodian da toushi* (Remolding the government: An analysis of governmental reform in 1998) (Beijing: Zhonghua gongshang lianhe chubanshe, 1998); Zhong Qiuju, *Kua shiji de xinyijie zhongguo zhengfu* (The new Chinese government at the turn of the century) (Beijing: Renmin chubanshe, 1998); and Yu Zhen and Shi Dazhen, *Buzhang yanzhong de weilai Zhongguo* (China from the eyes of ministers) (Changsha: Hunan chubanshe, 1995).

9. Guo Shuqing, *Zhengti de jianjin* (Integral gradualism) (Beijing: Jingji kexue chubanshe, 1998).

10. Also see Li, *Zhu Rongji renma*, 206–211.

11. Wu Yi, ed., *Nüshizhang: Zhongguo nüshizhang zhuizong shouji* (Woman mayors: Interview reports) (Beijing: Zhongguo funü chubanshe, 1999).

12. Ibid., 11.

13. *Zhonghua yingcai* (China's talents) 5 (March 1999): 12–13; 3 (February 1999): 24–26; 23 (December 1998): 40–42.

14. The first wave occurred in the late 1970s and early 1980s, largely as a result of the publication of Lu Xinhua's short story "The Wound." For more discussion of the topic, see Zhang Kai and Ji Yuan, *Youshuo laosanjie* (The three old classes revisited) (Beijing: Zhongguo Qingnian Chubanshe, 1997), 3–5.

15. The full name of the "sent-down" movement is "Up to the Mountain and Down to the Village Movement."

16. The exhibition, sponsored by those who previously lived in the great northern wilderness, included numerous photos, letters, and other material objects. See Jin Dalu, *Shiyun yu mingyun: Quanyu laosanjie ren de shengcun yu fazhan* (The time and fate: Survival and development of three old classes) (Shanghai: Shanghai renmin chubanshe, 1998), 2–3.

17. Ibid.

18. For example, Shi Xiaoyan, *Beidahuang fengyun lu* (Time and life in the great northern wilderness) (Beijing: Zhongguo qingnian chubanshe, 1990); Jin Dalu, ed., *Dongfang shiritan: Laosanjie ren de gushi* (Stories of the people of the three old classes) (Shanghai: Shanghai renmin chubanshe, 1997); Jin Dalu, *Ku'nan yu fengliu* (The miserable and admirable) (Shanghai: Shanghai renmin chubanshe, 1994); Gu Hongzhang, *Zhongguo zhishi qingnian shangshan xiaxiang shimo* (The whole story of the "sent-down" movement of Chinese youths) (Beijing: Zhongguo jiancha chubanshe, 1997); and Zhong Qiang, *Disidairen de jingshen* (The spirit of the fourth generation) (Lanzhou: Gansu wenhua chubanshe, 1997).

19. Jin, *Shiyun yu mingyun*, 19.

20. Xu Youyu, *1966: Women zheyidai de huiyi* (1966: Reminiscences of our generation) (Beijing: Zhongguo wenlian chuban gongshi, 1998).

21. *Beijing qingnian bao* (Beijing youth), 18 May 1995. Quoted from Jin, *Shiyun yu mingyun*, 9–10.

22. The Chinese title of the film series is *Laosanjie: Yu gongheguo tongxin.*

23. *Laosanjie*, pt. 20.

24. Chen Yixin, "Lost in Revolution and Reform: The Socioeconomic Pains of China's Red Guards Generation, 1966–1996." *Journal of Contemporary China* 8, no. 21 (1999): 219.

25. Ibid.

26. According to Chen Yixin, there were approximately 1.4 to 1.5 million members of the Red Guard generation (5 percent of their total) who later obtained a college-level education. Ibid., 227.

27. Zhong Yan, *Zhongguo xinsanji xueren* (China's new three classes of scholars) (Hangzhou: Zhejiang remin chubanshe, 1996).

28. Wen Lin and Hai Tao, eds., *Zhongguo xinyidai sixiangjia zibai* (Recollections of China's new generation of thinkers) (Beijing: Jiuzhou Tushu Chubanshe, 1998); and Li Hui and Ying Hong, *Shiji zhiwen: Laizi zhishijie de shengyin* (The question of the century: Voices from the intellectual community) (Zhengzhou: Daxiang chubanshe, 1999).

29. Many autobiographies written by the members of the CR generation illustrate how and why young students in the mid-1960s served as "Mao's ideal agents." See, for example, Jung Chang, *Wild Swans: Three Daughters of China* (New York: Doubleday, 1991), 283; and Liang Heng and Judith Shapiro, *Son of the Revolution* (New York: Knopf, 1983).

30. *Laosanjie*, pt. 1.

31. For violence and social and political backgrounds of the Red Guard movement, see Jing Lin, *The Red Guards' Path to Violence: Political, Educational, and Psychological Factors* (New York: Praeger, 1991); Anita Chan, *Children of Mao: Personality Development and Political Activism in the Red Guards Generation* (Seattle: University of Washington Press, 1985); and Lynn White, *Policies of Chaos: The Organizational Causes of Violence in China's Cultural Revolution* (Princeton: Princeton University Press, 1989).

32. *Laosanjie*, pt. 1.

33. Chen, "Lost in Revolution and Reform," 237.

34. The famous slogan of the blood theory was: Father is a hero, so is his son; father is a counterrevolutionary, his son must be a bad egg. He Pengfei, for example, led the Red Guards in Qinghua and other universities to torture "class enemies" and their children. Chen Xiaolu, who was only a student in the Beijing No. 8 Boys School, was elected head of the school. See He and Gao, *Zhonggong "Taizidang,"* 224, 348.

35. Ibid. For the violence committed by children of high-ranking officials, also see Li and Ying, *Shiji zhiwen*, 165.

36. *Shijie ribao*, April 23, 2000, A8.

37. It is estimated that 800,000 young people lost the opportunity for a higher education as a result of the CR. *Laosanjie*, pt. 1.

38. Among the 27,800 Beijing youths who were sent to Yan'an in the late 1960s, only 423 (about 1.5 percent) remained there by the middle 1990s. Jin, *Shiyun yu mingyun*, 7.

39. Chen, "Lost in Revolution and Reform," 228.

40. Ibid., 222.

41. *Laosanjie*, pts. 7, 14.

42. Ibid., pt. 2.

43. Ibid., pt. 3.

44. Ibid., pt. 17.

45. Ibid., pt. 6.

46. Ibid., pt. 20.

47. *Zhonghua yingcai* (China's talents) 5 (March 1999): 12.

48. Ibid.

49. *Laosanjie*, pt. 16.

50. Ibid., pt. 10.

51. Xing, *Zhongguo ershiyi shiji jingji zouxiang*; Zhang, *Chongsu zhengfu*; Zhong, *Kua shiji de xinyijie zhongguo zhengfu*; and Yu and Shi, *Buzhang yanzhong de weilai Zhongguo; Laosanjie*.

52. For detailed interview reports, ses Li, *Buzhang fangtan lu*.

53. Li, *Buzhang fangtan lu*, 104.

54. This spontaneous incident was later widely publicized in the country. See Zhong, *Zhongguo xinsanji xueren*, 1.

55. Ibid., 13.

56. Ibid., 33.

57. Chen, "*Dalian shizhang Bo Xilai*," 34–36.

58. Li, *Zhu Rongji renma*, 193–199.

59. He and Gao, *Zhonggong "Taizidang,"* 216–219.

60. Ibid., 219–220.

61. Li, *Zhu Rongji renma,* 233–240.

62. He and Gao, *Zhonggong "Taizidang,"* 110.

63. Ibid., 555.

64. For a discussion of intellectual and political discourse in post-Deng China, see Cheng Li, "Promises and Pitfalls of Reform: New Thinking in Post-Deng China," in *China Briefing 2000,* ed. Tyrene White (New York: M. E. Sharpe, in press).

65. Hu Angang, *Zhongguo fazhan qianjing* (Prospects of China's development) (Hangzhou: Zhejiang renmin chubanshe, 1999), 14.

66. Jin, *Shiyun yu mingyun,* 258.

67. Xu Jilin, "Qimeng de mingyun: Ershinian lai de Zhongguo sixiang jie" (The fate of enlightenment: The Chinese intelligentsia during the past two decades), *Ershiyi shiji* (Twenty-first century), December 12, 1998, 4–13.

68. *Laosanjie,* pt. 12.

69. Li and Ying, *Shiji zhiwen,* 173.

70. For example, *Laosanjie,* pt. 3; Zhong, *Zhongguo xinsanji xueren,* 27.

71. Wang Yizhou, "Shixi guoji zhengzhixue de meiguo zhongxin" (The American center of gravity in the study of international politics), *Meiguo yanjiu* (American studies) 1 (March 1998): 57–78.

72. Wang, "*Shixi guoji zhengzhixue de meiguo zhongxin,*" 64–65.

73. *Laosanjie,* pt. 6.

74. For example, *No Regret for One's Youth: An Exhibition of the Twentieth Anniversary of Sichuan Youth Participation in the "Up to the Mountain and Down to the Village Movement" in Yunnan* was held in Chengdu in 1961. See Jin, *Shyuni yu mingyum,* 5.

75. *Laosanjie,* pt. 6.

76. Ibid.

77. Ibid., pt. 16.

78. Ibid.

79. Ma Xiaojun, Party secretary of the Mining Bureau of Northwestern China, said that members of three old classes usually do not have high expectations for material needs to be met and their demand for survival is minimum. *Laosanjie,* pt. 6, pt. 10.

80. Ibid., pt. 16.

81. Ibid., pt. 10.

82. Hu did not spend much time in Tibet during the second half of his tenure due to his illness.

83. It may be argued that neither Lou nor Guo would have spent time in Guizhou if the CCP Organization Department had not objected to their early promotion to top positions in China's financial administration. But both Lou and Guo could certainly have found other important—and more comfortable—leadership posts in Beijing or Shanghai if they had tried.

84. The author is grateful to Joseph Fewsmith for drawing attention to this paradox.

85. Wen and Hai, eds., *Zhongguo xinyidai sixiangjia zibai,* 29.

86. Zhong, *Zhongguo xinsanji xueren,* 23.

87. Ibid., 21.

88. *Laosanjie,* pt. 6.

89. Yahuda, "Political Generations in China," 802.

90. *Laosanjie*, pt. 20.

91. Yang Fan, "Caogen yishi: Zhiqing baogui de jingshen caifu" (Grassroots consciousness: Precious essence of "sent-down" youths), *Jinri mingliu* (Contemporary celebrities) 10 (1998): 16.

92. Ibid.

93. Ibid.

94. Zhong, *Zhongguo xinsanji xueren*, 261.

95. Ibid., 231–232.

96. For more discussion of Qin Hui and his studies of Chinese peasantry, see Wen and Hai, eds., *Zhongguo xinyidai sixiangjia zibai*, 483–497.

97. Ibid., 13.

98. Ibid., 26.

99. Ibid., 529.

100. Zhong, *Zhongguo xinsanji xueren*, 261.

101. Ibid., 264.

102. Hu, *Zhongguo fazhan qianjing*, 6.

103. Wu An-chia, "Leadership Changes during the Fourth Plenum," *Issues and Studies* 30, no. 10 (October 1994): 134. Hu Angang also argues that the Financial Committee of the National People's Congress should consist of thirty members (each province has one representative on the committee). Hu Angang, *Zhongguo fazhan qianjing*, 312.

104. *Shijie ribao*, January 12, 2000, A9.

105. Hu, *Zhongguo fazhan qianjing*.

106. Ibid., 8.

107. Xin, "*Jing Yidan de zhiqingwei*," 4.

108. Ibid., 5.

109. Yang Dongping, "Conghong daolü" (From red to green), in *Zhongguo xinyidai sixiangjia zibai*, 269–306.

110. Yuan Zhengming and Liang Jianzeng, *Jiaodian fangtan* (Focus) (Heibei: Zhongguo dabaike quanshu chubanshe, 1999), 5.

111. Yang, "*Conghong daolü*," 302.

112. Wen and Hai, eds., *Zhongguo xinyidai sixiangjia zibai*, 281.

113. Xiao Chong, ed., *Beijing zhinangqun* (Beijing's think tanks) (Hong Kong: Xiafeier guoji chubangongsi, 1999), 233–238.

114. This discussion is based on Xiao, *Beijing zhinangqun*, 234.

115. For example, see Joseph Fewsmith, "Historical Echoes and Chinese Politics: Can China Leave the Twentieth Century Behind?" in *China Briefing 2000*, ed. Tyrene White (New York: M. E. Sharpe, 2000), 11–48.

116. Maggie Farley, "'One Less Movie at Cannes,'" *Los Angeles Times*, 7 May 1999, F1.

117. *Zhonghua yingcai* 5 (March 1999): 12.

118. Laosanjie, pt. 12.

119. Xiao Yandeng, *Zhongguo meiyou qiyejia: Zhongguo disidai qiyejia quexian fenxi* (China has no entrepreneurs: An analysis of the deficiencies of the fourth generation of entrepreneurs) (Nanchang: Jiangxi renmin chubanshe, 1999), 270.

120. *Renmin ribao*, 27 September 1999, 1.

121. For a further discussion of technocratic politics, see James Burnham, *The Managerial Revolution* (New York: John Day, 1941); John Kenneth Galbraith, *The New Industrial State* (Harmondsworth, U.K.: Penguin, 1969); and Galbraith, "Motivation of Technos-

tructure," *Personal Administration* 31 (November-December 1968): 4–15; Jacques Ellul, *The Technological Society*, trans. John Wilkinson (New York: Knopf, 1964); Daniel Bell, *The Coming of the Post-Industrial Society* (New York: Basic, 1973); *Frank Fischer*, Technocracy and Political Expertise (Newbury Park: Sage, 1990); Zbigniew Brzezinski, *Between Two Ages: American's Role in the Technetronic Era* (New York: Viking, 1970); and John Naisbitt, *Megatrends* (New York: Warner, 1982).

122. Ronald M. Glassman, "Conflicts between Legal and Bureaucratic Systems of Authority." In Ronald M. Glassman, William H. Swatos, Jr., and Paul L. Rosen, (eds.) *Bureaucracy Against Democracy and Socialism*. (New York: Greenwood Press, 1987), 49.

123. Robert B. Reich, "The Rise of Techno-Nationalism," *Atlantic Monthly* 259, no. 5 (May 1987): 63–69.

124. Ibid., 66.

125. Robert Gilpin, *France in the Age of the Scientific State* (Princeton: Princeton University Press, 1968).

126. For a further discussion of techno-nationalist views, see Thomas L. McNaugher, "U.S. Military Forces in East Asia: The Case for Long–Term Engagement" (paper presented at the Eighty-Fourth American Assembly, Columbia University, New York, November 11–14, 1993).

127. Michla Pomerance uses these phrases to refer to the diversification of intellectuals. See "The Intellectual in American Politics: An Irreverent Look," in *Religion, Ideology, and Nationalism in Europe and America: The Historical Society of Israel* (Jerusalem: Graph Chen, 1986), 294, 297.

128. This point is based on Syed Hussein Alatas, *Intellectuals in Developing Societies* (London: Frank Cass, 1977), xiv.

129. Li and White, "The Fifteenth Central Committee of the Chinese Communist Party," 235.

130. According to Li Rui, a leading critic and former vice minister of water resources, the fact that over 400 technocrats had the same hydraulic engineering background in the bureau that is in charge of the planning of the Three Gorges Dam is a main factor in its construction. This is based on an interview I conducted with Li Rui in Beijing, June 1995.

131. For a further discussion of this topic, see Li, *Rediscovering China*, 193–210.

132. Frederick Taylor, *The Principles of Scientific Management* (New York: Viking, 1911); Alvin Toffler, *The Third Wave* (New York: William Morrow, 1980); Gan Shijun, Yu Jianhua, and Cui Guanjie, *Ruan kexue zai Zhongguo* (Soft science in China) (Wuhan: Huazhong ligong daxue chubanshe, 1989); and Feng Zhijun, "Renzhong daoyuan de Zhongguo ruankexue" (China' soft science: Mission and path), *Xiandai lingdao* (Modern leaders), February 15, 1998, 4–5.

133. For a detailed discussion of the 863 Project, see Li Mingsheng, *Zhongguo Baliusan* (China's 863) (Taiyuna: Shanxi jiaoyu chubanshe, 1997).

134. Ibid., 19.

135. China's plan to launch its own spacecraft accelerated in January 1992, which gave the program the title of "the 921 project."

136. *Renmin ribao*, May 24, 1991, 1.

137. *Remin ribao*, August 24, 1999, 1.

138. For a detailed discussion of this trend, see Xiao, *Beijing zhinangqun*.

139. *Huanan xinwen* (South China news), 12 November 1999, 3.

140. Ibid.

141. Harlan W. Jencks, "Chinese Evaluations of 'Desert Storm': Implications for PRC Security," *Journal of East Asian Affairs* 6, no. 2 (Summer-Fall 1992): 462–468.

142. *Gongdang wenti yanjiu* (Studies of problems of the Chinese Communist Party), August 1993, 59.

143. Zhong, *Zhongguo xinsanji xueren*, 33.

144. *Shijie jingji daobao* (The world economic herald), 29 November 1982, 3.

145. *Guang Jiao Jing* (Wide angle) June 16, 1983, 40.

146. Wen Yuankai, *Buke nizhuan de lishi langchao* (Irreversible historical trend) (Hefei, Anhui: University of Science and Technology of China Press, 1986), 16–17.

147. Li and White, "The Thirteenth Central Committee of the Chinese Communist Party: From Mobilizers to Managers," *Asian Survey* 28, no. 4 (April 1988): 394.

148. *Laosanjie*, pts. 6, 20.

149. *Jingji cankao bao* (Economic reference), 27 January 1999, 6.

150. For the details about her appointment, see Li, *Zhongguo Baliusan*, 70–124.

151. Zhong, *Zhongguo xinsanji xueren*, 262.

152. Phillip Saunders, "China's America Watchers: Changing Attitudes toward the United States," *China Quarterly* 161 (March 2000): 58. For similar observations made by Chinese scholars, see Zhang Ming, "Public Images of the United States," in *In the Eyes of the Dragon*, ed. Yong Deng and Fei-Ling Wang (Lanham, Md.: Rowman & Littlefield, 1999), 141–158.

153. Ibid.

154. Ibid.

155. Fewsmith, "Historical Echoes and Chinese Politics."

156. Hu Fan and Li Daguang, *Daguo de zunyan: Gouzhu ershiyi shiji guojia anquan de jiangu baolei* (The dignity of a big country: Building a firm fortress of national security for the twenty-first century) (Shenzhen: Haitian chubanshe, 1999), 402–403.

157. *Shenghuo shibao* (Life time), 6 February 2000, 1.

158. Ibid. According to a recent study in the West, in terms of arms transfer, in 1997 the United States had 45 percent of the world market while China accounted for 2.2 percent. See Gerald Segal, "Does China Matter?" *Foreign Affairs* 78, no. 5 (September-October 1999): 30.

159. *Liaowang* (Outlook), 24 May 1999, 3–6.

160. Ibid., 6.

161. Zhao Xiaochun, "Xinxi geming dui dangdai guojiguanxi de yingxiang" (The impact of the information revolution on contemporary international relations), *Guoji guanxi xueyuan xuebao* (Journal of University of International Relations) 4 (1998): 1–6.

162. Jiang Yuncai and Tan Jianfeng, *Shiji tiaozhan: Zhongguo fuxing qidai zhishi jingji* (The challenge of the century: China's rejuvenation calls for knowledge economy) (Beijing: Lantian chubanshe, 1998), 221.

163. Tang Yongsheng, "Zhongguo guofang gongye de fazhan licheng jiqi zhanlue sikao" (The development path and strategic thinking of China's defense industry), *Shidaichao* (Coming era) 8 (1999): 1–2.

164. Xie Dajun, "Qiantan zhishijing ji jiqi dui junshigeming de yingxiang yu tiaozhan" (Knowledge economy: Its influence on and challenge to the military), *Guofan daxue xuebao: Zhanglue wenti yangjiu* (Journal of National Defense University: Study of strategic issues) 1 (1999): 25–28; and Zhang Zichun, "Toushi zhishijingji shidai de junshi biange" (Insight into military reform in knowledge economy era), *Guofan daxue xuebao: Zhanglue wenti yanjiu* (Journal of National Defense University: Study of strategic issues) 3 (1999): 25–27.

165. Wang Fa'an and Zhang Jie, "Guofang zhengti shili wushinian fasheng zhi de feiyue" (The fundamental change in national defense strength over the past fifty years), *Liaowang* (Outlook), July 26, 1999, 10.

166. Wu Jisong, *Zhishi jingji: Ershiyi shiji shehui de xingqushi* (Knowledge economy: The new social trend of the twenty-first century) (Beijing: Beijing kexuejishu chubanshe, 1998), iii.

167. The other terms included "Y2K" and "sexual harassment" (in the case of Bill Clinton). *Kua shiji* (Cross-century) 3 (March 1999): 19.

168. *Kua shiji* 3 (March 1999): 19. For example, Wu, *Zhishi jingji: Ershiyi shiji shehui de xingqushi*; Zhao Yunxi, *Zhishi zibenjia: Zhongguo zhishifenzi miandui zhishi jingji de jueze* (Knowledge capitalists: Chinese intellectuals' choices in the era of knowledge economy) (Beijing: Zhonghua gongshang lianhehui chubanshe, 1998); and Jiang Yuncai and Tan Jianfeng, *Shiji tiaozhan: Zhongguo fuxing qidai zhishi jingji* (The challenge of the century: China's rejuvenation calls for knowledge economy) (Beijing: Lantian chubanshe, 1998).

169. Zhao, *Zhishi zibenjia*, 4.

170. Ibid., 16.

171. Wu, *Zhishi jingji*, 2–3. Also see Bell, *The Coming of the Post-Industrial Society*; Brzezinski, *Between Two Ages*; Toffler, *The Third Wave*; and Naisbitt, *Megatrends*.

172. Yang Fujia, "Zhishi jingji chujian duanni" (The coming of knowledge economy), *Xin shiji lingdao zhe* (The leaders of new century) 11 (November 1998): 58–59.

173. *Kua shiji* 3 (March 1999): 19.

174. Jiang and Tan, *Shiji tiaozhan*, 6. Also see Wu, *Zhishi jingji*, 12–23.

175. Zhao, *Zhishi zibenjia*, 16–17.

176. Ibid., 8.

177. Walter B. Wriston, "Technology and Sovereignty," *Foreign Affairs* 67, no. 2 (Winter 1989): 63.

178. Si Jiangwei and Zheng Qixu, "Zhishijingji de jueqi yu renliziyuan kaifa" (The rise of the knowledge economy and the use of human resources), *Zhongguo rencai* (China's talents) 10 (1998): 5.

179. Si and Zheng, "Zhishijingji de jueqi yu renliziyuan kaifa," 4–6; Zhao, *Zhishi zibenjia*, 50; Jiang and Tan, *Shiji tiaozhan*, 27; Zhao, "Xinxi geming dui dangdai guojiguanxi de yingxiang," 5; Chen Lumin, "Zhishi jingji: Ershiyi shiji de zhaohuan" (Knowledge economy: The calling of the twenty-first century), *Makesi zhuyi yu xianshi* (Marxism and reality) 3 (1998): 35; and Shi Qingqi, "Ershiyi shiji gaojishu chanye fazhan zhong de renli ziben" (Human capital in the development of high-tech industry in the twenty-first century), *Zhongguo renli ziyuan kaifa* (Human resource development of China), August 1999, 6.

180. For conventional arguments in favor of technocracy, see Howard Scott et al., *Introduction to Technocracy* (New York: Technocracy, 1938); and Henry Elsner Jr., *The Technocrats: Prophets of Automation* (Syracuse: Syracuse University Press, 1967), 1–3.

181. *Xinhua wenzhai* (Xinhua news digest) 1 (1999): 169.

182. Jiang and Tan, *Shiji tiaozhan*, 32.

183. Yang, "Zhishi jingji chujian duanni," 59.

184. Shi, "Ershiyi shiji gaojishu chanye fazhan zhong de renli ziben," 6.

185. Ibid.

186. *Xinhua wenzhai* 4 (1999): 187.

187. Zhou Guangzhao, "Zhishi jingji shidai yijing daolai" (The era of knowledge economy has already arrived), *Xiandai lingdao* 3 (March 1998): 8.

188. *Jiefang ribao*, 23 August 1999, 2.

189. *Zhognguo qingnian bao* (China's youth daily), November 23, 1999, 1.

190. *Renmin ribao* (overseas edition), 23 November 1999, 1.

191. For example, Wu Jisong wrote that during his years in Xinjiang as a sent-down youth, he came to realize that "fifty strong laborers were not good enough to equal a tractor in farming." See Wu, *Zhishi jingji*, 3.

# 7

# Intra-Generational Diversity and Its Implications

The well-bred contradict other people. The wise contradict themselves.
—Oscar Wilde

At 30, one should have a career, at 40 one should not have any puzzles; at 50 one should know the "Mandate of Heaven."
—The *Analects* of Confucius

What is most distinctive about the fourth generation of leaders is their own diversity rather than their differences from previous generations. Although this chapter considers *inter*-generational differences, its emphasis is on *intra*-generational heterogeneity within the fourth generation leadership. The thesis is that the members of the fourth generation of leaders are more diversified than those in previous generations of CCP leadership in terms of political solidarity, educational background, career path, and policy preferences. The chapter concludes with a discussion of the political implications of the fourth generation leaders' coming of age.

## DIVERSITY WITHIN THE FOURTH GENERATION OF LEADERS

Members of the fourth generation of leaders all experienced their formative years during the CR, which had a strong impact on all of them, as discussed in chapter 6. Although these leaders share similar memories of the CR, they had diverse political affiliations during these chaotic years. Unlike the previous generations of leaders who usually shared strong bonding experiences such as the Long March, the Anti-Japanese War, or the Socialist Transformation, this generation of leaders lacks political solidarity. In fact, members of the fourth generation leadership were often on opposite political sides during the CR.

Compared with the usually undifferentiated recruitment channels of previous generations of leaders, there are now more diversified paths through which elites can advance their political careers. Informal networks, such as school ties, blood ties (*taizi*), patron–client ties (*mishu*), and birthplace ties (*tongxiang*), have played a pivotal role in elite promotion of the fourth generation of leaders, as analyzed in earlier chapters. But at the same time, there has been strong resistance, even in the political establishment, to control nepotism and favoritism. In addition, there are some formal channels, more professional paths, that new leaders can use in order to advance their political careers.

More importantly, because of different political affiliations during their formative years and various channels through which they later advanced their careers, the fourth generation of leaders lacks shared convictions and a commitment to the existing political system. Probably similar to the leadership in post-Communist Russia, the fourth generation of PRC leaders lacks a fundamental consensus on major socioeconomic policies, although for the time being they may continue to call their party Communist and their system socialist. This intra-generational diversity is very important for an assessment of the transformation of Chinese politics in the years ahead.

## The Lack of Political Solidarity

The different periods in which members of the fourth generation leadership joined the CCP illustrates the diverse spectrum of political affiliations during their formative years. More specifically, this generation of leaders can be divided into three distinct groups based on the period in which they obtained their Party membership: before, during, or after the CR. Chinese politics underwent substantial changes during these three periods.

Table 7.1 shows that the majority of the fourth generation of leaders—50.9 percent in the 1994 pool and 47.3 percent in the 1999 pool—joined the Party during the decade of the CR, especially during the early 1970s. This is surprising because one of the major criteria for elite recruitment during the Deng era, particularly in the early 1980s, was to eliminate the so-called beneficiaries of the CR, which included people who advanced their political careers during that decade, though many of them also experienced some hardships, such as being sent down to the countryside. Deng's cohorts consisted mainly of elites who suffered politically during the CR, not those cadres who survived intact or advanced their political status.[1]

The discrimination that Deng and his revolutionary veterans practiced against "beneficiaries" of the CR did not seem to apply to the fourth generation of leaders. Perhaps Deng and his veteran associates were only after "bigger fish," and they

**Table 7.1  Periods during Which the Fourth Generation of Leaders Joined the Chinese Communist Party**

|  | 1994 Pool | | 1999 Pool | |
| --- | --- | --- | --- | --- |
| *Period* | *Number* | *%* | *Number* | *%* |
| Prior to the Cultural Revolution | | | | |
| 1956–1959 | 2 | 0.7 | 0 | 0 |
| 1960–1965 | 95 | 34.1 | 79 | 35.3 |
| During the Cultural Revolution | | | | |
| 1966–1969 | 39 | 14.0 | 35 | 15.6 |
| 1970–1975 | 103 | 36.9 | 71 | 31.7 |
| After the Cultural Revolution | | | | |
| 1976–1979 | 26 | 9.3 | 20 | 8.9 |
| 1980–1985 | 13 | 4.7 | 18 | 8.0 |
| 1986–1989 | 1 | 0.4 | 1 | 0.4 |
| Total | 279 | 100.0 | 224 | 99.9 |

*Source:* Liao and Fan, *Zhongguo renming da cidian* (1994); Shen, *Zhonggong di shiwujie zhongyang weiyuanhui zhongyang jilü jiancha weiyuanhui weiyuan minglu.*
*Note:* The data were accumulated and tabulated by the author. Percentages do not add up to 100 due to rounding.

did not care about the cohort of young people who had just obtained Party membership during the CR. There is now no sanction against young political activists of the CR taking leadership positions, since about half of the fourth generation of leaders originally advanced their political careers during that period. They differ significantly from those who joined the Party either before or after the CR.

Those who joined the Party before 1966 were often labeled the "young followers of capitalist roaders" during the CR. Some were persecuted, as were their mentors and patrons, such as Deng Xiaoping and Hu Yaobang. For example, Chai Songyue, currently governor of Zhejiang Province, joined the CCP in 1961 and served as a Party secretary in a factory. During the CR, he was persecuted for his "revisionist views."[2] Lu Yongxiang, president of the Chinese Academy of Sciences, had a similar experience.[3] Those Qinghua graduates who joined the CCP before 1966, Hu Jintao, Jia Chunwang, Wu Shaozu, Tian Chengping, Li Jiating, Liu Yandong, and He Pengfei, were considered politically untrustworthy because of their close association with the "black line" of the Party committee of Qinghua University.

Those who joined the Party soon after the CR were mostly people who had long been denied the opportunity for political careers because of their class and occupational backgrounds. Liu Mingkang, vice governor of Fujian and a senior economist with an MBA from London University, did not join the Party until 1988. A number of top ministerial and provincial leaders, including Huang Zhendong (minister of transportation), Wang Xuebing (governor of the Bank of China), Ou Zegao (vice governor of Sichuan), Gao Guozhu (vice governor of Liaoning), Yao Zhongmin (vice governor of Henan), Chen Liangyu (executive vice mayor of Shanghai), joined the CCP in the 1980s. Xu Kuangdi, mayor of Shanghai, whom many see as a candidate to succeed Zhu Rongji in the future, did not join the Party until 1983. These people were politically inconspicuous before the 1980s, when many of them worked as senior engineers or college professors and were therefore labeled the "ninth stinking category" (*choulaojiu*) and considered "political aliens" (*zhengzhi yiji*). In about a decade they have risen to China's top leadership positions.

Because the fourth generation leaders have spent varying lengths of time in the Party and come from different backgrounds, they do not have the cohesive political solidarity that previous generations of CCP leaders had. For over half a century in CCP history, veteran revolutionaries who participated in the Long March dominated the CCP leadership. Almost all of the 8,000 Communist soldiers who survived the Long March later became the country's political elites. Their bonding experience during the incredible march became the foundation for the People's Republic of China, just as their hardship became the legitimate base for their rule. As Daniel Wright, an American scholar who recently hiked along the route of the Long March, observed, "the Long March veterans who were bound by this powerful shared experience, formed an unusual camaraderie and unity that lasted for 30 years, until the Cultural Revolution."[4] That powerful bonding experience continued into the post-CR era, when most veteran leaders returned to power along with Deng Xiaoping and remained influential for almost another twenty years.

In comparison, the Anti-Japanese War generation and the Socialist Transformation generation did not have such powerful bonding experiences to glue them together. But nevertheless, members of these generations were on the same side during these two events. Zhu Rongji, who was labeled a rightist, was an exception. Only a handful of former rightists entered China's provincial and ministerial leadership. But members of the fourth generation leadership actually belonged to opposing sides during the Cultural Revolution. Although they all experienced disillusionment and physical hardship, their experiences and sufferings during the CR were not identical and in many cases were quite different. Some were considered the "enemies of the people" because of their family background, their occupation, or their views and attitudes, while others were considered "revolutionary successors."

Variations in length of Party membership among the fourth generation of leaders have also had a strong effect on Party seniority, which hitherto depended on date of entry. A crucial factor in the promotion of political elites for most of the PRC history, seniority of Party membership, has now become less essential, or even irrelevant. Other factors, such as educational credentials and administrative experience, seem to be valued more highly than Party seniority.

In addition, nineteen leaders in the 1994 pool are not CCP members. Some of them hold important leadership positions: Pan Guiyu, vice governor of Hunan; Li Lanfang, vice governor of Guangdong; Zhang Rongming, vice governor of Liaoning; and Liu Hezhang, deputy auditor-general on the State Council. It is unlikely that these non-Communists will challenge Party authorities in any fundamental way, and they are not going to form an opposition party, but their political experience often differs from that of Communist elites.[5] In recent years, the authorities seem to have made a genuine effort to promote non-CCP officials to high positions. Over the past five years the number of non-CCP leaders who currently serve as vice governors of provincial governments has increased from seventeen to twenty-two.[6] The Chinese authorities now require each provincial government to have one non-Party member serving as vice governor. Provincial elections are held to select some of those non-Party leaders. This is a significant step toward more genuine elections and power sharing than presently exists.[7]

At present, members of the fourth generation leadership avoid talking about the differences in their political affiliations during the CR. Despite the fact that this generation of leaders experienced their formative years during the CR, they clearly lack political solidarity. They might have had some shared memories of this extraordinary event, but their political and professional careers were affected in profoundly different ways.

## Diversified Career Paths and Work Experiences

An enormous amount of evidence provided in chapters 3–5 supports the argument made in some previous studies of post-Mao leadership: China's new generation of technocratic elites rose to power only partly because of their educational and professional qualifications; many were protégés of veteran patrons.[8] Family background, school ties, regional connections, and work associations with senior leaders (e.g., serving as personal secretaries) are four major informal channels for the career advancement of technocrats. But this does not necessarily mean that nepotism and particularism are the most important factors for career advancement of fourth generation leaders, nor should other formal channels through which new leaders are promoted be overlooked. Some recent changes in elite recruitment, such as increasing diversity in terms of career paths, declining importance of political credentials, and increasing numbers of genuine experts in the new generation of leadership, all deserve serious attention.

Table 7.2 illustrates the promotion patterns of the fourth generation of leaders. Their careers follow one of three paths. On the first path, they are promoted step-by-step, moving from the grassroots (e.g., factory director) to a middle level (bureau/county/district head) and on to a top post (city head, provincial, or ministerial head). Vice Premier Wu Bangguo is a good example. After college graduation, he successively worked as a technician, engineer, factory director, head of an industrial company, head of an industrial bureau, and deputy Party secretary in the municipal Party committee, all in Shanghai, before becoming Party chief of the city. The same step-by-step promotion pattern can be found among other leaders: Li Changchun (Party secretary of Guangdong), Liu Qi (mayor of Beijing), Liu Haiyan (vice mayor of Beijing), Chen Liangyu (executive vice mayor of Shanghai), Bai Enpei (governor of Qinghai), Ji Yunshi (governor of Jiangsu), Niu Shaoyao (executive vice governor of Yunnan), Chai Songyue (governor of Zhejiang), Li Yizhong (president of China Petrochemical Corp), and Zhou Yongkang (minister of land and natural resources).

Another good example is Wang Lequan, current Party secretary of the Xinjiang Autonomous Region and member of the Fifteenth Central Committee. He started his career as a Party functionalist in a rural area of his native Shandong Province, where he moved from deputy head of the people's commune to Party secretary of the commune, deputy Party secretary of the county, Party secretary of the county, deputy Party secretary of the prefecture, vice governor of Shandong, and then to vice Party secretary of Xinjiang before being appointed to his current post. Similarly, other leaders such as Hui Liangyu (Party secretary of Anhui), Quan Zhezhu (vice governor of Jilin), Ou Guangyuan (vice governor of Guangdong), Zhao Jinduo (deputy Party secretary of Hebei), and Qian Yunlu (governor of Guizhou) had identical career paths. While some members of the fourth generation leadership, especially those *taizi* and *mishu*, lack grassroots-level experience and are often promoted very quickly (as discussed in previous chapters), others have long-term grassroots experience, especially those who were "sent-down youth" during the Cultural Revolution.

Fourth generation leaders have also been promoted from clerical positions, such as those who worked as personal secretaries or directors of an office before obtaining high-ranking leadership posts. For example, Li Jianguo, the new Party secretary of Shaanxi Province and a member of the Fifteenth Central Committee, started as deputy director in the office of the CCP Municipal Committee of Tianjin after graduating from college. Through office work, he eventually advanced to become deputy Party secretary of Tianjin and then was appointed Party boss of Shaanxi.

Another good example is Xu Yongyue, currently minister of state security. Born into a family of CCP intelligence agents, he is now in charge of China's KGB. His father, Xu Mingzhen, is currently secretary of the disciplinary committee of the State Commission of Industry of National Defense and has been actively involved

Table 7.2    Career Patterns of Members of the Fourth Generation Leadership

|  | 1994 Pool | | 1999 Pool | |
| --- | --- | --- | --- | --- |
| *Period* | *Number* | *%* | *Number* | *%* |
| Promotion patterns |  |  |  |  |
| Promoted step-by-step | 102 | 34.2 | 57 | 25.4 |
| Promoted through office work | 61 | 20.5 | 44 | 19.6 |
| Promoted irregularly | 135 | 45.3 | 123 | 54.9 |
| Total | 298 | 100.0 | 224 | 99.9 |

*Source:* Liao and Fan, *Zhongguo renming da cidian* (1994); Shen, *Zhonggong di shiwujie zhongyang weiyuanhui zhongyang jilü jiancha weiyuanhui weiyuan minglu.* The data were accumulated and tabulated by the author. Percentages do not add up to 100 due to rounding.

in China's "united front" work concerning Hong Kong and Taiwan affairs.[9] Xu Yongyue joined the PLA when he was eighteen years old and became a Party member at twenty. He studied at a public security school in Beijing and remained there as an instructor for ten years. In 1975, Xu started his *mishu* career, first for Zhou Rongxin, minister of education, then for Zhu Muzhi, minister of culture. Finally he worked for Chen Yun from 1983 to 1993. Before Chen passed away, Xu was appointed deputy Party secretary of Hebei Province. He was engaged in office work for much of his career, until assuming his current post.

Fourth generation leaders on the third path have been promoted irregularly, mainly those who were promoted directly from factory directors or college presidents to mayors or even provincial vice governors. Probably the most significant example is Wang Zhaoguo, who started his administrative career as a deputy director of a branch plant of China's No. 2 Motor Vehicle Plant. Wang impressed Deng during Deng's visit to the plant in the early 1980s and was promoted to first secretary of the secretariat of the CCYL Central Committee, then to director of the Central Office of the CCP Central Committee, then to governor of Fujian, and currently is head of the Department of United Front Work of the Central Committee of the CCP.

Another example of an "irregular" career path is that of Huang Huahua, who started his career as a CCYL official and Party functionalist in a factory after graduating from Zhongshan University as a mathematics major in 1968. After serving as deputy Party secretary in the workshop and deputy head of the factory, he was appointed secretary of CCYL in Zhaoguan city in 1978 and deputy secretary of CCYL of Guangdong in 1985. He attended a middle career training program at the Central Party School in 1983. After serving as secretary of CCYL of Guangdong for two years, he was appointed deputy Party secretary of Mei County in 1987. One year later he was appointed mayor of Meizhou. In 1992, he served as chief of staff for the Guangdong Province Party Committee, and in 1998 he was appointed Party secretary of Guangzhou.

The three types of career paths outlined above suggest that, compared to the Mao era, there are now more diversified channels through which cadres can advance their political careers. This trend echoes similar findings in studies of the career patterns of the post-Mao leadership, such as mayors and military officers.[10] The 1999 pool has a lower percentage of those who were promoted step-by-step than the 1994 pool. A main reason for this is that the Chinese authorities have made greater efforts in recent years to promote younger leaders to the top positions.

Table 7.3 shows the previous work experience that members of the fourth generation leadership have. There are several points worth noting. First, most of the fourth generation of leaders (68.5 percent) have had public administrative experience. They have usually been in charge of urban industrial work (62.1 percent), and many of them (51.7 percent) have had technical work experience, especially in engineering. Second, although a majority of them have had posts in Party leadership, only a small number have had experience in the organizational and ideological work of the Party (10.1 percent and 8.7 percent, respectively). Few have been involved in military service (5.4 percent) or mass organizations (6 percent). This is in sharp contrast to the Mao era, when most leaders claimed to specialize in these areas. Finally, while the above phenomena could also be found in Li and Bachman's study of Chinese mayors about ten years ago, there is an obvious decline in the number of people with experience in economic planning and an increase in the number who have worked in finance, banking, and law.[11]

Some recent studies of elite mobility in urban China argue that there are two distinct career paths to the top. According to Andrew Walder, one path requires both educational and political credentials and leads to administrative posts with considerable authority; the other path requires education but no political credentials and leads to professional positions with little authority.[12] While this may be characteristic of low-level administrative posts, such a distinction is not evident in high-level leadership positions. Walder observes quite accurately that the candidates for elite positions in the reform era are usually screened for educational credentials.[13] Walder also places much weight on political credentials in elite recruitment, but he seems to overlook the fact that the criteria for political credentials have become increasingly dubious. For instance, many prominent natural scientists and scholars, who

Table 7.3    Work Experience of Members of the Fourth Generation Leadership

|  | 1994 Pool (N=298) | |
| --- | --- | --- |
| Work Experience | Number | % |
| Public administration | 204 | 68.5 |
| Urban industry | 185 | 62.1 |
| Party leadership | 180 | 60.4 |
| Technical work (engineering) | 154 | 51.7 |
| Chief of staff or mishu | 66 | 22.1 |
| Rural agriculture | 62 | 20.8 |
| Communist Youth League | 56 | 18.8 |
| Party personnel and organization | 30 | 10.1 |
| Education (teaching) | 27 | 9.1 |
| Propaganda work | 26 | 8.7 |
| Mass Org. (women, union, etc) | 18 | 6.0 |
| Law and legal work | 16 | 5.4 |
| Military service | 16 | 5.4 |
| Academic/scientific research | 15 | 5.0 |
| Economic planning | 12 | 4.0 |
| Finance and banking | 11 | 3.7 |
| Editor and journalist | 6 | 2.0 |

Source: Liao and Fan, Zhongguo renming da cidian (1994).

Note: The data were accumulated and tabulated by the author. Percentages do not add up to 100 due to rounding.

did not have many political credentials, have been quickly promoted to top leadership positions during the past decade. Again, the mayor of Shanghai, Xu Kuangdi, is such a case. In terms of so-called political criteria, informal networks are more essential to the promotion of political elites than formal political credentials such as ideological loyalty, political identity, and leadership experience.

Furthermore, a number of scientists and other academics in the Fifteen Central Committee of the CCP have advanced their careers, both professionally and politically, largely through their academic research. Table 7.4 shows fourteen members of the fourth generation leadership on the Fifteenth Central Committee who are genuine experts in three areas: natural science, technology, and finance and banking. Many received advanced training abroad, either as degree candidates or visiting scholars, in advanced industrial countries. For example, Bai Chunli received his postdoctoral training at the California Institute of Technology, and Lü Feijie was a visiting scholar at the Massachusetts Institute of Technology. Both are now in charge of important scientific research projects in China. Zhang Huazhu, a graduate of Qinghua University, is now in charge of China's nuclear technology and defense industry. Some are members of the Chinese Academy of Science and Chinese Academy of Engineering, two of the most prestigious academic institutions in the country. Lu Yongxiang, to name just one, is currently president of Chinese Academy of Science. Some are presidents of universities or other research institutes. All of them have worked in their respective areas of research for a long time; most, for their entire career. They differ greatly from many other technocrats in their generation, as well as those in the third generation. Other technocrats have often shifted from technical work to political affairs while most of those listed in table 7.4 have been continuously engaged in scientific research.

The experts' takeover is particularly evident in finance and banking. All of them received their education in the same field in which they now are administrators. Similar to their counterparts listed under science and technology, they have usually worked in their own areas of finance, banking, and accounting for their entire careers. This allows them to develop expertise and to apply their knowledge to issues concerning China's banking and financial reforms.

In addition, as noted in chapter 5, Zhu Rongji's four top aides in economic and financial affairs, Lou Jiwei, Zhou Xiaochuan, Li Jiange, and Guo Shuqing, hold doctoral degrees in economics. Several top aides to Jiang Zemin were trained in law and social sciences. Wang Huning, a political scientist and former dean of the law school at Fudan University, and Cao Jianming, a law professor and former president of the East China Institute of Politics and Law, currently serve as deputy director of the General Policy Research Center and vice president of Supreme People's Court, respectively. Both Wang and Cao are in their early forties at the time of this writing and hold vice minister–level positions. Both lived in the United States as visiting scholars in the mid-1980s. Wang now has the official title "Assistant to the President of the PRC" as he travels with Jiang to foreign countries. Wang often identifies himself as a political scientist and claims that China's polit-

Table 7.4  Experts in the Fourth Generation Leadership Who Serve on the Fifteenth Central Committee of the CCP

| Name | Born | Current Position | Academic Title | Education Background | Main Work Experience |
|---|---|---|---|---|---|
| **Science** | | | | | |
| Bai Chunli | 1953 | Vice president, Chinese Academy of Science | Member, Chinese Acad. of Science | Postdoctoral at Cal Tech '85–87; Ph.D., Chinese Academy of Science, '85 | Chemistry Research Ins. (11 years) |
| Zhao Zhongxian | 1941 | Director, Ins. of Physics, Chinese Academy of Science | Member, Chinese Acad. of Science | Visiting School at Iowa Univ., '84–86. Cambridge Univ., '74–75, China's S&T Univ., '64 | Institute of Physics, Chinese Academy of Science (25 years) |
| Lü Feijie | 1943 | President, Chinese Academy of Agronomy | President | Visiting scholar at MIT, '82–84; South China Agricultural Research Institute, '64 | South China Agricultural Research Institute, and Chinese Academy of Agronomy (19 years) |
| Ma Qingsheng | 1944 | Deputy Party secretary of Guangxi | University president | Ph.D. in molecular genetics in England, '83 | President of Guangxi Institute of Agronomy (10 years) |
| Huang Jiefu | 1946 | President, Zhongshan Medical School | University president | Postdoctoral Sydney Univ., '84–87 M.A. Zhongshan Medical School, '82 | Zhongshan Medical School (17 years) |
| **Technology** | | | | | |
| Lu Yongxiang | 1942 | President, Chinese Academy of Science | Member, Chinese Acad. of Science, Chinese Acad. of Engineering | Ph.D. in engineering Aachen Industrial Univ., Germany, '81, Zhejiang Univ., '64 | Zhejiang Univ. and Chinese Academy of Science (25 years) |

| | | | | | |
|---|---|---|---|---|---|
| Liu Jie | 1943 | President, Anshan Steel Corp. | Member, Chinese Acad. of Engineering | Training in Japan, '73–76; postgraduate Beijing Institute of Iron and Steel, '68 | Engineering Research in Wuhan Steel Corp. and Anshan Steel Corp (21 years) |
| Zhang Huazhu | 1945 | Vice minister, Commission of Industry for National Defense | Senior engineer | Qinghua University, '70 | Nuclear research (19 years) |
| Finance/Banking | | | | | |
| Dai Xianglong | 1944 | Governor, People's Bank of China | Senior economist | China's Central Institute of Finance and Banking, '68 | People's Bank of China (31 years) |
| Li Jinhua | 1943 | Auditor general, State Council | Senior economist | China's Central Institute of Finance and Banking, '66 | Accounting work (23 years) |
| Jin Renqing | 1944 | Director, State Administration of Taxation | Senior economist | China's Central Institute of Finance and Banking, '66 | Finance and Accounting work (10 years) |
| Wang Qiren | 1941 | Director, Macao Affairs, State Council | Senior economist | China's Central Institute of Finance and Banking, '63 | People's Bank (17 years) |
| Wang Xuebin | 1952 | Governor, Bank of China | Senior economist | Beijing Institute of Foreign Trade, '76; training in New York and London, '76–83 | Bank of China (19 years) |
| Liu Tinghuan | 1942 | Governor, Industrial and Commercial Bank of China | Senior economist | Liaoning Ins. of Finance and Banking, '68 | People's Bank and Industrial and Commercial Bank of China (21 years) |

*Sources:* Shen, *Zhonggong di shiwujie zhongyang weiyuanhui zhongyang jilü jiancha weiyuanhui weiyuan minglu.*
*Note:* The data were tabulated by the author.

ical reform calls for rapid development of political science.[14] As a legal expert, Cao Jianming gives several lectures to top leaders about international affairs (e.g., legal issues related to the WTO).[15] At present, these top aides to Zhu and Jiang do not serve on the Central Committee of the CCP, but some of them have already held some of the most important leadership posts in financial and economic affairs in the country and others are in charge of political and legal reforms.

This new trend not only differs greatly from many other technocrats in the fourth generation, whose education and training do not bear much relevance to their current leadership posts, but is also in sharp contrast to the third generation of leaders, who were not trained in finance and banking but were in charge of these areas. As discussed in chapter 3, Li Guixian, a Soviet-trained engineer, was governor of the People's Bank from 1988 to 1993, at a time when most bank loans and fixed asset investments went to the least productive part of the economy. Genuine financial experts cannot necessarily solve the tough and complicated socioeconomic problems that China faces. Yet China, like other countries in the world today, greatly needs knowledge and expertise in finance and banking, since the powerful flow of global capital has reached unprecedented levels.[16] What is important is the fact that China's fourth generation of leaders exhibits diversity in terms of work experience and professional expertise, and includes many capable economic and financial experts who are already part of the decision-making circle.

### Different Policy Preferences

Chapter 6 presents shared technocratic worldviews of the fourth generation leadership. Just as the intellectual and political discourse about the technological revolution in the 1980s paved the way for the technocratic takeover in Chinese leadership during the Deng era, the more recent discussion of the so-called knowledge economy has been accompanied by the rapid rise of the fourth generation of leaders, especially those with professional backgrounds in economics, finance, law, and computer technology.[17] To a certain extent, the technocratic worldviews of the fourth generation leaders should be seen as political tactics for claiming power, rather than a belief system that guides their policy preferences. Except for some shared concerns for social stability, economic and technological development, and national security, members of the fourth generation leadership are more diversified in their policy preferences than any previous CCP generation.

There are various reasons for the diversity in policy preferences among the fourth generation leaders. Some characteristics of this generation discussed earlier in the book, such as the lack of political solidarity, the absence of a strong and coherent ideology, and the differences in political affiliations, career paths, and professional expertise, all contribute to the diversity of their policy preferences. In addition, some shared characteristics are often subject to modifications and variations. For instance, technocratic worldviews are certainly elitist by nature, but the grassroots consciousness that some members of the fourth generation leadership obtained during the CR may modify these elitist attitudes. Their firsthand knowledge of economic disparity, difficulties in the transition of the economic structure, and especially many unintentional side effects of the two-decade-long reform, such as deficiencies in the social safety net and high unemployment rates, may help them come to recognize their own limitations. Some technocrats realize that there is no such thing as either a master science or an all-purpose technology that can solve dilemmas of human values.

Some technocrats understand that their technical education does not prepare them well for the administrative jobs that they now hold. For example, Xu Kuangdi, when he became mayor of Shanghai, told a journalist, "Natural scientists and engineers are usually concerned about micro-level, specific problems while statesmen are required to be concerned with macro-level, strategic issues. As a natural scientist, I need to learn a great deal, including political and sociological studies."[18] Xu was inspired by Albert Einstein's remark about the relationship between nature science and politics. Einstein was once asked why, if he could solve the secrets of the universe, he could not devise a plan for the prevention of war. His answer was that "politics is more complicated than the rules of physics."[19] Xu believes that the overrepresentation of those trained in natural science and engineering in the current Chinese leadership reflects the need for present-day rapid economic growth. In fifteen to twenty years, when China's development becomes more sustainable and more balanced, a large number of specialists in economics, social studies, and law will become leaders.[20]

As noted in chapter 6, because of their early life experience, educational background, and recent international events, the fourth generation of leaders is strongly influenced by techno-nationalism. But techno-nationalism is not the only perspective that Chinese leaders hold; its contending viewpoint, techno-globalism, which also emphasizes the role of technology, sounds persuasive for many.[21] From the techno-globalist point of view, technological development is an international endeavor, a joint product of multinational institutions—universities, research laboratories, and business firms—that links scientists and engineers from all corners of the globe through a vast network of telecommunications.[22] For techno-globalists, the world is faced with common problems such as environment degradation, resource depletion, population explosion, international migration and refugees, nuclear proliferation, narcotics, and the spread of AIDS. All these urgent problems are global in scale, and dealing with them requires collective action—cooperation across economic and political boundaries. Both the 1986 Chernobyl incident and the 1999 nuclear accident in Japan showed that in today's world no country lives in isolation from its neighbors. Lives on earth are inextricably intertwined. As some public intellectuals in both China and abroad have stated, "It is one planet with one fragile environment."[23]

Among Chinese leaders, techno-globalist views are most prevalent in the areas of foreign trade and economic globalization. For example, Min Weifang, executive vice president of Beijing University, commented in the influential Chinese magazine *Outlook*, "The knowledge economy is global in nature. The Internet, which links millions of computers around the world, makes investment, production, market management and sales, labor, and technology all activities that cross national borders. This is an irreversible global trend. Economic interdependence of nation-states has become increasingly evident."[24] In a Politburo meeting held in the spring of 2000, Jiang Zemin said that "to better respond to tomorrow's challenges, we should select those younger leaders who have a global vision and are enthusiastic about the close integration with the outside world."[25]

As some foreign observers have noted, the Internet has indeed brought about a rapid and profound cultural revolution in China, "influencing the way people live and think."[26] By the end of 1999 there were about 9 million Internet accounts in China, in contrast to 17 million in Japan and 35 million in the United States. The number of China's Internet accounts reached 16.9 million in August 2000 and will surpass the number in the United States in 2005.[27] The total number of Web sites based in China increased from 9,906 in June 1999 to 15,153 in December 1999. The estimate is that e-commerce will increase from $8 million in 1998 to $3.8 billion in 2003. Similarly, China now has 50 million mobile phones, but the number will increase to 200 million within ten years. Although Chinese leaders are concerned about the political implications of this telecommunications revolution, they generally are enthusiastic about this so-called Internet start-up boom.[28]

China's determination to enter the WTO and its recent agreement with the United States on this matter reflects Chinese leaders' positive outlook toward economic globalization and foreign trade. The WTO negotiation lasted for thirteen years. The timing of this agreement is particularly revealing. China experienced tremendous difficulties in its application for WTO membership, especially during the past decade as Sino-U.S. relations deteriorated. From the Chinese perspective, the demonization of China in the American media after the Tiananmen incident, the U.S. role as a world police force, the U.S. plan to incorporate Taiwan into its theater missile defense (TMD) system, allegations of illegal campaign contributions and technological espionage, and Zhu Rongji's unsuccessful trip to the United States have further damaged the already troubled relationship. The bombing of the Chinese embassy and the subsequent mass protest in China crushed the myth of the so-called constructive strategic partnership between the United States and China (though arguably it never started).[29]

Anti-American sentiment and the new wave of nationalism in China have placed much pressure on Chinese policy makers. As the Western media accurately observed, Zhu and his associates have become the "focus of criticism from nationalists who think the WTO will infringe on Chinese sovereignty, and from vested economic interests threatened by foreign competition."[30] It is not surprising that some hard-liners in the Chinese government (e.g., Li Peng) have intensified their criticism of the "pro-American" foreign policy adopted by President Jiang Zemin and Premier Zhu Rongji.[31]

Chinese policy makers have placed many alternative policy options on the table.

Some argue that China should return to Maoist tactics in order to form a "third world coalition" with China as a leader, based on its advantageous position as a permanent Security Council member. Others believe that China and Russia should establish a "real" strategic partnership in dealing with NATO in Europe and TMD in Asia.[32] Still others want to accelerate China's military buildup in preparation for an arms race or even a confrontation with the United States. As discussed in chapter 1, the proposal that two middle-level PLA officers made in the recent book *Beyond the Rule of War* reflects this radical view of China's foreign policy strategy.[33]

As many Chinese leaders and public intellectuals argue, none of these policy options are appealing. In a recently published book entitled *Voices*, Ling Zhijun and Ma Licheng, two senior reporters from the *People's Daily*, criticize the rise of nationalism in China's foreign policy. They argue that isolationism reflects only traditional agrarian ways of thinking. It is particularly inappropriate at a time of industrial civilization, marketization, and economic globalization.[34] Responding specifically to the above policy options, the authors believe that the first will prevent China from achieving its number one objective—domestic economic development and foreign trade, in which third world countries are usually rivals. The second option is too unpredictable to adopt, since Russia under Vladimir Putin is a big question mark. The third is too costly, as China does not want to follow the former Soviet Union's military overspending, a misstep that at least partially caused Russia's economic collapse. For a large number of Chinese leaders and public intellectuals, the most appealing option for China is to play the European card. For example, China has recently offered a deal to Airbus rather than to Boeing. State visits between China and European nations have become increasingly frequent. The Chinese leaders believe that the interests of the European Union are not completely identical to those of the United States. Playing the European card, however, also means that China still aims to have a constructive economic relationship with the United States.

These recent incidents should not raise apprehension about how quickly and unpredictably Sino–U.S. relations can change, but rather how rationally and capably current top leaders, on both sides, are able to respond to crises. After all, in Sino–U.S. relations there is the very powerful common ground of trade, which is mutually beneficial, as most leaders on both sides agree. The fourth generation of leaders (some of them are actually the "brains, hands, and ears" of Zhu Rongji and Jiang Zemin) will likely continue this cooperative foreign policy. Because of their backgrounds and experiences, they hopefully will be more flexible and more capable of finding a middle ground between techno-nationalism and techno-globalism.

Ling Zhijun and Ma Licheng's book *Voices* expresses even stronger concerns about China's domestic affairs. The authors claim that the book "combines both praise and criticism of the reform." The authors observe that five voices coexist in post-Deng China: (1) the voice of the mainstream that follows Deng's reform policies, (2) the voice of dogmatism that advocates a return to a socialist planned economy, (3) the voice of nationalism, (4) the voice of feudalism influenced by neo-Confucianism and Asian values, and (5) the voice of democracy. The authors argue unambiguously that pluralist outlooks should be greatly appreciated while presenting the voice of democracy in a remarkably positive tone. Both of these messages would have been considered taboo during the Deng era, but, interestingly, it is reported that this book has been endorsed by the Chinese authorities, especially by Jiang Zemin.[35]

All this evidence suggests that pluralism has become a prevalent value among China's intellectual and political elites, including some policy makers. This does not necessarily mean that the Chinese authorities will no longer suppress criticism from the public, especially from critical intellectuals. For example, in the spring of 2000, the Chinese Academy of Social Sciences, under pressure from the CCP Propaganda Department, fired four prominent intellectuals, including Li Shenzhi, former vice president of CASS, and Fan Gang, former deputy director of the Institute of Economics. The authorities accused Li Shenzhi of launching "personal attacks" against top Chinese leaders, including Mao, Deng and Jiang, and expressing "bourgeois liberalism"[36] This new antibourgeois liberalism movement, however, differs profoundly from the previous political and ideological campaigns. As Liu Junning, one of the four scholars who were fired by CASS, recently said to a Taiwanese newspaper, "If it had happened during the Mao era, I would have been sent to a labor camp."[37] During the Deng era, these critical intellectuals would also have been subjected to political persecution, or at least more public criticism, as was true for Fang Lizhi and Liu Bingyan in the late 1980s.

One reason for the development of a more tolerant political environment is the fact that the current top leaders are not able to control the mass media or the intellectual community. This is also partially due to the increasing diffusion of power and the dynamism of factional politics within the new Chinese leadership. For example, the February 2000 issue of the Chinese magazine Yanhuang chunqiu (Chinese era) called for more political reform and freedom of the press.[38] More specifically, one article in the issue stated that China should avoid repeating the mistake of "overcentralization of power," which characterized the Mao era. According to the Hong Kong media, this article was interpreted as a "message to urge Jiang Zemin not to seek another term as general secretary of the CCP."[39] This magazine, as some believed, is backed by many political leaders who want to restrain Jiang's power.

One may reasonably expect that, compared to previous generations, the fourth generation of leaders will be even more aware of their own limitations and more inclined to assess costs versus benefits when they make decisions. In the future, different options and voices will likely be heard more frequently in both the public and decision-making circles.

## CONCLUSION AND IMPLICATIONS: WILL NEW LEADERS MAKE A DIFFERENCE?

What do all the data and analysis tell us about the real nature of the fourth generation of leaders, and what are the implications for Chinese politics in the future? The sociopolitical scene in China during the reform era is fascinating because of its seemingly contradictory trends and paradoxical developments. This is particularly evident in the characteristics of the fourth generation leadership. These new leaders share memories of the Cultural Revolution but have varying individual experiences and political associations. Calls for regional representation in the selection of new leaders are made at the same time that restraints are placed on the rise of localism. The ubiquitous role of informal networks, such as *taizi* and *mishu*, has met with both a growing public demand for more representative leadership and increasingly strong opposition, even within the political establishment. Lawyers and economists have emerged as political leaders while technocrats still manage to dominate most government and Party posts. New leaders have often expedited their political careers through *guanxi*, yet they are far more interested than their predecessors in seeking their legitimacy through institutional channels. The technocratic worldviews of the fourth generation leaders have led them to pursue some gigantic technological projects and have caused large-scale dislocations of people, but at the same time the "grassroots consciousness" and "common touch" nurtured during their humble experience in the CR have made them aware of the needs and concerns of ordinary people.

Not surprisingly, these paradoxical developments have often led students of Chinese politics to reach many contrasting interpretations. While no one seems to doubt the significance of the rise of the fourth generation leadership for the future political course of the country, China watchers differ profoundly regarding its implications. For example, some argue that this new generation of technocratic leaders will be more accountable to the Chinese people and more capable of dealing with the challenges that the country faces because of generational differences in terms of formative experience, political socialization, educational backgrounds, career paths, and worldviews. But others believe that, because of the prevalence of various forms of nepotism in elite recruitment (e.g., *taizi*, *mishu*, the Qinghua clique, the Shanghai gang), members of this generation should be known for their mediocre abilities, their lack of independence, their conservative stance toward sociopolitical change, and their obsession with political networking.

The development of the new generation leadership, like China's reform itself, is an open-ended and ongoing process and thus gives rise to sharply contrasting interpretations. But this does not mean that any assessment of this generation of leaders or any prediction about their effect on China's future is a subject to be shunned. In May 1990, when the former Soviet Union was undergoing fundamental changes, Walter Laqueur, a student of Russia, expressed his hesitancy to make political predictions about the Soviet Union. He wrote, "Political predictions are easiest to make when they are least needed, when the political barometer points to continuity. They become more difficult at a time of rapid and violent change."[40]

This is also true in the case of China. During the first few decades of the PRC, nothing seemed possible except perpetuation of the status quo. No one had the slightest doubt about the continuation of socialist planning in China's economy and Communist rule in the political life of the country. Today, however, there are a variety of possibilities. With their extraordinary formative experiences and diversified backgrounds, this new generation of leaders contributes to uncertainty about both the direction in which China is heading and their role in affecting it.

While recognizing the danger of hasty generalizations, this study takes an optimistic view of the coming of age of the fourth generation leadership. Three broad assessments loom large as all the data and evidence about the new generation of leaders are assembled. This generation of leaders will likely contribute to the following three changes: (1) greater collective leadership, (2) a more representative and democratic political system, and (3) a better international image of China.

## Toward Greater Collective Leadership

What is most evident in Chinese politics at present is the broad shift from an all-powerful single leader, such as Mao or Deng, to greater collective leadership, as is now characteristic of the Jiang era. It seems highly likely that post-Jiang leaders, the fourth generation, will make even greater progress toward collective leadership.

Some recent studies of Mao, including the memoirs of Mao's private doctor, show that Mao did not run the government in a modern and rational way.[41] As Lucian W. Pye observes, decision making in the Mao era "did not involve a professional review of facts and evidence, and systematic checking about the likely consequences of alternative policy choices, or any careful follow-up on the implementation of policies. Decisions were made by whim, and were guided by Mao's personal instincts and intuition."[42]

Although Deng Xiaoping claimed that China should adopt scientific decision-making strategies and give more attention to institution building, he never hesitated to exercise his personal "supreme power." As Kenneth Lieberthal characterizes it, under Deng, the "Politburo became a committee of protégés who answered to the real power behind the scenes."[43] Deng's departure signified an end to the age of a single, charismatic, all-encompassing strongman rule, which was based on both revolutionary legacy and idiosyncratic attributes. As Robert A. Scalapino recently argued, "The Great Leader is gone. . . . the primary characteristics of leaders have changed" in post-Deng China.[44]

Jiang's leadership relies heavily on power sharing and consensus building. This certainly does not mean the end of the power struggles. As noted in chapter 2, during the past decade, Jiang was engaged in a number of conflicts with his political rivals, such as the Yang brothers, the Deng children, Chen Xitong, and Qiao Shi. Except in the case of Chen Xitong, who was later jailed on a corruption charge, other conflicts were often resolved through negotiation and compromise. Yang Baibing lost power in China's military during the Fourteenth Party Congress, but he "obtained" a seat in the Politburo. Qiao Shi was not able to keep his seat on the Standing Committee of the Politburo during the Fifteenth Party Congress, but he passed this seat onto Wei Jianxing, his protégé.

Jiang has never been a strong leader. With no charisma and no solid basis of power in the military or Party hierarchy, Jiang's main advantage has been his willingness to share power with other factions, for example, deciding to keep Wen Jiabao as chief of staff of the General Office of the CCP; selecting Hu Jintao, the leader of the Qinghua clique, as his successor; and maintaining collegial relationships with Li Peng and Zhu Rongji. Another important development under Jiang's leadership involves the increasing influence of think tanks in making policy recommendations and evaluations.[45]

It seems highly likely that post-Jiang leaders, the fourth generation, will rely more on power sharing, negotiation, consultation, and consensus building than their predecessors. As detailed in the previous chapters, there are multiple reasons for this assessment:

- There is an absence of legendary backgrounds among members of the fourth generation leadership, since they were too young to join the Communist revolution. During the past two decades, there has been no major event, such as a war or domestic turmoil, in which any fourth generation leader could emerge as a distinctive figure.
- There is a lack of political solidarity among the fourth generation leaders, since many of them were on opposite political sides during the Cultural Revolution. The incohesiveness of the fourth generation leadership has prevented the ascent of a Great Leader.
- Many *mishu*-turned-leaders in the fourth generation, especially those members of the *taizi* (e.g., Zeng Qinghong and Xu Yongyue), often play the role of coalition builders in power politics; because of their political and administrative backgrounds, they are more inclined to contribute to negotiation and compromise in the Chinese political process.
- Members of formal bureaucratic institutions and informal networks have often overlapped. As a result, a complex interdependence among various factions has formed. No faction, no institution, no region, and no individual can really dominate power.
- Some institutional developments during the reform era (e.g., term limits, the growing role of people's congresses at various levels, election of members of the Central Committee and the Politburo) also curtail the influence and power of any individual top leader or a particular faction.
- Public opinion in today's China does not call for the rule of a strongman. Cynicism about Deng in his final years and the lack of respect for Jiang at present reflect this social mode. The decline of ideology in Chinese society makes the growth of a personality cult, which is often essential for the birth of a Great Leader, more difficult.

All these factors suggest that the diminishing role of strongman politics in China, which started during the final years of the Deng era, will likely continue as the fourth generation of leaders comes to the fore. Hu Jintao, Zeng Qinghong,

Wen Jiabao, and some other front-runners in the fourth generation may play bigger roles than their peers, but it is unlikely that any one of them will attain the prestige and power that Mao and Deng enjoyed. They may not even claim that they hold tremendous power, unlike Jiang, who currently pretends that he does. This does not deny the possibility that a younger, dynamic Chinese leader, a figure like Mikhail Gorbachev in the mid-1980s or Bill Clinton in the early 1990s, can emerge among the fourth generation leadership. But a "Chinese Gorbachev" or a "Chinese Clinton" will probably reflect, rather than counteract, the broad trend. Political power will increasingly be shared by a collective leadership as well as by various political factions and bureaucratic institutions.

### Toward a More Representative and Democratic Political System

In any society, the replacement of an older generation of leaders by a younger one can be viewed as a "regenerative force" for a stagnant country or as a potential for greater change. This is particularly relevant for China today, when the country is undergoing rapid transformation and faces many perplexing economic and political choices. After two decades of remarkable socioeconomic changes, reform is at a crossroads.

In the economic arena, many solutions to the old problems of socialism have themselves turned into new problems, and the undesirable side effects of the rush to Chinese-style capitalism have become acute. During the past two decades, China has changed from one of the world's most egalitarian nations to one of the least in terms of income distribution, though the number of people in absolute poverty has decreased significantly.[46] Disparity exists in various forms: between coastal region and interior, between urban and rural, between joint ventures and SOEs. During the past few years, the growth in China's GDP has slowed, as has the growth of the township and village enterprises (TVEs). In the early years of the reform, TVEs absorbed a large number of rural surplus laborers and were seen as a major contributing factor to China's economic miracle.[47] In addition, foreign trade, especially in China's exports, has also decreased. The decline in consumer spending has been even more evident, despite the fact that the bank interest rate is only about 2 percent, the lowest in the past two decades. The absence of a social safety net and the increasing cost of major living expenses, such as urban housing, children's education, and medical care for the elderly, have made the public very nervous. As if these problems are not serious enough, the high unemployment rate and the stagnation of the state-owned enterprises (SOEs) have surely become nightmares for Chinese leaders. A leading think tank for the Chinese government recently reported that unemployment has risen to its highest level since the founding of the PRC in 1949.[48]

The economic slowdown and socioeconomic problems, such as income disparity, the lack of a social safety net, high unemployment rates, and the stagnation of the SOEs, suggest an urgent need for major changes in China's economic structure and economic policies. China's recent agreement with the United States and other countries for entry into the WTO indicates the courageous efforts of Chinese leaders to seek international input in restructuring and stimulating the Chinese economy. China's economic problems not only have sociopolitical implications but are also closely interwoven with political problems. Their remedies should be found beyond the realm of economics. Official corruption, for example, has become such a serious problem that China's top leaders have depicted corruption as a "cancer within" and a "life-and-death" issue for the CCP and the state.[49] With public resentment of official corruption, in addition to the huge numbers of unemployed urban workers and surplus rural laborers, the Chinese regime seems to sit atop a volcano of mass social disturbance, just as its Nationalist and imperial predecessors did earlier in the century. This is the reason that the Chinese government sees the Falun Gong as a major threat and has recently decided to suppress it in a strong and decisive manner.

All these economic problems and sociopolitical challenges are so overwhelming that the third generation leadership cannot be expected to solve any of them. The task of responding to these difficult issues will likely pass on to the fourth generation leadership. The legitimacy of the new leaders will be based largely on how skillfully and effectively they handle these serious challenges. Will new leaders make a difference? More specifically, will the fourth generation leadership, because of its distinctive characteristics, contribute to a more representative and democratic political system?

This study provides a positive answer to these questions. One of the most important changes that has occurred in the late 1990s is the consensus within Chinese society, especially among the new generation of political leaders and public intellectuals, that economic reform cannot go forward unless accompanied by political reform. During the 1980s, Wen Yuankai, then vice president of China's University of Science and Technology and an adviser to policy makers, argued that all dimensions of China's reform—politics, economy, society, and culture—like the small squares of a Rubik's Cube, are interrelated. When Wen first proposed this idea, it was controversial, but it has now become common sense. What makes this moment in the reform process truly extraordinary, and this emerging generation of leaders particularly promising, is the fact that all the problems mentioned above, along with their ramifications, are not only known to the Chinese public but are also frequently and fervently debated in today's China.[50] This fact alone may be one of the most promising aspects for the future of China's democratic development.

Democracy is often defined as a political system that includes three interrelated traits. First, democracy must be based on rational respect for law; the people are governed by law, and government itself must be ruled by and subject to the law. Second, institutions must offer genuine political choices, and such choices must be made available through regular and fair elections. According to E. E. Schattschneider, democracy is a competitive political system in which competing leaders and organizations define the alternatives of public policy; the public can participate in the decision-making process through votes.[51] Third, democracy not only involves competition and participation but also emphasizes the role of political institutionalization. Democracy requires institutions that support conflict and disagreement as well as those that sustain legitimacy and consensus.[52] Institutions must permit important kinds of freedom (e.g., civil liberties, freedom of the press), promote respect for political diversity in terms of values and outlooks, and stress institutional means for solving socioeconomic problems.

In the strictest sense of this definition, China may seem far from establishing a democratic system. Party and government leaders are still often above the law, and rampant official corruption reflects the weakness of the legal system. A competitive multiparty system does not exist, and elections usually do not provide genuine choices. The government still controls the media and does not allow freedom of the press. The right to political socialization and organized protest is not granted.

Furthermore, a majority of members of the fourth generation leadership are technocrats. At the root of the problem of technocratic rule, as Frank Fischer has noted in a more general context, is the tendency to deny the importance of political interest groups and to claim that technically trained experts should "stand above" the political process.[53] Technocratic thinking, as some argue, inherently respects expert authority rather than legal authority. Technocrats not only emphasize unequal capabilities of human beings, but also hold the view that they have a privileged knowledge of truth. According to Robert Dahl, the development of Western democracy was a process by which a political system, dominated by one cohesive set of leaders, had given way to a pluralist system dominated by many different sets of leaders, each having access to a different combination of political resources.[54] The democratic pluralist system disperses power, influence, authority, and control away from any single group of power elites sharing the same social background toward a variety of individuals, groups, associations, and organizations.

But if we define democracy in a directional and evolutionary way, China seems to be on its way toward the establishment of a representative and democratic system, even according to the above traits, which are based mostly on Western perceptions of democracy. Evidence provided in the previous chapters and the earlier part of this chapter supports this assessment:

- During the reform era, especially since the mid-1990s, China has made substantial progress in the construction of a legal system. China has probably issued more laws and regulations during the 1990s than any other country. The issuance of laws and regulations may be seen as a small step on paper, but it is one that can have profound long-term implications. Meanwhile, the number of lawyers in China has increased from 3,000 in the early 1980s to 150,000 this year. Those who have trained in law and political science have emerged in the fourth generation leadership, including some top aides to Jiang Zemin and top provincial and ministerial leaders. The market economy's need for law will further consolidate China's establishment of a sound legal system.

- The fourth generation of leaders is more diversified than previous generations of CCP leaders in terms of formative experiences, political solidarity, career paths, occupational backgrounds, and worldviews. Also compared with their predecessors, the fourth generation of leaders is far more flexible, more open-minded, more pragmatic, and less dogmatic in responding to socioeconomic pressures and political demands within the country. Similar to the leadership in post-Communist Russia, China's fourth generation leaders lack a common ideology and a willingness to commit to the existing political system. They also lack a fundamental consensus on major socioeconomic policies. Their diversity, which should be seen as strength rather than a weakness, may constitute a major factor leading toward political democracy.
- The diversity of the new generation of leaders echoes pluralistic development in Chinese society. The overarching trend in Chinese society at the turn of the century is pluralism, which can be seen in virtually all aspects of life: fashion, music, dance, diet, arts, advertisements, social interaction, and social tolerance. In the wake of official ideology and dominant social values, the general public has become indifferent to ideological indoctrination, be it patriotism, Marxism, Confucianism, liberalism, socialism, or capitalism. None of these ideologies can dominate in today's China. Pluralism in Chinese society is also evident in the rise of new forces. Entrepreneurs and public intellectuals, for example, who were suppressed during the first three decades of the PRC, have become increasingly active in the political life of the country. The diversity of leaders and pluralism in society will likely reinforce one another.
- *Taizi* background, *mishu* experience, school and business firm affiliations, birthplace ties, and other bases of nepotism in elite formation will likely continue in the future. But institutional measures to curtail nepotism will probably be even stronger in the years to come. Some of these institutional measures have been part of the Chinese political system for many years now. In addition to measures such as term limits and elections, the NPC will play an even more important role in the future, aiming to provide institutional checks and balances with the CCP. Deputies of the NPC will likely voice different views about Party policies and use their votes to fight against nepotism and favoritism. In fact, deputies of the Party congress and members of the Central Committee of the CCP have been doing the same for their own elections.
- Regional representation has become the norm; the Central Committee now includes two full members per province and two per military district. Such a norm is not, however, already democratic. It does not mean that all representatives are equally powerful—except perhaps in the actual process of balloting. But in the long run, this practice may help to legitimate more effective electoral machinery.

Transition to democracy in any authoritarian political system should address priority, timing, and coordination among economic, social, and political changes.

China is certainly not an exception. At present, Chinese political leaders, both the third and fourth generation, believe that the time is not ready to lift the ban on political opposition. But at the same time, no one seems to question the need for further political reform. It remains to be seen whether or not the fourth generation leaders will make prompt and right decisions, constructing a regime that is more accountable to the Chinese people.

### Toward a Better International Image of China

The fourth generation leaders will work hard to change China's international image. They will likely be more flexible and more capable than the third generation leadership in handling China's foreign affairs. For example, Yang Jiechi, a newly appointed vice minister of foreign affairs and a member of the fourth generation, said that China's policy makers should learn from Deng's strategy, which represented "a marvelous combination of principles and flexibility."[55]

Compared with their predecessors, new leaders have a number of advantages in terms of their effort to improve China's international image:

- Unlike Deng Xiaoping and Yang Shangkun in the second generation, or Li Peng and Jiang Zemin in the third generation, who have always been under the cloud of the Tiananmen tragedy during the past decade, most of the fourth generation leaders, who were not involved in the crackdown, do not have similar hurdles to overcome.
- Among the third generation of leaders, Zhu Rongji is famous for his intelligence, his eloquence, and his human touch. There are more leaders like Zhu in the fourth generation leadership; this is partially due to their training and work experience (e.g., serving as political counselors at college and enduring hardship in the sent-down movement during the Cultural Revolution). They will be more comfortable in dealing with the media, both domestic and foreign.
- While this generation of leaders will be diversified in their foreign policies as well, most of them tend to emphasize (or perhaps overemphasize) the importance of economic and military might, more specifically, the role of science and technology in the information age.
- In contrast to the third generation of leaders who were usually trained in the former Soviet Union and other Eastern European Communist countries, the fourth generation of leaders have more contact and exposure with the West. Some studied in the United States as degree candidates or visiting scholars. This may help them communicate more effectively with the West.
- More exposure to the West among the fourth generation leaders does not necessarily mean that they are pro-Western. In fact, because of some recent troubling events in U.S.–China relations, China's new leaders are cynical about the moral superiority of the West, resentful of Western arrogance, and doubtful about the total adoption of a Western economic and political sys-

tem. Yet, even in the face of a crisis such as the tragic incident in Belgrade, they understand the need for cooperation instead of confrontation. A review of the recent writings and interviews of the fourth generation of leaders in chapter 6 seems to affirm this observation. Their policies toward the United States will be firm but not aggressive.

The full ramifications of the rise of the fourth generation of leaders, of course, await further study. Although this study provides an overall positive assessment of the characteristics of the fourth generation leaders, it also reveals some of their inherent limitations and weaknesses. During these uncertain times, it is important to also consider some less optimistic possible scenarios. This study regards the diversity among the fourth generation of leaders as a political strength, rather than a fundamental weakness. However, some cleavages within this generation (e.g., the lack of consensus on major social and economic policies) are so fundamental that compromise becomes very difficult, if not impossible. Another reason for skepticism about this generation of leaders is simply the fact that there is no obvious pecking order. Why should one new leader obey another with comparable accomplishments? Indeed, Jiang Zemin faced this problem in establishing his authority, but he had the advantage of serving in office for eight years (until Deng's death). During this time he was able to consolidate his power. It remains to be seen whether Jiang's successors will have the same luxury.[56]

More importantly, both domestic problems, such as the high unemployment rate and economic disparity, and troubling international issues, such as U.S.–China relations and the Taiwan Strait crisis, are far more difficult to handle now than during any previous period in the reform era. Taiwan's growing demand for independence and the mainland's uncompromising sovereignty claim on the island have placed fourth generation leaders in a very difficult situation. Any major policy mistake from either side of the Taiwan Strait may profoundly jeopardize the course of China's modernization.

As an economically strong China enters a new century, we need to know more about how intra-generational differences among new leaders affect the way in which the country is ruled; how new leaders in power interact with new forces in society, especially entrepreneurs and public intellectuals; how this generation relates to the fifth generation of leaders, which differs profoundly from the fourth generation; and in what ways they respond to all kinds of modern challenges in an increasingly integrated world.

The epigraph at the beginning of this chapter from the *Analects* of Confucius seems to echo the life experience of the fourth generation leaders. Because of the Cultural Revolution, they did not really start their careers until they were thirty. When they reached forty, the age of "no puzzles," they actively participated in the reform era, another period of far-reaching transformation in the country. Now at fifty, they have become the nation's leaders, possibly with the "mandate of heaven."

Intelligent and farsighted leaders in this generation (technocrats or not) should realize that attainment of their objectives may depend on their commitment to the political institutions that make group conflict institutional and make the legal system meaningful in the lives of all people. China is in the midst of rapid changes. Greater changes seem inevitable as this more diversified, more energetic, more committed, and less dogmatic generation of leaders aggressively rises to power in China at the beginning of a new century.

## NOTES

1. C. Montogomery Broaded, "The Lost and Found Generation: Cohort Succession in Chinese Higher Education," *Australian Journal of Chinese Affairs* 23 (January 1990): 77.
2. http://web1.peopledaily.com.cn/province. Last accessed 12 May 2000.
3. Xiao Chong, ed., *Beijing zhinangqun* (Beijing's think tanks) (Hong Kong: Xiafeier guoji chubangongsi, 1999), 155.
4. Daniel Wright, "A Walk into the Past: Hiking the Long March," *Institute of Current World Affairs Report,* July 1998, 5–7.
5. In 1998, five vice governors were actually nominated by delegates of the provincial people's congress, and they defeated candidates appointed by the Party. *Renmin ribao,* August 3, 1998, 1.
6. *Renmin ribao,* August 3, 1998, 1.
7. Erik Echholm, "Chinese Book on Political Reform Stirs Hopes for More Debate," *New York Times,* August 25, 1998, 3.
8. Li Cheng and Lynn White, "The Thirteenth Central Committee of the Chinese Communist Party: From Mobilizers to Managers," *Asian Survey* 28, no. 4 (April 1988): 371–399; and "The Army in the Succession to Deng Xiaoping: Familiar Fealties and Technocratic Trends," *Asian Survey* 33, no. 8 (August 1993): 757–786, for remarks and tables about the nontechnocratic connections of technocrats.
9. For a detailed discussion of Xu Yongyue and his father, see Li Xiaozhuang, *Zhu Rongji renma* (Zhu Rongji's men) (Taibei: Dujia chubanshe, 1998), 133–149.
10. For example, Li Cheng and David Bachman, "Localism, Elitism, and Immobilism: Elite Formation and Social Change in Post–Mao China" *World Politics* 42, no. 1 (October 1989): 77–79; and Li and White, "The Army in the Succession to Deng Xiaoping," 774–775.
11. Compared with the study of Chinese mayors, the percentage of those who have had experience in economic planning declined 14.1 percent to 4.0 percent. Li and Bachman, "Localism, Elitism and Immobilism," 78.
12. Andrew G. Walder, "Career Mobility and the Communist Political Order," *American Sociological Review* 60, no. 3 (June 1995): 309–328.
13. Ibid., 312.
14. Xiao, *Beijing zhinangqun,* 85.
15. *Shijie ribao,* 1 November 1999, A8. For a detailed discussion of Cao Jianming, see Xiao, *Beijing zhinangqun,* 177–185.
16. George Soros, *The Crisis of Global Capitalism: Open Society Endangered* (New York: Public Affairs, 1998).
17. For a detailed discussion of intellectual and political discourse on the "new technological revolution" and its significance to the rise of technocratic elites, see Li Cheng and

Lynn White, "China's Technocratic Movement and the World Economic Herald," *Modern China* 17, no. 3 (July 1991): 342–388.

18. Xiao, *Zhong gong disidai mengren*, 119.

19. Ibid. For the original quote by Albert Einstein, see James Forman, *That Mad Game: War and the Chances for Peace* (New York: Scribner's, 1980), ix.

20. Xiao, *Zhong gong disidai mengren*, 119–120

21. Some members of the three old classes who later became leaders of the fourth generation argued that their dramatic life experience encouraged them to pursue two objectives: first, to fulfill their individual values and, second, to look at the outside world. See Zhong Yan, *Zhongguo xinsanji xueren* (China's new three classes of scholars) (Hangzhou: Zhejiang renmin chubanshe, 1996), 63.

22. For a further discussion on the topic, see Cheng Li, "Techno-Nationalism vs. Techno-Globalism: East Asia in Search of a New Vision for the 21st Century," *Institute of Current World Affairs Report*, July 1994.

23. Frederic S. Pearson and J. Martin Rochester, *International Relations: The Global Condition in the Late Twentieth Century*, 3d ed. (Newburyport, Mass.: McGraw-Hill, 1992), 519–554. Du Xian, the well-known anchorwoman of Chinese Central Television who was fired because of her sympathetic tone in reporting on the Tiananmen tragedy, recently began hosting a new program on environmental protection called *We Have Only One Earth*.

24. *Liaowang*, 10 August 1998, 9.

25. *South China Morning Post*, May 4, 2000, 1.

26. John Pomfret, "A New Chinese Revolution," *Washington Post* (National weekly edition), 21 February 2000, 17.

27. "Zhongguo wuniannei jiancheng quanqiu zuida wangluo shichang" (China will become the largest Internet market in five years), 13 February 2000. http://www.chinese-newsnet.com; http://www.chinaonline.com/issues/internet_policy (last accessed 13 August 2000); also see China Securities Regulatory Commission, Staff Report, 2000.

28. Pomfret, "A New Chinese Revolution," 17.

29. Cheng Li, "The End of China's 'Strategic Partnership' with the U.S.," *Changing United Nations*, May-June 1999, 7–12.

30. Zhu Rongji reportedly offered to resign twice after the bombing incident. *Newsweek*, 29 November 1999, 57.

31. After signing the WTO agreement with the United States, Jiang Zemin and Zhu Rongji immediately convened the CCP national conference on economic affairs, trying to reduce criticism from the establishment. *Shijie ribao*, 18 November 1999, A9.

32. He Xin, a close aide to Li Peng, recently argued that China should keep all options open and redesign its foreign policy strategy. Tang Dianwei, "Duoqian dongwu He Xin" (He Xin: A man of many capacities), *Shijie zhoukan* (World journal weekend), 23–29 May 1999, 26.

33. Qiao and Wang, *Chaoxian zhan*; also see *Shijie ribao*, November 15, 1999, A9.

34. Ling Zhijun and Ma Licheng, *Huhan: Dangjin Zhongguo de wuzhong shengyin* (Voices: Five voices in present China) (Guangzhou: Guangzhou chubanshe, 1999), 252.

35. Ibid. Also see *Shijie ribao*, January 16, 1999, A2.

36. *Lianhe bao*, 2 April 2000, 1–2.

37. Ibid.

38. *Hong Kong Standard*, 18 April 2000, 1.

39. Ibid.

40. Walter Laqueur, "Forecasting the Soviet-Russian Future," *Encounter*, May 1990.

41. Zhisui Li, *The Private Life of Chairman Mao: The Memoirs of Mao's Personal Physician*, trans. Tai Hung-chao (New York: Random House, 1994).

42. Lucian W. Pye, "Rethinking the Man in the Leader," *China Journal* 35 (January 1996): 111.

43. Kenneth Lieberthal, *Governing China: From Revolution through Reform* (New York: Norton, 1995), 224.

44. Robert A. Scalapino, "The People's Republic of China at Fifty," *National Bureau of Asian Research Analysis* 10, no. 4 (October 1999): 7.

45. For a further discussion of the growing importance of think tanks, see Li, "Promises and Pitfalls of Reform."

46. He, *Xiandaihua de xianjing*, 218–244.

47. Li, *Rediscovering China*, 75–92.

48. Hu, *Zhongguo fazhan qianjing*, 35–36.

49. Jiang Zemin made these remarks. Quoted from *Far East Economic Review*, 2 March 1995, 15.

50. Li, "Promises and Pitfalls of Reform"; He, *Xiandaihua de xianjing*.

51. E. E. Schattschneider, *The Semisovereign People: A Realist's View of Democracy in America* (Hinsdale, Ill.: Dryden, 1960), xiii–xiv.

52. Seymour Martin Lipset, "The End of Ideology?" in *The End of Ideology Debate*, ed. Chaim I. Waxman (New York: Funk & Wagnalls, 1968), 69–70.

53. Frank Fischer, *Technocracy and the Politics of Expertise* (Newbury Park, Calif.: Sage, 1990), 24.

54. Robert Dahl, *Who Governs? Democracy and Power in an American City* (New Haven: Yale University Press, 1961), 86.

55. *Zhonghua yingcai* (China's talents) 3 (February 1999): 26.

56. This discussion is based on comments by Joseph Fewsmith, for which the author is very grateful.

# Bibliography

## ENGLISH LANGUAGE

Aberbach, Joel, et al. "American and German Federal Executives: Technocrats and Political Attitudes." *International Social Science Journal* 42, no. 1 (February 1990): 3–18.

Aberbach, Joel D., Robert D. Putnam, and Bert A. Rockman. *Bureaucrats and Politicians in Western Democracies*. Cambridge: Harvard University Press, 1981.

Akin, William E. *Technocracy and the American Dream: The Technocrat Movement, 1900–1941*. Berkeley: University of California Press, 1977.

Alfven, Hannes. "Science, Technocracy, and the Politico-Economic Power." *Impact of Science on Society* 22 (January-June 1972): 85–94.

Armytage, Walter Harry Green. *The Rise of the Technocrats: A Social History*. Toronto: University of Toronto Press, 1965.

Ascher, William. "Planning, Politics, and Technocracy in Argentina and Chile." Ph.D. diss., Yale University, 1975.

Bachman, David. *Bureaucracy, Economy, and Leadership in China: The Institutional Origins of the Great Leap Forward*. Cambridge: Cambridge University Press, 1991.

———. "The Chinese Communist Party: Forty Years in Power." *Fletcher Forum of World Affairs* 14, no. 1 (Winter 1990): 10–17.

———. "Succession, Consolidation, and Transition in China's Future." *Journal of Northeast Asian Studies* 15, no. 1 (Spring 1996): 89–106.

Bachman, David, and Yang Dali L., eds. *Yang Jiaqi and Chinese Struggle for Democracy*. Armonk, N.Y.: M. E. Sharpe, 1991.

Bachrach, Peter. *The Theory of Democratic Elitism: A Critique*. Washington D.C.: University Press of America, 1980.

Bailes, Kendall E. *Technology and Society under Lenin and Stalin: Origins of the Soviet Technical Intelligentsia, 1917–1941*. Princeton: Princeton University Press, 1978.

—————. "The Politics of Technology: Stalin and Technocratic Thinking among Soviet Engineers." *American Historical Review* 79, no. 2 (April 1973): 445–469.

Barnett, A. Doak. "Social Stratification and Aspects of Personnel Management in the Chinese Communist Bureaucracy." *China Quarterly* 28 (October-December 1966): 8–39.

Bartke, Wolfgang. *Who's Who in the People's Republic of China.* Armonk, N.Y.: M. E. Sharpe, 1981.

Baum, Richard. "China after Deng: Ten Scenarios in Search of Reality." *China Quarterly* 145 (March 1996): 153–175.

—————. "China in 1985: The Greening of the Revolution." *Asian Survey* 26, no. 1 (January 1986): 30–53.

—————. *Burying Mao: Chinese Politics in the Age of Deng Xiaoping.* Princeton: Princeton University Press, 1994.

—————. *Scientism and Bureaucraticism in Post-Mao China: Cultural Limits of the "Four Modernizations."* Lund, Sweden: Research Policy Institute, University of Lund, 1981.

Baylis, Thomas. *The Technical Intelligentsia and East German Elite.* Berkeley: University of California Press, 1974.

Beck, Carl. *Comparative Communist Political Leadership.* New York: David McKay, 1973.

Beissinger, Mark R. *Scientific Management, Socialist Discipline, and Soviet Power.* Cambridge: Harvard University Press, 1988.

—————. "In Search of Generations in Soviet Politics." *World Politics* 28, no. 2 (January 1986): 288–314.

Bell, Daniel. "The End of Ideology Revisited." *Government and Opposition* 23, no. 2 (Spring 1988): 131–150; no. 3 (Summer 1988): 321–331.

—————. *The Coming of the Post-Industrial Society.* New York: Basic, 1973.

—————. "Technocracy and Politics." *Survey* 16, no. 1 (Winter 1971): 1–24.

—————. "The Balance of Knowledge and Power." *Technology Review* 71, no. 2 (June 1969): 38–47.

—————. "The Post-Industrial Society." In *Technology and Social Change*, ed. Eli Ginzberg, 44–59. New York: Columbia University Press, 1964.

Ben-David, Joseph. *The Scientist's Role in Society: A Comparative Study.* Chicago: University of Chicago Press, 1984.

Bengtson, Vern L., et al. "Generations, Cohorts, and Relations between Age Groups." In *Handbook of Aging and the Social Sciences.* Edited by Robert H. Binstock and Ethel Shanas. New York: Van Nostrand Reinhold, 1985.

Bennett, Gordon A. "Elite and Society in China: A Summary of Research and Interpretation." In *Elites in the People's Republic of China*, edited by Robert A. Scalapino, 3–37. Seattle: University of Washington Press, 1972.

Bialer, Seweryn. *Stalin's Successors: Leadership, Stability, and Change in the Soviet Union.* Cambridge: Cambridge University Press, 1980.

Bian Yanjie. "Chinese Occupational Prestige." *International Sociology* 11, no. 2 (June 1996): 161–186.

Bian Yanjie and John R. Logan. "Market Transition and the Persistence of Power: The Changing Stratification System in Urban China." *American Sociological Review* 61, no. 5 (October 1996): 739–758.

Bickford, Thomas J. "The Chinese Military and Its Business Operations: The PLA as Entrepreneur." *Asian Survey* 34, no. 5 (May 1994): 460–474.

Bo Zhiyue. "Economic Performance and Political Mobility: Chinese Provincial Leaders." *Journal of Contemporary China* 5, no. 12 (1996): 135–154.

Broaded, C. Montgomery. "The Lost and Found Generation: Cohort Succession in Chinese Higher Education." *Australian Journal of Chinese Affairs* 23 (January 1990): 77–95.

Brook, Timothy, and B. Michael Frolic, eds. *Civil Society in China*. Armonk, N.Y.: M. E. Sharpe, 1997.

Brzezinski, Zbigniew. *Between Two Ages: America's Role in the Technetronic Era*. New York: Viking, 1970.

Buckley, Christopher. "Science as Politics and Politics as Science: Fang Lizhi and Chinese Intellectuals' Uncertain Road to Dissent." *Australian Journal of Chinese Affairs* 25 (January 1991): 1–36.

Bullard, Monte Ray. "People's Republic of China Elite Studies: A Review of the Literature." *Asian Survey* 19, no. 8 (August 1979): 789–800.

Burnham, James. *The Managerial Revolution*. New York: John Day, 1941.

Burns, John P. "Chinese Civil Service Reform: The Thirteenth Party Congress Proposals." *China Quarterly* 120 (December 1989): 739–770.

———. "China's Nomenklatura System." *Problems of Communism* 36, no. 5 (September-October 1987): 36–51.

———. "Strengthening Central CCP Control of Leadership Selection: The 1990 Nomenklatura," *China Quarterly* 138 (June 1994): 458–491.

Caldwell, James Timothy. "Elite Specialization, Bureaucracy, and Modernization: The Case of China, 1949–1969." Ph.D. diss., University of Texas, 1980.

Cavey, Paul. "Building a Power Base: Jiang Zemin and the Post-Deng Succession." *Issues and Studies* 33, no. 11 (November 1997): 1–34.

Centeno Gutierrez, Miguel Angel. "The New Cientificos: Technocratic Politics in Mexico 1970–1990." Ph.D. diss., Yale University, 1990.

Chan, Anita. *Children of Mao: Personality Development and Political Activism in the Red Guard Generation*. London: Macmillan, 1985.

———. "Dispelling Misconceptions about the Red Guard Movement: The Necessity to Re-Examine Cultural Revolution Factionalism and Periodization." *Journal of Contemporary China* 1, no. 1 (September 1992): 61–85.

Chang Chung-li. *The Chinese Gentry: Studies on Their Role in Nineteenth-Century Chinese Society*. Seattle: University of Washington Press, 1955.

Chang, Donald Heng. "In Search of Trends and Patterns: Elite Change in the Chinese Communist Party, 1945–1973." Ph.D. diss., Ohio State University, 1976.

Chang, Parris. "From Mao to Hua to Hu to Zhao: Changes in the CCP Leadership and Its Rules of the Games." *Issues and Studies* 25, no. 1 (January 1989): 56–72.

Chen Feng. "The Dilemma of Eudaemonic Legitimacy in Post-Mao China." *Polity* 29, no. 3 (Spring 1997): 421–439.

Chen Shi. "Leadership Change in Shanghai: Toward the Dominance of Party Technocrats." *Asian Survey* 38, no. 7 (July 1998): 671–687.

———. "Municipal Leadership and Interest-Oriented Mass Participation: The Process of Housing Reform Plan in Shanghai." *Journal of Contemporary China* 10 (Fall 1995): 45–65.

Chen, Theodore Hsi-en. *The Maoist Educational Revolution*. New York: Praeger, 1974.

Chen Yixin. "Lost in Revolution and Reform: The Socioeconomic Pains of China's Red

Guards Generation, 1966–1996." *Journal of Contemporary China* 8, no. 21 (1999): 219–239.

Cherrington, Ruth. *Deng's Generation: Young Intellectuals in 1980s China*. London: Macmillan/St. Martin's, 1997.

———. "Generational Issues in China: A Case Study of the 1980s Generation of Young Intellectuals." *British Journal of Sociology* 48, no. 2 (June 1997): 302–320.

Ch'i Hsi-sheng. *Politics of Disillusionment: The Chinese Communist Party Under Deng Xiaoping, 1978–1989*. Armonk, N.Y.: M. E. Sharpe, 1991.

Chu Tung-tsu. *Local Government in China under the Ch'ing*. Cambridge: Harvard University Press, 1962.

Chung Jae Ho. "The Politics of Prerogatives in Socialism: The Case of the Taizidang in China." *Studies in Comparative Communism* 24, no. 1 (March 1991): 58–76.

Cleveland, Harlan. *The Knowledge Executive: Leadership in an Information Society*. New York: Truman Talley, 1985.

Curtis, Gerald L. *The Logic of Japanese Politics*. New York: Columbia University Press, 1999.

Dai Qing, ed. *Yangtze! Yangtze! Debate over the Three Gorges Project*. London: Probe International/Earthscan, 1994.

Deng Xiaoping. "Deng's 16 June Speech: Establish the Third-Generation Collective Leadership Now." *World Affairs* 152, no. 3 (Winter 1989–1990): 159–162.

———. "On the Reform of the System of Party and State Leadership." *Beijing Review* 26, no. 40 (October 3 1983): 14–22, 26; 41 (October 10 1983): 18–22.

DeSario, Jack, and Stuart Langton. "Citizen Participation and Technocracy." In *Citizen Participation in Public Decision Making*. Edited by Jack DeSario and Stuart Langton. New York: Greenwood, 1987.

Dickson, Bruce J. "Unsettled Succession: China's Critical Moment." *National Interest*, no. 49 (Fall 1997): 64–72.

Ding Xue Liang. *The Decline of Communism in China: Legitimacy Crisis, 1977–1989*. Cambridge: Cambridge University Press, 1994.

Dittmer, Lowell. "Patterns of Elite Strife and Succession in Chinese Politics." *China Quarterly* 123 (September 1990): 405–430.

———. "Reform, Succession, and the Resurgence of Mainland China's Old Guard." *Issues and Studies* 24, no. 1 (January 1988): 96–113.

———. "The 12th Congress of the Chinese Communist Party." *China Quarterly* 93 (March 1983): 108–124.

Dittmer, Lowell, and Yu-Shan Wu. "The Modernization of Factionalism in Chinese Politics." *World Politics* 47, no. 4 (July 1995): 467–494.

Djilas, Milovan. *The Unperfect Society: Beyond the New Class*. London: Unwin, 1957.

———. *The New Class: An Analysis of the Communist System*. New York: Praeger, 1972.

Dreyer, June Teufl. "The New Officer Corps: Implications for the Future." *China Quarterly* 146 (June 1996): 315–335.

Dunham, Charlotte C., and Vern L. Bengtson. "Generational Continuity and Change." In *Encyclopedia of Adolescence*, edited by Richard M. Lerner, Anne C. Petersen, and Jeanne Brooks-Gunn, 392–396. New York: Garland, 1991.

Duvall, Raymond D., and John R. Freeman. "The Techno-Bureaucratic Elite and the Entrepreneurial State in Dependent Industrialization." *American Political Science Review* 77, no. 3 (1983): 569–587.

Durkheim, Emile. *Emile Durkheim on Morality and Society: Selected Writings.* Edited by Robert N. Bellah. Chicago: University of Chicago Press, 1973.

Elsner, Henry, Jr. *The Technocrats: Prophets of Automation.* Syracuse: Syracuse University Press, 1967.

—. "Messianic Scientism: Technocracy, 1919–1960." Master's thesis, University of Michigan, 1962.

Emerson, John Philip. "Manpower Training and Utilization of Specialized Cadres, 1949–68." In *The City in Communist China,* edited by John Wilson Lewis, 183–214. Stanford: Stanford University Press, 1971.

Engelborghs-Bertels, Marthe. "The New Man or a Lost Generation? Education in the Four Modernizations Program of the PRC." *Issues and Studies* 21, no. 9 (September 1985): 87–118.

Etzion-Halevy, Eva. *The Knowledge Elite and the Failure of Prophecy.* Boston: Allen & Unwin, 1985.

—. *Bureaucracy and Democracy: A Political Dilemma.* London: Routledge & Kegan Paul, 1983.

—. *Political Manipulation and Administrative Power: A Comparative Study.* Boston: Routledge & Kegan Paul, 1979.

Eyal, Gil, Ivan Szelenyi, and Eleanor Townsley. "The Theory of Post-Communist Managerialism." *New Left Review* 222 (March-April 1997): 60–92.

Falkenheim, Victor. "Bureaucracy, Factions, and Political Change in China." *Pacific Affairs* 57, no. 3 (Fall 1984): 471–479.

Fei Xiaotong [Fei Hsiao-T'ung]. *China's Gentry.* Chicago: University of Chicago Press, 1953.

Feldman, Elliot J. *Technocracy versus Democracy: The Comparative Politics of International Airports.* Boston: Auburn, 1982.

Fewsmith, Joseph. "Historical Echoes and Chinese Politics: Can China Leave the Twentieth Century Behind?" In *China Briefing: A Century of Transformation.* Edited by Tyrene White. Armonk, N.Y.: M. E. Sharpe, 2000.

Fischer, Frank. "American Think Tanks: Policy Elites and the Politicization of Expertise." *Governance* 4, no. 3 (July 1991): 332–353.

—. *Technocracy and the Politics of Expertise.* Newbury Park, Calif.: Sage, 1990.

Foucault, Michel. *Power/Knowledge.* New York: Pantheum, 1980.

Galbraith, John K. *The New Industrial State.* Harmondsworth, U.K.: Penguin, 1969.

Gilley, Bruce. *Tiger on the Brink: Jiang Zemin and China's New Elite.* Berkeley: University of California Press, 1998.

Gilpin, Robert. "The Computer and World Affairs." In *The Computer Age: A Twenty-Year Age View,* edited by M. L. Dertouzos and Joel Moses, 229–253. Cambridge: MIT Press, 1979.

—. *France in the Age of the Scientific State.* Princeton: Princeton University Press, 1968.

—. *American Scientists and Nuclear Weapons Policy.* Princeton: Princeton University Press, 1962.

Gilpin, Robert, and Christopher Wright. *Scientists and National Policy-Making.* New York: Columbia University Press, 1964.

Girvetz, Harry K. *Democracy and Elitism: Two Essays with Selected Readings.* New York: Scribner's, 1967.

Gold, Thomas. "Youth and State." *China Quarterly* 127 (September 1991): 594–612.

Goldstein, Avery. "Trends in the Study of Political Elites and Institutions in the PRC." *China Quarterly* 139 (September 1994): 714–730.

Gouldner, Alvin W. *The Future of Intellectuals and the Rise of the New Class.* New York: Seabury, 1979.

Gu, Edward X. "The Economics Weekly, the Public Space and the Voices of China's Independent Intellectuals." *China Quarterly* 147 (September 1996): 860–888.

————. "Elitist Democracy and China's Democratization: A Gradualist Approach towards Democratic Transition by a Group of Chinese Intellectuals." *Democratization* 4, no. 2 (1997): 84–112.

Gu Xin and David Kelly. "New Conservatism: Ideological Program of a New Elite." In *China's Quiet Revolution: New Interactions between State and Society.* Edited by David S. G. Goodman and Beverly Hooper. Melbourne: Longman Cheshire, 1993.

Guillermaz, Jacques. *The Chinese Communist Party in Power, 1949–1976.* Translated by Anne Destenay. Boulder: Westview, 1972.

Gunnell, John G. "Technocratic Image and the Theory of Technocracy." *Technology and Culture* 23, no. 3 (July 1982): 392–416.

Gupta, Kirshna Prakash. "Tsinghua Experience and Higher Education in China." *China Report* 7, no. 1 (January-February 1971): 2–14.

Haas, Ernest. *Beyond the Nation-State: Functionalism and International Organization.* Stanford: Stanford University Press, 1964.

Hahn, Bae-ho, and Kyu-taik Kim. "Korean Political Leaders (1952–1962): Their Social Origins and Skills." *Asian Survey* 3, no. 7 (July 1963): 312–323.

Halpern, Nina Phyllis. "Making Economic Policy: The Influence of Economists." In *China's Economy Looks toward the Year 2000*, edited by the Joint Economic Committee, U.S. Congress, 132–146. Washington, D.C.: GPO, 1986.

————. "Economic Specialists and the Making of Chinese Economic Policy, 1955–1983." Ph.D. diss., University of Michigan, 1985.

Hamrin, Carol Lee. "Perspectives on Generational Change in China." Unpublished scope paper for the workshop organized by the Paul H. Nitze School of Advanced International Studies, Johns Hopkins University, June 1993.

Hamrin, Carol Lee, and Zhao Suisheng. *Decision Making in Deng's China: Perspectives from Insiders.* Armonk, N.Y.: M. E. Sharpe, 1995.

Hanson, Leung C. K. "The Role of Leadership in Adaptation to Change: Lessons of Economic Reforms in the USSR and China." *Studies in Comparative Communism* 18, no. 4 (Winter 1985): 227–246.

Harding, Harry. *China's Second Revolution: Reform after Mao.* Washington D.C.: Brookings Institution, 1987.

Henley, Lonnie D. "Officer Education in the Chinese PLA." *Problems of Communism* 36, no. 3 (May-June 1987): 55–71.

Hinton, William. *Hundred Day War: The Cultural Revolution at Tsinghua University.* New York: Monthly Review Press, 1972.

Ho Ping-ti. *The Ladder of Success in Imperial China: Aspects of Social Mobility, 1368–1911.* New York: Columbia University Press, 1962.

————. "Aspects of Social Mobility in China, 1368–1911." *Comparative Studies in Society and History* 1, no. 4 (June 1959): 330–359.

Holheinz, Roy, and Kent Calder. *The Eastasia Edge.* New York: Basic, 1982.

Hooper, Beverley. "Chinese Youth: The Nineties Generation." *Current History* 90, no. 557 (September 1991): 264–269.

Houn, Franklin W. "The Eighth Central Committee of the Chinese Communist Party: A Study of Elite." *American Political Science Review* 51, no. 2 (June 1957): 392–404.

Israel, John, and Donald Klein. *Rebels and Bureaucrats: China's December 9ers*. Berkeley: University of California Press, 1976.

Joffe, Ellis. "Ruling China after Deng." *Journal of East Asian Affairs* 11, no. 1(Winter-Spring 1997): 183–220.

Johnson, Chalmers. *MITI and the Japanese Miracle: The Growth of Industrial Policy, 1925–1975*. Stanford: Stanford University Press, 1982.

Kau Ying-mao. "Patterns of Recruitment and Mobility of Urban Cadres." In *The City in Communist China*, edited by John W. Lewis, 97–121. Stanford: Stanford University Press, 1971.

———. "The Urban Bureaucratic Elite in Communist China: A Case Study of Wuhan, 1949–65." In *Chinese Communist Politics in Action*, edited by A. Doak Barnett, 216–264. Seattle: University of Washington Press, 1969.

Keum, Hieyeon. "Policy Conflicts and Leadership Changes in Chinese Politics: The Falls of Hu Yaobang and Zhao Ziyang and the Retreat from the Post-1978 Reforms." Ph.D. diss., Miami University, 1991.

Klein, Donald W., and Anne B. Clark. *Biographical Dictionary of Chinese Communism, 1921–1965*. Vols. 1–2. Cambridge: Harvard University Press, 1971.

Kornad, George, and Ivan Szelinyi. *The Intellectuals on the Road to Power Class*. New York: Harcourt Brace Jovanovich/Harvest, 1979.

Kwok, D. W. Y. *Scientism in Chinese Thought, 1900–1950*. New Haven: Yale University Press, 1965.

Lam, Willy Wo-Lap. *China after Deng Xiaoping: The Power Struggle in Beijing since Tiananmen*. Singapore: Wiley, 1995.

Lamb, Malcolm. *Directory of Officials and Organizations in China 1968–1983*. Armonk, N.Y.: M. E. Sharpe, 1983.

Lampton, David M. *Paths to Power: Elite Mobility in Contemporary China*. Ann Arbor: Center for Chinese Studies, University of Michigan, 1986.

Lee, Hong Yung. "China's New Bureaucracy?" In *State and Society in China: The Consequences of Reform*, edited by Arthur L. Rosenbaum, 55–76. Boulder: Westview, 1992.

———. "China's 12th Central Committee: Rehabilitated Cadres and Technocrats." *Asian Survey* 23, no. 6 (June 1983): 673–691.

———. "Deng Xiaoping's Reform of the Chinese Bureaucracy." *Journal of Northeast Asian Studies* 1, no. 2 (1982): 21–35.

———. "Evaluation of China's Bureaucratic Reforms." *Annal of the American Academy of Political and Social Science* 476 (November 1984): 34–47.

———. *From Revolutionary Cadres to Party Technocrats: The Changing Cadre System in Socialist China*. Berkeley: University of California Press, 1991.

———. "The Implications of Reform for Ideology, State, and Society in China." *Journal of International Affairs* 39, no. 2 (1986): 77–89.

———. "Mainland China's Future Leaders: Third Echelon of Cadres." *Issues and Studies* 24, no. 6 (June 1988): 36–57.

Leung Laifong. *Morning Sun: Interviews with Chinese Writers of the Lost Generation*. Armonk, N.Y.: M. E. Sharpe, 1994.

Li Cheng. *Chinese Elite Transformation on the Two Sides of the Taiwan Strait: An Empirical Analysis of the Theory of Technocracy.* M. A. thesis, University of California, 1987.
————. "'Credentialism' Versus 'Entrepreneurism': The Interplay and Tensions between Technocrats and Entrepreneurs in the Reform Era." In *Chinese Business Networks: State, Economy and Culture.* Edited by Chan Kwok Bun. New York: Prentice Hall, 1999.
————. "Promises and Pitfalls of Reform: New Thinking in Post-Deng China." In *China Briefing: A Century of Transformation.* Edited by Tyrene White. Armonk, N.Y.: M. E. Sharpe, 2000.
————. *Rediscovering China: Dynamics and Dilemmas of Reform.* Lanham, Md.: Rowman & Littlefield, 1997.
————. "The Rise of the Fourth Generation of Leaders in the PRC." *China Quarterly* 161 (March 2000): 1–40.
————. "University Networks and the Rise of Qinghua Graduates in China's Leadership." *Australian Journal of Chinese Affairs* 32 (July 1994): 1–32.
Li Cheng and David Bachman. "Localism, Elitism, and Immobilism: Elite Formation and Social Change in Post-Mao China." *World Politics* 42, no. 1 (October 1989): 64–94.
Li Cheng and Lynn White. "The Army in the Succession to Deng Xiaoping: Familiar Fealties and Technocratic Trends." *Asian Survey* 33, no. 8 (August 1993): 757–786.
————. "China's Technocratic Movement and the World Economic Herald." *Modern China* 17, no. 3 (July 1991): 342–388.
————. "Elite Transformation and Modern Change in Mainland China and Taiwan: Empirical Data and the Theory of Technocracy." *China Quarterly* 121 (March 1990): 1–35.
————. "The Fifteenth Central Committee of the Chinese Communist Party: Full-Fledged Technocratic Leadership with Partial Control by Jiang Zemin." *Asian Survey* 38, no. 3 (March 1998): 231–264.
————. "The Thirteenth Central Committee of the Chinese Communist Party: From Mobilizers to Managers." *Asian Survey* 28, no. 4 (April 1988): 371–399.
Li Nan. "Organizational Changes of the PLA, 1985–1997." *China Quarterly* 158 (June 1999): 314–349.
Li Wei. "The Role of the *Mishu* (Staff) Institution in Chinese Politics." Ph.D. diss., Massachusetts Institute of Technology, 1994.
Li Wei and Lucian Pye. "The Ubiquitous Role of the *Mishu* in Chinese Politics." *China Quarterly* 132 (December 1992): 913–936.
Li Xiaoxiong. "Rise of a New Elite in Rural China and Its Characteristics." *Journal of Northeast Asian Studies* 15, no. 3 (Fall 1996): 100–115.
Lieberthal, Kenneth. *Governing China: From Revolution through Reform.* New York: Norton, 1995.
Lieberthal, Kenneth, and David M. Lampton, eds. *Bureaucracy, Politic, and Decision Making in Post-Mao China.* Berkeley: University of California Press, 1992.
Lieberthal, Kenneth, and Michel Oksenberg. *Policy Making in China: Leaders, Structures and Process.* Princeton: Princeton University Press, 1988.
Lin Nan and Xie Wen. "Occupational Prestige in Urban China." *American Journal of Sociology* 93, no. 4 (January 1988): 793–832.
Macfarquhar, Roderick. *The Hundred Flowers Campaign and the Chinese Intellectuals.* New York: Praeger, 1960.
Manion, Melanie. *Retirement of Revolutionaries in China: Public Policies, Social Norms, Private Interests.* Princeton: Princeton University Press, 1993.

Mannheim, Karl. "Consciousness of Class and Consciousness of Generation." In *Essays on Sociology of Knowledge*. Edited by Karl Mannheim. London: RKP, 1952.

———. *Ideology and Utopia: An Introduction to the Sociology of Knowledge*. New York: Harcourt and Brace, 1936.

Marsh, Robert. *The Mandarins: The Circulation of Elites in China, 1600–1900*. Glencoe, Ill.: Free Press, 1961.

Martin, Roberta. *Party Recruitment in China: Patterns and Prospects: A Study of the Recruitment Campaign of 1954–56 and Its Impact on Party Expansion through 1980*. Occasional Papers of the East Asian Institute. New York: Columbia University, 1981.

Massey, Andrew. *Technocrats and Nuclear Politics: The Influence of Professional Experts in Policy-Making*. Brookfield, Vt.: Avebury, 1988.

McCormick, Barrett. *Political Reform in Post-Mao China: Democracy and Bureaucracy in a Leninist State*. Berkeley: University of California Press, 1990.

McNeill, Pat. "The Changing Generation Gap." *New Statesman & Society* 1, no. 16 (September 1988): 30.

Meynaud, Jean. *Technocracy*. London: Feber, 1968.

Miller, Lyman. "Overlapping Transitions in China's Leadership." *SAIS Review* 16, no. 2 (Summer-Fall 1996): 21–42.

———. "Preparing for Change with Promises of Continuity: Jiang Zemin Managed to Maintain His Centrist Position at the 15th Party Congress." *China Business Review* 25 (January-February 1998): 8–10.

———. *Science and Dissent in Post-Mao China: The Politics of Knowledge*. Seattle: University of Washington Press, 1996.

Milles, C. Wright. *The Power Elite*. New York: Oxford University Press, 1956.

———. *White Collar: The American Middle Class*. New York: Oxford University Press, 1951.

Min, Yinhay Ahn. "Elite Politics in China: Its Relationship to Economic Reform and Sino-Japanese Economic Relations during 1978–1989." Ph.D. diss., George Washington University, 1991.

Mok, Ka-ho. *Intellectuals and the State in Post-Mao China*. London: Macmillan/St. Martins, 1998.

Moore, Barrington, Jr. *Political Power and Social Theory*. Cambridge: Harvard University Press, 1958.

Morgenthau, Hans Joachim. *Science: Servant or Master?* New York: Norton, 1972.

———. *Scientific Man versus Power Politics*. Chicago: University of Chicago Press, 1946.

Mosca, Gaetano. *The Ruling Class*. New York: McGraw-Hill, 1936.

Mulvenon, James C. *Professionalization of the Senior Chinese Officer Corps: Trends and Implications*. Santa Monica, Calif.: Rand Corporation, 1997.

Muttalib, M. A. *Democracy, Bureaucracy, and Technocracy: Assumptions of Public Management Theory*. New Delhi: Concept Publishing, 1980.

Nagle, John D. "A New Look at the Soviet Elite: A Generational Model of the Soviet System." *Journal of Political and Military Sociology* 3, no. 1 (1975): 1–13.

Nathan, Andrew J. "China's Path from Communism." *Journal of Democracy* 4, no. 2 (April 1993): 30–42.

———. *China's Crisis: Dilemmas of Reform and Prospects for Democracy*. New York: Columbia University Press, 1991.

Nee, Victor. "The Emergence of a Market Society: Changing Mechanisms of Stratification in China." *American Journal of Sociology* 101, no. 4 (January 1996): 908–949.

———. "Social Inequalities in Reforming State Socialism: Between Redistribution and Markets in China." *American Sociological Review* 56, no. 3 (June 1991): 267–282.

Nee, Victor, and Frank W. Young. "Peasant Entrepreneurs in China's 'Second Economy': An Institutional Analysis." *Economic Development and Cultural Change* 39, no. 2 (January 1991): 293–310.

Nee, Victor, and Rebecca Matthews. "Market Transition and Societal Transformation in Reforming State Socialism." *Annual Review of Sociology* 22 (1996): 401–435.

Nelson, Daniel N. *Elite–Mass Relations in Communist Systems.* Houndmills, U.K.: Macmillan, 1988.

———. "Charisma, Control, and Coercion: The Dilemma of Communist Leadership." *Comparative Politics* 17, no. 1 (October 1984): 1–15.

North, Robert, and Ithiel Pool. *Kuomintang and Chinese Communist Elites.* Stanford: Stanford University Press, 1952.

Odgaard, Ole. "Entrepreneurs and Elite Formation in Rural China." *Australian Journal of Chinese Affairs* 28 (July 1992): 89–108.

O'Donnell, Guillermo A. *Bureaucratic-Authoritarianism.* Berkeley: University of California Press, 1988.

———. *Modernization and Bureaucratic-Authoritarianism: Studies in South American Politics.* Berkeley: University of California Press, 1973.

Oksenberg, Michel. "China's Political Future." *JETRO China Newsletter* 120 (January-February 1996): 2–11.

Ou-yang Hsin-yi. "The Impact of the Tiananmen Incident on Mainland China's Provincial Leadership Appointment: A Brief Explanation of Second-Generation Elite Studies." *Issues and Studies* 31, no. 7 (July 1995): 100–117.

Pareto, Vilgredo. *The Rise and Fall of the Elites: An Application of Theoretical Sociology.* Totowa, N.J.: Bedminster, 1968.

Pearson, Margaret M. *China's New Business Elite: The Political Consequences of Economic Reform.* Berkeley: University of California Press, 1997.

Pei Minxin. *From Reform to Revolution: The Demise of Communism in China and the Soviet Union.* Cambridge: Harvard University Press, 1994.

Price, Donald K. *The Scientific Estate.* Cambridge: Harvard University Press, 1965.

———. *Government and Science.* New York: New York University Press, 1954.

Price, Jane L. *Cadres, Commanders, and Commissars: The Training of the Chinese Communist Leadership, 1920–45.* Boulder: Westview, 1976.

Primack, Joel, and F. Von Hippel. *Advice and Dissent: Scientists in the Political Arena.* New York: Basic, 1974.

Putnam, Robert D. "Elite Transformation in Advanced Industrial Societies." *Comparative Political Study* 10, no. 3 (October 1977): 383–412.

———. *The Comparative Study of Political Elites.* Englewood Cliffs, N.J.: Prentice-Hall, 1976.

Pye, Lucian W. *The Mandarin and the Cadre.* Ann Arbor: Center for Chinese Studies, University of Michigan, 1988.

Rigby, Thomas Henry. *Political Elites in the USSR: Central Leaders and Local Cadres from Lenin to Gorbachev.* U.K.: Edward Elgar, 1990.

Rintala, Marvin. "Generations: Political Generations." In *The International Encyclopedia of the Social Sciences.* New York: Macmillan/Free Press, 1968.

Rona-Tas, Akos. "The First Shall Be the Last: Entrepreneurship and Communist Cadres in the Transition from Socialism." *American Journal of Sociology* 100, no. 1 (July 1994): 40–69.

Saich, Tony. "The Fourteenth Party Congress: A Programme for Authoritarian Rule." *China Quarterly* 132 (December 1992): 1136–1160.

Saint-Simon, Henri comte De. *Social Organization, the Science of Man, and Other Writings.* New York: Harper, 1964.

Saunders, Phillip. "China's America Watchers: Changing Attitudes toward the United States." *China Quarterly* 161 (March 2000): 41–65.

Scalapino, Robert A. *Elites in the People's Republic of China.* Seattle: University of Washington Press, 1972.

Schattschneider, E. E. *The Semisovereign People: A Realist's View of Democracy in America.* Hinsdale, Ill.: Dryden, 1960.

Schell, Orville. *Mandate of Heaven: A New Generation of Entrepreneurs, Dissidents, Bohemians, and Technocrats Lays Claim to China's Future.* New York: Simon & Schuster, 1994.

Schumpeter, Joseph. *Capitalism, Socialism, and Democracy.* London: Allen & Unwin, 1961.

Schurmann, Franz. *Ideology and Organization in Communist China.* 2d enl. ed. Berkeley: University of California Press, 1968.

Segal, Gerald. "Does China Matter?" *Foreign Affairs* 78, no. 5 (September-October 1999): 24–36.

Shambaugh, David. "The CCP's Fifteenth Congress: Technocrats in Command." *Issues and Studies* 34, no. 1 (January 1998): 1–37.

———. "China's Military in Transition: Politics, Professionalsm, Procurement, and Power Projection." *China Quarterly* 146 (June 1996): 265–298.

Shirk, Susan L. *Competitive Comrades: Career Incentives and Student Strategies in China.* Berkeley: University of California Press. 1982.

———. "Educational Reform and Political Backlash: Recent Changes in Chinese Educational Policy." *Comparative Education Review* 23, no. 2 (1979): 183–217.

Silva, Patricio. "Technocrats and Politics in Chile: From the Chicago Boys to the CIEPLAN Monks." *Journal of Latin American Studies* 23, no. 2 (May 1991): 385–410.

Simis, Konstantin. "The Gorbachev Generation." *Foreign Policy* 59 (Summer 1985): 3–21.

Simon, Denis Fred. "China's S and T Intellectuals in the Post-Mao China: A Retrospective and Prospective Glimpse." *Journal of Northeast Asian Studies* 4, no. 2 (Summer 1985): 57–82.

Simon, Denis Fred, and Merle Goldman. *Science and Technology in Post-Mao China.* Cambridge: Harvard University Press, 1989.

Smith, Peter. *Labyrinths of Power: Political Recruitment in Twentieth-Century Mexico.* Princeton: Princeton University Press, 1979.

Snow, C. P. *Science and Government.* Cambridge: Harvard University Press, 1961.

Solinger, Dorothy J. "Urban Entrepreneurs and the State: The Merger of State and Society." In *State and Society in China: The Consequences of Reform*, edited by Arthur L. Rosenbaum, 121–142. Boulder: Westview, 1993.

Strauss, William, and Neil Howe. *Generations: The History of America's Future, 1582–2069.* New York: William Morrow, 1992.

Suleiman, Ezra N. *Elites in French Society: The Politics of Survival.* Princeton: Princeton University Press, 1978.

———. "The Myth of Technical Expertise: Selection, Organization, and Leadership." *Comparative Politics* 10, no. 1 (October 1977): 137–158.

Swaine, Michael D. *The Military and Political Succession in China: Leadership, Institution, Beliefs.* Santa Monica, Calif.: Rand Corporation, 1992.

———. *The Role of the Chinese Military in National Security Policymaking.* Santa Monica, Calif.: Rand Corporation, 1998.

Tanner, Murray Scott, and Michael J. Feder. "Family Politics, Elite Recruitment, and Succession in Post-Mao China." *Australian Journal of Chinese Affairs* 30 (July 1993): 89–120.

Taylor, Frederick. *The Principles of Scientific Management.* New York: Viking, 1911.

Teiwes, Frederick C. "The Paradoxical Post-Mao Transition: From Obeying the Leader to "Normal Politics." *China Journal* 34 (July 1995): 55–94.

Ting Wang. "An Analysis of the P.R.C.'s Future Elite: The Third Echelon." *Journal of Northeast Asian Studies* 4, no. 2 (Summer 1985): 19–37.

Toffler, Alvin. *The Third Wave.* New York: William Morrow, 1980.

Tsai Wen-hui. "Patterns of Political Elite Mobility in Modern China, 1912–1949." Ph.D. diss., University of California, 1974.

Tucker, C. Robert. *Political Culture and Leadership in Soviet Russia: From Lenin to Gorbachev.* New York: Norton, 1987.

Volti, Rudi. *Technology, Politics, and Society in China.* Boulder: Westview, 1982.

———. "Technology and Polity: The Dynamics and Dilemmas of Managed Change." *Studies in Comparative Communism* 15, no. 1–2 (1982): 71–94.

———. "Organizations and Expertise in China." *Administration and Society* 8, no. 4 (February 1977): 423–458.

Walder, Andrew. "Career Mobility and the Communist Political Order." *American Sociological Review* 60, no. 3 (June 1995): 309–328.

Waller, D. J. *Revolutionary Intellectuals or Managerial Moderniser?* Beverly Hills: Sage, 1975.

———. "The Chinese Communist Political Elite: Continuity and Innovation." In *Comparative Communist Political Leadership,* edited by Carl Beck, 154–201. New York: David McKay, 1973.

Wang Hsueh-wen. "Peking and Tsinghua Universities: 1966–1976." *Issues and Studies* 13, no. 6, (June 1977): 75–90.

Weart, Spencer R. *Scientists in Power.* Cambridge: Harvard University Press, 1979.

Weber, Max. *Protestant Ethic and Spirit of Capitalism.* London: Unwin Paperbacks, 1982.

———. *Economy and Society.* Edited by Guenther Roth and Claus Wittich. 2d ed. Berkeley: University of California Press, 1978.

———. *The Theory of Social and Economic Organizations.* Edited by Talcott Parsons. New York: Free Press of Glencoe, 1964.

Welsh, William A. "Elites and Leadership in Communist Systems: Some New Perspectives." *Studies in Comparative Communism* 9, no. 1–2 (1976): 162–186.

———. "Toward a Multiple-Strategy Approach to Research on Comparative Communist Political Elites: Empirical and Quantitative Problems." In *Communist Studies and the Social Sciences: Essays on Methodology and Empirical Theory,* edited by Frederic J. Fleron Jr., 318–356. Chicago: Rand McNally, 1969.

White, Gordon. *Party and Professionals: The Political Role of Teachers in Contemporary China.* Armonk, N.Y.: M. E. Sharpe, 1981.

White, Lynn T., III. *Policies of Chaos: The Organizational Causes of Violence in China's Cultural Revolution.* Princeton: Princeton University Press, 1989.

———. "Chinese Intellectuals and Party Policy." *Issues and Studies* 20, no. 10 (October 1984): 11–30; no. 11 (November 1984): 12–32.

———. "Diversification among Mainland Chinese Intellectuals." *Issues and Studies* 24, no. 9 (September 1988): 50–77.

Whiting, Allen S. "Chinese Nationalism and Foreign Policy after Deng." *China Quarterly* 142 (June 1995): 295–316.

——. "The Scholar and the Policy-Maker." In *Theory and Policy in International Relations*, edited by Raymond Tanter and Richard H. Ullman, 229–247. Princeton: Princeton University Press, 1972.

Whitson, W. William. "The Concept of Military Generation." *Asian Survey* 11, no. 8 (November 1968): 921–947.

*Who's Who in Communist China*. Hong Kong: Union Research Institute, 1970.

Wilhelm, Alfred D. "Chinese Elites and Comparative Elite Studies: A Progress Report." *Studies in Comparative Communism* 13, no. 1 (1980): 63–81.

Wilson, Ian, and You Ji. "Leadership by 'Lines': China's Unresolved Succession." *Problems of Communism* 39, no. 1 (January-February 1990): 28–44.

Wong, Paul. *China's Higher Leadership in the Socialist Transition*. New York: Free Press, 1976.

Yahuda, Michael. "Political Generations in China." *China Quarterly* 80 (December 1979): 792–805.

Yang Guansan, et al. "Enterprise Cadres and Reform." In *Reform in China: Challenges and Choices*, edited by Bruce Reynolds, 74–85. Armonk, N.Y.: M. E. Sharpe, 1987.

Yang, Martin M. C. "The Formation of China's New Intelligentsia in the Early Twentieth Century." *Soochow Journal of Social and Political Sciences*, December 1980, 1–17.

Yu, Peter Kien-hong. "Lee Teng-hui (and His Successors?) versus Jiang Zemin (and His Successor!): Dialectical Games." *Asian Affairs: An American Review* 23, no. 1 (Spring 1996): 64–79.

Zang Xiaowei. "Elite Formation and the Bureaucratic-Technocracy in Post-Mao China." *Studies in Comparative Communism* 24, no. 1 (March 1991): 114–123.

——. "Ethnic Representation in the Current Chinese Leadership." *China Quarterly* 153 (March 1998): 107–127.

——. "The Fourteenth Central Committee of the CCP: Technocracy or Political Technocracy." *Asian Survey* 33, no. 8 (August 1993): 787–803.

——. "Professionalism and the Leadership Transition in the Post-Mao Chinese Army." *Journal of Northeast Asian Studies* 10, no. 3 (Fall 1991): 46–60.

——. "Provincial Elite in Post-Mao China." *Asian Survey* 31, no. 6 (June 1991): 512–525.

Zhang Ming. "Public Images of the United States." In *In the Eyes of the Dragon*, edited by Yong Deng and Fei-Ling Wang, 141–158. Lanham, Md.: Rowman & Littlefield, 1999.

Zhang Zhongliang. "People and Science: Public Attitudes in China toward Science and Technology." *Science and Public Policy* 18, no. 5 (October 1991): 311–317.

Zhou Xueguang, Nancy Brandom Tuma, and Phyllis Moen. "Institutional Change and Job-Shift Patterns in Urban China, 1949 to 1994." *American Sociological Review* 62, no. 3 (June 1997): 339–365.

Zubek, Voltek. "The Rise and Fall of Rule by Poland's Best and Brightest." *Soviet Studies* 44, no. 4 (1992): 579–608.

## CHINESE LANGUAGE

Chang Ching-chien. *Zhongguo wenguan zhidu shi* (The history of the Chinese civil service system). Taibei: Chinese Culture Press, 1955.

Chen Fang. *Tiannu: Shizhang yaoan* (The wrath of God: A mayor's severe crime). Hong
Kong: Taipingyang shiji chubanshe, 1997.

Chen Hanzhong. "Zheyidai: Xiagang gongren" (This generation: Laid-off workers). *Zhongguo Zhichun* (China spring), November 1998.

Chen Hong and Yao Shiguang. *Jinxi qinghua* (The past and present of Qinghua). Beijing:
Beijing Press, 1958.

Chen Lumin. "Zhishi jingji: Ershiyi shiji de zhaohuan" (Knowledge economy: The calling
of the twenty-first century). *Makesi zhuyi yu xianshi* (Marxism and reality) 3 (1998):
34–37.

Cheng Xiaoying. "Yazhou zhongguo jueqi de 'jiliyidai'" (The rise of "Genie" in China and
Asia). *Haishang wentan* (Literary forum of Shanghai) 8 (August 1997): 4–11.

Cui Zhiyuan. "Zhongguo zhengzhi gaige de xinsilu: Feizhengdang shi jingzheng xuanju"
(New ideas for China's political reform: Nonpartisan competitive elections). *Zhongguo
yu shijie* (China and the world) 17 (March 1998).

Dai Qing. *Changjiang, Changjiang* (Yangzi River, Yangzi River). Guiyang: Guizhou chubanshe, 1989.

Fan Hengshan. *Biewu xuanze: Tan danqian jingji gaige* (No alternative: On current economic
reform). Beijing: Zhongguo jingji chubanshe, 1999.

Fang Xingdong and Wang Junxiu. *Qilai* (Get up). Beijing: Zhonghua gongshang lianhe
chubanshe, 1999.

Feng Zhijun and Zhao Hongzhou. *Xiandai hua yu kexuexue* (Modernization and science of
sciences). Shanghai: Zhishi Press, 1985.

Gan Shijun, Yu Jianhua, and Cui Guanjie. *Ruankexue zai zhongguo* (Soft science in China).
Wuhan: Central China Institute of Technology, 1989.

Gao Xin. *Jiang Zemin de muliao* (Jiang Zemin's counselors). 4th ed. Hong Kong: Mingjing
chubanshe, 1997.

———. *Xiangfu Guangdong bang* (Taming the Guangdong gang). Hong Kong: Mingjing
chubanshe, 2000.

Gao Xin and He Pin. *Zhu Rongji zhuan: Cong fandang youpai dao Deng Xiaoping jichengren*
(Biography of Zhu Rongji: From anti-Party rightist to Deng's successor). Taibei: Xinxinwen wenhua chubanshe, 1992.

Gu Hongzhang. *Zhongguo zhishi qingnian shangshan xiaxiang shimo* (The whole story of the
sent-down movement of Chinese youths). Beijing: Zhongguo jiancha chubanshe, 1997.

Guo Shuqing. *Zhengti de jianjin* (Integral gradualism). Beijing: Jingji kexue chubanshe, 1998.

He Pin and Gao Xin. *Zhonggong "Taizidang"* (China's communist "princelings"). Taipei:
Shih-pao Ch'u-pan Kung-ssu, 1992.

———. *Zhonggong "Taizidang"* (China's communist "princelings"). Rev. ed. Taibei: Shibao
chubanshe, 1999.

———. "Taizidang jieban de shishi yu kenengxing" (The succession of the "party of
princes": Reality and possibility). *Dangdai* (Contemporary monthly), April 1992, 40–58.

He Qinglian. "Caifu yu pinkun: Xian jieduan pinfu fenceng pingxi" (Wealth and poverty:
An analysis of China's current polarization). *Zhongguo yu shijie* (China and the world)
22 (August 1998).

———. *Xiandaihua de xianjing: Dangdai Zhongguo de jingji shehui wenti* (The pitfall of modernization: Economic and social problems of contemporary China). Beijing: Jinri Zhongguo chubanshe, 1998.

———. *Zhongguo de xianjing* (China's pitfall). Hong Kong: Mingjing chubanshe, 1998.

Hu Angang. *Zhongguo fazhan qianjing* (Prospects of China's development). Hangzhou: Zhejiang renmin chubanshe, 1999.

Hu Fan and Li Daguang. *Daguo de zunyan: Gouzhu ershiyi shiji guojia anquan de jiangu baolei* (The dignity of a big country: Building the firm fortress of national security for the twenty-first century). Shenzhen: Haitian chubanshe, 1999.

Hu Yaobang. "Makesizhuyi weidazhenli de guanghui zhaoyao women qianjin" (Great truth of Marxism moves us forward). *Hongqi* (Red flag) 6 (March 1983): 2–13.

Ji Ye and Zhang Ximing. *1999 nian Zhongguo fazhan zhuangkuang yu qushi* (The status and trend of China's development in 1999). Beijing: Jingji ribao chubanshe, 1999.

Jia Hao. "Dui dangqian woguo liuxue renyuan zhuangkuang de fenxi he jidian jianyi" (Analysis of Chinese study abroad and some recommendations). *Shehui kexue* (Social science) 6 (1997): 58–62.

Jiang Yuncai and Tan Jianfeng. *Shiji tiaozhan: Zhongguo fuxing qidai zhishi jingji* (The challenge of the century: China's rejuvenation calls for knowledge economy). Beijing: Lantian chubanshe, 1998.

Jin Dalu. ed. *Dongfang shiritan: Laosanjie ren de gushi* (Stories of the people of the three old classes). Shanghai: Shanghai renmin chubanshe, 1997.

———. *Ku'nan yu fengliu* (The miserable and admirable). Shanghai: Shanghai renmin chubanshe, 1994.

———. *Shiyun yu mingyun: Guanyu laosanjie ren de shengcun yu fazhan* (The time and fate: Survival and development of three old classes). Shanghai: Shanghai renmin chubanshe, 1998.

Li Dongsheng, ed. *Buzhang fangtan lu* (Interview with ministers). Beijing: Zhongguo Jiancha Chubanshe, 1998.

Li Erhua, Zhang Liucheng, and Zhao Xiaoyan. *Zhongguo gaige kaifang ershinian dashiji* (Chronicle of China's twenty-year reform). Beijing: Zhongzhou guji chubanshe, 1998.

Li Hui and Ying Hong. *Shiji zhiwen: Laizi zhishijie de shengyin* (The question of the century: Voices from the intellectual community). Zhengzhou: Daxiang chubanshe, 1999.

Li Mingsheng. *Zhongguo baliusan* (China's 863). Taiyuan: Shanxi jiaoyu chubanshe, 1997.

Li Qiang. "Zhengzhi fenceng yu jingji fenceng" (Political stratification and economic stratification). *Shehuixue yanjiu* (Sociological research) 4 (1997): 32–41.

———. "Naoti daogua" yu woguo shichang jingji fazhan de liangge jieduan." ("Misplacing the body above the brain" and two stages of the development of China's market economy). *Shehui xue yanjiu* (Sociological research) 6 (1996): 5–12.

Li Tongwen, ed. *Zhongguo minsheng baogao: Zhongguo shehui gejieceng de xianzhuang yu weilai* (Report on the Chinese people's livelihood: The current situation and future of social strata in China). Beijing: Jincheng chubanshe, 1998.

Li Xiaozhuang. *Zhu Rongji renma* (Zhu Rongji's men). Taibei: Dujia chubanshe, 1998.

Liao Gailong and Fan Yuan, comps. *Zhongguo renming da cidian* (Who's who in China). Vol 3. Shanghai: Shanghai Dictionary Publishing House, 1989.

———. *Zhongguo renming da cidian xiandai dangzhengjun lingdaorenwujuan* (Who's who in China: Current party, government, and military leaders). Beijing: Foreign Languages Press, 1994.

Lie Xing. "Zhonggong disidai hexin daremen Hu Jintao" (Hu Jintao: A front-runner of the fourth generation of leaders). In *Zhonggong disidai mengren* (The fourth generation of leaders of the Chinese Communist Party), edited by Xiao Chong, 7–17. Hong Kong: Xiafeier guoji chubangongsi, 1998.

Lin Jiacheng. "Keji zhuanjia jieceng zhi jueqi, liudong ji yingxiang" (The rise and influence of technocrats). *Dongwu zhengzhi shehui xuebao* (Soochow journal of political science and sociology) 7 (December 1983): 81–98.

Ling Zhijun and Ma Licheng. *Huhan: Dangjin Zhongguo de wuzhong shengyin* (Voices: Five voices in present China). Guangzhou: Guangzhou chubanshe, 1999.

Liu Ningrong. "Niuzhuan guoyun de liumei xuesheng" (American-trained Chinese students are changing China). *Yazhou zhoukan* (Asia week), 8 November 1998.

Long Xiong. "Sanshinian wandong, sanshinian wanxi" (Thirty years live east, thirty years live west). *Haishang wentan* (Literary forum of Shanghai) 2 (Febuary 1997): 5–11.

Lu Xinger. "Laosanjie de ernümen" (Children of the three old classes). *Haishang wentan* (Literary forum of Shanghai) 1 (January 1996): 4–10.

Ma Guiqiu. *Keji rencaixue* (Modern study of talented scientists and technologists). Hangzhou: Zhejiang jiaoyu chubanshe, 1987.

Ma Hong and Sun Shangqing. *Zhongguo fazhan yanjiu: Guowuyuan fazhan yanjiu zhongxin yanjiu baogao xuan* (China development studies: The selected research reports of the Development Research Center of the State Coucil). Beijing: Zhongguo fazhan chubanshe, 1996.

Ministry of Education, comp. *Qinghua daxue dishisanci jiaoxue yanjiuhui, disici kexue baogaohui lianhe dahui ziliao xuanbian* (The collection of the reports presented in the Thirteenth Conference of Educational Research and the Fourth Conference of Science at Qinghua University, December 1959–January 1960). Beijing: People's Educational Press, 1960.

Qiao Liang and Wang Xianghui. *Chaoxian zhan* (Beyond the rule of war). Beijing: Jiefangjun wenyi chubanshe, 1999.

Qinghua daxue (Qinghua University). *Qinghua Daxue* (Qinghua University). Beijing: Zhishi Publishing House, 1982.

Qinghua daxue Jiang Nanxiang jinian wenji bianji xiaozu (Editorial group for the commemorative collection of Jiang Nanxiang at Qinghua University). *Jiang Nanxiang jinian wenji* (A commemorative collection of Jiang Nanxiang). Beijing: Qinghua University Press, 1990.

Qinghua daxue xiaoshi bianxie zu (Writing group for the history of Qinghua University). *Qinghua daxue xiaoshi gao* (A draft of Qinghua University history). Beijing: Zhonghua Press, 1981.

Qinghua daxue xiaoshi bianyan zu (Research group for the history Qinghua University). *Zhandou zai yi'er jiu yundong de qianlie* (Fighting at the front of the December Ninth movement). Beijing: Qinghua University, 1985.

Qinghua daxue xiaoshi zu (Writing group for the history of Qinghua University). *Renwu zhi* (Personage). Beijing: Qinghua University Press, 1983.

Qiu Liping. "Shanghai shimin zhiye diwei pingjia jiqi yiyi" (The evaluation of occupational status of Shanghai residents and its implications). *Shehui* (Society) 7 (1996): 4–6.

Qu Taifeng. *Qingjie laosanjie* (The complex of the three old classes). Xian: Shaanxi renmin chubanshe, 1996.

Ren Zhichu. *Hu Jintao: Zhongguo kuashiji jiebanren* (Hu Jintao: China's first man in the twenty-first century). Hong Kong: Mirror Books, 1997.

Shen Xueming et al., comps. *Zhonggong di shiwujie zhongyang weiyuanhui zhongyang jilü jiancha weiyuanhui weiyuan minglu* (Who's who of the members of the Fifteenth Central Committee of the Chinese Communist Party and the Fifteenth Central Commission for Discipline Inspection). Beijing: Zhonggong wenxian chubanshe, 1999.

Shi Qingqi. "Ershiyi shiji gaojishu chanye fazhan zhong de renli ziben" (The human capital of the development of high-tech industry in the twenty-first century). *Zhongguo renli ziyuan kaifa* (Human resource development of China), August 1999, 4–7.

Shi Xiaoyan. *Beidahuang fengyun lu* (Time and life in the great northern wilderness). Beijing: Zhongguo qingnian chubanshe, 1990.

Shu Zhan et al. "Guofang daxue jiangjun de yaolan" (The University of National Defense: The cradle of generals). *Zhonghua yingcai* (China's talents) 171 (August 1997): 40–42.

*Shuangjiantiao: Qinghua daxue xuesheng fudaoyuan gongzuo sishinian de huigu yu tansuo* (Double-load on shoulders: Retrospect and exploration of the forty-year work by student political counsellors at Qinghua University). Beijing: Qinghua daxue chubanshe, 1993.

Song Qiang et al. *Zhongguo keyi shuo bu* (China can say no). Beijing: Zhonghua gongshang lianhe chubanshe, 1996.

————. *Zhongguo hai neng shuo bu* (China can still say no). Beijing: Zhongguo wenlian chubanshe, 1996.

Sun Daiyao and Wang Wenzhang. *Julong de suxing* (Dragon wakes). Beijing: Wenjin Publishers, 1993.

Tang Bo. *Zhonggong yu zhishi fenzi* (The Chinese Communist Party and intellectuals). Taibei: Youshi Press, 1989.

Tang Dianwei. "Duoqian dongwu He Xin" (He Xin: A man of many capacities) *Shijie zhoukan* (World journal weekly), May 23–May 29, 1999, 24–27.

Wang Jun. *Zhonggong gaodeng xuexiao gaikuang zhilu* (An empirical survey of colleges and universities under the Chinese Communist Party). Hong Kong: Zhongshan Books, 1972.

Wang Junxian and Cui Wunian. "Zhongguo ganbu jigou de bianqian: Quanguo liuqianerbai ge dixianji lingdao banzi de diaocha yu shizheng fenxi" (Changes in the structure of China's cadres: An investigation and analysis of 6,200 leading bodies at county and prefectural levels). *Zouxiang weilai* (Toward the future) 2, no. 2 (1988): 22–31.

Wang Keliang and Bo Liangze. "Shilun zhishi jingying yu zhengzhi jingying de jiehe" (The Integration of intellectual elites and political elites). *Zhengzhixue yanjiu* (Studies in political science) 2 (1989): 22–25.

Wang Shan. *Disanzhi yanjing kan Zhongguo* (China through the third eye). 3d ed. Hong Kong: Mingbao Press, 1994.

Wang Ya'nan. *Zhongguo guanliao zhengzhi yanjiu* (A study of Chinese bureaucratic politics). Shanghai: Time and Culture Press, 1948.

Wang Yizhou. "Shixi guoji zhengzhixue de meiguo zhongxin" (The American center of gravity in the study of international politics). *Meiguo yanjiu* (American studies) 1 (March 1998): 57–78.

Wen Lin and Hai Tao, eds. *Zhongguo xinyidai sixiangjia zibai* (Recollections of China's new generation of thinkers). Beijing: Jiuzhou Tushu Chubanshe, 1998.

Wu Guoguang. *Zhulu shiwuda: Zhongguo quanli qiju* (Toward the Fifteenth Party Congress: Power game in China). Hong Kong: Taipingyang shiji chubanshe, 1997.

Wu Jisong. *Zhishi jingji: Ershiyi shiji shehui de xinqushi* (Knowledge economy: The new social trend of the twenty-first century). Beijing: Beijing kexuejishu chubanshe, 1998.

Wu Yi, ed. *Nüshizhang: Zhongguo nüshizhang zhuizong shouji* (Women mayors: Interview reports). Beijing: Zhongguo funü chubanshe, 1999.

Xia Yulong et al. *Xiandai zhinangtuan* (Modern brain trust). Shanghai: Zhishi Press, 1984.

Xiang Wenhua, ed. *Shijimo de sikao* (Thoughts at the end of the century). Beijing: Zhongyang bianyi chubanshe, 1998.

Xiao Chong, ed. *Beijing zhinangqun* (Beijing's think tanks). Hong Kong: Xiafeier guoji chubangongsi, 1999.

———. *Zhonggong disidai mengren* (The fourth generation of leaders of the Chinese Communist Party). Hong Kong: Xiafeier guoji chubangongsi, 1998.

Xiao Yandeng. *Zhongguo meiyou qiyejia: Zhongguo disidai qiyejia quexian fenxi* (China has no entrepreneuers: An analysis of the deficiencies of the fourth generation of entrepreneuers). Nanchang: Jiangxi renmin chubanshe, 1999.

Xie Dajun. "Qiantan zhishijingji jiqi dui junshigeming de yingxiang yu tiaozhan" (Knowledge economy: Its influence and challenge to the military). *Guofang daxue xuebao, zhanglue wenti yanjiu* (Journal of National Defense University: Study of strategic issues) 1 (1999): 25–28.

Xie Lizhong. "Dangdai zhongguo shehui jiegou de bianqian" (Transformation of the social structure in contemporary China). *Nanchang daxue xuebao* (Nanchang University journal) 2 (1996): 13–22; 3 (1996): 15–25.

Xin Mao. "Chaoyue zuoyouyi haishi bei zuoyouyi chaoyue: Ping Yan Fan 'Zhongguo de weiji: Quanli ziben exing pengzhang'" (Transcend left–right division or be transcended by the left and right: A comment on Yang Fan). *Zhongguo yu shijie* (China and the world) 23 (September 1998).

Xing Junfang. *Zhongguo ershiyi shiji jingji zouxiang: Busheng ji lingdao ganbu fangtanglu* (The direction of China's economy in the twenty-first century: Interviews with ministerial and provincial leaders). Beijing: Central Party School Publishers, 1997.

Xing Wuyi. "Wang Dazhong: Wei qinghua ganhao jintian, mouhua mingtian" (Wang Dazhong: All for Qinghua's today and tomorrow). *Zhonghua yingcai* (Chinese talent) 142 (May 1996): 31–33.

Xu Fuguan et al. *Zhishi fenzi Yu Zhongguo* (Intellectuals and China). Taibei: Shibao Press, 1980.

Xu Jilin, "Qimeng de mingyun: Ershinian lai de zhongguo sixiang jie" (The fate of enlightenment: The Chinese intelligensia during the past two decades). *Ershiyi shiji* (Twenty-first century), December 12, 1998, 4–13.

Xu Youyu. *1966: Women zheyidai de huiyi* (1966: The reminiscences of our generation). Beijing: Zhongguo wenlian chuban gongsi, 1998.

Yang Fan. "Caogen yishi: Zhiqing baogui de jingshen caifu" (Grassroots consciousness: The precious essence of sent-down youths). *Jinri mingliu* (Contemporary celebrities) 10 (1998): 16.

———. "Wei 'disandai ren' zheng gongdao." (Justice for the "third generation"). *Zhongguo yu shijie* (China and the world), December 1997.

Yang Fan et al. *Zhongguo: 1990–2020* (China: 1990–2020). Shenyan, China: Liaoning renmin chubanshe, 1991.

Yang Fujia, "Zhishi jingji chujian duanni" (The coming of knowledge economy). *Xin shiji lingdao zhe* (The leaders of the new century) 11 (November 1998): 58–59.

Yang Guansan et al. "Dangqian woguo qiye ganbu suzhi de diaocha yu chubu fenxi" (The survey and preliminary analysis of enterprise cadres of China). In *Gaige women mianlin de tiaozhan yu xuanze* (Reform: Challenges and choices), edited by Research Group of Chinese Economic System Reform Research Institute, 270–305. Beijing: Chinese Economy Press, 1986.

Yang Yiyong. *Gongping yu xiaolü: Dangdai zhongguo de shouru fenpei wenti* (Justice and efficiency: Income and distribution in contemporary China). Beijing: Dangri zhongguo chubabshe, 1997.

Yang Zhongmei. *Zhonggong kuashiji jiebanren: Hu Jintao* (Hu Jintao: The cross-century successor of China). Taibei: Shibao chubanshe, 1999.

Yu Zhen and Shi Dazhen. *Buzhang yanzhong de weilai Zhongguo* (China from the eyes of ministers). Changsha: Hunan chubanshe, 1995.

Yu Zuyao, "Zhuanxing shiqi baofahu qunti de zhengzhi jingjixue fenxi" (A political and economic analysis of the new rich in the era of transition). *Jingji yanjiu* (Economic research 2 (1998).

Yuan Zhengming and Liang Jianzeng. *Jujiao: Jiaodian fangtan* (Focus). Heibei: Zhongguo dabaike quanshu chubanshe, 1999.

Zhai Ligong and Guo Daofu. *Zhongguo redian* (China's heated issues). Beijing: Zhongguo tongji chubanshe, 1999.

Zhang Bingliang. "Xinzhongchanjieji de maoqi yu zhengzhi yingxiang" (The rise of the new middle class and its political influence). *Mingbao yuekan* (Mingbao monthly) (Hong Kong) 1 (January 1987): 10–15.

Zhang Jianhua. *Zhongguo mianlin de jinyao wenti* (The crucial issues that China faces). Beijing: Jingji ribao chubanshe, 1998.

Zhang Kai and Ji Yuan. *Youshuo laosanjie* (The three old classes revisited). Beijing: Zhongguo Qingnian Chubanshe, 1997.

Zhang Yuan. *Chongsu zhengfu: '98 zhengfu jigou gaige jiaodian da toushi* (Remolding the government: An analysis of governmental reform in 1998). Beijing: Zhonghua gongshang lianhe chubanshe, 1998.

Zhang Y. and Y. Cheng. *Disidai ren* (The fourth generation). Beijing: Dongfang chubanshe, 1988.

Zhang Zichun, "Toushi zhishijingji shidai de junshi biange" (Insight into military reform in the knowledge economy era). *Guofan daxue xuebao, zhanglue wenti yangjiu* (Journal of National Defense University: Study of strategic issues) 3 (1999): 25–27.

Zhao Yunxi. *Zhishi zibenjia: Zhongguo zhishifenzi miandui zhishi jingji de jueze* (Knowledge capitalists: Chinese intellectuals' choices in the era of knowledge economy). Beijing: Zhonghua gongshang lianhehui chubanshe, 1998.

Zhao Xiaochun. "Xinxi geming dui dangdai guojiguanxi de yingxiang" (The impact of the information revolution on contemporary international relations). *Guoji guanxi xueyuan xuebao* (Journal of University of International Relations) 4 (1998): 1–6.

Zhong Qiang. *Disidairen de jingshen* (The spirit of the fourth generation). Lanzhou: Gansu wenhua chubanshe, 1997.

Zhong Qiuju. *Kua shiji de xinyijie zhongguo zhengfu* (The new Chinese government at the turn of the century). Beijing: Renmin chubanshe, 1998.

Zhong Yan. *Zhongguo xinsanji xueren* (China's new three classes of scholars). Hangzhou: Zhejiang renmin chubanshe, 1996.

Zhongguo chengshi fazhan yanjiuhui, zhongguo xingzheng guanli xuehui (The council of China's urban development and the association of China's public administration), comp. *Zhongguo chengshi nianjian* (The almanac of China's cities). Beijing: Zhongguo chengshi nianjian chubanshe, 1994.

Zhongguo chengshi jingji shehui nianjian lishihui (The council of the almanac of China's urban economy and society), comp. *Zhongguo chengshi jingji shehui nianjian 1986* (The almanac of China's urban economy and society). Beijing: Zhongguo chengshi nianjian chubanshe, 1986.

Zhongguo gaodeng jiaoyu xuehui he qinghua daxue, comp. *Jiang Nanxiang wenji* (Collections of Jiang Nanjiang). Beijing: Qinghua University Press, 1998.

*Zhonggong renminglu* (Who's who in Communist China). Taibei: Institute of International Relations, 1983.

Zhou Gucheng. *Zhongguo shehui zhi jiegou* (The structure of Chinese society). Shanghai: New Life Press, 1935.

Zhou Lindong. "Dui kexue zhuyi de piping yao shenzhong" (Be cautious in criticizing scientism). *Fudan xuebao* (Fudan journal, social sciences edition) 2 (1997): 10–11.

Zhou Shaosen and Chen Dongyou. *Kejiao xingguo lun: You Zhongguo tese shehuizhuyi luncong* (On technocracy: Collections on Chinese-styled socialism). Jinan: Shandong renmin chubanshe, 1999.

Zhu Guanglei. *Dangdai zhongguo shehui gejieceng fenxi* (Analysis of social strata in China). Tianjin: Renmin chubanshe, 1998.

# Index

# About the Author

Cheng Li grew up in Shanghai during the Cultural Revolution. He left China in 1985 to pursue graduate study in the United States. Li received an M.A. from the University of California, Berkeley, and a Ph.D. from Princeton University. He is currently professor of government at Hamilton College in Clinton, New York, and a fellow of the Institute of Current World Affairs, Hanover, New Hampshire. He is also the author of *Rediscovering China: Dynamics and Dilemmas of Reform* (1997).